Survival Schools

SURVIVAL SCHOOLS

The American Indian Movement
and Community Education
in the Twin Cities

JULIE L. DAVIS

University of Minnesota Press
Minneapolis
London

Published by the University of Minnesota Press
111 Third Avenue South, Suite 290
Minneapolis, MN 55401-2520
http://www.upress.umn.edu

A Cataloging-in-Publication record for this book is available from the Library of Congress.

ISBN 978-0-8166-7428-2 (hbk.)
ISBN 978-0-8166-7429-9 (pbk.)

Printed in the United States of America on acid-free paper

The University of Minnesota is an equal-opportunity educator and employer.

20   19   18   17   16   15   14   13   10   9   8   7   6   5   4   3   2   1

For my grandmother,
who will be so happy to know
that I finally finished The Book.
Eleanor Eide Trent, "Muga," 1916–2002

Though last in the order of creation,

least in the order of dependence,

and weakest in bodily powers,

man had the greatest gift—the power to dream.

—Basil Johnston, *Ojibwe Heritage*

Contents

PREFACE   *xi*

INTRODUCTION Not Just a Bunch of Radicals: A History of the Survival Schools   *1*

1   The Origins of the Twin Cities Indian Community and the American Indian Movement   *11*

2   Keeping Ourselves Together: Education, Child Welfare, and AIM's Advocacy for Indian Families, 1968–1972   *53*

3   From One World to Another: Creating Alternative Indian Schools   *99*

4   Building Our Own Communities: Survival School Curriculum, 1972–1982   *127*

5   Conflict, Adaptation, Continuity, and Closure, 1982–2008   *173*

6   The Meanings of Survival School Education: Identity, Self-Determination, and Decolonization   *195*

CONCLUSION The Global Importance of Indigenous Education   *239*

ACKNOWLEDGMENTS   *247*
NOTES   *251*
BIBLIOGRAPHY   *287*
INDEX   *301*

Preface

T HIS PROJECT began in ignorance, and it was driven by unanswered questions. While reading about the American Indian Movement years ago, I came across a brief mention of two "survival schools" that AIM members had founded in Minneapolis and St. Paul in the early 1970s. Given what I thought I knew about AIM, this was so unexpected that I did a mental double take: "They did *what*??" When I looked for additional information about the schools, I found little, either in the scholarship on AIM or in general histories of Indian activism. I became determined to find out more.

In my research I sought answers to the questions that interested me as a historian: What might have motivated a group of Indian people to create their own independent schools in the heart of the Twin Cities? Who led this bold action, and what were their personal histories? What kind of education did they provide, and how did they do it? What were their most significant successes, challenges, and shortcomings, and how did the schools change over time? What have they meant to the people who created, attended, worked in, and were influenced by them? And how do they help us better understand AIM and its place in Native American history?

The first answers I found only fueled my curiosity, leading me to dig deeper into the layers of the schools' history. Learning what had motivated people to found the schools made me examine the relationship between their personal experiences, the conditions of postwar urban Indian life, and Indian people's collective history in the upper Midwest. Hearing the schools' origin stories made me ask why the Twin Cities public schools were failing Indian students so spectacularly in the 1960s and 1970s and why so many Indian families were losing their children to the child welfare system. Analyzing the schools' structure and philosophy made me wonder what educational models they might have drawn from. Considering the circumstances around the schools' closure made me examine their long-term challenges for the roots of later problems. Listening to people talk about what the schools meant to them made me question how we determine the purpose of schooling in this country and reconsider how we might measure educational success. Above all, exploring the survival schools' history forced me to ask, What is the place of Native people in American society? How can we make more room for them, and how might we help their children thrive?

I could not have answered any of my initial research questions without talking to the people who were closest to the survival schools. The oral history interviews that I conducted with school founders, parents, administrators, teachers, and students provide this book's methodological backbone, as well as its narrative heart. I have brought my own analysis to the process, and I have drawn my own conclusions. But I also allowed the interviews to shape the questions that I asked, how I answered them, and what parts of the story I emphasized. As I spoke with survival school people—those who imagined, created, and maintained the schools, those who volunteered and worked in them, and those who attended them—though I asked about the past, they persistently pulled our conversations into the present tense. They also pushed the discussion further back in time than I had anticipated. The interviews thus reminded me that the schools' story is ongoing, and they revealed the powerful place that historical experience still holds in modern Indian people's lives.[1]

The people who talked to me in oral history interviews provided otherwise inaccessible information about the schools' founding, development, and outcomes. Because I am interested not just in what happened, but also in how people experienced it and what it has meant to them, using oral history methodology was essential to this project. Its very subjectivity became its strength, as it grounds the schools' story in a more humanized, intimate understanding of the past. Oral history is a particularly powerful tool for documenting the experiences of people who remain on the margins of the historical record. It becomes especially important when considering those whose cultural traditions privilege oral rather than written expression.[2] As Ojibwe language and culture teacher Dennis Jones insists, "Oral history is not only a valid tool for understanding Indian peoples; it is an essential tool. Everything does not have to be written down in order to be true." Oral tradition and storytelling remain central to Indigenous knowledge and social systems and to Native people's understanding of their own histories. Using oral history methodology helped me write a version of the survival schools' story that more closely reflects Indigenous historical experiences and perspectives.[3]

In addition to oral history interviews, I also conducted archival research in the written record of the survival schools' history, had informal conversations with survival school people, visited the Heart of the Earth school when it was still open, made visits to other Twin Cities Indian schools, and, when invited, attended community events and ceremonies. These research methods allowed me to construct a narrative of the schools' history and analyze their meanings within their local and regional context.

I also use the theoretical insights of settler colonial studies and Indigenous decolonization theory to place the survival schools' story within the larger framework of Indigenous history. Scholars' analysis of settler colonialism as a persistent and protean project to displace and replace Indigenous people reveals the connection between the nineteenth-century U.S. policies of dispossession and assimilation and the post–World War II urban environment in which AIM and the survival schools emerged. Indigenous decolonization theory situates AIM's activism within Indigenous peoples' global movements to reclaim not only their lands and political sovereignty, but also their social structures, cultural knowledge, and distinctive identities. Scholarship in both of these fields emphasizes the centrality of education within Indigenous historical experiences, both as an instrument of colonization and as a tool for decolonization. In the Twin Cities survival schools, then, the histories of American settler colonialism, Indian education, and Indigenous decolonization converge.[4]

Comparative and transnational theory frames the American Indigenous experience in a way that transcends myopic nationalism and challenges notions of American exceptionalism. These mind-sets have impoverished both scholarly analysis and public understanding of Native American history and limited Indigenous people's struggles for justice in the United States. This book, however, is neither primarily a work of theory nor a comparative study. While I use theoretical and comparative analysis to contextualize AIM and the survival schools, my narrative focuses on people's lived historical experiences in a particular local place.

In the writing of Indigenous histories, labeling never has been a neutral act. The words used to describe Native peoples are deeply embedded in historical relationships of power and laden with political significance. Thus I have chosen my terminology with care, while also realizing that the terms I use are imperfect and burdened with unintended connotations. I use "Indian" and "Native American" in reference to the Indigenous people of the Americas who now reside within the national boundaries of the continental United States (as opposed to Canada, where I would use First Nations, and distinct in both historical experience and legal status from Alaska Natives and Native Hawaiians). When I use "Indigenous" it is meant to convey something of the common cultural orientations, historical experiences, and/or contemporary concerns among the world's Indigenous peoples, though I also recognize the differences across cultural and national contexts. At times I follow Seminole scholar Susan Miller's lead in using the phrase "American Indigenous" (rather than "Indigenous American") to reveal the transnationality of Indigenous experience and identity, and to highlight Native Americans' existence outside of and in opposition to the American nation-state. When I quote Canadian scholars who use the term "Aboriginal" in the same way that I use "Indigenous," I leave the original language intact.[5]

Clearly, this naming business is complicated. Narrowing the focus to the level of tribe—or "nation" or "people"—does not simplify things. I generally use "Ojibwe" to refer to members of the largest tribe in Minnesota, rather than the more Europeanized "Chippewa" or the self-designation *Anishinaabe* (in the plural, *Anishinaabeg*). I do use the more amorphous *Anishinaabe(g)*—variously translated as "the first people," "the original people," or "the good people"—to refer to the ethnohistory and identity of the Algonquian-speaking peoples who migrated west from the eastern coastal regions of North America prior to European colonization. Over centuries of adaptation to places in what became the upper Midwest of the United States and south-central Canada, with populations particularly concentrated around the western Great Lakes, these related peoples developed into the modern Native nations of the Ojibwe, the Odawa, and the Potawatomi. "Anishinaabe" sometimes refers to these three tribes, who forged a historical alliance known as the Council of the Three Fires or Three Fires Confederacy. In recent decades some descendants of these Anishinaabeg have used this terminology to reclaim a precolonial Indigenous identity and mobilize it for spiritual and social revitalization.

Although it is possible that I have Anishinaabe or other Indian ancestors, I was not raised as a Native person, and I never have claimed an Indian identity. I do not write as an Indigenous scholar. But I did grow up on the Leech Lake reservation in north-central Minnesota, where I lived in the small town of Cass Lake from the time I was born until I graduated from high school. Many of my friends and schoolmates and the members of their extended families were Ojibwe people. Although I did not realize it at the time, this environment significantly shaped who I am, what I care about, and how I see the world. Undoubtedly, it influenced my decision to study Native American history in graduate school; certainly, it has made my work as a historian more than an academic exercise. When I read and write about Indian history, I am not dealing in abstract concepts. I am reading the history of people I grew up with. I am writing about processes, policies, and interactions that shaped the shared heritage and collective identity of the region I was born into and created the place that I call home.

Ojibwe storyteller Ignatia Broker tells us that long ago, Ojibwe children were taught, "Listen, and you will hear the patterns of life." Literary scholar J. Edward Chamberlin has written that "every culture not only hears but also listens to things—one of the problems being that we are not very good at doing so across times and places and across cultures." I have listened to Indigenous people talk about their experiences, and I have tried to interpret what I heard faithfully in the writing of this book. In the end this is my version of the schools' history; those who lived it might choose to tell it differently. I have done my best, however, to answer Indigenous education scholar K. Tsianina Lomawaima's call for research that is "guided by locally meaningful questions and concerns."[6]

Like Indigenous historian Susan Miller, I believe that the meaningful questions for Native people include, "What have they seen and felt?" and "What kinds of lives have they created?" as well as "What have they needed? What have they wanted?" and "What do their histories mean to them?" In exploring such questions I hope that what Heart of the Earth teacher Johnny Smith called my "inquisitive ways" have not hurt anyone. Perhaps my efforts can be of some use as Native people reflect on the past and work for the good of their families and communities. I also hope that this book will help non-Native people—students, teachers, school administrators, education policy makers, and general readers—come to a better understanding of Indigenous people's history and gain new perspective on their place in American society.[7]

Not Just a Bunch of Radicals:
A History of the Survival Schools

IN THE FALL OF 2011, I called Pat Bellanger, a Leech Lake Ojibwe activist, at her home in Minneapolis. As a longtime Twin Cities resident, an early American Indian Movement organizer, and a survival school founder, teacher, and parent, she had a long term perspective on AIM and the schools that she generously had shared with me over the course of multiple interviews. Because she recently had spent weeks of rehabilitation recovering from an injury, I wanted to see how she was doing.

As I should have anticipated, rather than recuperating quietly at home, Bellanger was busy organizing something. When I first met her ten years earlier, though she was then in her sixties and not in good health, she was planning events for Indian youth and elders, supporting Native language programs, developing diabetes education initiatives with doctors at the Native American Community Clinic, and lobbying the state government on water quality issues. At the time, Bellanger did most of her organizing from the back room of her brother's Native arts and gift shop on Franklin Avenue in Minneapolis; this recently revitalized urban corridor lined with Native agencies and businesses once had been the heart of the "Indian ghetto." Every time I went to see her there she was smiling and laughing, her black eyes bright with purpose, wearing a T-shirt supporting an Indian cause or proclaiming Indian pride, and in the middle of organizing something for the Twin Cities Indian community. As I got to know her, I came to see Bellanger's activism as the continuation of a forty-year-long

1

commitment to working for the well-being of Indian people that had begun as an AIM organizer in the 1960s.

When I called her on this November day in 2011, Bellanger was applying her organizing skills to a project designed to tell the story of AIM itself. She was planning for the American Indian Movement Interpretive Center, an ambitious initiative that she and other AIM founders and supporters had launched to collect, preserve, and exhibit AIM's history. As envisioned by Bellanger and other members of the executive board, the Center would hold an extensive archive of documents, artifacts, photographs, and audiovisual media and provide space for interpretive exhibits, community meetings, and public programs. That winter the group was developing plans and raising funds for the renovation of a nineteenth-century mansion to house the Center. The building, located in the Dinkytown neighborhood near the University of Minnesota's East Bank campus in Minneapolis, sits across the street from the former site of the Oh Day Aki/Heart of the Earth survival school, which Bellanger had helped found in 1972.

Over the time that I had known her, Pat Bellanger had spent hours talking to me about AIM's early history in the Twin Cities and its work to improve the lives and conditions of Indian people there. She had shared stories of the AIM survival schools' founding, development, and decline, and explained what they meant to those who created them and whose lives they influenced. Through these interviews and conversations, she had helped me understand the history of AIM and the survival schools so that I could tell their story to the world. Now, through the American Indian Movement Interpretive Center, she and other AIM founders and supporters were working to create a space in which they could tell their own story, on their own terms. Together, this book on the survival schools and the archives and exhibits of the AIM Interpretive Center will offer vital new perspectives on the American Indian Movement, its contribution to educational self-determination for Indian people, and its place in Indigenous history.

THE HISTORY of the American Indian Movement, as most Americans understand it, goes something like this: AIM was organized in Minneapolis in July 1968 by local Indian people fed up with the racism, discrimination, and socioeconomic disparities they experienced in the city and seeking to secure and expand Native American civil rights. Local leaders Clyde Bellecourt and Dennis Banks soon began organizing national protest actions to assert treaty rights and demand reforms in federal Indian policy.

By the early 1970s, AIM had become the most prominent Indian organization of the "Red Power" activist movement, with multiple national chapters and significant media attention. Between 1969 and 1973, AIM members participated in the occupations of Mount Rushmore and Alcatraz Island, organized the Trail of Broken Treaties, spearheaded the occupation of the Bureau of Indian Affairs headquarters in Washington, D.C., and led the occupation of Wounded Knee on the Pine Ridge reservation in South Dakota, resulting in an armed standoff with U.S. military forces. After the Wounded Knee takeover of 1973, AIM splintered under the pressure of federal prosecution, FBI infiltration, and internal dissension. By the mid-1970s, it had dissolved as a national organization.

While this is on the surface a true history of AIM, it is incomplete. It ignores the vigorous and wide-ranging local activism in the Twin Cities of Minneapolis and St. Paul that both preceded and outlasted the movement's national political actions. This version of AIM's history also oversimplifies organizers' concerns, motivations, and goals. It fails to fully explain the movement's origins, inadequately answering the question of just how and why this movement came into being in the summer of 1968.

Origins can be tricky things to trace. When the historical record consists largely of multiple individual memories rather than a single official document, finding the beginning becomes even more complicated. AIM emerged from a collection of experiences, an accumulation of choices, that developed and converged over time. So it is difficult to answer the question simply of how and where the movement really began.

According to one version of its origin story, AIM was formed at a community meeting held in north Minneapolis on July 28, 1968.[1] A group of Minnesota Ojibwe people, including Dennis Banks and George Mitchell from the Leech Lake reservation and Clyde Bellecourt from White Earth, organized the meeting for local Indian people to discuss the many challenges of life in the Twin Cities, and to find new solutions to the problems they faced. Some two hundred people attended the meeting, most of them Ojibwes with ties to Minnesota reservations. During the gathering, people voiced their frustrations with slum housing conditions, unemployment, police harassment, and discrimination by employers and landlords as well as in the schools, the welfare system, and the courts.[2]

During the meeting, Clyde Bellecourt rose to speak. In his 2004 memoir, Dennis Banks remembered Bellecourt urging people to take immediate action on the problem of police harassment. Describing Bellecourt as a "man in a hurry to get things done," Banks recalled that "he spoke with such intensity that his enthusiasm swept over us like a storm. In that moment, AIM was born."[3]

As Bellecourt has remembered it, he delivered a more wide-ranging "firebrand talk" in which he decried the damage done to Indian people by the federal government, the Christian church, and the Euro-American educational system. In an interview he described the argument he made that night:

> ... that these three institutions worked hand in hand, day in and day out, to strip us of our language, our culture; remove us from our land, our home; relocate us into large urban areas and then go in and steal what we had left. That we had to look at these three institutions as the three worst enemies of Indian people, that's the way I looked at it. I got up and gave this in my talk: these are our enemies, this is what we have to deal with every day, these three agencies work hand in hand to take what we have from us, and we had to design a program to confront every one of them, and to change the lives and conditions of Indian people.

By the end of the meeting, many of those in attendance had committed themselves to creating a new organization, with Bellecourt as chairman and Banks as field director. Charles Deegan, another White Earth Ojibwe man, was named vice chairman. Other early AIM organizers included Leech Lake Ojibwe Patricia (Pat) Bellanger and an Ojibwe man from the Lac Courte Oreilles reservation in northern Wisconsin named Edward (Eddie) Benton-Banai. All of them were in their early thirties at the time that AIM formed.[4]

As for a name, they first called themselves "Concerned Indian Americans," but after someone pointed out that this had the unfortunate acronym of "CIA," they reconsidered. Dennis Banks and Clyde Bellecourt both credit one of the group's elder women for suggesting "AIM." Banks remembered her saying, "You always 'aim' to do this and to do that. Why don't we just call ourselves 'AIM'?" So they did, and within a few weeks they had become the American Indian Movement. Then and later, calling themselves a "movement" was critically important for people who sought to create not just another organization, but a new collective force for change. The desire to create such a movement began well before the first organizing meeting in July 1968. For both Banks and Bellecourt, it began in prison.[5]

By the early 1960s Dennis Banks was living in the Minneapolis "Indian ghetto," working intermittently, drinking hard, and finding camaraderie through the struggles of city life with other Minnesota Ojibwes he knew from boarding school and military service. Like many other young Indian men, Banks spent time in prison. In 1966 he was arrested for burglary and spent two and a half years at Stillwater State Prison, where he "became politicized." He followed the social and political movements gathering strength outside the walls of Stillwater: the African American civil rights movement, Black Power, the student movements on college campuses, and the growing antiwar protests against U.S. involvement in Vietnam. He also read American Indian history and researched Indian civil rights issues. As Banks described it in his 2004 memoir, "Inside Stillwater, I made a commitment to myself that there would be an Indian movement." After his release from prison in May 1968, Banks reconnected with his old boarding school friend and fellow Leech Laker George Mitchell; together they organized "a series of meetings to get the Indian community in Minneapolis behind an effort to begin making the changes that we needed." That summer, Banks and Mitchell helped convene the meeting where AIM was formed.[6]

By the time Dennis Banks arrived at Stillwater State Prison, Clyde Bellecourt already had served his time there. Bellecourt was sentenced to Stillwater for robbery in 1962. Because he frequently broke prison rules, he spent considerable time in solitary confinement. While in solitary he was approached by Lac Courte Oreilles Ojibwe Eddie Benton-Banai and an Irish-American caseworker named James Donahue, who wanted to create an Indian cultural studies group for Native prisoners. Bellecourt helped organize the group, which brought him a sense of identity and purpose. After his release from prison in 1964, he organized efforts to improve Indian life in the Twin Cities and introduce urban Native people to knowledge about their cultural heritage. This work eventually brought him together with Dennis Banks, George Mitchell, and others at AIM's first organizing meeting. As Bellecourt once told a reporter, "People always say that the American Indian Movement started in 1968. But to me it started in the hole at Stillwater in '62."[7]

With its seeds planted in prison and cultivated through years of community organizing, AIM took root in Minneapolis in the summer of 1968. Soon Dennis Banks, Clyde Bellecourt, and other AIM leaders would become the public face of a national Indian movement that forcefully rejected the status quo, both in the conditions of Indian people's lives and in Native activists' responses to them. In their first few years in the Twin Cities, AIM organizers launched multiple community initiatives to improve Native

5

people's lives in Minneapolis and St. Paul, including the founding of two alternative schools in 1972: first the A.I.M. Survival School (later named Heart of the Earth, then Oh Day Aki) in Minneapolis, followed by the Red School House in St. Paul. AIM's origins and its local work in the Twin Cities are much less well understood than its national politics, and the schools that AIM people founded have received little attention in either scholarly or popular histories.[8]

This book provides a history of the Twin Cities survival schools from their opening in 1972, through the closing of Red School House in 1996, to the closing of Oh Day Aki/Heart of the Earth in 2008. In telling this story, I also illuminate the origins and the early work of the American Indian Movement in Minneapolis and St. Paul from AIM's founding in 1968 to the schools' creation in 1972. Examining AIM through the lens of the survival schools reveals a group of parents and community activists working to nurture Native youth, strengthen and protect Indian families, and achieve self-determination within urban institutions. The survival schools' story demonstrates that rather than disappearing in the mid-1970s, AIM people continued to work for change in Minneapolis and St. Paul for decades. Thus the movement's long-term impact on Indian people's lives becomes more clear. While AIM is best known for its national protests and political demands, the schools foreground its local and regional engagement with issues of language, culture, spirituality, and identity.

The survival schools also allow us to see Native women's importance as community organizers and cultural leaders. Ojibwe historian Brenda Child has noted the lack of attention to women's roles in the American Indian Movement, despite women's significant contributions to AIM's community activism in the Twin Cities. She notes in particular how women's work during AIM's early years in Minneapolis and St. Paul "laid a foundation for new institutions for education and social welfare that have been extraordinarily long-lived in the Indian community." While AIM's male leaders made public speeches and got the attention of the national media, Child argues that "women held the majority of sustained leadership roles in the community through their participation in the less sensational but no less important or visionary work of organizing new schools" and advocating for the rights of Native families and children. "Their body of work," Child asserts, "is a breathtaking achievement that led to increased well-being for Indians in Minnesota and greater sovereignty for Indian people nationwide." The survival schools were part of this important work.[9]

On one level we can trace AIM's origins, and those of the survival schools, to a particular time, place, and set of conditions within the Indian communities of Minneapolis and St. Paul in the 1960s. Yet, as the schools' story demonstrates, AIM also responded to the long history of Euro-American efforts to sever Native people's ties to their homelands, eradicate their distinctive societies, and transform their cultural identities, a campaign waged most aggressively within the federal boarding schools of the late nineteenth and early twentieth centuries. Indian people in the Twin Cities organized AIM in part as an antidote to the long-term effects of historical assimilation policies. They also resisted ongoing systemic efforts to assimilate Indian people in the postwar urban communities where they lived. In this way, the AIM survival schools are part of the story of Indigenous colonization, resistance, survival, and revitalization in the United States. Because these also have been transnational processes, we must understand the AIM schools in the larger context of the Indigenous decolonization movements that began taking shape around the world in the 1960s. The history of the survival schools, then, is both intensely local and thoroughly global.

Through the AIM survival schools, I illuminate the postwar experiences of Indian people in Minneapolis and St. Paul, including Native families' relationships to Twin Cities public schools. Although not a comprehensive local study, this contributes to our understanding of the history of urban Indian communities. My book also helps bring the history of Indian education beyond the federal boarding schools and into the twenty-first century. At the same time, it reveals how profoundly and persistently the legacy of boarding school education has continued to shape Indian people's lives.

By telling the survival schools' story, I also make a significant contribution to the scholarship on postwar Indian activism. Most studies of the "Red Power" movement have focused on the high-profile protest actions of the 1960s and 1970s: the fish-ins in the Pacific Northwest, the occupations of Alcatraz and the BIA headquarters, and the confrontation at Wounded Knee. Yet the same period saw the beginnings of a national movement for educational self-determination among Indian people and the emergence of the first community-controlled Indian schools. Listening to the voices of those who criticized mainstream education and created their own alternatives reveals another kind of activism during this time, with a sustained focus on familial, cultural, and community-based concerns.

Both the substance and the style of AIM's activism have generated controversy since its founding in 1968. In my hometown of Cass Lake on the

Leech Lake reservation in northern Minnesota, a 1972 AIM protest over the tribal council's position on treaty rights met resistance from both Indian and non-Indian residents, who questioned AIM activists' motivations and challenged their right to speak for local people. The Cass Lake protest and its aftermath raised racial tensions and created social conflicts that still shape reservation politics today, and some locals remain critical of AIM's long-term impact on the community. Some critics have faulted AIM spokesmen like Clyde Bellecourt and Dennis Banks for creating images of militant Indianness that garnered national media attention but accomplished little of real value for Indian people. Others have criticized some of AIM's most prominent male leaders for the size of their egos, their treatment of women, their substance abuse, and their criminal records.

Although these are legitimate critiques, the picture they paint is incomplete. Over time, the perpetuation of such a one-dimensional public image—owing in part to the actions of some AIM leaders themselves—has obscured a much more complex historical reality and limited both academic and popular understanding. This book tells a different story: of AIM's origins and its early activism in the Twin Cities, of the survival schools and their meanings for Indian people, and of the place they hold in Indigenous history.

Seminole historian Susan Miller asserts that "the ultimate purpose of Indigenous historiography is to place Indigenous peoples and communities at the center of historical narratives and to reflect their behavior and motives in terms of their own realities." I have told this story as much as possible from the perspectives of those who were close to the schools, drawing from the memories of those I was able to talk to and the voices that spoke most clearly from the written records. While I acknowledge other points of view, I do not develop them as thoroughly. Although I have not ignored the conflicts and disappointments present in the schools' history, overall I have interpreted their story as one of perseverance, creativity, and hope. In the end, my position is a relatively sympathetic one. I did not set out to valorize AIM organizers or survival school founders, any more than I would want to villainize them. But I listened when Clyde Bellecourt told me that they "were not just a bunch of radicals," that they "were sincere about our children, and our family, and our community."[10]

This is not the whole history of the American Indian Movement. AIM people will continue to tell their own story, in speeches and presentations, in interviews with journalists, at conferences, and now through the American

Indian Movement Interpretive Center. I would not presume to write their history for them. But I do have what I believe is an important story to tell about the AIM survival schools, one that draws from multiple conversations and extended interactions with AIM organizers and other survival school people. I also have a deep knowledge of American Indigenous history and a broad theoretical perspective gained from comparative analysis of global Indigenous experiences. My perspective also has been shaped by the personal experience of growing up in the part-Indian community of Cass Lake and spending years living in Minneapolis, both places that I love. I have brought all these dimensions of my intellectual and emotional self to the task of researching and writing a history of the survival schools. This book is the result.

CHAPTER 1

The Origins of the Twin Cities Indian Community and the American Indian Movement

O N A MONDAY MORNING IN NOVEMBER the students, staff, and guests of Heart of the Earth school in Minneapolis gathered in their lunchroom to listen to a guest speaker, a Lac Courte Oreilles Ojibwe man named Eddie Benton-Banai. Before the talk, cultural instructor Johnny Smith, a Red Lake Ojibwe, led a group of Indian boys in drumming and singing while other Native children danced, dressed in colorful regalia. Among the drummers, ten-year-old Mukwah Bellanger sang with enthusiasm while his eleven-year-old sister Binaishi, danced gracefully in a jingle dress. Their mother, Leech Lake Ojibwe Lisa Bellanger, watched proudly from the back of the room.

After the performance Clyde Bellecourt, a large, imposing, White Earth Ojibwe man in his early sixties, stood before the students and introduced Benton-Banai as the founder and longtime director of Heart of the Earth's former sister school in St. Paul, the Red School House. Bellecourt praised Benton-Banai as a great spiritual leader and honored him as the Grand Chief of the Midewiwin lodge, the spiritual center of traditional Anishinaabe society. Then he explained to the audience how the two men had first met back in 1962, when both were incarcerated at Stillwater State Prison. Benton-Banai had organized the American Indian Folklore Group for Native prisoners to learn about their history, culture, and spiritual traditions. During their first meeting, Bellecourt recalled, Benton-Banai had drawn a picture of a Midewiwin ceremonial lodge on the chalkboard. "Someday," Benton-Banai had promised the men, "we're going to be back in that lodge."

At the time, Bellecourt told the Heart of the Earth students, he had no idea what Benton-Banai meant. He knew little about his Ojibwe heritage and nothing about the ceremonies that would take place in such a lodge. He had spent his adolescence in correctional institutions and most of his adult life finding trouble on the streets of Minneapolis and moving in and out of jail. At twenty-six years old, in prison, in despair, how could he know what was to come?

THE SURVIVAL SCHOOLS began with two Indian families. They began in the Hennepin and Ramsey County welfare agencies and in juvenile court. They began in the hallways and classrooms of the Minneapolis and St. Paul public schools. They began in the offices of the American Indian Movement. They began in Stillwater State Prison. They began in the government boarding schools.

To understand AIM's emergence, its early work in Minneapolis and St. Paul, and the creation of the survival schools, we need to consider them in historical context. What brought so many Indian people to a community meeting on a July night in 1968, and what led AIM's organizers to call them together? What compelled them to take on the responsibility of educating their community's children three and a half years later? To answer these questions, we need to listen to the expressions of frustration and desire, and trace the convergence of local circumstances and national historical developments, that made AIM and the survival schools both possible and necessary.

AIM formed in part as a response to the conditions of postwar urban Indian life in the Twin Cities of Minneapolis and St. Paul. Socioeconomic disparities and anti-Indian prejudice, combined with the disorienting experience of cultural dissonance and the cross-generational impact of cultural loss, made life in the city a struggle for many Native people in the post–World War II period. Conflicts within the criminal justice, child welfare, and public school systems would become especially pressing concerns for Native Twin Citians by the late 1960s.

The Twin Cities Indian community itself went back to the early twentieth century, and it had developed out of the historical experiences of Ojibwe and other Native people in Minnesota and elsewhere in the upper Midwest since the mid-nineteenth century. Beginning in the 1830s, generations of Native people in the region dealt with the intensifying consequences of American colonialism: the dispossession of their lands, the appropriation of their resources, the disruption of their economic and social systems, and the assimilationist assault on their cultural identities. After 1900, in response to these disruptive forces, increasing numbers of Indian people migrated to and made their lives in Minneapolis and St. Paul; there they built a tradition of collective activism to better their lives and conditions in the city and to create a new place for themselves in American society. AIM's organizers thus stood on a historical foundation of colonization, survival, activism, and urban community that was decades in the making. While building on this foundation, the people of the American Indian Movement also engaged in a new kind of local activism, driven by their personal experiences and shaped by postwar circumstances.

Colonialism and Its Consequences in the Upper Midwest, 1830–1900

The history of Indigenous people in America always has been a story of interaction, adaptation, and migration. Centuries before the first Europeans arrived, Native peoples had built complex societies adapted to particular physical environments and interacted with one another through trade, political alliances, warfare, intermarriage, and other forms of political, economic, social, and cultural exchange. While finding ways to survive in their environments and adjust to each other, Indigenous communities undertook many migrations, some small-scale and temporary, others of epic proportions across long spans of time. When European explorers, missionaries, traders, and settlers arrived and began to implement their nations' colonial projects, Native peoples continued patterns of selective adaptation and strategic migration in response to the newcomers' presence, their new technologies, and their desire for land and resources. In many places, and in some cases for long periods of time, these strategies helped Indigenous people survive and even thrive in the new worlds created by European colonization. Over time, as the number of European and then American settlers and their demand for land and resources increased, Indigenous people's options dwindled. The necessary adaptations incurred greater losses and the migrations became more drastic and more difficult. As American power and expansionist ambitions grew, more migrations were undertaken by force or out of desperation, and they had increasingly devastating consequences.

The colonization of Indigenous people's lands and lives in what became the United States did not end after the thirteen colonies won their independence from Britain; rather, it accelerated its pace and expanded its reach. After the Louisiana Purchase of 1803 and the War of 1812, the shifting balance of power among the French, British, and Americans that previously had afforded Native people strategic political advantages gave way to American dominance and removed barriers to U.S. territorial expansion west of the Appalachians and then across the Mississippi River. As U.S. policy makers sought to bring more territory and resources under national control and open more areas to Euro-American settlement, they worked to restrict Indigenous people's political sovereignty and remove them from their homelands.

In the upper Midwest the pressures of American colonization began to escalate for the region's Native people in the 1820s, as U.S. expansion and Euro-American settlement intensified in the region. In subsequent decades it became increasingly difficult for Indigenous people of the western Great Lakes and northern Plains regions to maintain the integrity of their traditional economies and the political and social structures that had sustained them for generations. It also became impossible to remain in full occupation of their homelands. From the 1830s to 1900, the Indigenous people in what became Michigan, Wisconsin, Minnesota, and eastern North and South Dakota—the Potawatomis, Menominees, Ho-Chunks, Ojibwes, and Dakotas—went from a position of relative political and economic strength and cultural integrity to one of dispossession and social crisis.

With the regional decline of the fur trade and the collapse of the interdependent alliances that had supported it, the Indigenous people of this region lost their primary source of economic and political power. At the same time, the federal government and territorial and state legislatures, along with timber and mining companies and Euro-American settlers, all sought increasing control over Native people's lands. The establishment of statehood for Michigan, Wisconsin, and Minnesota between 1837 and 1858 encouraged new waves of Euro-American settlement into the region, increasing demands to open access to Indian-controlled land. Between the 1830s and the 1860s, Native people signed treaties that ceded most of the land in the upper Midwest to the U.S. government. The stipulations of some treaties required tribal people to leave their homelands for reserved areas to the west, while others retained reservations within their home territories. In return, tribes were supposed to secure federal trust protection over reservation lands and receive annuities in cash, food, and material goods as well as agricultural training, education, and services such as blacksmiths and mills. The Ojibwes, who maintained the largest Native land base in the region, also retained rights to continue traditional economic practices of hunting, fishing, and gathering in certain ceded territories.

The Dakota War, fought against the U.S. government and settlers in southern Minnesota in 1862, both resulted from and accelerated the patterns of land loss, economic disruption, and cultural conflict for the region's Native people. After the Dakotas' defeat, Minnesotans' reactions to the recent hostilities, combined with the drive for territorial expansion west of the Mississippi River, led the federal government to nullify its most recent treaty with the Dakotas, abrogate their reservations along the Minnesota River, and forcibly remove most of them from the state. Pressures to remove other Indian tribes from the region also increased, fueled by the desires of traders and speculators and the owners of lumber and mining companies for Native land.

By 1890, most Dakota people had either fled or been exiled from Minnesota to reservations in North and South Dakota and Nebraska or reserves in Canada. The majority of Ho-Chunks and Potawatomis had been removed to reservations in Nebraska and Kansas. Those who remained in Wisconsin in defiance of removal orders had no reservation land base. The Ojibwes largely were confined to reservations in northern Minnesota, Wisconsin, and Michigan, while the Menominees retained a small reservation in Wisconsin.

Even for those who held on to some reservation territory, the reduction of their land base through treaty cessions severely compromised Native people's ability to sustain themselves through their traditional seasonal round of subsistence activities. The viability of the Native economy also suffered from the effects of American logging and mining operations, which destroyed the resources that had provided food, medicines, clothing, housing, tools, and weapons. As a result, the Native people of the upper Midwest became increasingly dependent on treaty annuities. But the unauthorized alteration of treaty provisions, the diversion of annuity monies to pay off inflated trade debts, the corruption among government agents, and the tendency for payments to be distributed late—or sometimes not at all—rendered the annuity system an unreliable source of economic survival. By the turn of the twentieth century, Native communities across the region suffered from hunger, destitution, and epidemic disease.

At the same time that Euro-Americans took possession of Native people's land and resources and undermined their economies, they also worked to change their social systems and transform their cultural identities. Federal

Indian agents implemented policies designed to turn the members of tribal communities into individualized, market-oriented, Christian farmers. Missionaries established reservation churches and mission schools to convert Native people to Christianity and to inculcate new value systems and forms of social organization. By the late nineteenth century, Native people across the upper Midwest lived under a heavy blanket of cultural repression.

The U.S. government's policies toward Indigenous people in the nineteenth century constituted a complex and evolving relationship of settler colonialism. In the British colonies that formed the seed of the United States, a significant settler population had come to stay in North America, seeking to build farms and towns and permanent lives, bringing settlers into escalating conflict with Indigenous populations over access to and control of land and resources. This contrasted with the extraction colonialism that characterized the French and Spanish colonies, where a smaller and more transient European population exploited the colonial territory primarily for the extraction of resources and used Native people for the labor to acquire them. When the United States declared its independence from Britain, leaders of the new nation conceptualized Indigenous American people and formulated national Indian policy within the framework of a settler state, intent on asserting sovereignty over its territory and gaining control over Indian-occupied lands. Thus U.S.–Indian relations developed within a particular historical circumstance of settler colonialism; this was one expression of a larger transnational process that also shaped the development of nation-states in former British colonies such as Canada, Australia, New Zealand, and Northern Ireland.

According to historian Patrick Wolfe, the essential characteristic of settler colonialism is what he calls the "logic of elimination," through which the settler state and its citizens seek to "displace and replace" the Native population in the territories they want to occupy and control. Thus the logic of elimination functions through the "attempt to remove Native societies from their land and replace them with settler ones." As Wolfe insists, "the primary motive for elimination is . . . access to territory. Territoriality is settler colonialism's specific, irreducible element." Therefore, Indigenous people's occupation of desirable territory, and their profound cultural attachment to their homelands, drive the settler imperative of displacement and replacement.[1]

Settler colonial relations do not end once the "frontier" disappears and Indigenous people have been conquered. In a settler state like the United

States, where Native people still occupy remnants of their original homelands, national political and economic forces continue to try to dispossess them. As long as Indigenous people remain within the nation's borders, and as long as they maintain some degree of the distinctive social and economic systems and cultural identities that tie them to the land, elements within the settler society will seek to get rid of them. Historically, the methods for displacing and replacing Indigenous peoples have taken multiple malleable forms, and they have proven remarkably persistent over time. From the late eighteenth through the mid-nineteenth centuries in the United States, the government worked to eliminate Indigenous people—physically, politically, economically, socially, and culturally—through military conquest, treaties, removal, reservations, and assimilation policies.[2]

In the upper Midwest, both the scope of American settler colonialism and the enormity of its consequences for Native people intensified after 1880. In the late nineteenth century, federal policy makers developed the policy of allotment, which worked to displace and replace Indian people through the privatization of reservation land and resources. The Dawes Act of 1887 allotted most collectively held reservation lands in the region into individually owned parcels, distributed mostly to male heads of households. Federal and state allotment legislation also authorized the sale of remaining "surplus" land to state governments, speculators, farmers, and logging and mining interests. Initial protective provisions that restricted the sale or lease of allotments were subsequently lifted through state and federal legislation, rendering reservation land vulnerable to exploitation.

As elsewhere in the country, land allotment in the upper Midwest proceeded in tandem with a more aggressive federal assimilation policy. Allotment, proponents believed, would encourage Native people to reject their commitment to collectivism in favor of individualism, private property ownership, and the patriarchal nuclear family. In turn, the replacement of collective societies with individualized citizens was intended to loosen Native ties to the land and facilitate its expropriation. In the late nineteenth and into the early twentieth centuries, federal and state policy makers accelerated efforts to make tribal people abandon their traditional communal economies, as well as their entire cultural systems.

For the Ojibwes, who had retained the most reservation land in the region, allotment resulted in what historian Brenda Child has called "a devastating loss of country." Land loss, combined with state game and fish laws that restricted treaty rights to hunt, fish, and gather in their former homelands, made the traditional subsistence economy nearly impossible to sustain after the turn of the twentieth century. At the same time, despite the plans and promises of American policy makers, the quality of most reservation land allowed few residents to make a living from farming. Assimilation programs and the repression of non-Christian religious practices made Native spiritual traditions as difficult to maintain as their traditional economies. For Ojibwes and other Native people in the region, poverty took a firm hold over their lives and the social and spiritual fabric of their communities became stressed and torn.[3]

Indigenous Survival and the Twin Cities Indian Community, 1900–1940

Indigenous people did not give way passively to U.S. colonialism. As they faced the forces of chaos and change, they devised creative ways to maintain the integrity of their way of life for as long as possible. Individuals, families, and political and spiritual leaders weighed options and made decisions in an effort to shape their own futures during these troubled times. As it had in the past, migration emerged as a key survival strategy. In the early twentieth century, growing numbers of Ojibwes, along with some members of other upper Midwestern tribes, began migrating to the "Twin Cities" of Minneapolis and St. Paul, where they established a small urban Indian community and continued to adapt to a changing world.

After the turn of the twentieth century, economic conditions on Ojibwe reservations made it increasingly difficult for people to sustain themselves or to see much hope for the future on reservation land. Even those who had become most open to change found that the profits of a market economy mostly benefited Euro-American companies, settlers, and speculators. Many people also became frustrated with the federal control and political divisiveness that pervaded reservation society. After 1900, some moved from within reservation boundaries to settle in nearby small towns and midsized cities, seeking work.

The best chance for economic opportunity lay in the Twin Cities, an urban center at the confluence of the Minnesota and Mississippi rivers. Prior to American colonization, Dakota people had lived in villages in the area and had become deeply rooted in the land and waters there, which they used for transportation, subsistence, and trade and invested with meaning as places of spiritual and ancestral significance. After decades of coexisting with the growing American presence that spread out from Fort Snelling and founded the cities of St. Paul and Minneapolis, most Dakotas were expelled from the area in the wake of the 1862 war.

In the 1910s and 1920s, Ojibwe people from Minnesota reservations began moving to the Twin Cities in growing numbers. In the 1920s and 1930s, Dakotas and Lakotas from North and South Dakota and Ho-Chunks and Menominees from Wisconsin began joining them, though in significantly smaller numbers. By the end of the 1920s, according to one historian's estimate, just under a thousand Indian people lived in the Twin Cities, among a total population of almost 736,000. From the 1910s to the early 1940s, most of the Indian residents were Ojibwes, most came from Minnesota, and many had migrated from the White Earth reservation, where allotment had been especially devastating to the reservation land base and had fostered deep social divisions.[4]

These early urban residents had mixed experiences. Many of them found economic stability and some achieved a middle-class standard of living. Most Ojibwes lived in South Minneapolis, especially in the Stevens Square and Phillips areas south of downtown. There they rented and owned dwellings in mixed neighborhoods of working-class and lower-middle-class Whites, a few Blacks, and a smattering of Indian people. Along with their neighbors, many of these urban Ojibwes found good work in the 1920s, then struggled with common economic hardship in the 1930s.[5]

Frederick Peake, his wife Louise, and his daughter Natalie moved to Minneapolis from the White Earth reservation in 1914. During the 1920s, Peake worked as an inspector at a flour mill, and the family, including second daughter Emily, established a comfortable residence in a duplex in the Stevens Square neighborhood. With the onset of the Depression, Peake lost his job, worked as a day laborer, then suffered a period of unemployment. To help support the family, Louise took on work cleaning houses. During the lean years of the 1930s, the Peake family's circumstances mirrored those of their non-Indian neighbors. While attending grade school and high school in Minneapolis, Emily did well academically and had many non-Indian friends.[6]

Not all Native people, however, found the same degree of economic opportunity or social acceptance in the Twin Cities during this time. Winnie Jourdain moved from White Earth to Minneapolis in the mid-1920s, looking for work. Her husband had died of tuberculosis, leaving her at age twenty-five to support herself and her young son. Late in her life, Jourdain told a reporter that at the time she moved to Minneapolis, "The city was full of prejudice." When it came to employment, "Indian people were the last ones hired and the first ones fired." Another Minneapolis Indian resident, Sophia White, recalled widespread anti-Indian discrimination in the early 1940s in both employment and housing. She also recounted that "many restaurants and taverns turned Indian people away," leaving them to gather in the "Indian bars" like the Harbor Bar and Tony's in South Minneapolis. Even Frederick Peake's daughter Emily seems to have run up against prejudice when she graduated from high school in 1938 and began looking for a job. Despite good grades, solid clerical skills, and a stabilizing local economy, Peake struggled to find work, while all of her non-Indian friends quickly landed jobs.[7]

Even when migration to the city offered economic gains to Indian people, it could bring other kinds of losses. Minneapolis and St. Paul lay hundreds of miles from some of the reservations that urban migrants had called home. The move to the Cities distanced Native people from their extended families and familiar environments, and from the shared history and social system of reservation life. While traditional ways had been seriously weakened in reservation communities, in Euro-American urban society they were nonexistent. Those who moved to the city also found that their off-reservation status threatened their rights to tribal membership and treaty-based federal benefits.[8]

Confronted with the uncertainties that characterized urban life, Native people worked to create the best lives possible for themselves and their families. In keeping with traditional Native values of sharing and cooperation, established residents like Frederick and Louise Peake, Winnie Jourdain, and others opened their homes to more recent arrivals to the city, offering shelter, food, and tips on finding jobs and housing. Louise Peake hosted gatherings of Ojibwe women to talk about their common experiences and offer mutual support. Winnie Jourdain organized efforts to help the children of impoverished families succeed in the city's public schools. She and other Native women made and sold quilts and held rummage sales and potluck dinners to raise money for textbooks and eyeglasses. Jourdain also tutored struggling Indian students and helped recent high school graduates find housing.[9]

In addition to these mutual-assistance networks, Ojibwe people in the Twin Cities also formed more formal organizations. Some of these groups, such as the Twin Cities Chippewa Council, had political agendas. Founded in the 1920s by Frederick Peake, the Council lobbied for the tribal and treaty rights of Ojibwe people living off the reservation. Other organizations sponsored dances and other social gatherings, promoted language preservation, and worked to increase public knowledge of Minnesota's Indian heritage and Indian people's contributions to American society.[10]

By 1940, an urban Indian community had taken shape in the Twin Cities. It was a community of common background, composed primarily—though not exclusively—of Ojibwe people who had migrated from Minnesota reservations. It was a community of broadly shared urban experiences: the adjustment from reservation to city life, the need to find work and housing, the problem of anti-Indian prejudice, the threats to tribal rights. Finally, it was a community of individuals working collectively to improve conditions and create better lives for themselves and their fellow urban Indian people.

Development of the Twin Cities Indian Community, 1940–68

After the United States entered into World War II, the Twin Cities Indian population grew significantly. Across the country, the war years transformed the lives of many Native people through military service, war work, and intensified patterns of migration. Nationally, more than twenty-five thousand Indian men served in the military during the war, while several hundred women served as nurses and in the WAC and WAVES. Another forty thousand Indian men and women worked in defense plants and other war-related industries. Most of them moved to major cities for these jobs.[11]

As in other urban areas, Indian people in Minneapolis and St. Paul found employment in war-related industries. One historian estimates that 1,800 Native people worked in defense industries in Minnesota during World War II, most of them in the Twin Cities. They worked in factories for such companies as Honeywell, Northern Pump, Minneapolis Moline, and Crown Iron Works, where they labored as mechanics, assemblers, riveters, welders, and electricians. Indian women as well as men worked in wartime factories. Frederick and Louise Peake's daughter Emily got a job making parachutes at the Honeywell plant, while other Native women worked as welders for U.S. Air Conditioning in Minneapolis. Native women also worked as nurses and cooks and found employment in domestic service during the war years.[12]

The Twin Cities Indian population rose dramatically during World War II and in the postwar period, as it did in other American cities. According to one estimate, because of employment in war industries, the Indian population of Minneapolis and St. Paul increased from under a thousand in the 1920s, to about six thousand by 1945. Once the war ended, many of them stayed, and some of the more than a thousand Indian people from Minnesota who served in the armed forces during the war also moved to the city after they returned to the United States. For many American Indian people, their war service had brought them away from the reservation and into close and sustained contact with non-Indian society for the first time. Serving and fighting for the United States also raised many young veterans' hopes about what they might achieve and what American society might offer them. After the war, rather than return to their reservations, some Indian people chose to try their luck in cities like Minneapolis and St. Paul.[13]

In the 1950s, Indian migration to American cities skyrocketed. From 1945 to 1958, about a hundred thousand Indian people nationwide left reservation communities for urban areas. By 1960, the census reported that one-third of the nation's Indian people lived in cities; by 1970, that number rose to 45 percent. These statistics reflect developments in national Indian policy. In the late 1940s and early 1950s, policy makers sought to reduce or eliminate federal responsibility for Indian affairs, break up the reservation system, move Indian people to cities, and assimilate them into mainstream American life. These goals became manifested in the federal policies of the 1950s: compensation, termination, and relocation. Relocation policy, which encouraged Indian people across the country to leave their reservations for life in the city, significantly accelerated existing patterns of urban Indian migration.

After piloting smaller-scale, more localized efforts, the Bureau of Indian Affairs (BIA) launched its national relocation program in 1952. BIA officials and relocation propaganda promised relocatees good jobs, pleasant homes, adventure, excitement, and the opportunity to achieve an integrated, middle-class lifestyle, as well as social equality and freedom from the restrictions of reservation life. The program provided transportation to the city, assistance finding jobs and housing, and a small stipend to help relocatees get through the first transitional weeks. The relocation program began in seven major cities, including Los Angeles, Denver, and Chicago, then expanded over the course of the decade. Attracted by the promises of relocation, and frustrated with the economic limitations and political tensions on many reservations, thousands of Indian individuals and families migrated to urban areas in the 1950s and 1960s. By the end of 1954, more than six thousand American Indians had relocated to cities in twenty states. Although the BIA did not designate the Twin Cities an official relocation site, public and private agencies in Minneapolis and St. Paul initiated smaller-scale relocation programs, and the BIA area office in Minneapolis opened an employment placement office for new arrivals in 1948.[14]

Even without a full-blown relocation effort, the Twin Cities absorbed a tremendous influx of American Indian migrants from the early 1950s through the 1960s. For Minneapolis, the federal census reported a rise in the Indian population from 145 in 1949, to more than 2,000 in 1960, and up to 5,829 by 1970. In St. Paul, the census counted 60 Native people in 1940, 524 in 1960, and 1,906 in 1970. The actual population certainly exceeded the census numbers, which chronically undercounted Native people in this period. The Minnesota Council of Churches, for instance, estimated 8,000 Indians in the Twin Cities in 1955. By 1969, a research team from the University of Minnesota placed the Minneapolis Indian population at somewhere between 8,000 and 10,000, just under 2 percent of the city's total population of 489,000. Another university report counted about 3,000 Indian residents in St. Paul in 1965, climbing to 4,000 by 1969, when the city had a total population of about 300,000. Drawing from these higher numbers, a different group of researchers estimated that by 1970, 43 percent of Minnesota's Indian people were living in the Twin Cities, up from 21 percent just ten years earlier.[15]

By the 1960s, the Twin Cities Indian population had not only grown larger, it also had become younger and more diverse. While a small number of Indian people had lived in Minneapolis and St. Paul since the 1910s and 1920s, now a younger group of recent migrants comprised the majority of the urban Indian community. The range of Native nations, homelands, and reservation communities from which people migrated also proliferated. In the postwar period, though most urban Indian residents still were Ojibwes, the numbers of Dakotas, Lakotas, Ho-Chunks, and Menominees increased. Other Twin Cities residents identified themselves as Oneida, Cree, Iroquois, Arikara, Cherokee, Ponca, Omaha, Blackfeet, and Tlinget. Although most Twin Cities Indians still came from reservations in Minnesota, Wisconsin, and the Dakotas, others hailed from Nebraska, Oklahoma, Mississippi, Kentucky, Washington, Alaska, and Canada. Some differences existed between the Indian populations in Minneapolis and St. Paul. In Minneapolis, the great majority of Indian people were Ojibwe, followed by Dakotas and

Lakotas. In St. Paul, a higher percentage of Dakota and Lakota people and a significant number of Ho-Chunks joined a slimmer Ojibwe majority.[16]

"I Felt Like Walking Right Out of Minneapolis": Socioeconomic Struggles in the Native Twin Cities, 1945–68

Despite their growing diversity, Indian people in Minneapolis and St. Paul had many things in common in the postwar years. Like the migrants of earlier decades, most of them came to the city seeking employment. As their numbers grew, some also moved to join family or friends. By the 1950s, most Twin Cities Indian people also encountered a similar set of socioeconomic challenges in their attempts to build lives for themselves and their families. They struggled to find work and adequate housing, suffered from poor health, lacked access to social services, and ran into trouble with the justice system.[17]

Members of the postwar Indian community faced what historian Nancy Shoemaker calls a "radically different urban environment" than that of the 1920s and 1930s. Prior to World War II, many Indian people rented and owned residences in integrated, working-class and lower-middle-class areas of Minneapolis and St. Paul. While some Native people encountered prejudice and discrimination among employers, others found good jobs, and the overall economic opportunities of the city's Indian population generally resembled those of their non-Indian neighbors. After the war, both stable employment and decent housing became increasingly scarce for Twin Cities Indian people, and their social conditions diverged from those of working- and middle-class Whites.[18]

Although most postwar Indian migrants moved to the Cities for better economic opportunities, by the 1960s many of them struggled to find employment, or to find work that paid a living wage. One study from 1965 estimated that half of employable Indian people in St. Paul were unemployed, at a time when the national average stood at just 4 percent. In 1970, census figures reported that the average income for St. Paul Indian families was half that of the general population. In Minneapolis, an early 1970s civil rights commission found that in both the private and public sectors, Indian workers generally held the lowest-paying positions. A university research team wrote in late 1969 of "the overwhelmingly preponderant numbers of urban Indians who live in poverty or at least in the status of low-income recipients." The researchers concluded that "although there are *some* middle-class urban Indians in Minneapolis, there do not appear to be many."[19]

Growing anti-Indian prejudice as well as the changing urban economy worked to the disadvantage of Indian job seekers in postwar Minneapolis and St. Paul. Some employers openly refused to hire any American Indian applicants. Pat Bellanger, an Ojibwe woman from the Leech Lake reservation in northern Minnesota, lived in St. Paul in the 1960s. She remembers how "in the paper there would be want ads that would say, 'Indians need not apply.' That was a real hard thing to face, to try to get a job." Increased competition for jobs after the war—as those who had served in the armed forces returned and as overall migration to the city increased—made discrimination against Indian applicants more acute. The kind of work available also shifted from unskilled labor to more skilled, specialized, and professional positions. Many Indian people lacked the formal education and the job training necessary to secure anything other than unskilled positions. Unskilled jobs also paid less than they did in the prewar years, and by the mid-1950s most of the good jobs were located in the rapidly developing suburbs. Because so many Twin Cities Indians lived in inner-city neighborhoods and did not own cars, many jobs became inaccessible to them.[20]

Postwar conditions also worked against Indian people in their search for housing. The influx of new migrants in the 1940s and 1950s, both Indian and non-Indian, led to housing shortages. Housing availability shrank further in the late 1960s because of urban renewal and freeway construction projects that destroyed thousands of low-income units. Within this tight housing market, landlords practiced both overt and covert discrimination against Native people. While some bluntly advertised their policies against renting to Indians, others put up barriers by requiring large rent deposits and extensive credit checks. Some would not rent to anyone with several children, disqualifying many Indian families. For those who refused to accept unsafe or unsanitary conditions, it could take months to find a decent place to live. As one Native woman described, "It took me a whole year to find a place ... I went on the North side and South side. I would have to find a babysitter and then walk and walk. Sometimes I felt like walking right out of Minneapolis."[21]

By the 1960s, Native people had become heavily concentrated in what a university research team described as "the worst housing in the worst neighborhoods in the city." A 1969 report characterized more than 70 percent of Indian rental housing in Minneapolis as substandard. The report cited nonfunctioning refrigerators in one-third of Indian rental units, no plumbing in 36 percent, and 75 percent with broken doors or stairs or no working lights. Another group of researchers reported in 1971 that "uncollected garbage, mice, cockroaches, exposed wiring, and debris piled in the yards of the old houses plague Indian tenants" in both Minneapolis and St. Paul.[22]

The Minneapolis Indian population became increasingly centralized in North Minneapolis and in the Elliot Park and Phillips neighborhoods southeast of downtown. Phillips in particular became known as the "Indian ghetto." By 1970, about two-thirds of Minneapolis Indian people lived in this area, comprising somewhere between 10 and 50 percent of the total Phillips population. Franklin Avenue, an east–west street that forms the neighborhood's northern boundary, turned into an Indian skid row. Lined with bars and boarded-up businesses, Franklin Avenue was equated with urban poverty and crime. Most of the city's Indians who did not live in Phillips lived in North Minneapolis, an area northwest of downtown composed of American Indian and African American residents and similarly known for slum conditions.[23]

In St. Paul, the Indian population was less concentrated than in Minneapolis. Most Indian people lived in three areas: around the intersection of Dale and Selby Avenues (also known as Summit Hill), in the Dayton's Bluff neighborhood, and in the Mount Airy projects north of downtown. St. Paul Indians generally lived in neighborhoods with a mix of American Indian, African American, and Hispanic residents.[24]

In addition to economic hardships and poor living conditions, Indian people in postwar Minneapolis and St. Paul experienced striking health disparities. In the early 1970s, the Minnesota State Medical Association reported that Minnesota Indians lived with significantly lower levels of health than their White counterparts. In Minneapolis, the infant death rate was more than 50 percent higher for Indians than for non-Indians. Indian people were three to five times more likely to die between the ages of fifteen and fifty-four, and they were more likely to die younger of heart disease and cancer. Twin Cities Indian people also suffered more often from poor vision and hearing. Researchers also noted that alcoholism and chemical dependency were more widespread and more severe problems for urban Indians than for non-Indians.[25]

Rather than receiving long-term treatment for alcohol and drug abuse, Indian people became disproportionately high statistics in county detoxification and detention centers. This in turn contributed to their troubled relationship with the Twin Cities criminal justice system. As a civil rights commission observed:

> No matter what aspect of the justice system is examined in relationship to Native American people—law enforcement, courts, or corrections— Native Americans are disproportionately represented compared with their numbers in the Minnesota population. They are grossly under-represented as employees; they are significantly overrepresented in the numbers of arrests and convictions.[26]

Research by the League of Women Voters in Minneapolis corroborated the commission's findings. The League also found evidence that Indian people served longer sentences than non-Indians for similar crimes.[27]

The growing social problems faced by Twin Cities Indian people in the postwar years proved closely interrelated. Unsafe, unsanitary, and overcrowded housing conditions undermined Native people's health. Inadequate housing and chronic health problems made it more difficult for Indian people to find employment. The lack of stable income, in turn, made it harder to afford decent housing and procure adequate health care. With their multiple and interconnected struggles, many Twin Cities Indian people needed the help of social-service agencies. Yet, every study in the 1960s and early 1970s found that local agencies—whether public or private, and on local, state, and federal levels—were not meeting Indian people's needs.

During this period, researchers found widespread confusion regarding which services applied to urban Indians, not only among those who needed help, but also among Bureau of Indian Affairs and Indian Health Service (IHS) employees. At the time, the federal services provided specifically for Indian people through agencies like the BIA and the IHS did not extend to those who moved off the reservation. Although the BIA area office in Minneapolis operated an Employment Assistance Branch for new arrivals, it usually required them to prove a minimum of one-quarter blood quantum to qualify for services, which not all applicants could do. Native people also found it difficult to access the social services aimed at the general urban population. Some municipal agencies would not serve anyone unless they had lived in the city or the county for six months or a year. This disqualified many Indian applicants who had arrived more recently or whose mobility within the city or between city and reservation left them without a long-term urban address. Urban Indian residents also encountered prejudice and discrimination from social-service workers, which discouraged them from seeking help when they needed it.[28]

Most of the social problems experienced by Native people in Minneapolis and St. Paul—unemployment and underemployment, substandard housing, poor health, disproportionate arrest and incarceration rates, prejudice and discrimination—also plagued Indian migrants to other cities across the country in the 1950s and 1960s. Some places proved worse than others, however. In Chicago, for instance, the Indian population seems to have experienced better employment and housing and less discrimination than in the Twin Cities. Official BIA relocation sites such as Chicago also offered more social services to Indian migrants. In cities without official relocation centers, Native people had to rely more on themselves, on each other, and on an urban social-welfare system that was ill-equipped to deal with an influx of Indian residents.[29]

Indian Community Activism in the Twin Cities, 1945–68

As their numbers increased in the postwar period, their living conditions and economic prospects worsened, and existing social-service agencies failed to meet their needs, Twin Cities Indians came together in the 1950s and 1960s to work for change. As they had for decades, more established Indian residents shared housing, food, and information with recent arrivals. Groups of Native people gathered in each other's homes to share stories of reservation and urban life and offer mutual support. Louise Peake, for instance, continued to host gatherings of urban Indian women. In the 1950s, her adult daughter Emily's home in the Stevens Square neighborhood of South Minneapolis also became a meeting place and a source of community organizing.[30]

In the 1950s and early 1960s, a new generation of young Indian leaders like Emily Peake began to work more closely with non-Indian religious and civic groups as well as city, county, and state agencies to address the social welfare needs of urban Indians. In 1952, members of the Indian community, along with a group of interdenominational religious leaders affiliated with the Minnesota Council of Churches, established the Department (later Division) of Indian Works in Minneapolis. Originally created to connect Indian families with local churches, the office began offering counseling services and referring them to Twin Cities social-service agencies. Eventually, a

Division of Indian Works office also opened in St. Paul. Indian community leaders also forged alliances with settlement houses such as Unity House in North Minneapolis and Elliot Park Neighborhood House (later Waite House) in South Minneapolis. The settlement houses extended employment services and organized social gatherings such as powwows, as well as camping trips and other activities for young people.[31]

Twin Cities Native people also created new Indian organizations in the postwar period. Some of these had a social and cultural agenda, such as the Ojibway–Dakota Research Society, which worked for language preservation, and the St. Paul Indian Dance Club, which sponsored monthly powwows. Other groups had broader concerns. American Indians, Incorporated formed in 1950 to create a sense of fellowship through potluck suppers, Christmas parties, and dances. Its members also sought political equality for urban Indians, wanting to secure for them "the rights and privileges enjoyed by all other citizens." This was in keeping with the goals of postwar federal Indian policy, and it reflected the approach of African American activists in the early civil rights movement in the South. American Indians, Incorporated also educated non-Indian urban residents about the culture and social contributions of their Indian neighbors.[32]

In the early 1950s, long-term Minneapolis Ojibwe residents Emily Peake and James Longie, along with other Ojibwe and Dakota people, began meeting regularly in each other's homes to plan the creation of a new organization. Like the members of American Indians, Incorporated, they wanted to foster fellowship among Twin Cities Indians; indeed, they sought to create a broad-based sense of community among urban Indian people, one that would cross divisions of band, nation, and economic status. They also shared other organizations' goals of protecting urban Indians' treaty rights, preserving elements of Indian cultures, and promoting understanding between Native and non-Native people. In addition, these emerging leaders of the Minneapolis Indian community wanted to help other Native people procure much-needed social services. Increasingly, they talked of the need for an Indian center, a multipurpose community institution that could serve as a social and cultural gathering place, information hub, and referral center for welfare services.

In 1961, these ongoing discussions led to the formation of the Upper Midwest American Indian Center (UMAIC). Lacking sufficient funds for a physical center or paid employees, in its first several years the UMAIC moved its programs around among various sponsoring organizations in

Minneapolis and depended entirely on volunteers. The UMAIC helped new urban arrivals find jobs and temporary shelter, gave food and clothing to the needy, and provided referrals to social-welfare agencies. It also sponsored a drum club, a multitribal singing group, monthly powwows, sewing classes, and children's activities, and published a newsletter. UMAIC organizers worked with local religious leaders and received assistance from Waite House, which provided space for some programs. In 1966, the UMAIC received a federal grant from the Office of Economic Opportunity that allowed its members to rent dedicated space in North Minneapolis, hire a director, and expand services. In 1968, however, the organization lost this funding. UMAIC founders and other community leaders began talking about ways to create a new, more stable Indian center in Minneapolis.[33]

Twin Cities Indian leaders of the 1950s and 1960s continued a decades-long tradition of urban Indian activism that had begun in the early twentieth century. In some ways, though, the activism of this period differed from the prewar past. Urban Indian organizations had become more intertribal, and they devoted more attention to burgeoning economic and social problems than had their predecessors. Postwar Indian activists also engaged in more cooperative efforts with non-Indian individuals, institutions, and agencies. At the same time, there was a growing interest in creating an Indian-run institution—an Indian center—to serve the range of urban Indian needs.

The changing nature of Indian activism in the postwar period both reflected and shaped the development of the Twin Cities Indian community. The Native residents of Minneapolis and St. Paul became more numerous and more diverse after World War II. They shared a growing sense that any urban Indian identity they might forge must incorporate multiple affiliations of band, reservation, and tribe. They also lived in more concentrated numbers in more identifiable Indian neighborhoods, which contributed to a more physical sense of geographic community within the city. By the 1960s, many Twin Cities Indians also faced common struggles while trying to make a life in the city: severe economic hardship, terrible housing conditions, confrontations with police, and pervasive prejudice and discrimination. These collective experiences fashioned a community that was increasingly defined by its marginalization and by a shared sense of embattlement. Their collaborative efforts to improve conditions for themselves, their families, and their neighbors also created an activist community, one that became increasingly organized.[34]

"We Became That Voice": The American Indian Movement in the Twin Cities, 1968–72

In Minneapolis and St. Paul the work of community activists in the 1950s and 1960s educated non-Indians about the needs of the city's Native population and provided much-needed assistance to many individuals and families. Yet the scale of the problems plaguing Twin Cities Indian people far outweighed the help that the members of the UMAIC or other organizations could provide. In July 1968, the American Indian Movement emerged in part out of these long-standing socioeconomic concerns, and its organizers worked to alleviate them.

Initially, AIM leaders focused on police discrimination and harassment against Indian people, particularly in the Phillips neighborhood of South Minneapolis. Organizers objected to local law-enforcement practice that targeted "Indian bars" along Franklin Avenue—places like Bud's Bar and the Corral—for weekend arrests on "drunk and disorderly" charges. AIM cofounder Dennis Banks, an Ojibwe from the Leech Lake reservation, later said that at the time, "there were as many as two hundred arrests every weekend of Indian people," which he claimed filled quotas "to provide unpaid labor for the work house and various city projects." According to Banks, Indian men in their twenties and thirties frequently were arrested, assigned to a short-term labor project at the work house or a public building, then released. As he described it in his 2004 memoir:

> During the early sixties, I got caught in that dragnet maybe twenty-five times. Monday mornings I would sometimes end up at the work house or they would put me to work on a farm. . . . Once this happened to me three weekends in a row. I would go back to the same bar and get caught again. . . . It took me a while to realize that the police raided only the Indian bars and never the white ones.

AIM's organizers also objected to the racial slurs, abusive language, and excessive force that some officers used against Indian people.[35]

In response to these long-standing conditions, AIM brought complaints to the chief of police and denounced police treatment of Indians as racial discrimination. It also confronted the problem of police relations directly on the streets. Drawing on the examples of the local Black Patrol in North Minneapolis and the Black Panthers' police patrol in Oakland, AIM members used observation, documentation, and their own physical presence to prevent police mistreatment of Indian residents. Beginning in late August 1968, they formed the "Indian Patrol," cruising Franklin Avenue and nearby streets in cars painted red and equipped with two-way radios, tape recorders, and cameras. They documented incidents of harassment, recording the license plate numbers of offending officers and filing complaints with accompanying evidence at precinct headquarters. Inside and outside of Franklin Avenue bars, they intervened before police could make arrests by offering intoxicated Indians rides home and breaking up fights. When Native people were arrested, AIM members recorded police behavior and provided those arrested with free legal assistance. Night after night, wearing bright red jackets with "Indian Patrol" on the back, the men and women of AIM sent a message that Indian people in Minneapolis would no longer accept the status quo.[36]

Soon AIM members' efforts expanded to encompass the whole interconnected tangle of Indian people's problems in the Twin Cities. They worked to improve Native people's housing conditions, find them jobs, get them access to health care, educate them about their legal rights, and provide them with legal assistance and more effective representation in court. In the same spirit that they had faced the police on the streets of Phillips, AIM activists directly confronted city hall, county and state agencies, and other urban institutions over their shortcomings and demanded more responsiveness to Indian people's needs and desires. AIM members also personally accompanied Indian people into employment centers, welfare agencies, and courtrooms to advocate for their interests, and they went into juvenile detention centers and prisons to counsel and connect with Native inmates.[37]

In 1970, AIM members created a St. Paul chapter with its own office to focus specifically on the needs of the St. Paul Indian community. As AIM organizer Pat Bellanger explained, "The St. Paul Indian community was different than the Minneapolis community, although we met together on a lot of things." Ojibwe people from Minnesota reservations still comprised most of the Minneapolis Indian community, while St. Paul had more of a mixture, with more Ho-Chunks, Dakotas, and Lakotas. As AIM members assisted families in the two cities, they also confronted different municipal and county agencies. According to Bellanger, "It was like two different fights—or two different arenas, maybe" of the same fight. Pat Bellanger and Eddie Benton-Banai assumed leadership roles within St. Paul AIM, while Clyde Bellecourt and Dennis Banks remained leading figures in Minneapolis.[38]

In many ways, AIM organizers continued the work of previous Indian

Dennis Banks, a Leech Lake Ojibwe, helped organize the meeting that led to the founding of the American Indian Movement in Minneapolis in July 1968. He was an active leader in the local Indian community through the early 1970s. Associated Press, Bettmann/Historical Archive, 1974.

Clyde Bellecourt's discovery of his Native identity while an inmate at Stillwater State Prison inspired him to become a community activist in the Twin Cities. The White Earth Ojibwe's impassioned speech at AIM's first organizing meeting in 1968 made him one of the movement's early local leaders. He became the founding director of Heart of the Earth school in Minneapolis in 1972. Associated Press/Jim Wells, Bettmann/ Historical Archive, 1973.

Eddie Benton-Banai, a Lac Courte Oreilles Ojibwe, worked with Clyde Bellecourt to organize the American Indian Folklore Group for Native inmates at Stillwater State Prison in 1962. He attended AIM's founding meeting in Minneapolis in 1968 and was a leader in AIM's St. Paul chapter. In 1972 he became the founding director of the Red School House in St. Paul. From "We, Yesterday, Today, Tomorrow: Red School House Yearbook 1977–78," published by Indian Country Communications, Inc.; reprinted with permission.

leaders and organizations. They shared some similar concerns—the need for more jobs, adequate housing, and better services from social agencies—and they had decided to come together to try to make things better for themselves and for their community. In the organization's early days, AIM members gave carless Indian people rides, helped them find housing, helped them move, and provided food and money for those in need. In these ways, AIM's efforts resembled those of other Twin Cities Indians who had created informal assistance networks. Although AIM founders were overwhelmingly Ojibwe, like the generation of urban Indian leaders that emerged in the post–World War II period, the group was multitribal. They came together as Indian people addressing Indian problems, rather than organizing by tribal affiliation.[39]

At the same time, the founders of the American Indian Movement brought a new kind of Indian activism to the Twin Cities. AIM organizers tackled issues that they believed other Indian leaders had not addressed adequately. They took a much more confrontational approach to urban institutions, challenging directly and forcefully the discrimination and disparities that they found there. They also insisted on more Indian control over urban services for Indian people.

AIM founders Dennis Banks and Clyde Bellecourt both have asserted that, in the 1960s, existing Indian activism was inadequate. In his 2004 memoir, Banks explained its limitations:

we had no organization to address social reform, human rights, or treaty rights. We had . . . Indian organizations for social welfare and gathering clothes. These were needed, but there was no movement specifically addressing the police brutality that was an everyday fact for Indian people or the discrimination in housing and employment in Minneapolis.[40]

Bellecourt told a journalist in 2000, "Back then, there were only two Indian organizations in town, and they weren't concerned about police brutality and racism. So we became that voice."[41] In a 2003 interview, Bellecourt elaborated on his frustration with other Indian organizations of the late 1960s such as the Upper Midwest American Indian Center and the Twin Cities Tribal Council:

It was kind of like, you know, social-service agencies: put out food baskets, beg the churches for help, send people to the BIA. Nobody was dealing with the racism, the police brutality, the dual system of justice, the poor housing conditions . . . Nobody was dealing with those kinds of issues; they just were too scared to stand up to the system.[42]

AIM's first priority, in contrast, had been to challenge racial discrimination in the justice system, as well as in local housing, health care, and employment.

Historian Rachel Buff's research on the Twin Cities Indian community also reveals a growing frustration with the limitations of the Upper Midwest American Indian Center in dealing effectively with the challenges they faced. She argues that by the late 1960s, "many charged that this center was inadequate to the needs of the Indian community." In her interviews with Twin Cities Indian residents from that time, she heard criticisms that the UMAIC had "functioned mainly as an information and referral agency for Indians" and that it had been too conservative in its approach to change.[43]

The people of AIM also believed that the urban agencies charged with helping Twin Cities Indian people should incorporate substantially more input from Native people themselves. When existing institutions would not change fundamentally or quickly enough, AIM members created their own Indian-controlled institutions as alternatives to those that they saw as dominated by Whites and compromised by ignorance and anti-Indian prejudice. In 1970, in cooperation with the North Minneapolis African American organization The Way and members of the Hennepin County Bar Association, AIM organizers helped create the Legal Rights Center. The Center provided free legal advice and representation in criminal cases for poor residents of Minneapolis, including many American Indians. In 1971, AIM organizer Charles Deegan helped establish the Indian Health Board (IHB) in Minneapolis, the first urban Indian health-care facility in the United States; he also served as its first executive director. To ensure Indian control, the IHB had an all-Indian advisory board with the authority to direct institutional policy. In 1971, AIM members secured funding from the Department of Housing and Urban Development for Indian-controlled housing units in South Minneapolis for low-income Indian tenants; this became the Little Earth housing project.[44]

AIM's work in the Twin Cities reflected larger historical developments within the Indian activism of this period. In the early 1960s, young, college-educated Indian people had begun to push for a different kind of change than that pursued by existing national Indian organizations, which they criticized as too conservative, too conciliatory, and not focused enough on their generation's concerns. A conference of American Indian leaders held in Chicago in 1961 had galvanized these young activists to speak out and to organize themselves into the National Indian Youth Council (NIYC). NIYC leaders such as Clyde Warrior, a Ponca from Oklahoma, and Hank Adams, an Assiniboine/Sioux from Washington, wanted more attention and resources devoted to the needs of urban Indian people. They made more direct challenges to individuals and institutions of authority, and they practiced a more confrontational style of activism. In 1964, the NIYC began staging high-profile "fish-ins" in the Pacific Northwest to reassert Indian treaty rights.

NIYC leaders also called for Indian people to exercise greater self-determination over their own lives and communities and insisted that they must shape their own destinies. They wanted greater input from Indian people in the management of Indian affairs and more community control over the administration of funds and services. Such efforts bore fruit with higher Native employment in agencies like the Bureau of Indian Affairs and contributed to a shift in federal policy toward self-determination, as formalized in President Nixon's message to Congress in 1970. Indian leaders on both national and local levels also used the Johnson administration's War on Poverty programs and the framework of the Great Society to empower Native people in reservation and urban communities in the creation and administration of local programs and services in the 1960s.

Calls for self-determination and the assertion of community control also echoed the message of other minority activists in the 1960s and early 1970s. The Black Power movement that developed in the late 1960s encouraged African Americans to create and control their own community institutions rather than seek equality and integration within the White-dominated system. Black Panthers chapters in northern cities established legal rights centers and medical clinics and provided drug and alcohol counseling in African American communities, and the Black Panther Party advocated Black-owned businesses and alternative party politics. The Brown Berets and other activists in the Chicano movement provided similar services in urban Latino communities in the West and Midwest beginning in the late 1960s. Both the Brown Berets and the Black Panthers also organized against police brutality and challenged racial discrimination in housing, employment, social-services agencies, and the court system.

While AIM's approach reflected national trends, it created conflict with other local Indian activists. AIM leader Russell Means identified the willingness to "stand up to the system" as the defining characteristic of Clyde Bellecourt and of early AIM:

> He wasn't afraid of the police and he wasn't afraid of jail. . . . He was such a confrontational person, such a righteous person. I think Clyde's personality gave that aura of righteousness to the American Indian Movement.[45]

But community leaders like Emily Peake, while equally committed to improving the lives of urban Indian people, preferred to work more cooperatively with non-Indian individuals and agencies. They favored tactics of negotiation and compromise over confrontation and righteous anger. Some who had worked on urban Indian problems for years resented what they perceived as an effort to squeeze them out of leadership positions in the community. At the time, Peake criticized AIM as "a relatively small group of militant Indians" who did not represent the majority of Native Twin Citians.[46]

These conflicts intensified during the planning process for a new Indian center, which began in 1968 and culminated in the opening of the Minneapolis Regional Native American Center (later the Minneapolis American Indian Center) on Franklin Avenue in 1975. Peake and other like-minded community leaders, who felt that AIM had taken over the creation of the center, eventually retreated from the process. They chose instead to revitalize the Upper Midwest American Indian Center, opening a new physical location for the organization on West Broadway Avenue in North Minneapolis.

U.S. Assimilation Policies and Indigenous Cultural Loss, 1880s–1940s

AIM's founders diverged from other local Indian leaders in more than their style and tactics. In the Twin Cities, while targeting the socioeconomic disparities that had motivated other urban activists, they also focused on the cultural struggles experienced by many Indian residents. These struggles stemmed in part from the legacy of multigenerational cultural alienation and loss that resulted from the federal assimilation policies of the late nineteenth and early twentieth centuries.

As the alienation of Native land and resources had escalated in the late nineteenth and early twentieth centuries, pressures also had increased on Native people to abandon their traditional ways of life. Government agents, policy makers, and missionaries had been working toward this goal for decades. By the late nineteenth century, the assaults against Indigenous cultures had focused into a concerted assimilation campaign, driven by federal policy. Policy makers argued that in order for Indian people to survive in American society, they had to replace their political institutions, social structures, cultural practices, and spiritual beliefs with "civilized" Euro-American ways. Rather than have them do so slowly in protectively isolated areas—which had been part of the rationale for reservations—federal officials now determined to dismantle the reservation system and push Native people more quickly into mainstream society.

This accelerated assimilation policy reveals the process of settler colonialism at work through Patrick Wolfe's "logic of elimination":

What's to be eliminated is Native societies, as autonomous polities originating independently of the settler social contract, rather than necessarily individual human beings. If the human beings can be reclassified on an individual basis so that the fragment of Native society that they represent effectively ceases to present an independent alternative to the settler social monopoly, then all well and good. This is why Colonel Richard Pratt's famous phrase "Kill the Indian, Save the Man" is so revealing. You could hardly express the eliminatory ambition of assimilationist policies more concisely.

According to Wolfe, "settlers also seek to assimilate Native institutions to the settler civic environment," which is "another way of seeking to eliminate Native polities' independently—which is to say, sovereignly—constituted sources of legitimacy." An aggressive assimilation policy, tied to the elimination of the reservations, also served the federal and corporate agendas of opening up land and resources for settlement, private acquisition, and profit.[47]

American policy makers in the late nineteenth century argued that in order to ensure the assimilation of Indian people, they had to target the children. To this end the federal government created a system of day schools and boarding schools aimed at the eradication of Indigenous societies and cultures through formal education. By the end of the 1880s, policy makers focused on the off-reservation boarding school as the most effective way to carry out assimilation policy, by separating Indian children from the influences of their families and communities, severing their ties to tribal cultures, and inculcating the values, beliefs, practices, and priorities of Euro-American society. By 1900, of the twenty-one thousand Indian children in school, eighteen thousand were in boarding schools, more than a third of which were located off-reservation. By 1920, there were more than two dozen off-reservation government boarding schools, and they remained the keystone of the federal Indian education system through the 1920s.[48]

The federal schools of the late nineteenth and early twentieth centuries incorporated significant numbers of Native children from the upper Midwest. They attended government day schools and boarding schools on reservations throughout the region. Many Native children also traveled far from their homes to attend such schools as Wahpeton in North Dakota, Flandreau in South Dakota, Haskell in Kansas, and Carlisle in Pennsylvania. By 1900 it was preferred policy to send Indian children to schools as far away from their reservations as possible, to keep them isolated from their families and tribal traditions. In these schools Ojibwe, Ho-Chunk, Menominee, Lakota, and Dakota children joined students from dozens of other tribes across the United States.[49]

Many Indian children who attended off-reservation boarding schools in this period experienced them as disorienting, humiliating places of cultural alienation. In their first days at school, teachers replaced their tribal names with English ones. School officials also worked hard to take away their languages. Most government schools in this period followed a strict English-only policy, and students who spoke their Native languages were shamed and physically punished. Boarding school life also challenged the central values and beliefs of traditional Indigenous cultures. Euro-American education introduced students to a linear rather than a circular orientation to the world. It taught them that, rather than living in interdependence and balance with the natural world, human beings should control nature and its resources. Conceptions of time changed from natural daily and seasonal rhythms to the tyranny of the clock, the linearity of the school calendar, and the regimentation of every aspect of students' lives in an institution modeled on the U.S. military. Native children also learned to abandon their traditional spiritual system in favor of Christianity. The expression of Indigenous spiritualities, like the speaking of their languages, was punished. Through these practices, school policies sought to erase children's Indigenous identities. In the process, they also undermined their sense of self-worth.

While the off-reservation boarding schools challenged Native children, they also imposed great hardships on their families. Some parents chose to send their children away to school to escape the increasingly desperate conditions on the reservations or as a way to help them adapt to and succeed in a rapidly changing world. Other children were removed from their families through intimidation or force. Either way, parents of boarding school students often endured years of separation from their children. Most government schools in this period strictly limited both the frequency and the duration of home visits. They also required that parents pay the transportation costs for such visits, an impossibility for impoverished families. Many children spent four or more years away at school with no home visits and infrequent familial contact. Many young people suffered intense homesickness during these periods, and their families missed them terribly.[50]

Children who spent years away at school lost contact with the sources of cultural knowledge that had provided the foundation for a traditional Indigenous education. This distance, combined with school policies that denigrated and punished expressions of the old ways of life, caused many young people to lose their cultural grounding. They lost the ability to speak or understand their native languages. They forgot or never learned traditional skills, rituals, and ceremonies. They no longer were raised within the tribal system of values and beliefs, and they lost connection to networks of extended family and kinship.

When students finally left school and returned to their reservations, they became agents of further cultural change within their families and communities. Historian Brenda Child describes the "cultural chasm" that distanced returning Ojibwe boarding school students from their relatives on Minnesota reservations:

> many households became settings for dramas involving deep intergenerational and cultural conflict. Whereas the cultural clash between whites and Indians had once been fought on battlefields and in treaty councils, now it advanced to parent–child disagreements over campfires and across kitchen tables—whether to farm or lease an allotment, whether to boil the dishwater, whether to offer a prayer of thanks for a slain animal's spirit.

Young people introduced to new ways of thinking questioned the viability of the old ways. When former boarding school students grew up and became parents, many of them were unable or unwilling to provide their children with a traditional education. Some also sent their own children to government schools. Because of these intergenerational dynamics, the boarding school system proved the assimilationists' most powerful weapon against Indigenous culture. As Brenda Child observed, the government schools created "unprecedented sources of stress" for Native families and shook the "distinctive cultural foundation" of their communities.[51]

Policies enacted on reservations in the late nineteenth century furthered the process of cultural erosion. Beginning in the 1880s, state laws in the upper Midwest banned gatherings for feasts, dances, and ceremonies on reservations, criminalizing the public expression of Indigenous spirituality. Violators were harassed, arrested, and jailed by reservation agents and tribal police. Spiritual leaders had to perform their work in secret; eventually, many intimidated community members stopped attending ceremonies and other gatherings altogether. Over the years, embattled by economic hardship and the assimilationist siege, increasing numbers of Native people lost faith in their traditional belief systems. Some converted to Christianity as they sought meaning in a changing world. Others succumbed to despair.[52]

The deterioration of traditional ways of life proceeded with varied speed and intensity across the region, depending on the specific circumstances of each state, reservation, village, and family. Some resisted the destabilizing consequences of cultural repression longer and more successfully than others.[53] By the 1920s, though, and later with the added hardships imposed by the Great Depression, reservation communities throughout the region were in a state of crisis. Poverty and disease had taken deep root. The strength of the traditional economy, which had provided physical, social, and spiritual sustenance for generations, had nearly failed. Family and community instability, interpersonal violence, and alcoholism had become widespread problems.

The loss of cultural knowledge instigated within the boarding schools and enforced on reservations set in motion a process that would affect Native people for generations to come. By 1940, most people in reservation communities no longer openly practiced the celebratory and healing ceremonies of the Anishinaabe Midewiwin lodge and other traditional spiritual systems. As Ojibwe storyteller Ignatia Broker writes, "Those who knew about the old ways were silent." Ojibwe children, once eager pupils of their village elders, no longer "stood with eyes cast down before the Old Ones to ask about the old ways and the old people." These children "did not respect the Mi-de-wi-win people. Instead they feared them."[54]

In the years after World War II, many of the growing numbers of Indian people who moved to Minneapolis and St. Paul had become estranged from their Indigenous social and cultural systems. Young adults in their twenties and thirties, they were the product of several generations of mission and boarding school education, religious repression, land loss, and economic decline. Many of their parents, scarred by their own boarding school experiences or intimidated by government officials and Christian missionaries on the reservations, had not taught their children their Native languages or traditions. Coming into the city, these young people had little grounding in the skills, practices, beliefs, value systems, or linguistic worlds that had oriented their ancestors. Yet, for the most part, they also found it difficult to fit into the Euro-American economic or sociocultural mainstream. Marginalized by non-Indian society and severed from traditional life, many Native people drifted into the struggles of city life without a cultural anchor to steady them. This left them vulnerable to the alienation and hopelessness that could fuel alcoholism, drug abuse, criminal activity, and incarceration.

"I Was Gonna Save the World": AIM's Cultural and Spiritual Foundation

AIM founders Dennis Banks and Clyde Bellecourt had personal experience with the pattern of cultural loss, social alienation, and self-destructive behavior that many Native migrants to the Twin Cities in the 1960s experienced, especially young Indian men. Their years of living in a cultural and spiritual void provided motivation for the collective activism they began in their early thirties. In her analysis of AIM's origins, anthropologist Rachel Bonney argues that early organizers such as Bellecourt and Banks "had become alienated from their tribal traditions" and "ashamed of their Indian heritage, while simultaneously rejecting the dominant society"—a society that in many ways had rejected them as well. According to Bonney, "because of their own first-hand experiences with problems of adjustment . . . alienation, and discrimination, AIM leaders developed an ideology stressing pride in the Indian heritage and one's identity as an Indian."[55]

As a young boy, Dennis Banks was raised largely by his maternal grandparents, who were among the few elders still practicing the traditional ways of their ancestors on the Leech Lake reservation in the late 1930s. Although Banks's mother Bertha had lost her Native language while at the Flandreau boarding school in her youth, he learned to speak and understand Ojibwe from his grandparents. In 1941, when he was five years old, he was removed from his grandparents' home and sent to the federal boarding school at Pipestone, Minnesota, more than two hundred miles away. Banks spent nine years in boarding schools—six years at Pipestone, two at the Wahpeton school in North Dakota, and a year at Flandreau in South Dakota—without going home to Leech Lake. He tried to run away multiple times, but he was always caught and brought back to school.[56]

In Banks's years at boarding school, like his mother before him, he had his Native language disciplined out of him. The assimilationist curriculum and harsh punishments also taught him to reject his Ojibwe identity. As he recalled in his 2004 memoir:

> I began to hate myself for being Indian . . . My white teachers and their books taught me to despise my own people. White history became my history because there was no other. When they took us once a week to the movies . . . I cheered for Davy Crockett, Daniel Boone, and General Custer. I sided with the cavalry cutting down Indians. In my fantasies I was John Wayne rescuing the settlers from "red fiends." I dreamed of being a cowboy.[57]

At sixteen, Banks left Flandreau and returned to Leech Lake. He still felt drawn to his home community and the culture of his childhood. But he had lost his language, and the effects of reservation poverty, disease, and state and federal regulations had further diminished what traditional practices had remained. After a stint in the air force, Banks ended up living in the Twin Cities. He spent several years drifting and drinking, directionless, until he landed in Stillwater State Prison in 1968.[58]

Clyde Bellecourt's childhood on the White Earth reservation in the late 1930s and early 1940s lacked even the truncated traditional influence of Banks's early years. As a child, lying awake in bed late at night, Clyde overheard his parents and other adults speaking languages that he later realized were Ojibwe and French, yet they spoke nothing but English around the children. Bellecourt's parents raised him and his sibling without any knowledge of their Ojibwe heritage, and no one else on the reservation taught him anything about his Native language or cultural traditions.[59]

Bellecourt blames his early lack of cultural grounding on his mother's boarding school education. He has described her experience as one of harshly enforced cultural repression with lasting physical and psychological consequences:

My mom was actually crippled for life, because when they caught her
speaking Indian, she would have to scrub floors all day on her hands
and knees with a toothbrush and a bucket of water . . . And then toward
the end they actually tied sacks of marbles to her knees, and made her
do that, and that crippled her for the rest of her life.

According to Bellecourt, his mother's traumatic school experience poisoned
her relationship to her Indigenous culture. As an adult at White Earth, the
teachings of the Catholic missionaries at church and in the mission school
and repressive reservation policies further distanced her from the culture
of her youth. As a mother, she chose not to expose her children to the traditional ways and pushed them toward assimilation into non-Indian society. Bellecourt has remembered his mother telling him and his siblings,
"Forget about the past. Go to school, learn English, someday you might be
president."[60]

Bellecourt's own educational experiences undermined his sense of self
in ways that still raise painful memories. He first attended a public elementary school, where he frequently got into trouble. According to Bellecourt,
"I liked to go out bullhead fishing at night, camping out, and running in
the woods, that's the kind of person I was—I *hated* school." At the time, "If
you weren't making it in the public school, they would always threaten
you: We're gonna send you out to those *nuns,* and let those *nuns* take care
of you." The nuns in question ran the reservation mission school for the
Catholic Order of St. Benedict. When Bellecourt was in the second grade,
school officials made good on their threats and sent him to St. Benedict's
Mission School. Once there, he rebelled against the religious curriculum
and strict discipline and was punished frequently for skipping school, missing church, and other misbehavior. At age eleven in 1949, his chronic truancy brought him into juvenile court, where the judge gave him a choice:
either return to the mission school or go to the Red Wing State Training
School, a military-style reform school for boys southeast of the Twin Cities.
At the time, Bellecourt said, "I thought *anything* had to be better than the
mission school, so I was sent to Red Wing."[61]

Bellecourt expected to remain in reform school for a few months. In
fact, he spent the rest of his youth and most of his early adult years in a series of correctional institutions. After three years at Red Wing, he was transferred to the St. Cloud Reformatory. In his early adulthood, like Dennis
Banks, Bellecourt lived in the Twin Cities, abused alcohol, got into various

kinds of trouble with the law, and served several prison sentences. In 1962, when Bellecourt was twenty-six, he was sent to Stillwater State Prison for robbery. During his incarceration at Stillwater, Bellecourt made the discovery that would turn his life around and transform him into a community activist: he found out, for the first time, what it meant to be an Indigenous person. As he later explained, "I knew I was Indian, but I didn't know anything about 'Indian,' absolutely nothing—language, culture, tradition. . . . I would fight anybody that said anything bad about Indian people, but many times, I didn't know why I was fightin." Everything changed when he met Eddie Benton-Banai.[62]

Benton-Banai's personal history and his path to the American Indian Movement differed significantly from those of Bellecourt and Banks. He was born in 1934 on the Lac Courte Oreilles reservation in northern Wisconsin into an Ojibwe family that raised him fully within the language and Midewiwin traditions of his ancestors. The Midewiwin is the Anishinaabe spiritual system, a way of living that grounded precolonial Native societies throughout the Great Lakes region of what later became the United States and Canada. It encompasses cultural knowledge, social teachings, collective values, ceremonial practices, and a personal growth process that form the foundation of a traditional Anishinaabe life. Benton-Banai's parents and grandparents told him the Ojibwe creation story, sang him the songs of the fish clan to which he belongs, and surrounded him with the Ojibwe language, from the time when he was in the womb throughout his childhood. They kept him out of Euro-American schools until he was nine years old and thereafter still kept him closely connected to his Anishinaabe language and traditions. Benton-Banai thus grew into adulthood with a degree of cultural continuity and a strong sense of identity that Dennis Banks, Clyde Bellecourt, and most Native people of their generation lacked.[63]

Benton-Banai was raised with the understanding that he was meant to carry on the Midewiwin teachings and other Anishinaabe traditions of his ancestors, a responsibility that he embraced. In the early 1960s, when he was in his late twenties, he decided to bring those teachings to the Native men incarcerated at Stillwater State Prison, most of whom were Ojibwes from upper Midwestern reservations. James Donahue, an Irish-American caseworker who worked with Native inmates at Stillwater, had found that the majority were there for alcohol-related crimes, they tended to serve disproportionately long sentences, and they received little useful job training while in prison. Donahue wanted to help Indian inmates break these destructive patterns and build new lives for themselves outside of prison. Benton-Banai believed that teaching the Native prisoners about their heritage might provide a way to do this. As Clyde Bellecourt has explained, Benton-Banai and Donahue thought that if they "sat 'em down, taught 'em about their culture, and their traditions, the contributions that they made to today's society, start makin' 'em feel good about themselves, then they would want to deal with the issues that brought 'em in there." As it turned out, Bellecourt himself enabled them to put their plan into action.[64]

During his sentence at Stillwater Bellecourt spent considerable time in solitary confinement for disciplinary infractions. As he has told the story, one day in 1962 he was in his cell in solitary when he heard a man singing and calling out to him by name. When he looked out the peephole in his cell door, there was Eddie Benton-Banai. Benton-Banai and Donahue saw Bellecourt's relationships with the other Indian inmates, formed during his years spent in correctional school and the reformatory, as essential to the formation of their cultural study group:

> They couldn't organize it . . . because they didn't know these Indian inmates. I knew every single one of 'em, I'd spent time with them from when I was eleven years old until they approached me when I was twenty-six years old . . . So they knew that they needed somebody like me to get out and help them.

Bellecourt struck a deal that if they got him out of solitary confinement and helped him get training as a boiler engineer in the prison's power plant, he would help organize the program. Prison authorities approved the plan, and the three men formed the American Indian Folklore Group, with more than eighty Indian inmates organized by Bellecourt into a study group under Benton-Banai's guidance. Together these Native men, most of them Ojibwes in their twenties and thirties, learned about the history, culture, and spiritual traditions of the Anishinaabeg and other Native American people.[65]

As he participated in the Folklore Group at Stillwater, Bellecourt discovered "a whole newfound awareness" of what it meant to be a Native person, and he acquired a powerful sense of identity, pride, and self-worth. He also began to understand how the absence of a positive sense of self had hurt him throughout his life. As a boy, Bellecourt says, "I was not *allowed* to be an Indian." The lack of cultural identity, the experience of regimentation and punishment in school, and a sense of hopelessness about his future led to desperation:

> I used to feel alone, I used to feel like killing myself . . . I wanted to hang myself, I wanted to die. You know, I cut my wrists when I was a young boy, because of the loneliness, and the despair, and the thought that I would be in jail the rest of my natural-born life.[66]

As he connected with other prisoners in the Folklore Group at Stillwater, Bellecourt realized that other young Indian people had experienced a similar kind of despair.

Through the Midewiwin teachings of Eddie Benton-Banai, Bellecourt now awakened to a whole new way of looking at the world and at himself. As he has described it, "Here I am, twenty-six years old, and I found out who I am." Other Indian men in the group were coming to similarly transformative realizations. Through their contributions to this collective experience, Bellecourt and Benton-Banai found the motivation to help others who had suffered similar pain.

> So it was kind of based on that newfound freedom, and awareness, and pride, that we felt in there, that we made a commitment to one another that we were gonna do the same thing out here on the streets, and try to block, and stop, young men and women from experiencing what we did: the loneliness, and the despair, of being separated from home, and community, and nation . . . And so, when I got out of Stillwater, I had accumulated close to sixteen years of my life in correctional institutions. But I was very excited when I got out, I was gonna save the world, you know, especially our own Indian people.

This desire to help others discover their cultural identity and fight despair drove Bellecourt to help organize AIM; it also brought Benton-Banai to that first organizing meeting in the summer of 1968. As he later explained, "The American Indian Movement was saying something that I thought was very important, so I went there." Benton-Banai became a spiritual adviser and local organizer for the new movement. As he tells it, this role "came through inspiration. It came through revelation . . . and through the willingness to pick it up." His leadership within AIM emerged as an enactment of the cultural responsibility inculcated in him throughout his youth, to share the teachings of his elders, "to do the work."[67]

The experiences of individual AIM founders helped motivate their decision to work for change. Beyond personal history, the movement's origins also lie in the collective, cross-generational experiences of Indigenous people across the country who had suffered from the losses of the past. In this sense, AIM organizers worked against the legacy of colonialism—the physical, psychological, and spiritual separation "from home, and community, and nation"—endured by American Indigenous people through the dispossession of their lands and the assimilationist assault on their societies.

When AIM people talk about Indian history, the federal boarding schools surface quickly and repeatedly, both as an agent of cultural loss and as a motivation for AIM's early commitment to cultural and spiritual regeneration. Clyde Bellecourt speaks about the multigenerational consequences of Euro-American education in ways that weave together his personal story, his mother's boarding school experience, and Indian people's collective past:

> When I speak about my mother . . . I say I'm speaking for every Indian in America. Because *every one* of us—our parents, our grandparents—*every one* of them went through that system. And because of that, we're all suffering today. We lack our language, we lack our culture, our tradition . . . We're all crippled today, we're all handicapped, every one of us Indian people. I don't care . . . how smart you are, we're *handicapped* because we *lack* our spiritual foundation, our spiritual base.[68]

As an AIM activist, Bellecourt targeted the lack of a spiritual foundation as a critical factor in Indian people's struggles to make good lives for themselves, in the Twin Cities and elsewhere.

Early AIM organizer Pat Bellanger also speaks frequently about the boarding school system of the late nineteenth and early twentieth centuries as an agent of multigenerational cultural loss. She talks about the "backlash" that emerged out of boarding school education, in which "the values that you learned in K through 12, those are the values that they were taught was *good; nothing else was good.*" For many boarding school graduates, their response "was to . . . try and teach their kids what they saw working," which meant the denial of their Native languages, traditions, and beliefs. Like Bellecourt, Bellanger identified this collective historical experience as a motivation for founding AIM. "When the movement started," she explained, "we were reacting to that kind of reality. We just refused it."[69]

Responding to their own troubled pasts, reflecting on Native people's shared history of colonization, and wanting to build a positive Indian identity for others, AIM organizers grounded their activism in the revitalization of Indigenous cultures. Beyond the surface of surviving traditions, they sought to revive the heart of the old ways of life, the core values and the comprehensive spiritual systems that had oriented their ancestors' entire existence. Clyde Bellecourt believed in the late 1960s that "our community was totally spiritually bankrupt" and says that "we knew from day one that we couldn't move forward until we developed a spiritual base." Pat Bellanger remembers that as early AIM organizers talked about the conditions facing urban Indian people, "one of the things we said was *missing*, that we could see, were . . . the cultures, the language, and also the religious part." In 1977, Eddie Benton-Banai told a journalist that "the founding principle of AIM was spiritualism."[70]

To foster a cultural and spiritual revival among urban Indian people, AIM organizers began sponsoring community powwows. They revived the use of the drum within its powerful traditional context, as the spiritual heartbeat of Native people and the heart of all creation. They incorporated drumming and singing into protests and other public actions throughout the Twin Cities. They hosted community feasts with traditional seasonal foods from the reservation, such as "Miigwetch Mahnomen" feasts in the fall

The American Indian Movement logo displayed on this banner was worn with pride on shirts, jackets, buttons, patches, and headbands by Twin Cities AIM organizers and supporters in the late 1960s and early 1970s. From "Heart of the Earth Survival School Yearbook, 1979–80," published by Heart of the Earth Survival School, Inc.; reprinted with permission.

49

to give thanks for the first wild rice harvest. They also revived open observance of the sacred seasonal ceremonies and teachings of the Anishinaabe Midewiwin lodge. With the revival of these ceremonies, AIM leaders rejected decades of state and federal policies designed to stamp out the practices of Ojibwe medicine people and other spiritual leaders. They also broke laws that, until the passage of the American Indian Religious Freedom Act in 1978, criminalized public expressions of Indigenous spirituality. According to Pat Bellanger, AIM leaders did so deliberately and defiantly: "See, it was illegal ... but in 1971 and '72 we were doing it anyway, and daring them to come and arrest us."[71]

AIM organizers' concern with the legacy of assimilationist policies set them apart from other Native activists in the Twin Cities. They fostered a fundamentally different kind of relationship to their ancestral cultures than those who had preceded them, as well as most other community leaders of their time. These efforts generated resistance from some local Indian people. Clyde Bellecourt recalls this resistance as driven by fear:

> When the American Indian Movement formed in 1968, one of the first things we did, was build a [sacred] drum. Other people were scared. Indian people said, Oh, you can't do that drum, they're gonna punish you—'cause here they'd all been punished for that, when they went to school.

Despite the opposition from some community members AIM leaders persisted, driven by their conviction that a movement grounded in knowledge of ancestral traditions and a connection to Indigenous identity had the power to change Indian people's lives. According to Bellecourt:

> a lot of people, when we started, they doubted us ... they were tellin' me, others: You've gotta forget about the past, think about the future! Those days are gone! And my answer to that all the time was, If we forget about the past, we'll never have a future. 'Cause I knew that forgetting about my past put me in prison. And I know that *learning* about being an Indian in prison gave me my freedom. I'll never forget that.[72]

Benton-Banai has expressed his enduring gratitude for the spiritual grounding that his parents and grandparents provided him in his youth, which protected him from the cultural alienation experienced by Bellecourt, Banks, and so many other Indian people of his generation. Without those teachings, he asks, "where would I be? In prison doing life? . . . Long dead and buried?" For helping him avoid this fate, he thanks his family "every day" of his life.[73]

Conclusion

Like other local activists, AIM organizers wanted to improve the lives and conditions of Twin Cities Native people. In order to do so, they tackled the socioeconomic disparities and fought the racial discrimination that characterized urban Indian life in the late 1960s. But they also looked beyond contemporary circumstances, back to their people's history. Within Indian people's shared historical experiences of colonialism and cultural loss they found the deep roots of their current struggles. In the traditional ways of their ancestors, they identified a source of strength as they transformed their own lives and built a collective movement for social change.

For some Twin Cities Indians, the challenges of contemporary urban life stemmed not only from cultural *loss*, but also from Native people's cultural *persistence*. Those who came into the city carrying traces of a traditional cultural orientation and maintaining elements of an Indigenous identity experienced a profound cultural dissonance. They also encountered individuals and institutions intent on neutralizing or eradicating their remaining sociocultural differences. As AIM organizers mobilized to help Twin Cities Indian people navigate the challenges of urban life in the late 1960s, they confronted settler colonialism's "logic of elimination," now manifested as the assimilationist imperative of the postwar American city.

In response, AIM organizers mobilized their commitment to revitalizing the cultural and spiritual systems eroded by past U.S. policies. They also actively resisted ongoing Euro-American colonialism in Native people's encounters with child welfare workers, the juvenile justice system, and the Twin Cities public schools. In a society that denigrated and sought to eliminate what set Indian people apart, the people of AIM renounced accommodation and rejected assimilation. In the process, they formed a new kind of activist community, one that reclaimed their Indigenousness and asserted their right to difference. The members of the AIM community considered this work a fight for survival. In 1972, it would lead them to found the survival schools.

CHAPTER 2

Keeping Ourselves Together:
Education, Child Welfare, and AIM's Advocacy
for Indian Families, 1968–1972

E VERY TIME I TALKED TO CLYDE BELLECOURT, he told a story about school. He told me the first story on a chilly October weekend when I attended the fall Midewiwin ceremonies in northern Wisconsin. During an afternoon break, people filtered outside from the teaching lodge into the damp cold to stand in small groups, chatting and drinking coffee. As I spoke with Pat Bellanger's daughter Lisa, we decided it was a good time for me to meet Bellecourt, whom I hoped to interview about the survival schools. We walked over to where Bellecourt stood and Bellanger introduced me.

As we exchanged greetings, Bellecourt noticed a woman walking by behind me, dressed in a long black robe with a hood. "There goes that nun," he said, shaking his head. We laughed at the joke, because the woman obviously was not a nun; most likely she had dressed for warmth. Bellecourt continued, "I see her, and I—"; he did a double take, and flinched, putting his hands up as if to shield himself from a wrathful ruler whistling through the air toward his head. "It takes me right back to Catholic school."

A month later I had lunch with Bellecourt, Eddie Benton-Banai, and a group of other survival school people. The two AIM organizers reminisced about the movement's early days: the pranks they had pulled, the battles they had fought, and the things they had accomplished. Bellecourt recalled AIM's role in the revival of some of the old ceremonial songs. Back in those days, he said, most Indian people did not know their traditional songs; instead they were singing "God Bless America." "Or," he said, "they were singing," and he began to sing, "Jesus loves me, this I know . . ." Everyone at the

table laughed. A pause, then he continued, "For the Bible tells me so ..."
More laughter. He continued, slowly, with a gleam in his eye. "Little ones
to him belong..." He paused again, for dramatic effect. "They are weak but
he is strong..." Someone begged Bellecourt to stop. But he sang the entire
song, loudly, deliberately, pausing between lines just long enough to make
us think he might stop, then continuing on.

When he finished, he asked, "You want me to sing it in Latin? Because I
can." Then, more quietly, "Yeah, I had that drilled into me." This led to a story
about how, in Catholic school, the nuns constantly punished him for "being
bad." Almost every night he had to say his Hail Marys and do the rosary as
penance. He always cheated, he confessed, by skipping beads; he did two at
a time, and finished half an hour before anyone else—that is, until a nun
caught him, and beat him for it.

Two months after hearing Bellecourt's rendition of "Jesus Loves Me,"
I met with him at a Baker's Square restaurant in Minneapolis for a three-
hour recorded interview about the history of the American Indian Movement and the survival schools. Sitting in a booth with a pot of weak coffee
on the table and lite rock music piped in overhead, I turned on my tape
recorder, and Bellecourt began to speak. Within thirty seconds, he was talking about school.

BY THE LATE 1960s, the long-term consequences of the federal assimilation campaign of the late nineteenth and early twentieth centuries had
combined with postwar assimilationist policies and practices in ways that
placed Twin Cities Indian people under great stress. Disconnected from
the sociocultural environments that had sustained their ancestors, but marginalized and pathologized by the dominant society for their persistent
Indigenousness, growing numbers of Indian families found themselves in
crisis. For Indian youth and their families, the difficulties of urban life became concentrated within the Hennepin and Ramsey County child welfare systems and the Minneapolis and St. Paul public schools. As they came
under the scrutiny of these powerful urban institutions, growing numbers
of Indian families felt that they were under siege.

After the American Indian Movement organized in July 1968, these families had a new place to turn for help. In the late 1960s and early 1970s, AIM
organizers challenged the public school systems to serve Indian students better. They also became advocates for Native youth and parents in their interactions with welfare workers and in the juvenile courts. AIM activists' work

in these areas provided a new kind of community support network for local Indian people. AIM's activism in these years was distinguished by its fierce and wide-ranging opposition to assimilation, in its historical forms as well as its contemporary manifestations, and by its attention to the cultural and spiritual dimensions of the problems that urban Indian people faced. In 1972, these elements of AIM's local work—education, child welfare, and cultural identity—converged in the creation of the Twin Cities survival schools.

"A Severe Dissonance": Cultural Conflict in the Native Twin Cities, 1945–68

By the 1920s, decades of American colonialism had severely diminished the viability of Indigenous social systems in the upper Midwest. Through war, treaties, fraud, sales, and allotment, Native people in the region had been dispossessed of most of their land. Land loss limited access to the resources on which traditional economies had depended and undermined the foundation of Indigenous identities. Assimilation policies enacted in the boarding schools and on reservations and the effects of economic hardship eroded Native languages, ceremonies, values, beliefs, and traditions, and disrupted the family and community dynamics that passed Indigenous knowledge from one generation to the next. Reflecting on the difficult years of the early twentieth century on Minnesota reservations, historian Brenda Child observes that "the fabric of Ojibwe community life persisted only under great stress."[1]

Yet somehow, it did persist. In her study of Ojibwe experiences with federal boarding schools, Child argues that the schools could not completely sever the cultural and emotional ties between students and their families and communities. Ojibwe scholar Thomas Peacock reminds us that despite the best efforts of the assimilationists, Native traditions "endured through this difficult period." In Ojibwe and other Native communities in the region, some people still held on to their ancestral values and belief systems and maintained elements of Indigenous social systems. Some adults maintained a version of the traditional seasonal economy, and a few spiritual leaders kept practicing the ceremonies of the Midewiwin lodge and other Indigenous spiritual systems in secret. The elders remembered the stories of their people's history, and they harbored knowledge of their ancestors' ways of life. As Ojibwe storyteller Ignatia Broker has written, as long as at least one young person in each generation asked about the old ways, they could not die out completely.[2]

55

Pat Bellanger grew up on the Leech Lake Ojibwe reservation in northern Minnesota in the 1940s and 1950s, where her family lived in the small, isolated community of Onigum. Her childhood memories reveal both the consequences of cultural repression and the traces of cultural persistence on Minnesota reservations in the postwar period. During Bellanger's childhood, a few community elders continued to perform the ceremonies of the Midewiwin lodge, the spiritual heart of traditional Ojibwe culture. Other local Native people warned Bellanger and her brothers against any contact with them. In a 2002 interview, she remembered "being told that it was wrong." Some of the warnings were especially ominous:

> they called them witches. . . . [W]e were told we couldn't even look at 'em when they walked down the street, walked down the road at Onigum: Don't look at 'em. Because they were witches, and they had all this power.

Clyde Bellecourt has recalled similar warnings about "bad medicine" being practiced on the White Earth reservation in his youth. As these narratives reveal, by this time it was not only Euro-Americans who perpetuated the repression of traditional culture; Indian people also enforced it.[3]

Despite the intimidation, the old ways persisted. Bellecourt has childhood memories of "drumming and high-pitched singing . . . coming from the deep forest where the older, more traditional . . . people lived" on the White Earth reservation.[4] In Onigum at Leech Lake, traditional elders also continued practicing their culture in secret, and they carried that spiritual power with them as they walked down the road before the downcast eyes of frightened yet curious children. In Pat Bellanger's own family, even some of those who had embraced Christian beliefs and institutions did so selectively, and they continued to introduce the next generation to the old ways:

> my grandfather was an Episcopalian minister. But also, he's the one that took me to the Mide ceremonies. I mean, he was really in that generation of change, I think, . . . where he was told he *couldn't* [maintain Native traditions], but did it anyway, because he knew it was right, for him.[5]

Some of the generation who grew up on upper Midwestern reservations in the 1940s and 1950s, such as Dennis Banks at Leech Lake and Eddie Benton-Benai at Lac Courte Oreilles, also had grandparents who still spoke Native languages, maintained traditional economic and social practices, and told stories to their grandchildren about the way things used to be.[6]

Even in the federal Indian schools of this period there were opportunities to retain ties to a Native cultural orientation. By the 1940s, some boarding schools had become less repressive than in earlier decades. The federal Merriam Report of 1928, which exposed the negative effects of poor housing, malnutrition, substandard education, hard physical labor, and harsh discipline in the boarding schools, had inspired reform. Bureau of Indian Affairs policies in the 1930s that moved away from full-scale, forced assimilation and encouraged the preservation of some aspects of Indigenous cultures included educational reforms that modified the federal curriculum to include bilingual and bicultural materials. As the federal schools employed more Native teachers, some of them incorporated elements of Indian cultures into their teaching and helped their students maintain aspects of their tribal identities. Shoshone educator Essie Horne taught at the Wahpeton boarding school in North Dakota in the 1940s and 1950s, where her students included AIM founders Dennis Banks and George Mitchell. Horne encouraged their interest in Indian history and traditions and worked to bolster their self-esteem in ways that later led Banks to tell Horne that she "might well have been called the mother of AIM."[7]

Because of this cultural persistence, some of the Native people who moved to St. Paul and Minneapolis in the decades following World War II had what historian Donald Fixico has called a "quasi-traditional" cultural orientation. Some even had what historian Rachel Buff has described as "substantial memories of language and culture." While migration to the Twin Cities distanced Native people from the pockets of traditional culture that had survived on upper Midwestern reservations, urban Indians were not cut off entirely from their communities, especially those who came from Ojibwe reservations in Minnesota. Many of them made periodic return migrations for births, deaths, wild rice harvests, and other family and community events.[8]

Like those who had been alienated entirely from their tribal traditions, those who maintained aspects of Indigenous identity had difficulty adjusting to life in the Twin Cities. Rather than a cultural vacuum, they experienced a multifaceted, pervasive cultural conflict. Their lives became filled with dissonance between the cultural orientation of their ancestors and Native communities, and that of postwar urban society.

For many, the conflict began with the initial jarring transition from a small, close-knit reservation or other rural community to the strangeness of the urban environment. Pat Bellanger explained what the Leech Lake reservation borders represented for her as a child in the 1940s and 1950s:

> Any reservation, you've gotta understand, there's kind of a boundary around it. So, when you're in there, you're safe. And you walk to the road, and all of a sudden you're not safe anymore; you're subjected to anything and everybody. And the White community doesn't understand the Indian community.

Although she had contact with non-Indian people in Walker, a small town just off the reservation, Bellanger never developed any sort of meaningful relationships with them. When she moved to the Twin Cities in the early 1960s to attend the University of Minnesota, Bellanger found a world even more different from the reservation than what she had experienced in Walker: "An urban area is unlike a reservation; on a reservation, you know, everybody's the same." In many reservation communities, Indian people lived in a world composed primarily of other Indian people, many of them relatives. In the city, they suddenly found themselves a minority in a predominantly non-Indian environment full of strangers. As Bellanger noted, Native migrants experienced this difference as "a culture shock."[9]

When Bellanger first moved to the Twin Cities in the early 1960s, Charlotte Day and her children were living in the small town of Angora just outside the borders of the Nett Lake Ojibwe reservation in far northern Minnesota. When they moved to St. Paul in 1967, they also experienced a difficult adjustment. After staying with relatives for a few weeks, the Days moved into an efficiency apartment on Dayton Avenue in the Summit Hill neighborhood of St. Paul. With Charlotte and six children, as youngest sibling Dorene recalled, "We were pretty stuffed in there. We had two roll-away beds, the kids slept on the floor. We shared a bathroom with other tenants." Compared to the isolation, quiet, and familiarity of northern Minnesota, the city seemed crowded and full of danger. Dorene remembered that "my mom was scared for us to go to the bathroom." For everyone, she said, "it was pretty traumatic, from being in this home you always knew, and then coming to some place that was strange."[10]

Charlotte put her name on a housing list for the Mt. Airy projects near Jackson Street and University Avenue, north of downtown St. Paul. After a few months, an apartment became available, and the Days moved again.

Although they had more space, the family still struggled to adjust to their surroundings. Charlotte missed preparing wild rice, venison, duck, and other foods familiar to an Ojibwe family in the north woods. Dorene and her siblings made friends with the Wind children, who had moved to the projects from the Leech Lake reservation. Rather than hang out at the playground near their apartments, they would walk under Interstate 35, cross a frontage road, and climb a hill to play in a small wooded area. Dorene explained:

> That was the only place we wanted to play, because that was what we knew. We knew how to play in the woods; we knew how to find great big jack pines and play house underneath them, on this rust-colored carpet of needles. That's how we used to play up north, so that's what we looked for here.[11]

In reservation and rural communities throughout the upper Midwest, families like the Days lived in close contact with the natural places of their north woods and prairie environments. Coming into the city, they found themselves detached from nature, surrounded instead by concrete, brick, glass, and steel.

For families like the Days and Winds, the transition to city living brought longing for the wooded places of the North. It also meant contending with pervasive anti-Indian hostility. The children played among the trees up the hill from the projects not only because this environment felt familiar, but also because it felt safer than the playground near their apartments, where other children harassed them because they were Indian, and they "always had to defend themselves." Charlotte cautioned her children not to go out alone to play, because "then we weren't going to be protected."[12]

In a 2002 interview, Dorene Day vividly remembered a particularly painful encounter with anti-Indian prejudice. Her friend Michelle, who was from one of the few White families at the Mt. Airy projects, had tried for months to convince her mother to allow Dorene to stay overnight. When Michelle's mother finally relented, Dorene discovered the reason for her reluctance:

> Their house was immaculate, just her and her mother. So, you know, I went, in my raggedy little pajamas . . . And so we're up in her room, and her mom comes and says, "Okay, you guys have got to get ready for bed." So, I didn't bring a brush, I brought a toothbrush. So I used her

brush, and then her mother said she wanted me to brush my teeth in
the kitchen. So, I go to the kitchen, and then she fumigates the kitchen.
After I used [Michelle's] brush, she put bleach and Lysol in the sink, and
she's soaking these brushes . . . And I didn't even really want to tell my
mother, because I knew . . . she wouldn't let me go there again.[13]

Certainly, Indian people who lived on or near reservations had encountered
prejudice from local Whites. But in the city, closer proximity, more frequent
interaction, and extreme minority status made encounters with racist hostility more frequent and more intense.

Anti-Indian prejudice was fueled by the cultural differences that set
Indian people apart within postwar urban society. The Twin Cities Indian
population in the 1950s and 1960s represented a wide range of Native cultures, each with its own distinct traditions. Despite their diversity, many
of those who came to the city with at least some connection to their traditional cultures shared a common value system and a similar social orientation that differed significantly from the Euro-American, middle-class,
urban social norm. Native cultures favored cooperation over competition
and respected generosity and sharing rather than material consumption
and accumulation. They valued communal identity and collective responsibility more than individualism. They also prioritized loyalty and hospi-
tality to extended family and kin networks rather than the primacy of the
nuclear family.[14]

For many Indian people accustomed to the social dynamics and cultural values of the reservation, immersion in the urban heart of mainstream
society felt profoundly disorienting. Researchers from the University of
Minnesota found in the late 1960s that "a severe dissonance exists between
the culture of the American Indian in Minnesota and non-Indian styles
of life." A civil rights commission studying the Minneapolis Indian community in the early 1970s concluded that, because of this cultural conflict,
urban Indian migrants were "hard-pressed to 'bridge the gap' between reservation and metropolis."[15]

The clash of cultural values encountered by Indian people in the city
exacerbated other problems of urban life such as the search for housing,
employment, and help from social-service agencies. Many new Indian arrivals to the city stayed with relatives or friends while they looked for places
of their own. This practice reflected traditional American Indian conceptions of social obligation, which emphasized responsibility to the extended

family as well as the wider community. But the resulting overcrowding of small apartments angered landlords and encouraged discrimination against Indian renters.

While looking for work, many Indian applicants' indifference to White, middle-class standards made it difficult for them to make a good impression in job interviews. Some young Indian people without a family to support preferred to take on short-term work to make the next month's rent or earn gas money for a trip back to the reservation, rather than seek and maintain a steady job. Many Native people viewed a job as a temporary means to a particular, practical end rather than a long-term commitment in pursuit of material consumption or socioeconomic mobility. This put Native people at a disadvantage with employers looking for a stable workforce.[16]

Some employers, though initially willing to hire Native people, became frustrated when their Indian employees did not fulfill their expectations. For many Indian people, responsibilities to family, friends, or neighbors took priority over obligations to employers. If someone became ill, needed a ride, or asked for help with a move, providing that assistance was more important than going to work or getting there on time. This led employers to stereotype Indian people as lazy and unreliable workers, and made them unwilling to hire other Indian people in the future.[17]

Indian people also faced cultural dissonance within the offices of social-service providers in Minneapolis and St. Paul. The League of Women Voters found in the late 1960s that most Twin Cities welfare workers had little or no training in working with Indians. A team of researchers that interviewed members of the Indian community in the early 1970s reported a frequent criticism of social-service agencies as "operated by non-Indians insufficiently sensitive to Indian culture." According to an Indian man who worked with Native people in alcohol and chemical dependency programs during this period, the requirements for successful completion of such programs—adhering to a forty-hour workweek, proving a long-term fixed residence, and demonstrating a good credit rating—were "totally irrelevant to Indian life styles." Another contemporary researcher noted that "differing value systems and communication skills" as well as "a lack of mutual trust and understanding" complicated relationships between social workers and their Indian clients. As increasing numbers of Native people moved into the Twin Cities and as more of them needed assistance from social-service agencies in the postwar period, these cultural conflicts became more common.[18]

"To Come in Whole": The Assimilationist Imperative in the Twin Cities, 1945–72

In the decades following World War II, federal policies, state and county agencies, and urban institutions across the country worked to diminish Indian people's cultural distinctiveness and absorb them into mainstream society. This period continued a long history of Euro-American efforts to undermine Indigenous people's traditional ways of life and eradicate their cultural difference. These efforts began with the first European missionaries to enter Indian country in the sixteenth and seventeenth centuries and continued with American missionaries, policy makers, reservation agents, and educators through the 1920s. In the 1930s, a window of cultural tolerance had opened during John Collier's administration as Commissioner of Indian Affairs. After World War II that window closed and more thoroughly assimilationist policies returned.

The renewal of assimilationist pressures in the postwar period reveals the enduring "logic of elimination" that has characterized the relationship between Indigenous people and the dominant society in the American settler state. Historian Patrick Wolfe insists that "it's crucial to recognize the uninterrupted operation of the logic of elimination after the frontier, including into the present." Historian Lorenzo Veracini also has argued that rather than being confined to the past, "the settler colonial situation retains an extraordinary capacity to impinge on the present" and that "settler colonialism is a resilient formation that rarely ends." This illuminates Euro-Americans' tenacious efforts over nearly two centuries to transform Native people into something else, as well as the multiple forms that desire took in policy and practice over time. According to Wolfe, what persisted past the period of military conquest and beyond the boarding school era was "the attempt to eliminate the Native alternative" to the political, economic, and social dominance of Euro-American society.[19]

The sources of assimilationist pressures in the postwar period were diffuse and decentralized yet cumulatively powerful. Some came from the federal government in the form of the termination and relocation policies of the 1950s and 1960s, when policy makers sought to "get out of the Indian business" by terminating tribal status, releasing the federal trust responsibility, depopulating the reservations, and detribalizing Native people by moving them into cities. Termination and relocation policies were bolstered by the belief that Indian people's service during World War II had proven them capable of integration and the hope that Indian citizens could both contribute to and benefit from a prosperous postwar economy. Under relocation, federal policy makers pursued these goals through BIA offices and programs in designated relocation cities as well as in cities that were not official relocation centers, such as Minneapolis and St. Paul.

Broader political and social forces in the postwar United States also supported the push for American Indian assimilation. Anticommunist fears fueled suspicion of tribal people's collectivism. The assimilationist agenda also reflected the postwar period's emphasis on cultural conformity and a desire to break down ethnic divisions and merge diverse groups into a common "American" identity. During these years, assimilationist pressures came to bear heavily on Indian people living in American cities, who came into frequent contact with agencies and institutions invested in changing them. Taken together, these political, social, and cultural forces added up to a powerful assimilationist imperative that intruded deeply into the lives of urban Indian people.[20]

The assimilationist imperative clearly asserted itself in the lives of Indian people in postwar Minneapolis and St. Paul. From 1969 to 1971, sociologist Joseph Westermeyer conducted a comprehensive study of the relationship between Indian people and social institutions in the Twin Cities and elsewhere in Minnesota. He investigated state, county, city, public, and private agencies, including police departments, welfare offices, schools, health-care providers, legal services, and church groups. Despite hearing a range of professed opinions about Indian people, Westermeyer argued that, across the board, "Social institutions practice gross discrimination against Indian people in Minnesota—and they do so in the name of equality. Besides ignoring the real social needs of Indians, they often attempt to undermine Indian mores and values." Westermeyer went on to explain how an attitude of "pseudo-egalitarianism" actually resulted in discrimination against Indian people:

> Since all people in Minnesota were *not* the same in regard to their cultural mores and social problems, gross inequality in services resulted from treating everybody as though they were 'the same.' In effect, the true needs of Indian people were blatantly ignored or poorly handled.... In order to benefit from social institutions as constituted, Indian people were expected to behave in ways which are odious to them.

Westermeyer concluded that this kind of treatment "amounted to de facto attempts at ethnicide."[21]

Other assessments also reveal the pressure for cultural change faced by Twin Cities Indian people in the postwar period. Historian Pauline Brunette writes of the 1950s and 1960s that "many white people working on 'the Indian problem' continued to define urban success by degree of assimilation into the white urban culture," and charges Twin Cities social agencies with "promoting assimilation and eradication of Indian ethnicity." A civil rights commission investigating the Twin Cities Indian community in the early 1970s concluded that urban Indians "cannot easily adapt to this new society without abandoning their culture."[22]

Even within the reports of researchers who seemed genuinely concerned with Twin Cities Indians' problems and displayed some cultural sensitivity, there is the unshakable assumption that Indigenous cultural perspectives, values, and priorities could not survive in a modern world. While understanding that cultural differences underpinned many problems of urban Indian life, the point of most contemporary studies was to learn how to *overcome* those differences, not to legitimate them as a viable alternative to the social norm. This mind-set is consistent with the purpose that drove most research on urban Indians in the 1960s. Government-funded studies gathered data on urban Indian people in order to identify the obstacles the hindered their adaptation to city life and develop programs and services that would assimilate them more effectively into mainstream urban society.[23]

Settler colonialism's intolerance for the persistence of Indigenous difference and the assimilation required by the mid-twentieth century's version of the "logic of elimination" lay at the heart of many Indian people's struggles in postwar Minneapolis and St. Paul. Members of an early 1970s civil rights commission found that "the predominant fear of all Indians interviewed during this project dealt with 'forced assimilation.'" At an open meeting held in the Indian community, one Native resident "expressed this concern quite clearly" when asked to explain the conflict between Indian culture and urban life:

> I guess the primary difficulty is the fact that our Indian community would prefer to come in whole . . . They don't want to leave what is unique about them behind them at the borders of this community, and yet people want us to become assimilated and join that polluted mainstream and strip ourselves of everything that is unique about us, and we are not about to do that.[24]

Researchers for the League of Women Voters wrote in 1971 that "while most Indians want to raise their standard of living, they do not see that assimilation is required to do so."[25]

Not all urban Indians experienced the same degree of cultural dissonance, and not all objected entirely to cultural change. Differences in tribal background, home community, gender, age, marital status, socioeconomic position, and length of urban residence created various perspectives on the city, reservation life, traditional culture, and mainstream society. By the late 1960s, as Pauline Brunette observes, "many urban Indians retained strong ties with the reservations and traveled 'home' to educate their children about seasonal and traditional activities." For others, however, "the city had been home for many generations, and other families had ties to several reservations and minimal connection with any particular reservation." Those who had not grown up on or near a reservation, who were not as attuned to the ways of their traditional culture, who already had spent considerable time in a non-Indian-oriented environment because of wage work or military service, who had more formal education, and who embraced more of the dominant society's values, had an easier time adjusting to life in the city.[26]

Yet even some of those who appeared to blend in experienced a sense of disjuncture. Vernon Bellecourt, brother of AIM founder Clyde Bellecourt, experienced feelings of alienation despite attaining social integration and economic success while living in Denver in the 1960s. In a 1973 interview, Bellecourt recalled, "I was assimilated into the mainstream of White America. And I was *dis*enchanted. There was always an emptiness inside me. I wasn't really complete." Certainly, the majority of Twin Cities Indians in this period had not adjusted successfully, even on the surface, to the imperatives of urban life. Those who struggled the most, and especially those who most consciously resisted the pressure to assimilate, found urban life the most difficult.[27]

In the late 1960s and early 1970s, American Indian Movement activists supported those who resisted the pressure exerted by Twin Cities agencies and institutions to assimilate Indian people into the Euro-American sociocultural norm. They insisted that Native people should be able to retain a fundamentally different set of values, beliefs, priorities, and social structures, even as they pursued economic stability and worked to make good lives for themselves and their families in a modern urban environment. Indian people, AIM leaders believed, had the right to improve their political and economic status while remaining socially and culturally distinct.

In their resistance to assimilation, the people of AIM resembled the leaders of the National Indian Youth Council (NIYC) and others who had shifted the focus of Indian activism in the early 1960s. NIYC leaders like Clyde Warrior and Hank Adams had criticized existing national Indian organizations such as the National Council on American Indians as too conservative, too conciliatory, and not focused enough on issues of culture and identity. They called on Indian people to resist assimilation, to keep their cultural traditions alive, and to retain their own unique ways of being in the world. They advocated a kind of self-determination and a form of Indian nationalism that included reconnection to a distinctive Indigenous identity, rooted in the ways of their ancestors, as well as political sovereignty and economic self-sufficiency.

AIM organizers' strong stance against assimilation, while not unprecedented nationally, set them apart from other Indian leaders and organizations in Minneapolis and St. Paul. Each generation of Native people in the Twin Cities had experienced the effects of cultural difference to some degree and had confronted the questions of how much to adapt to the dominant society and whether to preserve distinctly Native traditions. They continued Indigenous people's centuries-long survival strategies as they struggled to retain elements of traditional cultures while also adapting to new social, political, and economic realities. Some had clung more tightly to the old ways; some had embraced new values, economies, and social structures; and some had tried to strike a balance somewhere in between.

Twin Cities Indian associations of the 1920s and 1930s had promoted substantial accommodation to Euro-American urban society and embraced many dominant cultural values such as individual self-reliance, hard work, and self-sufficiency. They aspired to middle-class economic status and sought equality as American citizens within the existing political and economic structure. Where they sought improved conditions for American Indians, they did so with a strong faith in working through the channels of legislative reform. At the same time, they wanted to secure the rights of tribal membership for urban Indians and they advocated the preservation and public awareness of some aspects of Native culture.[28]

Within the Indian organizations of the 1950s and early 1960s, there was some ambivalence toward the question of assimilation. Many activists of this period spoke of wanting equal rights and opportunities for Indian people, including the ability to join the economic mainstream and achieve a middle-class lifestyle. They worked closely with local religious leaders, and some were practicing Christians. Yet they also encouraged the expression of Native cultures through powwows and other social gatherings. They saw these activities as a way to build an urban Indian community through intertribal cultural exchange. By laying the foundation for the building of an Indian center, they also fostered the creation of a uniquely Indian urban space. At the same time, they operated within a social and political climate that exerted more concerted pressure on urban Indian people to assimilate into the dominant society. Twin Cities Indian leaders of the early postwar period did not promote the wholesale revival of traditional spiritual systems and generally did not address cultural dissonance or assimilation as central concerns of their community work.[29]

AIM organizers in contrast targeted the postwar assimilationist imperative as a root cause of the socioeconomic and psychological problems that plagued the Twin Cities Indian community. They wanted to preserve what remained of traditional Indian cultures within the urban environment. Moreover, they sought to revitalize the spiritual core of those cultures, strengthen it, and build their people's future on it. In AIM leaders' estimation, Indian people needed to learn more about their Native languages, histories, value systems, and spiritual traditions. They believed that Native people's survival depended on reclaiming this knowledge and using it as the foundation and central orientation of their lives. They also wanted Indian people to stop feeling ashamed and inferior because they were Indian. AIM organizers worked to cultivate a sense of Indigenous identity, pride, and self-worth among urban Native people, to combat cultural alienation and its psychological and social consequences. In this way, they resisted the ongoing attempts within American settler society to eliminate the Indigenous alternative that persisted within the borders of the United States. These commitments led them to become educational activists and brought them into confrontation with the child welfare system in Minneapolis and St. Paul.

"Almost Completely Unsuccessful": Crisis in Indian Education, 1960–72

By the 1950s, the majority of American Indian children attended school in public school systems. The shift from federal day schools and on- and off-reservation boarding schools to public schools began after the turn of the century, then accelerated after 1930. In 1930, 53 percent of the country's Indian children attended public schools; by 1970, it was 65 percent.[30]

The public educational system in the Twin Cities exerted tremendous influence over the lives of Indian families. Researchers from the University of Minnesota who carried out multiple studies of Indian education in Twin Cities public schools from the late 1960s to the early 1970s wrote that "for many Indian families, the school may be potentially the single most important urban institution in terms of its impact upon daily life." Within the public schools, the combined effects of economic and health disparities, cultural dissonance, individual prejudice, institutional bias, and the assimilationist imperative manifested themselves, with numerous negative consequences for Native students. Indian public school students in this period suffered from disproportionately high truancy and dropout rates and low academic achievement as well as prejudice, discrimination, and sociocultural alienation.[31]

A high dropout rate provided the most obvious evidence of Indian students' educational struggles. Estimates of the Indian dropout rate varied widely as student population statistics, dependent largely on sight counts, consistently undercounted Indian students. Native students also proved difficult to track through the system because of their families' high mobility, both within the city and between the city and the reservations. It is likely, however, that the Indian dropout rate in the Twin Cities in the 1960s and early 1970s was at least 60 percent, and perhaps as high as 80 percent.[32]

These numbers contrast starkly with the general student population. In the Minneapolis public schools, the overall dropout rate was 15 percent in this period; the statewide rate stood at 7 percent, which in 1969–70 was the lowest state average in the country. Even other disadvantaged student populations did not fare as badly: in four Minneapolis high schools with significant minority and low-income enrollments, the overall dropout rate stood at 26 percent. Researchers also found in the early 1970s that Indian attrition rates rose as children aged. While Indian children accounted for more than 18 percent of prekindergarten students in Minneapolis, by twelfth grade Native students composed only 1.4 percent of the total.[33]

Other statistics that signaled Indian public school students' difficulties in the 1960s and early 1970s included high rates of tardiness, frequent absenteeism, lack of participation in the classroom, and lower levels of academic success compared to other students. Schools also placed Native children in special education classes at higher rates than other students. The studies that uncovered these problems also found that teachers and administrators were well aware of them. In one study of a Minneapolis junior high school in 1969, University of Minnesota researchers found that all of the employees and administrators interviewed felt that their school "was not effectively meeting the needs of its Indian population. In fact, they evaluated the school as almost completely unsuccessful with Indian youth."[34]

Native students' high rates of tardiness, absenteeism, and attrition and their low levels of academic engagement and performance had many causes. In most Twin Cities public schools, Indian children made up only a small percentage of the student body. One group of researchers asserted in the 1970s that "Indians receive a better education when they attend schools with a concentration of Indian students than when they are a small minority within the school." In the few schools with higher numbers of Indian students, they found that those students "have a lower dropout rate and are less likely to be assigned to special education classes."[35]

Native students' low numbers, combined with anti-Indian prejudice, made them vulnerable to hostility and harassment from other students. A university research team, reflecting on a series of studies of Indian education in Minneapolis, wrote in 1969 that Indian youth "often seem to feel discriminated against by non-Indian students," and that "they experience a general feeling of being disrespected and looked down upon." The same report noted "frequent conflicts between Indians and blacks" in the city's schools. In one St. Paul elementary school, Indian parents reported that African American students harassed Native students by calling them derogatory names like "dirty Indians," pulling their hair, physically attacking them, and picking fights. When fights broke out, parents complained that school officials punished only the Indian students. Mechanic Arts High School, located near the State Capitol building north of downtown St. Paul, was known for tensions between Indian youth and African American students. Reflecting these experiences, a civil rights commission listed "peer group hostility" as one of the primary contributing factors to high Indian dropout rates.[36]

Indian students and parents also reported discrimination by teachers and administrators. Throughout the 1960s and 1970s, the Twin Cities public school systems had few Indian employees. In 1969, university researchers found only nine Native teachers in the entire Minneapolis system of more than ninety schools, compared to 181 Black and twenty-six Asian; the overwhelming majority of teachers were White. Another study reported that only 1.3 percent of all Minneapolis public school personnel had Indian heritage in 1973 (when Indians comprised at least 4.3 percent of students), and found only two Native elementary schoolteachers. The authors of this report cited "the paucity of Native American staff in the school system" as a major reason for high attrition and dropout rates among Indian students. In St. Paul in 1968–69, an elementary school with at least 9.2 percent Indian students employed no Indian teachers.

All investigators of Twin Cities Indian education during this time noted the lack of sufficient training and understanding among public school employees regarding the cultural, social, and historical backgrounds of Native students and families. This problem also sparked criticism by Indian parents. Even educators admitted their own ignorance and its negative impact on Native pupils. Ignorance fed prejudice among teachers, some of whom expected less of their Native students.[37]

Native families' economic instability also posed problems for Indian students, creating multiple obstacles to academic success. Inadequate housing conditions necessitated frequent moves, which often required transferring to a different school. Older Indian students whose parents worked and did not have access to child care sometimes stayed home to care for younger siblings. School officials then punished these students for missing class. When they did attend school, their parents' inability to afford new clothing or school supplies made them vulnerable to teasing from other students and reprimands from classroom teachers.[38]

Unlike many Indian parents in the Twin Cities, Charlotte Day had a full-time job that provided a steady, if modest, income. Yet, despite this relative economic stability, her children experienced many of the problems noted by observers of Twin Cities Indian education in the 1960s. By the time Day settled her family in the Mt. Airy housing projects in St. Paul in 1967, she had five children attending Mechanic Arts High School in St. Paul: Sharon, Ross, Cheryl, Janet, and Charlene. Although her youngest child Dorene was still in elementary school at the time, she knew what her older siblings went through at Mechanic Arts. As she tells it, school was a daily battleground for the older Day children, who faced prejudice and hostility from both teachers and fellow students:

> That school was highly racist and discriminatory, and my sisters and brother were feeling, I guess, the brunt of that. They'd go through things like, they'd come into class and the teacher, instead of referring to them by their first name, would say, [sternly] "Day. Can't you afford a two-cent pencil." Or they'd actually be physically attacked by some-

body that didn't like Indians . . . People would write, you know, "Dirty Indians" on their locker.

Day understands her siblings' experience in a broader social context:

> In those years, there was this underlying feeling of, you know, continually being treated unfairly, or continually being disrespected, or continually being discriminated against. And that's the era, of the time, I mean, that's how they grew up.

Like other Indian students in the Twin Cities public schools, the Days "never got the respect they wanted. They just wanted to be left alone and respected for what they were, and they never really got that."[39]

Rather than quietly accept their place in the social order, the older Day children chose to resist it. As Dorene recounted, when other students harassed her brother and sisters for being Indian, "they weren't about to take that lying down; they'd fight back." This response did not sit well with school officials. Day recalls that "my older brother and sisters started getting into trouble, because they were defending who they were, they were defending their Indian heritage." According to Dorene, when her siblings got into fights with other students, "*they* were the only ones that would get expelled, or they were the only ones that would get in trouble."[40]

Her children's problems at school caused Charlotte Day great concern. Both Charlotte and her estranged husband Clyde believed in the importance of a good education. They had read to their children from an early age. At their childhood home in northern Minnesota, the Day kids had sat down at the family's long dining table every night to do their homework under the light of two kerosene lamps. Dorene remembers her father's attentiveness to his children's schoolwork:

> He was serving as a teacher, basically, going from this person to that person, and making sure that everyone had information if they needed it, or talking through problems with kids.

This nightly scene had a profound effect on her own intellectual development:

> I wanted homework, even though I wasn't old enough to go to school. So I learned how to count, I learned my colors, I learned how to even

do addition, before I went to kindergarten, only because I kept pestering my dad. You know, "I need work too, I need work too." So he'd sit me down, and he showed me numbers first, and then he introduced me into addition, so I already knew how to add, and was learning how to subtract by the time I went to kindergarten. So I was advanced for my age, *only* because my home environment was that my parents wanted everyone to get an education.

Given Charlotte's commitment to her children's education, their experiences at Mechanic Arts High School troubled her deeply. As Dorene Day observed, "She didn't like that my brothers and sisters had to fight all the time." Charlotte did her best to stay involved; she "was always mediating, because she had a bunch of kids that were really tired of being pushed around, and so they dealt with things kind of on their own." Still, "as things continued to escalate at the school, the more concerned my mother became."[41]

Although other Twin Cities Indian parents shared Charlotte Day's concerns, contemporary educators largely considered them obstacles to their children's education. The public school teachers and administrators, social scientists, and other researchers seeking causes for the problems in Indian education in the 1960s and early 1970s generally targeted two areas: Indian poverty, and Indian parents. University researchers spoke for many of their contemporaries when they asserted in 1969 that "all of the concomitants of low income—poor housing, inadequate diet, family disorganization, insufficient clothing, and lack of support for the education process at home, to name a few—constitute a drain upon the potential learning of Indian children." In survey after survey from this period, public school employees voiced their concern that the home life of Indian children hindered their chances for academic success, not only because of economic deprivation, but because of their parents' negative influence. One group of researchers remarked in 1970 that "negative opinion" of Indian parents' attitude toward education "abounds" in Twin Cities public schools.[42]

To be sure, some Indian families that struggled with poverty, chemical dependency, or domestic abuse lacked the stability to provide their children with much educational support. And certainly some Indian parents in Minneapolis and St. Paul saw little worth in a public school education for their children and failed to encourage regular attendance or academic success. Such attitudes stemmed in part from parents' own unpleasant experiences in boarding or public schools. Given the experiences of many urban

Indian people, they also might conclude that Euro-American society offered their young people nothing but a future of continuing socioeconomic marginalization, with or without an education. Yet Indian parents' negativity toward the Twin Cities public school system also had other sources. There was a deep gulf between Native parents and most public school employees in their beliefs about *what* and *how* Indian children should be taught—that is, about what their education should be.

Most of those who researched Twin Cities Indian education in the 1960s and early 1970s reported conflicting educational goals and cultural values between Indian homes and public schools. Stemming from this conflict, they also found evidence of a negative impact on Indian students' sense of themselves and their place in society. Some Twin Cities public school employees saw competing values as a key challenge to educating Indian students. At a South Minneapolis elementary school in 1969, nearly half of the teachers observed a conflict between what they taught Native children at school and what their parents taught them at home; most of them identified that conflict as one of the top two reasons for Indian students' poor academic performance and high dropout rate. In keeping with the teachers' assessment, the school's principal and social worker also listed "difficulties in acculturating" among the top four problems of their Indian students. They further defined those acculturation issues as "identity problems, poor self-image, value conflicts between home and school, and difficulty in relating to whites."[43]

While some school personnel recognized the different values that separated their educational institutions from many Indian students and parents, the real question was what school officials were willing to do about it. Would schools adapt to meet the needs of Indian families? Or would they force Indian students to conform to the system in order to succeed? For the most part, Indian people encountered in the public schools the same problem they faced elsewhere in the city: resistance to their cultural difference, and the pressure to assimilate into the dominant culture.

In several studies of Indian education in Twin Cities public schools in this period, investigators from the University of Minnesota asked administrators, teachers, and other staff members about their attitudes toward American Indian culture and its place in the lives of young Native people. While most responses did not completely reject the value of Indian culture, they indicate little willingness to challenge or change the status quo in order to accommodate significant sociocultural diversity. Those coming in with a different perspective would have to adjust if they wanted to "make it" in the schools or in the modern world.

When interviewers asked thirty-eight staff members at Bryant Junior High School in Minneapolis in 1969 whether Indian children should be brought up as Indians, only half of those interviewed said yes. When asked whether Indian children, when they became parents, should raise *their* children as Indians, the percentage dropped to one-third. At a South Minneapolis elementary school where more than 20 percent of the students were Indian, most of the teachers felt that, although Indian students should be able to retain *some* aspects of Indian culture, they still needed to adjust largely to White ways. None of the teachers interviewed believed that Indian students' *predominant* identification should be with Indian ways. A teacher at a St. Paul elementary school with close to 10 percent Indian students said that they "should always remember their Indian traditions and fit it in where it will work." Yet, ultimately, she believed, Indian children should "assimilate into city life."[44]

Most school personnel did not understand the depth of the cultural dissonance experienced by urban Indian students and their families, nor were they willing to make systemic changes to accommodate them. At a St. Paul elementary school with close to 10 percent Indian enrollment in 1969, most teachers shared the conviction that "the problems facing St. Paul Indians were no different from those of any poor minority group in the city." The principal of a South Minneapolis elementary school with more than 20 percent Indian enrollment in 1970 stated that the goals of Indian education "are not markedly different from the goals of any other school." Indian students, he insisted, "need to be able to compete." In order to do so, "they have to accept society's value structures to some degree and incorporate them into their lives." His responsibility to Indian students, as for all students, was "educating them to fit into society."[45]

Twin Cities public school educators equated Indian people's circumstances with those of other urban minority populations. This attitude corroborated what Joseph Westermeyer had found among local social workers. In the name of equality, of treating Indian people the same as everyone else, both social-service providers and educators ignored the ways in which Indian people were *not* the same—historically, culturally, socially, politically, and legally. Thus they failed to recognize the need for a different approach to helping them.[46]

The experiences of Native children enrolled in the Minneapolis and

St. Paul public school systems in the 1960s and 1970s echoed those of other American Indian students in public schools across the country. Nationwide, Indian children suffered from high dropout rates, low attendance and participation, poor academic achievement, and cultural alienation. When considering the reasons for these problems, contemporary observers targeted many of the same issues as those emphasized by researchers in the Twin Cities. They criticized the dearth of Indian teachers; the cultural ignorance prevalent among non-Indian teachers and administrators; the pervasiveness of prejudice, discrimination, and hostility toward Native students; the economic disadvantages among many Indian families; and the lack of parental involvement, input, and support. Research conducted nationally during these years also revealed the general tendency of public educational institutions to pressure Indian students toward assimilation into the dominant society.[47]

In the Twin Cities, just as Indian people had worked to alleviate other problems of urban life, they also tried to improve their children's education. Early-twentieth-century urban residents such as Winnie Jourdain and Louise Peake had tutored Indian students and raised money for school supplies. In the 1960s, Louise's daughter Emily Peake spoke out about the failure of the Minneapolis public school system to educate Indian children as well as other inner-city students. The high Indian dropout rate in Minneapolis public schools also prompted a group of Indian parents in North Minneapolis to take collective action. To help Indian students stay in school and graduate, they created Project STAIRS (Service to American Indian Resident Students), which offered tutoring services, field trips, a summer program, and other recreational activities. Project STAIRS was first implemented in a North Minneapolis elementary school in 1964, and it expanded to a South Minneapolis school in 1968 with funding from the Minneapolis Public Schools, the University of Minnesota, and the federal Office of Economic Opportunity. Also in 1968, a cooperative effort among members of the Indian community, the Minneapolis Public Schools, and the University of Minnesota created a similar program for Indian students at two Minneapolis junior high schools. Indian Upward Bound offered tutoring services, culture classes, teacher training, and a summer program held outside of the city. The program had an all-Indian staff and established an Indian parent board to increase participation in their children's education.[48]

During the late 1960s and early 1970s, in communities throughout Minnesota, Native parents began pushing public school systems to train and hire more Indian teachers, solicit more parental input, and include Indian culture and history in school curriculum. During these years, Minnesota Ojibwes Rosemary Christensen, Will Antell, and David Beaulieu also emerged as leaders in a national Indian educational reform movement. In 1969, Christensen and Antell organized the first national conference on Indian education. Held in Minneapolis, the meeting attracted more than nine hundred participants, including Indian educators and parents who had been working for educational reform in other communities. In 1970, after the second annual Indian education conference brought together more than two thousand people, Christensen and Antell helped found the National Indian Education Association (NIEA). The NIEA planned annual conferences, encouraged research, fostered the exchange of information, and lobbied for changes in federal Indian education policy.[49]

Non-Indian scholars, government agencies, and policy makers also paid increasing attention to the problem of Indian education during these years, and contributed to calls for national-level reform. From 1967 to 1971, the United States Office of Education funded the National Study of American Indian Education. Directed by Estelle Fuchs and Robert J. Havighurst and carried out through eight university field offices (including one in Minneapolis), the study compiled national facts and figures and conducted in-depth research in twenty-six communities. Between 1967 and 1969, the U.S. Senate Special Subcommittee on Indian Education sponsored its own national study, released in 1969 as *Indian Education: A National Tragedy—A National Challenge* (better known as the Kennedy Report). The results of these studies, which were highly critical of the state of Indian education in the country, facilitated the work of Indian educational activists, in Minnesota and elsewhere.[50]

"Totally against the System": AIM's Educational Activism, 1968–72

Soon after organizing in 1968, AIM members began their own efforts to improve Indian education in Twin Cities public schools. They confronted the Minnesota State Department of Education, along with the school boards, superintendents, and principals of the Minneapolis and St. Paul public schools, about the ways in which they were failing Indian students. They argued with public school officials for Indian boys' right to wear their hair long to school as an expression of their cultural identity without being punished for violating school policy. They pushed the schools to include more,

more accurate, and more positive Indian-related curriculum and to drop curriculum materials that denigrated or distorted Indian cultures and histories. They proposed that schools bring in Indian elders and community leaders to speak to students. They also helped organize a group called True American Native Students (TANS) at North and South High Schools in Minneapolis. TANS brought Indian students together to talk about their heritage and fostered cultural pride.[51]

The same mix of motivations that had driven AIM organizers to found their movement also led to their activism in Indian education. They were concerned about the current failures of public school education for Twin Cities Indian children in the 1960s and early 1970s. They also viewed the schools with a critical eye turned to the past, to the long history of assimilationist education in the federal boarding schools and other Euro-American educational institutions, which they saw perpetuated in a new form in public school classrooms and curriculum. AIM members' attention to education also stemmed in part from their personal histories, as the desire to protect Indian children from their own painful educational experiences helped motivate AIM organizers to work for educational reform.

While Clyde Bellecourt and Dennis Banks had their formative educational experiences in mission and boarding schools, Pat Bellanger attended the Walker public schools, just outside the Leech Lake Ojibwe reservation in north-central Minnesota. Like many Minnesota border towns, Walker in the 1940s and 1950s harbored racial divisions and sometimes open hostility between Native and non-Native people, which also extended into the schools. According to Bellanger, "there was definitely an Indian and a non-Indian partition in that school, very definitely." Even though she joined the band, choir, and other extracurricular groups, she did not find acceptance among the non-Indian students. "I don't care if we all were in the band," she insisted, "the Indians were not included, in any of the parties or anything. It was a really tough way to grow up." Dennis Banks, who attended the Walker high school for a short time in the early 1950s, also has recalled a racially segregated school experience: "I didn't have any white friends at Walker. There was a wall between us and them."[52]

Even the Native students who found some acceptance among their peers suffered from the prejudices of non-Indian administrators, teachers, and parents. Bellanger acknowledged that "there were a few people who could fit in with the other kids." Two of the more accepted Indian students were her brothers Ken and Ron, whose participation in sports eased their social interactions with White students. But, according to Ken's son Greg, "Dad used to tell me about when he became friends with the principal's daughter, when they were really young, but she told him he couldn't come over to her house, 'cause he was Indian. Her dad told her to stay away from him; she couldn't be friends with him anymore. That's kinda hard when you're eight or nine years old."[53]

Bellanger's struggles in the Walker public schools included her teachers' hostility toward her academic ambitions and resentment of her tendency to question authority. As Bellanger recounted in a 2002 interview:

> I was on the A honor roll all the time. I was *always* there . . . I aced their English. I aced their math . . . when they finished passing out the math tests at the end of the row, I'd have mine in. They *hated* that. [pause] So I'd do it again. [pause] *'Cause they hated it.*

In ninth grade, Bellanger remembers, "this English teacher hated me . . . and part of it was, he thought I was taunting him by turning my papers in early and things like that." Even in elementary school, Bellanger had conflicts with her teachers:

> They kept catching me in the library—I was too young to be reading these schoolbooks, and I'd already read all the [other] ones, and I was bored with them and wanted to read other literature—and they would kick me out of the library . . . I asked, "Why? Why can't I read these books?" I mean, I was mad, and I wanted to read something. And they said, "Well, if you read it now, what are you going to read when you're in twelfth grade?" I thought, Well, [laughing] I hope they'll find me something when I'm in twelfth grade that will be a challenge, you know? Not a good answer, not the answer they wanted to hear.

The memory of those painful experiences remained vivid more than twenty years later when, as a young parent, Bellanger determined not to see her own children suffer similar treatment in the public schools:

> I would *not let them* do that to my children. I was totally against the system. Because of what it did to me. . . . I had *such* a bad time in school, and *such* a bad time with the teachers . . . that it became an influence, because I was determined that my children were not gonna be subjected to that kind of feelings, and that kind of talk, and that kind of education.

Bellanger's own history made her "a fighter right from the beginning in education," and she was not alone. As she said of the Twin Cities Indian community, "We've all got bad images of grade school and high school in the regular school system." Those bad memories from their own public school experiences helped turn Bellanger and other AIM organizers into educational activists.[54]

In Minnesota, the criticisms of AIM members, other concerned Indian parents and community leaders, and non-Indian researchers began to have a noticeable effect, and opportunities for Indian input increased. The Minnesota Indian Education Committee formed in 1969 as the first all-Indian advisory committee to a state Department of Education in the United States. The same year, the state of Minnesota accomplished another national "first" by hiring a Native person as Director of Indian Education. Also in 1969, the University of Minnesota's Minneapolis campus established the country's first university Indian Studies Department. By the early 1970s, the Indian Section of the Minnesota State Department of Education, created in 1936 to direct the state's role in Indian education, had significantly increased the percentage of Indian people on its staff.

In 1968 and 1969, Twin Cities Indian people's calls for change led to the establishment of an Indian Advisory Committee to the Minneapolis Public Schools and an Indian Advisory Board to the St. Paul Public Schools. The first in the nation, these all-Indian committees evaluated and developed curriculum materials, planned and facilitated training workshops for teachers and staff members, and listened to the grievances of Indian parents. In 1969, Indian people also convinced both Minneapolis and St. Paul to hire Indian consultants as liaisons between their communities and the public school systems, also the first such positions in the United States. By 1970, both North and South High Schools in Minneapolis offered Indian studies classes, and all new teachers in the Minneapolis Public Schools received training in understanding Native cultures and working with Indian students.[55]

In 1971, a study by the League of Women Voters concluded that "Minnesota has put considerable effort into upgrading Indian education." Much of that effort had been focused on the Minneapolis and St. Paul public schools. Yet, despite the progress, the report's authors noted, "problems still loom large." As Indian people learned, there were limits to how much they could accomplish by working within the existing public school system. Most of the newly required cultural training applied only to new teachers and thus did not reach those already in the system. Advisory boards also had limited effectiveness. As sociologist Joseph Westermeyer pointed out, "these boards can only advise. Unlike real boards of education, they are unable to set policy and cannot hire or discharge school employees. Thus Indian parents had, in effect, no authority over their children's education."[56]

Resistance from individual school administrators and teachers also hindered the effectiveness of reform efforts within certain schools. One principal of a South Minneapolis school with high Indian enrollment told university researchers in 1969 that the Minneapolis Board of Education deserved praise for its responsiveness to Indian demands for educational reform. He stressed, however, that Indian parents could not expect school officials to respond to every criticism:

> For example, they might like to see some culture-thing retained, e.g. bow and arrow, but what practical use is there for such a thing?[57]

Training workshops, advisory committees, and Indian consultants increased Indian parents' opportunities to influence their children's education. By the early 1970s, the educational experiences of some Indian children in the public schools of Minneapolis and St. Paul had begun to improve. But substantial change would take time. And it would continue to confront those educators who persisted in their belief that Indian students needed to assimilate into the dominant society.

For some AIM organizers, the limitations of working within the system became frustrating. Beginning in 1970, seeking an alternative to the public schools, Pat Bellanger worked with other St. Paul parents to create the St. Paul Open School. These parents rejected the rigid structure and unindividualized pedagogy of the traditional public school. The Open School offered students more autonomy in choosing their classes, more flexible classroom structures, and more opportunities for artistic exploration and creative expression. Its founding in St. Paul reflected a larger national movement for "open schools," "open classrooms," and "open education" that emerged among educational reformers in the 1960s and 1970s. Both of Bellanger's elementary-age children, Lisa and Michael, attended the school after it opened in 1971.[58]

For Pat Bellanger, though, the open school experiment proved disappointing. The freedom of choice she had envisioned for students and parents regarding course requirements did not come to fruition. And the St. Paul

Open School had never been exactly the kind of education that Bellanger wanted for her children. It was not designed to serve the specific needs of Indian students, nor did it ground its educational philosophy in the teaching of Indian culture or the fostering of a positive Indian identity.[59]

For Bellanger and for other AIM organizers and supporters, it was these issues of culture and identity that most fundamentally influenced their approach to Indian education. Public school principals might dismiss the demands of Indian people for a different kind of education as an irrational attachment to "some culture-thing" like the "bow and arrow," an outdated artifact with "no practical use." But for Clyde Bellecourt, Pat Bellanger, and Eddie Benton-Banai, the point was not to cling to the bow and arrow but to retain the values and beliefs of traditional culture in the face of a society that worked to eradicate them. This would help Native students develop a positive sense of self, which in turn would allow them to learn and succeed in an academic environment. As Benton-Banai later explained to a journalist, "If you give people back their identity and their self-esteem, you give them something to be proud of . . . That's what culture-based education is. It ain't about beadwork and making moccasins. It's more than that."[60]

When AIM's founders rejected the educational models of their youth, they did so not just because they had been snubbed by White children or discriminated against by their teachers. Their deepest scars came from the denial of their cultural identity and the erosion of their self-worth. For their children and the children of other Indian families, they wanted an education that would foster a positive sense of identity and pride in their heritage, through the teaching of ancestral cultural knowledge. As Pat Bellanger recalls of AIM's early days:

> I was looking for the same thing that everybody else was as well. I wanted the kids to have that background; I wanted them never to forget who they were. . . . And so, when we would meet, we'd sit around and talk about all sorts of things, and it would come back to that, you know.[61]

Eddie Benton-Banai later said that because the public schools could not offer Indian children "identity and focus," he had been motivated "to organize a school where Indian students could learn with pride about their culture and backgrounds, develop self-esteem and enthusiasm for knowledge." Envisioning a completely different kind of education for Indian students, some AIM people began to discuss the possibility of creating their own school.[62]

In October 1970, Dennis Banks publicly announced the American Indian Movement's plans to develop a K–12 Indian school in Minneapolis. As Banks described it to a local reporter, such a school would provide a real alternative for the hundreds of Native children who struggled every day in the public schools, thereby significantly reducing the dropout rate. It would place the control of Indian education directly in the hands of Indian people through an all-Indian school board. It would employ Indian teachers to provide culturally sensitive and relevant instruction. Most important to AIM organizers, it would replace the public schools' assimilationist curriculum with one steeped in Native cultures, inclusive of Native languages, more focused on Indian history, and aimed at promoting a positive Indian identity.[63]

AIM's proposal for an all-Indian school met with both opposition and support from other members of the Twin Cities Indian community. When Banks unveiled AIM's plans, Ted Mahto, an Ojibwe working as a consultant to the Minneapolis Public Schools, expressed skepticism about their feasibility and concern about the dangers of educational self-segregation. Other local Indian leaders such as Dakota educator Chris Cavender criticized AIM's plans, as well as its generally confrontational tactics, as divisive and counterproductive. Cavender and others preferred to continue working for gradual changes within the existing system.[64]

Other Native people agreed about the need for an Indian school in the Twin Cities. When he announced AIM's plans to the press in October 1970, Dennis Banks cited the endorsement of Indian organizations in Minneapolis and elsewhere in the state, as well as the backing of local Indian parents. Clyde Bellecourt also remembers getting verbal support for the idea from state and national Indian organizations. Yet, even with others' tacit approval, AIM leaders lacked funding and other critical material support.[65]

"Great Power over Indian Lives": The Indian Child Welfare Crisis, 1945–72

In the end it was the desperate situation of two Indian families threatened with the removal of their children by the welfare system that provided the catalyst for AIM's founding of alternative schools in Minneapolis and St. Paul. AIM leaders had become educational activists for many reasons: because they objected to the public school curriculum; because Native students were struggling academically and psychologically; because of prejudice and discrimination; because of their own personal educational experiences.

But AIM activists also got involved with education because troubled Indian families who had become entangled in the child welfare system were coming to them for help.

The postwar assimilationist imperative that underpinned public education in Minneapolis and St. Paul also pervaded the cities' social-service agencies. In the opinion of many social-service providers, for Indian people to move from a "problem" population to a successful one, they were going to have to become less Indian. In the postwar Twin Cities, the welfare system's cultural and socioeconomic prejudices and the scrutiny of social workers intruded deeply into American Indian families and communities, with sometimes devastating consequences.

A high percentage of urban Indian people came into contact with social services while living in the Twin Cities, most of them with a division of the welfare departments of Hennepin County, where Minneapolis was located, or Ramsey County, which served St. Paul. In his study of relationships between Indian people and social institutions in Minnesota from 1969 to 1970, Joseph Westermeyer concluded that "welfare departments ranked second only to the police in number of contacts with Indian people in trouble or distress." Westermeyer also found that "social workers wielded great power over Indian lives in Minnesota" because "at one time or another the finances of virtually all Indians rested upon personal decisions made by social workers."[66]

The power wielded by social workers went beyond financial control. According to Westermeyer, "an even more important cudgel was the worker's capability to take children away from Indian parents." From the first visit urban Indian parents made to a welfare agency, their families were exposed to surveillance and vulnerable to intervention. Minnesota child welfare laws permitted welfare workers and the juvenile courts to remove children from their families if they considered a child neglected, abandoned, abused, or delinquent. In Hennepin and Ramsey counties, such a child might be placed in detention at the Juvenile Center pending court disposition of a case, held at the Minnesota Reception and Diagnostic Center north of St. Paul in Lino Lakes for several weeks of assessment, committed to the County Home School or the state reformatory, placed with a foster family, or put up for adoption.[67]

In the 1960s and 1970s, the Minnesota child welfare system removed Indian children from their families with astonishing frequency, at wildly disproportionate rates. A study conducted by the Association on American

Indian Affairs (AAIA) in 1969 concluded that Indian children in Minnesota were five times more likely to be adopted out or placed in foster care than non-Indian children. The same year, however, Joseph Westermeyer asserted that throughout Minnesota, "the rate of foster placement and state guardianship for Indian children ran twenty to eighty times that for majority children." In 1974, testimony at hearings before a U.S. Senate subcommittee stated that Minnesota Indian children were being placed in foster or adoptive homes at a rate twenty-two times higher than other children. In 1971–72, state statistics showed that nearly one-fourth of Indian children under the age of one lived with adoptive families; by 1977, one in eight Native children under eighteen had been adopted. The League of Women Voters found in 1966–67 that almost 11 percent of children under state guardianship in Minnesota, and almost 10 percent of those under county-supervised care, were Indian. In 1972, 12 percent of boys and 21 percent of girls held at the Minnesota Reception and Diagnostic Center in Lino Lakes were Indian. At the time, according to census data, Indian people made up less than 1 percent of the state's population.[68]

In almost all cases, Indian children who were fostered out or adopted in Minnesota were placed with non-Indian families. In 1969, Joseph Westermeyer discovered that of more than seven hundred foster homes known to have taken in Indian children in Minnesota, only two had an Indian parent. By 1977, more than 90 percent of adopted Indian children not residing with family members lived in non-Indian homes.[69]

Minnesota statistics reflected a broader national crisis. From the 1950s through the 1970s, the removal of Indian children from their families by welfare workers, county and state courts, and religious organizations throughout the United States reached epidemic proportions. Studies conducted by the AAIA in 1969 and 1974 estimated that 25 to 35 percent of Indian children nationwide had been taken from their families; in some states, the rates ran as high as 85 percent. On average, across the country, Indian children were twenty times more likely than non-Indian children to be placed in foster care. These numbers drove AAIA executive director William Byler to condemn "the wholesale separation of Indian children from their families" as "perhaps the most tragic and destructive aspect" of American Indian life in that period. The reasons for this tragedy, in Minnesota and throughout the country, included the legacy of past federal and state Indian policies, the prejudices of social workers, the failures of the legal system, and the "logic of elimination," in the form of the postwar assimilationist imperative.[70]

In the eighteenth and nineteenth centuries, the dispossession of reservation land and resources, the weakening of traditional economies, and assimilation policies that worked to replace extended kin networks with patriarchal nuclear family units all had undermined the integrity of Indian family structures. The off-reservation federal boarding schools, which removed Native children from their families and communities for years at a time, also weakened social structures in ways that reverberated across generations. Menominee activist Ingrid Washinawatok-El Issa has commented on the cross-generational consequences of boarding school education:

> For many in our society, the role of parenting was halted by boarding schools. Our great-grandparents were prevented from being parents. Both my grandmother and my grandfather were sent away. Then their kids were brought up in a regimented, abusive system of boarding schools. What that system has done to our grandparents, our parents, and then to us and our children is put holes in the fabric of our society.[71]

Ojibwe education scholar Thomas Peacock agrees that because of government policies, generations of boarding school students "grew into adults who did not know how to parent children."[72]

By the 1950s and 1960s, some of the generation of Indian people who moved their young families to urban areas like the Twin Cities lacked the personal memories and the psychological resources to raise their children in responsible, nurturing ways. The socioeconomic and cultural stresses of life in the city further strained Native families. Some parents struggled with alcohol abuse and chemical dependency, relationship conflicts, and domestic violence, with negative consequences for their children. Yet most social workers who witnessed the breakdown of Native families removed children from these environments without recognizing the historical processes that had helped create them.[73]

In some instances, the welfare workers who intervened in Indian families did so not because of abuse or acute endangerment to the child; rather, they removed Native children based on more subjective determinations of "neglect," "social deprivation," or "emotional damage." These judgments were influenced by White, middle-class bias. The vast majority of child welfare workers in postwar America were non-Indians, and most of them were White. By 1977, only about one hundred professionally trained Native social workers existed in the entire United States. Most non-Indian child welfare workers were well-intentioned individuals who believed they were acting in the "best interest of the child." Yet they largely failed to recognize how their own culture- and class-bound perspectives, and their misunderstanding of the social context of American Indian families, shaped their judgment of Indian parents as providing unfit homes for their children.[74]

American Indian concepts of kinship and approaches to child rearing conflicted with White, middle-class ideas about the nuclear family and parental responsibility. Many Indian families, even into the 1950s and 1960s, continued the traditional practice of leaving their children in the care of extended family members—grandparents, aunts, uncles, cousins, or other people in the community—on a daily basis or for an extended period of time. Many White social workers did not consider these acceptable childcare arrangements. Conflicting perspectives on aging also came into play. White social workers tended to consider grandparents and other elderly people unfit caretakers, whereas many Native people viewed elders not only as capable of caring for young children but as key contributors to their emotional and spiritual development. Different approaches to discipline and economic standards also led some child-care workers to label Indian people as unfit parents.[75]

Socioeconomic disparities also triggered social workers' concerns. AAIA executive director William Byler wrote in the 1970s that "poverty, poor housing, lack of modern plumbing, and overcrowding are often cited by social workers as proof of parental neglect and are used as grounds for beginning custody proceedings." In the 1970s, social workers in California removed a child from an Indian family on the grounds that White adoptive parents "were financially able to provide a home and a way of life superior to the one furnished by the natural mother." Their assessment concluded that "an Indian reservation is an unsuitable environment for a child." The collective message of child welfare policy and practices across the country in the postwar period was that an Indian *family* provided an unsuitable environment for a child. As Senator James Abourezk, chair of a Senate subcommittee investigating Indian child welfare, wrote in the 1970s, "public and private welfare agencies seem to have operated on the premise that most Indian children would really be better off growing up non-Indian."[76]

American Indian people made unfit parents because they were poor, and because they were *different*. To prove their suitability to raise their own children, they were expected to conform to the cultural and socioeconomic values and priorities of White, middle-class America. For many Indian parents during this time, their contact with social-welfare agencies confronted them with a wrenching choice: assimilate, or lose your children.

In many cases, in fact, it was not entirely a matter of choice. Postwar economic marginalization and racial prejudice rendered most Indian people unable to attain middle-class standards of living. As AAIA executive director William Byler explained in 1977, some Native families also experienced coercion from social-service providers:

> Indian parents dependent on social agencies for welfare payments or other economic assistance, and in communities characterized by police discrimination and disproportionately high incarceration rates, are vulnerable to coercion. . . . . [F]or many Indian parents . . . the primary service agency to which they must turn for financial help also exercises police powers over their family life and is, most frequently, the agency that initiates custody proceedings.

Indian parents sometimes reluctantly agreed to give up their children because they feared financial recrimination or incarceration if they did not agree to do so. Some Indian parents agreed to relinquish custody without understanding the legal ramifications or the permanence of what they were doing. In some cases where the state won only temporary custody, if the parents subsequently failed to meet stipulated requirements for proving themselves fit caretakers, the court terminated their parental rights altogether.[77]

Native American people's experiences within the U.S. child welfare system are strikingly similar to those of Indigenous people in other settler societies during this time. In his study of state social policies toward Indigenous peoples in Canada, Australia, and New Zealand, Andrew Armitage found that in all of these places in the 1960s and 1970s, Native children were removed from their families by child welfare workers and the juvenile justice system at rates significantly higher than non-Native children. Armitage attributes this disparity in part to the higher rates of alcohol and substance abuse among Native parents, and in Canada and Australia, to the multigenerational institutionalization of Native people in government schools, which prevented children's socialization in parenting skills. He also implicates the ignorance and sociocultural bias embedded within state welfare systems, where "responses to perceived problems of parental neglect and abuse contained no recognition of aboriginal cultures, values, extended families, communities, languages, or other relationships." He argues that because these societies applied to Indigenous families the same policies "designed to provide non-aboriginal children with the kind of parenting that would best prepare them for life as adults in mainstream society," their child welfare practices "had the same purpose and effect as did assimilation."[78]

In fact, Armitage analyzes postwar child welfare practices as just the latest phase within long-standing state policies of Indigenous assimilation. Although "the buzz-word was now 'integration,'" he argues, "the objective was still assimilation." Through the dismantling of specific services for aboriginal peoples and their incorporation into mainstream social-welfare systems, policy makers believed they would further their integration into the dominant society. In this way, "assimilation would be achieved, and aboriginal peoples would become invisible."[79]

In Australia, Canada, and New Zealand, as in the United States, the push to integrate Indigenous people into the postwar social fabric furthered efforts to diminish aboriginal rights to land and resources and terminate Indigenous people's unique legal status. As Armitage argues, the extension of "common services" was "part of a total social policy framework which was designed to repeal all recognition, including territorial recognition, of aboriginal status." With this accomplished, "there would then be no need for special land tenure, social policy, or political institutions." Thus, the policy of "integration," though promoted as "equality," in fact threatened what remained of Indigenous people's sovereignty as well as their distinctive cultural identities. Postwar integration policies, then, were the settler state's "logic of elimination"—or, as literary scholar Mark Rifkin has called it, the "domestication" of Indigenous people—at work in a new form.[80]

Within any period of a settler colonial history, most of those who function as the frontline agents of assimilation believe that what they are doing is in the long-term best interests of Native people. Missionaries, boarding and residential school teachers, public school educators, and welfare workers generally have not perceived the integrity of Indigenous cultures, nor have they anticipated the lasting psychological and social damage that assimilationist institutions would inflict across generations. As Armitage observed, these individuals "were usually sincere and well-motivated." They believed that, "given the right opportunities, education, and resources," Indigenous people "would become like them. They did not recognize the racial discrimination of their own societies, and they did not understand their own colonialism." Over time, however, their actions have proven "destructive to aboriginal cultures" while also failing "to offer aboriginal children any viable alternative." From the 1830s to the 1990s, Armitage argues, though social policies in Canada, Australia, and New Zealand were designed to serve policy makers' perceptions of "the aboriginal populations' 'best interests' . . . the results were always disappointing and often disastrous."[81]

Armitage's comparative assessment of Indigenous social policies clearly reveals parallels to the history of U.S. Indian policy. By the 1950s, as in other settler societies, American federal policy makers, as well as state, county, and local institutions, were pursuing the goal of "integration" in ways that amounted to assimilation. Social-welfare agencies, including those in urban areas, proved especially powerful agents of assimilation, particularly when it came to child welfare.

In the decades following World War II, conditions in cities like Minneapolis and St. Paul made Indian families particularly vulnerable to having their children taken away by the child welfare system. In the Twin Cities, many Indian people depended on welfare agencies for economic assistance. They experienced police discrimination and disproportionately high incarceration rates, and they lacked adequate legal representation. With no legal advocate for their cultural interests and little knowledge of how to argue their own case in an alien environment, Native people stood at a distinct disadvantage. Here the "great power" wielded by the social-welfare system over American Indian lives in Minnesota—a power derived from economic control, legal impenetrability, and the assimilationist imperative—overwhelmed some Indian families.

Native families in the Twin Cities encountered the scrutiny of child welfare workers when they tried to obtain economic assistance through social-welfare offices or when they came into conflict with the police. They also were exposed to family surveillance and the threat of custody proceedings through the Minneapolis and St. Paul public school systems. When an Indian child got into trouble at school for truancy, fighting, or another infraction of school policy, a social worker got involved. If the situation seemed serious enough or became chronic, the social worker and the principal might refer the case to the juvenile court system in either Hennepin County or Ramsey County. The court might classify the child as a delinquent, accuse the parents of violating the state's mandatory attendance laws, or charge them with some other form of parental neglect that provided grounds for removing the child from the family and into court custody. This might lead to incarceration in a juvenile correctional institution, placement in a foster home, or proceedings for adoption.

In the late 1960s, the Day children's conflicts at Mechanic Arts High School in St. Paul brought their mother Charlotte before school officials and a welfare worker from Ramsey County Family Services. In a 2003 interview, Dorene Day shared her memory of her mother's experience:

> When my older brother and sisters started getting into trouble, . . . that's when the social worker, and the counselor, and the principal at the school started kind of working together, and trying to—basically, they threatened her. They said, If your kids don't straighten up, then we're gonna—you know, they *must* be from an unfit home, you must drink— and these are the things they said to her. You must be an alcoholic. You must not be there. You must not know what they're doing. And my mother, she was shocked, because they threatened to take her kids away, because her kids were defending themselves.

Charlotte was especially horrified by the charges made against her as an unfit parent, because she had worked hard to provide a good life for her children. She had found adequate, if not ideal, housing for her family at the Mt. Airy projects, and she had a full-time job as a cook. The early hours allowed her to be home every day when her children returned from school. As Dorene Day recalled, even after a workday spent cooking for other people, her mother always had food waiting for her children's supper.[82]

Even as a single parent, Charlotte Day maintained a disciplined, stable home life for her family. She insisted that the girls clean the house on Saturday mornings before they could go out to play. She cautioned them against playing alone and lectured them about hanging around in what she considered dangerous areas. She also made a tremendous effort to protect the children from their father's alcoholism. Day had left Angora and moved to St. Paul in part because of her husband's drinking. Although he occasionally came to visit the family in the city, Dorene remembers a childhood in which his drinking did not intrude into family life:

> When my father came, she didn't let him actively drink [in the house]. So, when he was in the Cities, he had to go someplace and drink, and come home . . . and then basically she would lay him down, and he'd go to sleep, and then the next day, when he'd get up, she'd cook and we'd all eat together. . . . It wasn't like there was an alcoholic in our home that disrupted our lives continually; it wasn't like that.

In general, Dorene says, "it was a very normal kind of family atmosphere."[83]

Despite all of her efforts to be a good parent, Charlotte Day was being accused of neglecting her children. She found this difficult to comprehend:

> That was the most absurd thing to her, that she could be doing all these things for us, and someone could say that she was an unfit mother. Someone could *say* that she wasn't providing for us, and she wasn't disciplining us, and she wasn't doing all these other things that she was doing.

Unable to understand why the public school and welfare systems would cast her in this disparaging light, and lacking an advocate to represent her interests, Charlotte Day seemed on the verge of becoming yet another Indian child welfare statistic.[84]

"We Were Losing Our Children": AIM's Advocacy for Indian Families, 1968–72

As AIM gathered strength in the late 1960s, its organizers addressed the conflict between Indian families and welfare agencies and challenged the rate at which child welfare workers and the juvenile courts took Indian children from their parents. By this point, the threat to Twin Cities Indian families had created a collective sense of crisis. Clyde Bellecourt remembers that "we were losing our children during this time; juvenile courts were sweeping our children up, and they were fostering them out, and sometimes whole families were being broken up." Pat Bellanger recalls that AIM's child welfare activism developed in response to requests for help from desperate Indian parents. Often, the problem began within the public schools:

> because they knew I was an AIM member, a lot of people started calling me about children who couldn't make it in the regular schools.... [T]he social services of the counties, Ramsey and Hennepin . . . were taking Indian children from homes where they felt that the child wasn't being educated, that they were being made a failure, and so they were put into White homes. And so the parents were panicking, saying, you know, My child is good, I have a good kid, they just can't do it in that school.

In response to these calls for help, AIM members worked to stem the tide of child custody proceedings and prevent the separation of Indian families.

Local Native parents began to see AIM as the place to turn when there seemed no other alternative.[85]

AIM members attacked the child welfare problem on several fronts. They pushed Hennepin County and Ramsey County Family Services to provide their social workers with training in understanding Indian cultures and working with Indian families. Pat Bellanger, Clyde Bellecourt, Dennis Banks, and others provided legal counsel to threatened families. They also went to juvenile court to argue for the right of Indian families to stay together, despite cultural differences, economic disadvantages, and their children's struggles in the public schools. When a judge refused to reunite a child with the family, AIM members sometimes convinced the judge to release the child into their care.[86]

By 1970, Charlotte Day had learned of the work that AIM was doing to help families entangled in the child welfare system. She made contact with Billy Blackwell, an Ojibwe AIM member who was working with Indian parents in the St. Paul public schools. Blackwell became Day's advocate as she dealt with Mechanic Arts High School and Ramsey County Child Services. His education and his knowledge of relevant laws helped him deal effectively with school officials, and his experience with urban institutions had familiarized him with the effects of prejudice and cultural ignorance within them. He also understood Native culture and the dynamics of Indian families and he spoke Ojibwe, Day's first language. Dorene Day explained how Blackwell helped her mother:

> When they were at a hearing or something, he could speak to her in Ojibwe and have her understand exactly what was going on. So my mother had a good understanding from [that] point, versus before, when she felt like she was being ostracized—and the kids were—because they would tell her things that didn't make any sense to her. And Billy would explain it to this extent: "Okay, Charlotte, because they see all these other Indian families like this, they're thinking that you're like that. But I've explained to them that you're not."

In Blackwell, Charlotte had found someone that could speak effectively for her as a good parent. Gradually, the threat of family separation receded.[87]

In the early 1970s, AIM organizers also mobilized to help the family of Jerry and Patricia Roy, White Earth Ojibwes whose three sons attended public school in Minneapolis. In the winter of 1971, the Roys stopped sending their boys to school. Individual memories in oral interviews and written documents suggest a variety of reasons for this decision, which represent the range of frustrations among Twin Cities Indian parents about their children's experiences in the public schools. Clyde Bellecourt recalled in a 2003 interview that the Roys "*refused* to allow those kids to go to school because of the racism. They were gettin' their hair pulled, and being called names." In 2002 interviews, Pat Bellanger and former survival school teacher Vikki Howard remembered that the boys had been told that in order to continue attending school, they would have to cut their long hair. They refused, and their parents supported them. In a 1978 interview, Jim O'Brien, then director of Heart of the Earth School, recalled that the Roys had withdrawn their sons from the public schools because they were being taught "fallacies in American history." For one or more of these reasons, the Roys decided to stop sending their boys to school and began teaching them at home. In 1971, before home school legislation, this was against Minnesota state law.[88]

The Roys had been homeschooling their boys for several months when school officials reported them to Hennepin County Family Services for violating the state's mandatory attendance law; this brought them into juvenile court. The judge ruled in a preliminary hearing that if the Roys did not send their children back to school, they would be sentenced to the Minneapolis Workhouse and their children would be taken from them. The Roys, determined to keep their family together, went to members of the American Indian Movement and asked for help.[89]

"To Take Care of Our Own": Founding the Survival Schools, January–April 1972

When the Roys approached AIM for help in dealing with Hennepin County Family Services, Clyde Bellecourt and Dennis Banks agreed to accompany them to their next court hearing. In court, Banks and Bellecourt angrily challenged Judge Lindsay Arthur for forcing the Roys to send their children back to the public school. The judge called the two men into his chambers, where, as Bellecourt remembers, "He said he'd heard about us" and that "he appreciated what we were doing, but he said, 'I'm sorry, there's nothing I can do.'" Although somewhat sympathetic, Judge Arthur still considered it his responsibility to remove children from home environments that prevented them from attending school. Bellecourt remembers the moment when the confrontation came to a head in the judge's chambers:

We got really upset with him. We told him that we were sick and tired of them stealing our children, fostering them out ... and we told the judge we didn't want no more. We wanted to take care of our own. And the judge finally got to the point where he was so upset with us, he told me and Dennis Banks, "If *you guys* can come up with an alternative, I'll send them to you! *You* give them an education!"[90]

That night, a group of concerned people met in AIM's Minneapolis office on Franklin Avenue to discuss the situation. In a 2002 interview Pat Bellanger recalled the sense of urgency in the room:

we were all sitting around . . . and we were going to lose these kids, and these were parents that we knew were really good parents. And we couldn't get the kids to stay in school, but we all recognized that those schools weren't anything that *we* ever could live with anyway, *ever* . . .

As Bellanger described it, "all of a sudden, we just, we *had* to, I mean, it was like a *have* to. The only way we could keep our kids within the families was, they had to go to school. Well, then, let's *have a school*!" Early in January 1972, the A.I.M. Survival School opened in the American Indian Movement office at 1337 East Franklin Avenue.[91]

News of the school spread within the Minneapolis Indian community and its student population quickly grew, coming primarily from families who had been taken to court because their children were in trouble or had stopped attending the public schools. By one account, the AIM school had fifteen students within a week of opening. According to Clyde Bellecourt, "within one month, I had forty-five kids like that, boys and girls, right out of juvenile court."[92]

Indian families in St. Paul also heard about the Minneapolis school. By this time, Charlotte Day had, in her daughter Dorene's words, "aligned herself" with the American Indian Movement, attending protests and cooking for AIM powwows and feasts. Charlotte took great interest in the new school because her own children's education at Mechanic Arts High School continued to worry her. Altough Billy Blackwell's advocacy had helped Day negotiate a better relationship with school officials, her children's battles with prejudice and discrimination had continued. In the fall of 1971, they had erupted into violence.[93]

For weeks, Charlotte's daughter Janet had been tormented by a boy who pulled her hair and called her ugly names. One day, while standing in front of the boy in the lunch line, Janet reached her breaking point, and she struck back. As Janet's younger sister Dorene tells it, "She just turned around and decked him." Unbeknownst to Janet, the bully had a metal plate in his head from a previous injury, and her blow landed him in the hospital. Janet found herself in deep trouble with school officials, and the boy's parents threatened to sue Charlotte. Although the boy recovered and his parents did not take the Days to court, the incident troubled Charlotte deeply. As Dorene recalls, "She was very upset by that, that he bullied her, and she reacted that way, and that he was hurt."[94]

Her children's high school environment, long a source of concern for Charlotte, had become unbearable. "Things had gotten to the point where it just wasn't feasible for them to stay in the public school system," Dorene said. Now, thanks to her involvement with the American Indian Movement, Charlotte believed that she had an alternative:

> She finally saw that something could be different. I mean, she got enough information, she knew that the school had started in Minneapolis . . . so I think that was like the pivotal point for her, was that, Oh, I don't really need to keep fighting this losing battle; I can do something different.

Armed with outrage and fear for her children's well-being, and drawing strength from the existence and rapid growth of the AIM school in Minneapolis, Charlotte went to Eddie Benton-Banai, then director of the St. Paul AIM office, and urged him to start a school in St. Paul. Dorene recalls:

> She took me, my sister Janet, my sister Cheryl, my sister Charlene, and she marched down to the [St. Paul] American Indian Movement office; it was on the corner of Central and Fuller . . . She marched down there, and Eddie was sitting in the office . . . She walked up to him, and she sat us all down, and she said, "My kids are not going back to the public schools." She says, "I've heard you talk about wanting to start a school. We need to do that now. We need to start a school where my kids can be respected, and they don't have to be defending themselves every time they turn around. They don't need to be bullied, they don't need to be disrespected. And I want them in a safe place."

In April 1972, the second AIM survival school, the Red School House, began holding classes. According to Dorene Day, its origins were "a woman and her children, wanting them to be safe. Wanting them to be in a dignified place."[95]

The survival schools began because two families refused to continue putting their children through the daily trauma of attending public school. Dozens of other families joined them because their own problems with the public schools had brought them into conflict with Hennepin County and Ramsey County welfare offices and the juvenile courts. We must recognize the role of parents such as the Roys, the Days, and others in founding these schools. When asked to name the most important people in the creation of the schools, Pat Bellanger replied emphatically, "You can't forget the parents in this one." Their story challenges the assumptions of educators and social workers who stereotyped Indian parents as irresponsible and negligent. These Indian parents were anything but apathetic toward their children's education. Rather, they opposed the specific *kind* of education they received, and the hostile atmosphere in which they received it. When the system punished them for their children's struggles in that environment, they sought an alternative.[96]

The parents also needed help. They found it in AIM, whose local leaders had the organizing experience, the fearlessness, the motivation, and the preexisting commitment to take on the challenge of creating their own school. The AIM people who helped found the survival schools sought to protect the interests of local Indian families and worked for the collective good of the Indian community. AIM organizers also had a personal investment in the creation of a different kind of education for Indian children. Like the Roys and Charlotte Day, they also acted as parents, concerned about their own children. Clyde Bellecourt said in a 2003 interview that in forming the new schools "we were concerned with what was happening right here, in our own families, our own community, and our own children." When asked whether something had pushed her over the edge in the decision to found the first survival school, Pat Bellanger answered immediately, "Yeah, my own kids!" For Bellanger, the "survival" in survival schools was about "keeping families together, keeping ourselves together."[97]

Conclusion

Between 1968 and 1972, the Twin Cities Indian community underwent a transformation. In some ways, the conditions that had characterized the community since World War II remained. Indian people in Minneapolis and St. Paul still experienced the problems of socioeconomic disparities, discrimination, and cultural alienation that had plagued them since the 1940s.

Many of the Indian leaders and organizations that had worked against these conditions for years continued to do so. After 1968, however, a new activist community took shape, one composed of American Indian Movement founders, organizers, and supporters, as well as those who turned to them for help. AIM offered resources for those troubled Indian people who had not found relief for their problems elsewhere in the city, providing direct assistance in conflicts with the police, the courts, welfare agencies, and the public schools. AIM members engaged in a fundamentally different kind of activism, more confrontational and more sharply critical of urban systems and institutions. Those who practiced and benefited from this brand of activism formed a new kind of community, one that sometimes clashed with other local Indian leaders.

The community engendered by AIM's founding also became distinguished by its engagement with issues of culture, spirituality, identity, and history. AIM organizers addressed some of the deepest psychological and social conflicts of urban Indian life, those stemming from cultural dissonance and alienation, the ongoing effects of settler colonialism, and the legacy of Native people's collective history, marked by generations of cultural loss. By the early 1970s, the American Indian Movement had fostered the emergence of a new spirit among Twin Cities Indian people. Those who embraced this spirit shared a growing pride in cultural difference and engaged in a deliberate return to the ways of their ancestors.

As people like Charlotte Day caught this spirit, they joined the emerging AIM community—one of righteous anger and a newfound hope. Although not an AIM founder, Day became a faithful AIM supporter. AIM's activism confronted the conditions that she and her family struggled with on a daily basis. At AIM powwows and feasts, she cooked wild rice for dozens of Indian people who also searched for a better way of life. While she fed others, Day also found sustenance in the AIM community, for herself and for her children.[98]

As part of their work in the Twin Cities, AIM members founded Indian-controlled institutions that fostered this newly emerging Indian community through the practice of local self-determination. These included a legal rights center, a health facility, a housing complex, and, early in 1972, the survival schools. After struggling to stay afloat in their first few years, by the mid-1970s the schools would reach a level of stability that allowed their ambitious mission and their impact on the lives of local Indian people to become clear.

CHAPTER 3

From One World to Another: Creating Alternative Indian Schools

O<small>N A BRIGHT, INVIGORATING MORNING</small> in late September, a dozen Indian kindergarten students gathered in the cafeteria of the Heart of the Earth School in Minneapolis for a half hour of culture class with Johnny Smith. In one corner of the room, the boys sat in a circle of tiny blue plastic chairs with Smith as he taught them how to drum and sing. The girls assembled near the drum to dance. Occasionally, some of the boys got up to dance along with them.

Smith, a sixty-one-year-old Ojibwe man from the Red Lake reservation in northern Minnesota, was in his fourteenth year of teaching at Heart of the Earth. He had been drumming, singing, and dancing for decades at powwows across the country. A slight, wiry man with thick gray hair and a handsome, weathered face, he wore a crisp, long-sleeved cotton shirt, Wrangler jeans, cowboy boots, and a large silver belt buckle engraved with the words "Champion, Rocky Boy Powwow 1993." Between songs he joked gently with the students. Occasionally, he exclaimed "All right!" or "Wheee!" before taking a sip of his coffee, looking around the circle, and grinning. Clearly, he was having a good time. The class proceeded at a relaxed, unstructured pace until the children's teacher gathered them up and took them back to their classroom.

After the kindergartners left, Smith began teaching a group of older students. During this class, another teacher brought in a high school girl who had refused to participate in her classroom and left her to read a book in the back of the cafeteria. She had a small face and light brown hair pulled back in a thin ponytail; she wore jeans and a powder-blue nylon jacket and she looked both sullen and sad. After his class, Smith went back to find out what was wrong with her; he listened intently as she talked, counseled her for a few minutes, and when she seemed to feel better, sent her back to her classroom.

Earlier that morning Smith and I had chatted in his basement office, a cluttered space that looked like a cross between a used office furniture store and a powwow dressing room. Taped outside the door was a white piece of paper with "Johnny" written on it in black marker. As we talked, a young boy suddenly appeared in the hall just outside the open door. Smith called hello to him; the boy flashed a wide grin, jumped up and down a couple of times, and ran off.

During his long tenure at Heart of the Earth, Smith had served as a cultural instructor, history teacher, administrator, and board member. He had become closely woven into the lives of his students and deeply committed to their well-being. He tutored them after school, gave them rides home, took their calls at any hour, accompanied them to court hearings, and bought them groceries when their families were "hurting." During a previous interview, Smith had explained to me how he had first come to Heart of the Earth. Asked to join the staff as a culture teacher, he had reluctantly agreed, on the condition that he would stay no more than a year. The next year he returned; then he decided to get his teaching license. Fourteen years later, he was still there.

WHEN THEY WERE FOUNDED IN 1972, providing at-risk youth with the opportunity for an education and keeping their families together was the survival schools' most urgent mission. Variously described as "street kids," "hell-raisers," and "hard-core children," these young people grew up in inner-city Indian communities that struggled with poverty, discrimination, chemical dependency, and family violence. Many came from single-parent homes (most headed by women), and many had one or more family members in jail.

Not all survival school students had such unstable home lives, but all of them had struggled in the Minneapolis and St. Paul public schools. Many of these students came to the survival schools with a record of behavioral problems and they usually lagged behind their peer group in most academic subjects. Branded as "problem students" by public school officials and dismissed as incorrigible delinquents, many of these young Indian people had dropped out of school, and some already had spent time in juvenile court, detention facilities, reform school, or foster care. Others were in situations that seemed likely to lead to such outcomes.[1]

In order to reach these young people, to preempt their seemingly scripted unhappy endings—and to keep their families intact—the survival school founders believed that they had to provide them with a completely different kind of education. To do that, they had to create a very different kind of school. What they created, though, was more than just a stopgap response to an immediate crisis. They constructed a truly alternative school system with an institutional structure and environment and a set of governing principles that deliberately diverged from the public school model that had alienated many Native children. To construct this framework, survival school educators drew from multiple sources and acted on a complex mix of influences. The schools they created were open schools, and they were community schools. They were family schools, and they were Indian schools. Throughout their first decade, they also, fundamentally, were AIM schools.

By combining all of these elements into an alternative, urban educational system for Native students, survival school founders were helping to blaze a new trail for Indian education. This was not easy, and not everything worked perfectly. Survival school educators confronted many challenges. Sometimes they disagreed over goals and methods, and their efforts were not always successful. Their schools also came under criticism from outside observers. Still, the period from the mid-1970s to the early 1980s was the survival schools' most vibrant and cohesive time. These also were the years when AIM's educational philosophy most thoroughly permeated the schools and most profoundly shaped their development.

Early Years, 1972–75

From the schools' founding in 1972, the people of Heart of the Earth and Red School House endured several years of hardship, uncertainty, and opposition. At times, it seemed unlikely that the schools would survive these difficult early years. Yet they did survive, thanks to the tenacious commitment of the AIM organizers, parents, and community members who devoted themselves to this educational experiment. Because of their efforts, and thanks to the availability of new sources of funding, by the mid-1970s the Twin Cities survival schools would reach a point of relative stability.

The need for funding provided the schools' first (and, over time, most persistent) challenge. When AIM organizers founded the first survival school in Minneapolis in January 1972, they had received verbal endorsement but no financial backing from national Indian organizations. Because they started their school as an independent, alternative institution outside of the public school system, they could not receive state funds. As Clyde Bellecourt recalls, "We didn't have a penny. Absolutely didn't have a penny." Through appeals to religious organizations and private foundations, AIM leaders procured a few small grants in the school's first few months. The Akban Foundation gave $500 in January, the Lutheran church donated $500 in March, and in April the Annie Maytag-Shaker Foundation, the Elliot Foundation, and the Women's Club also contributed small amounts. Like the A.I.M. Survival School, Red School House also had no significant source of funds for its first year of existence.[2]

Because of their shoestring budgets, the survival schools' organizers faced many logistical challenges. Finding appropriate facilities was the founders' most pressing material need. The quest for safe, permanent buildings dominates the narratives of AIM people asked to recount the survival schools' early years. Clyde Bellecourt recalled the primitive conditions of the A.I.M. Survival School's first location below AIM's Minneapolis office at 1337 East Franklin Avenue. As he remembered, "There was no toilet—one little toilet that didn't work—one little lightbulb hanging from the ceiling, no windows, cockroaches crawling on the walls." In its first three years of existence, the school moved twelve times. Its temporary quarters included condemned buildings, basements, churches, drop-in centers, and a tent. Most of the buildings lacked proper plumbing, ventilation, and kitchen facilities. By January 1975, the school occupied a three-bedroom townhouse in the South High Housing Project, located in the heart of the Phillips neighborhood at 25th Street and 18th Avenue. Although safer than a condemned building, this overcrowded, inadequately furnished space hardly provided an ideal learning environment.[3]

When the Red School House opened in the spring of 1972, it shared a building with St. Paul AIM offices in the former North Central Baptist Church at 400 Central Avenue. Red School House organizers conducted some classes inside the tiny one-room church and held others outside on the wooded lot surrounding the church building. Soon after the school's founding, the director of the Ober Boy's Club across the street offered the use of their building during the day, because they held their programs in the evening. This arrangement provided the school with two more classrooms, a lunchroom, and a small gymnasium.

Even this additional space quickly proved inadequate and the Red School House cycled through its own series of temporary, flawed facilities, including church basements, storefronts, and condemned buildings. The Hallie Q. Brown Neighborhood House, located at 553 Aurora Avenue, housed the school from October 1972 to December 1974. It offered space for classrooms and offices as well as an auditorium and a gym, but it was an uncomfortable old building in need of serious repair. The boiler often broke down in the middle of winter, forcing students to bundle up in coats, hats, and mittens while they attended classes. By the fall of 1974, the building was scheduled for demolition to make way for a new shopping center. Once again, the people of the Red School House began searching for another facility for their students.[4]

Survival school organizers also wrestled with a lack of educational supplies and the difficulty of providing students with essential services. Pat Bellanger recalls the beginning of the A.I.M. Survival School in Minneapolis as a time of immediate material need: "I mean, it was just like, overnight, we had a school. And then, when overnight you have a school, then you've got to worry about having that many pens, and that many pencils, and that much paper, and start checking for books—what are we going to use for books?" Survival school organizers lobbied for help with these needs from the public schools, with limited success. The A.I.M. Survival School did receive some cast-off desks and chairs from the Minneapolis public schools, and both survival schools also used old books donated by the Minneapolis and St. Paul public school systems. Initial attempts to persuade the public schools to provide bus service and funding for a hot-lunch program proved less successful, and so school founders and parents did whatever it took to feed the kids:

> people who got food stamps would donate some of their food stamps to the school lunch program—and all of our money went to the school lunch program for a long time—and then it was like, we didn't know what we were going to have for lunch most of the time, so we had hunters out and everything.

In the beginning, Bellanger said with a chuckle, the students "ate a lot of soup and sandwiches."[5]

The organizers of the survival schools encountered a complex set of problems, from miniscule budgets to condemned buildings to the need for textbooks. They met these challenges with passionate commitment, creativity, and resilience, and with the conviction that without a different kind of education, their children, their families, and their cultures would not survive. As Pat Bellanger recalls, "the schools were kind of freewheeling" in their initial years. In retrospect, it seems remarkable that the schools' founders had the audacity even to consider starting their schools, let alone the community capital to sustain them in those first difficult years. In fact, low-income Native families did not find it easy to offer such dedication. Some eventually had to reduce their commitment to the schools in order to work a paying job, but many did what they could for as long as possible. For school supporters, the difficulty of keeping Indian kids in school, the threat to Indian families, and the desire for a different kind of Indian education had convinced them that they had to try something, even if they did not have adequate resources.[6]

Despite the hardships of their early touch-and-go years, the AIM schools survived. They also grew, in student enrollment, staff size, and the scope of their programs. The A.I.M. Survival School in Minneapolis, founded in January 1972, began with a few students, one certified teacher, and a handful of volunteers; by the spring of that year, it had about thirty-five students and four full-time teachers. In the fall of 1972, the school had about seventy students, and over the next year and a half enrollment fluctuated between seventy and eighty-five pupils. In March 1974, the school changed its name to Heart of the Earth Survival School (HOTESS), a name chosen by the students. By the fall of 1974, in addition to parent volunteers, HOTESS had eight staff members, including a project director and assistant project director, English and math teachers, an Ojibwe cultural instructor, and three home tutors. That year, the school also began offering a preschool program, beginning with eight children attending half days.[7]

The Red School House also grew in its first few years. By the summer of 1972, the school served more than twenty-five students. That fall, Red School House organizers formed their first parent advisory committee. In the fall of 1973, the school opened with more than sixty students in grades K–12, five teachers, and six teacher aides. That spring, the school faltered and canceled classes when its director, Eddie Benton-Banai, left for a semester to teach Indian studies at the College of St. Scholastica. By the fall of 1974, with Benton-Banai's return, the Red School House reopened with around forty students, ten staff members, and three new programs: preschool, drug education, and graphic arts.[8]

During the 1974–75 school year, HOTESS and Red School House both achieved a milestone that helped them reach an unprecedented level of stability: they finally found permanent homes. By the fall of 1974, the building at 553 Aurora Avenue where the Red School House had resided for more than two years was scheduled for demolition, and school leaders had to look for another facility. They found it in the former St. Vincent's Catholic School building at 643 Virginia Street. By December 1974, the school operated in its new building, which it eventually purchased in 1979. In the spring of 1975, Heart of the Earth representatives negotiated purchase of a permanent facility for their school, a building on Southeast Fourth Street near the University of Minnesota campus in Minneapolis. The deal was completed by the end of the summer, and HOTESS occupied its new home by the beginning of the 1975–76 school year.

Both of these buildings required renovations, and the old St. Vincent's School lacked a proper gymnasium. But they proved superior in many ways to previous facilities, and they provided a necessary foundation for further growth. A scholar looking back on HOTESS history from the vantage of the late 1970s wrote that the acquisition of the Fourth Street building "alleviated safety concerns . . . and a sense of chaos" and "allowed more energy to be put into development of an alternative educational program." An internal account of Red School House history written in the fall of 1975 highlights the move to the Virginia Street building as a similarly critical accomplishment:

> Our school building has four classrooms, office space, a cafeteria, a kitchen, and all the physical facilities necessary for forming a school. Our concerned people quickly supplied the spirit necessary to fill these spaces with good feelings and the program necessary to run our school. Within a week the Red School House was operating smoothly in its new facilities.

Looking ahead, the authors wrote, "The start of the 1975–1976 school year sees us with much enthusiasm."[9]

By that time, the people of the survival schools had many reasons for enthusiasm. Funding had increased over the years, thanks both to ongoing fund-raising efforts and to the effects of the 1972 Indian Education Act, which AIM organizers had lobbied for. Also known as Title IV, this legislation opened up new federal monies for Indian educational initiatives. Although it was passed in June 1972, the first appropriations were not released until early 1973. By their third full year of operation, both schools received significant grant money through Title IV, as well as substantial funding from the Department of Health, Education, and Welfare and the Office of Economic Opportunity. These higher levels of federal financial support translated into the ability to hire, train, and consistently pay more teachers, offer more diverse subjects of instruction and student services, and initiate community outreach programs.[10]

The schools' relationship to the Twin Cities public schools also had improved. In 1975, Heart of the Earth began participating in a program that provided breakfast and lunch for low-income students, administered by the Minneapolis public school system and funded by Title IV. That year, HOTESS also received public school busing services. Both schools also passed another important milestone during this period when they celebrated their first graduations. Heart of the Earth graduated its first students in 1974, while Red School House honored its first six graduates in June 1975.[11]

The Red School House occupied the former St. Vincent's Catholic School building at 643 Virginia Street in St. Paul from 1974 until it closed in 1995. Here students and staff members gather outside the school to celebrate the end of the 1977–78 academic year with drumming, singing, and dancing. From "We, Yesterday, Today, Tomorrow: Red School House Yearbook 1977–78," published by Indian Country Communications, Inc.; reprinted with permission.

From 1975 until the early 2000s, Heart of the Earth Survival School (HOTESS) was located at 1209 Fourth Street Southeast in Minneapolis in the Dinkytown neighborhood near the University of Minnesota's East Bank campus. From "Chimigezi Winage: Heart of the Earth Survival School Yearbook, 1983–84," published by Heart of the Earth Survival School, Inc.; reprinted with permission.

In September 1975, the organizers of the Twin Cities survival schools hosted an Indian education conference on the White Earth reservation in northwestern Minnesota. There, AIM leaders formed the Federation of Survival Schools and Indian-Controlled Alternative Schools, to assist other Indian communities in establishing alternative educational institutions for their children. The creation of the Federation signaled a hard-won level of confidence among AIM organizers in the viability of the survival school model. Their schools had survived, and now they had grown strong enough to provide inspiration and guidance to others.[12]

Open Schools: Academic Structure and Instruction, 1972–82

Survival school founders departed from the public school model in the way they structured their students' education and in the methods they used to teach them. Rather than adopt conventional grade levels, they organized

107

their students into broader modules or areas, based on age and academic ability. Students proceeded through the modules at their own pace and in their own time.[13]

School organizers' resistance to traditional grade structures stemmed in part from their commitment to individualized learning. Classes generally were divided into smaller groups according to individual ability and subject interest. A student with proficiency in math worked with other similarly advanced students during math instruction, and offered help to other classmates. The same student might not have equally advanced reading skills; in that case, he or she spent time devoted to reading instruction working with a different group of students of similar abilities, and receiving help from more advanced pupils. Teachers moved among the small groups, acting as facilitators and providing as much individualized attention as possible. An observer at Heart of the Earth in the late 1970s noted how teachers also individualized the evaluation process. They considered each student's unique strengths and weaknesses, focusing on individual progress rather than comparing students to each other or assessing them according to a standardized benchmark.[14]

At Red School House, a journalist who spoke with director Eddie Benton-Banai in 1978 reported that he "stressed the importance of adjusting the learning process to the student rather than the reverse. He said it recognizes that individuals are different with different needs at different times. Yet, he added, all are treated as equal, and are equally able to develop self-worth." A written statement of the Red School House philosophy from 1978 emphasized the "constant availability of instructors for a one-to-one communication with all students—not just 'problem students.'" In documents and interviews throughout the 1970s, Red School House people insisted that at their school, there was "no back row."[15]

The commitment to individualized learning and the "no back row" philosophy reflected broader developments in American educational reform taking shape in the 1960s and 1970s. Frustrated with many students' alienation within public school environments and influenced by innovations in British schools, Herbert Kohl and other American educators experimented with alternative approaches known variously as "open classrooms," "open schools," and "open education." Proponents of open education advocated informal class environments that encouraged unstructured exploration and self-directed, experiential learning. They wanted children to develop self-confidence and self-esteem within a holistic educational program. Believing that students learned best by proceeding at their own pace, in their own way,

Survival school teachers provided individualized instruction and close personal attention for their students, who worked through learning modules at their own pace. From "We, Yesterday, Today, Tomorrow: Red School House Yearbook 1977–78," published by Indian Country Communications, Inc.; reprinted with permission.

in activities of their own choosing, open education practitioners eschewed grades, standardized evaluation methods, and strict course requirements.[16]

While embracing an individualized structure and curriculum, survival school organizers also employed group learning. For some subject areas such as music or dancing, students from all areas or modules gathered in a common room for communal instruction. Survival school students also came together regularly in all-school assemblies held on Monday mornings, Friday afternoons, and at other times during the week.[17]

For young Indian people labeled as troublemakers and delinquents, and for those unused to academic success, the survival schools' unconventional structure was a radical and potentially empowering departure from the public schools, and some students responded favorably to this environment. But did the ideals of structural flexibility, informality, and individualized attention always work in reality? How did some of the most troubled students respond to the survival school system? Were staff members always able to accommodate them successfully? And did they always agree about

109

the best way to do so? These are difficult questions to answer. Neither interviews with survival school people nor school-generated documents have addressed them in depth. The opinions of contemporary outside observers, though useful, reflect the bias of those socialized within the culture of the public schools.

Outside visitors to the schools in the 1970s described the schools with an ambivalent mixture of criticism and praise. Journalist Dan Lounberg spent time at both schools in February 1977. At first the schools struck him as "undisciplined, ineffective efforts to teach basic skills to Indian children." He found the informal, unstructured environment particularly disconcerting:

> children . . . travel through the school as they like, sitting in classes when held, which is not at all times during the day. Older students often talk in small groups among themselves. The feeling sometimes seems to be one of a social gathering rather than a school. Pop cans and half-filled ashtrays ornament the rooms.

At the same time, Lounberg appreciated that "classes are small, and there is a palpable rapport between teachers and students."[18]

A representative from the Minnesota Department of Education recorded similar impressions of Heart of the Earth in May 1972:

> The children, apparently are free to wander when and where they feel like it. Several older students were observed ducking out to the street to buy a few donuts which they brought back to the building to rather reluctantly share with their friends. Boys restlessly wander during math class, feinting the air with imaginary guns, or lounging near the pool table to come back to the class minutes later.

Yet, the author also described the school's younger students as "friendly, open to visitors" and remarked that "they are as delightful as small children can be when they are unconstrained by formal classroom structure."[19]

The work of Sonja Schierle, a German Fulbright scholar who spent a semester conducting research at Heart of the Earth in 1977, offers a more in-depth exploration of how the ideals of the survival schools' structure and environment operated in practice. Schierle volunteered as a teacher's aide, observed classes and other school gatherings, interviewed staff members, and interacted with students. She knew some of the history behind the school's founding and understood its unconventional environment as the result of a deliberate effort to design a different kind of school. Schierle's perspective lends credence to her description of the challenges faced by teachers in Heart of the Earth classrooms.

In her observations of elementary-level classes, Schierle noted that truly individualized instruction sometimes proved difficult to sustain. The school's philosophy, as articulated to Schierle and others during that time by director Jim O'Brien, required teachers to shift gears as soon as they saw a single student losing interest in the lesson. In practice, that was impossible. Instead, teachers waited until concentration lagged among several children, then took a break, split the class into small groups, or moved to another subject. Other challenges arose when students worked in small groups. Because teachers could not give their attention to all groups simultaneously, this method allowed unruly students to act up. Schierle often saw a few children moving around the room, distracting other students, or leaving the classroom to wander the hallways. She noted that "such disruptions created continuous work" for teachers and made it difficult to complete lessons for the other pupils.[20]

Journalist Sally Thompson also documented the difficulty of maintaining discipline within Heart of the Earth classrooms when she visited the school in 1975. Thompson interviewed HOTESS teacher Charlotte Smith, who expressed frustration with her students' behavioral patterns:

> Although most Survival School teachers speak positively about students' progress in classes, Charlotte Smith, instructor for module two (roughly grades 4 to 6), has mixed feelings. "I came here intending to teach the kids basics, but at times I feel they don't want to learn them." . . . She says sometimes students tell her, "This is like a public school" when they don't want to do an assignment or be disciplined. "I think that's a cop-out excuse," Smith says.[21]

Despite the best efforts of survival school staff members to create a positive, flexible environment, some of their students struggled to maintain productive social behavior and focus on their studies.

Survival school staff members had several strategies for dealing with discipline problems. When disruptions threatened to take over a classroom at Heart of the Earth, the principal or director might personally come into the class to admonish the students, encourage them to cooperate with one another, and remind them that the school and their community had high expectations for them. At both survival schools, teachers and other staff members learned as much as they could about students' home lives and took their family situations into account if they acted out at school. When it became clear that children were responding to troubles at home, rather than punish them, staff members pulled them aside, talked to them, and offered to support them.[22]

Maintaining an alternative approach to discipline proved challenging, and staff members sometimes disagreed on the best strategies for managing troubled students' behavior. Sally Thompson found in her interview with Charlotte Smith that the teacher was frustrated by her colleagues' attitudes, as well as those of her students:

> When she began teaching at the Survival School in October 1974, Smith says she disciplined her students. "I believe, along with a lot of other educators, that kids need discipline and direction in school. But two staff members told me I was teaching 'too white.'"[23]

Even some of those who were fully committed to the survival school philosophy found it difficult to maintain the delicate balance between offering a welcoming environment and providing the structure necessary for meaningful learning. Over time, the effort could take a toll on staff members. While concluding that Heart of the Earth truly "tried to care for every individual student," Sonja Schierle also pointed out "the demands that places on the teachers and the administrators." In her time at the school, Schierle watched teachers struggle to help students negotiate the fallout of their embattled homes while also providing them with high-quality instruction. For some, Schierle found, the "high demands of the school" led them to leave their positions. Of the thirteen teachers on staff during Schierle's semester in residence, only five remained the following year.[24]

Outsiders' critiques of structure, pedagogy, student behavior, and discipline were, and still are, a sensitive subject for survival school people. One frustration expressed by school founders is that, rather than evaluate the schools according to their internal mission and goals, outside observers critiqued them according to their own criteria of what a school should look like, how it should function, and what it should be. They also emphasized that the concentration of at-risk youth in their programs posed challenges not faced by most public schools.

Most contemporary observers also probably did not understand the survival schools fully within their historical and social context. Native people's multigenerational experiences in reservation schools, federal boarding schools, and the public schools shaped the choices made by school founders and help explain the system they created. The conditions of urban Indian life in the Twin Cities and the actions that AIM took in response to contemporary local challenges also determined the schools' founding and shaped their development. Outside observers also might not have recognized the complex convergence of educational and pedagogical models manifested in the survival schools.

Community Schools: Parent–School Relationships and Community Control, 1972–82

In the beginning, having so many immediate needs and so little money, school founders adopted whatever roles necessary to get the schools off the ground and keep them going. Pat Bellanger remembered one of the first questions facing organizers of the Red School House: "Who's going to be the teacher? And [so] I became a math and English teacher." Bellanger and other AIM organizers became what she called "hit-and-run teachers" to provide instruction for their students before they had time or money to put together a teaching staff. In the first semesters at Red School House, Bellanger also helped write the articles of incorporation, organized a board of directors, served as the board's first chair, wrote early funding proposals, and lobbied the state board of education for books, supplies, and assistance with transportation and hot lunches.[25]

It wasn't just AIM organizers who did whatever was necessary to make the schools function; students' parents and extended family members and others from the local Indian community also took on these responsibilities. This was no accident, as founders deliberately built their system on a foundation of parental involvement and community control. Clyde Bellecourt remembered this as a key component of AIM organizers' early discussions about the need for an Indian school, saying, "We had to have something that was independent, that had parental control over it." Similarly, Eddie Benton-Banai had envisioned Red School House as "a neighborhood community presence controlled by its own people."[26]

As soon as the two schools were off the ground and running, AIM organizers began encouraging the parents of their first students and other local

Indian people to take an active part in the life of the schools. Clyde Bellecourt remembered these recruits as vital resources in the formative months of the A.I.M. Survival School in Minneapolis:

> All we had was a blackboard, a piece of chalk, and a young Indian woman—traditional woman, full-blooded Indian woman—named Ona Kingbird. We asked her if she'd come help us. She said, "Well, what am I gonna do? I'm not a teacher, I never went to school." "We want you to teach these kids about their culture, about their tradition, their language, about what it is to be an Indian." And we hired her, and another young man by the name of Chuck Robertson, and he became our principal.... We put them to work. And that was the beginning of the Heart of the Earth.

Community members and parents like Kingbird and Robertson quickly became the schools' backbone and a key to their survival in their first years. When there was no money for teacher salaries, parents volunteered their time to lead classes. Even when funds became available to compensate them, the schools' first teachers often donated their pay to buy supplies and cover utility bills. Early survival school parents also cooked, cleaned, acted as hall monitors, chaperoned field trips, made building repairs, and served on the first boards of directors, all on a volunteer basis.[27]

Pat Bellanger described parental involvement as integral to the daily life of Red School House in its first decade:

> We didn't have a PTA, ever, we never did have anything that was that isolated. I mean, it was the parents getting involved in any way they could. They might be teachers' assistants. They might be working with the real young children; if they didn't feel like they could be part of an English class, or a math class, or something, they might have been volunteering in the preschool program.

Throughout these years, parents and other family members maintained a constant presence in the schools, as teachers, teachers' aides, tutors, cooks, janitors, bus drivers, and school board members. Those with cultural knowledge instructed students in Native languages, dancing, drumming, and beadwork.[28]

School organizers fostered a very different kind of parent–school relationship than what Indian families had experienced within the cities' public school systems: less hostile, more open, more collaborative, and more intimate. From her semester of participant observation in 1977, Schierle concluded that at Heart of the Earth, all teachers were expected "to come to an understanding of each student's family situation, to make contact with the people the student lives with and to build a personal relationship based on mutual respect and trust." In a statement of the Red School House philosophy from 1978, the "human family" began with survival school students and teachers. It also included "parents, grandparents, uncles, aunts, cousins, friends and visitors."[29]

As the survival school system developed, the commitment to Native parental control became an important feature of institutional governance. The A.I.M. Survival School's articles of incorporation stipulated that general membership include "natural or adoptive parents or legal guardians," with at least two-thirds of Indian ancestry. As the school grew, its administrative structure for program and fiscal management expanded into a governing board, led by an executive committee. Membership on the governing board was open to any parent or guardian with children attending the school.

Members of the Red School House school board, including student representatives and special guest St. Paul mayor George Latimer, gather for a meeting and share a feast. Native parents and other local Indian people held most of the board positions at both survival schools throughout the 1970s and 1980s, ensuring both community control over school governance and parental involvement in children's education. From "We, Yesterday, Today, Tomorrow: Red School House Yearbook 1977–78," published by Indian Country Communications, Inc.; reprinted with permission.

115

All members had voting privileges, and any member could bring an issue before the board for discussion. Four of the ten positions on the executive committee were reserved for parent representatives. At the St. Paul school, all parents of Red School House students had voting privileges when electing members to the board of directors, which set policies, oversaw school operations, and controlled staffing decisions. Through the 1970s, most members of the board were, in fact, parents.[30]

The survival schools' commitment to community involvement and parental control, like their incorporation of open school pedagogy, reflected the broader context of education reform efforts in this period, as parents and educational activists led a national movement for greater community control over public school education. They worked to involve parents and local community members more actively in their schools and to give them more decision-making power over budgets, personnel, and curriculum. The movement for community control began in African American neighborhoods in New York City in the late 1960s and spread to other, primarily northern, cities in the early 1970s.[31]

In the Twin Cities public schools, many Indian parents had felt vilified by school officials and powerless to influence their children's education. Because of this, persuading parents and other family members to come into the survival schools sometimes took considerable effort, as Pat Bellanger recalled:

> A lot of them didn't feel like they could teach any of these particular subjects, so, if they didn't, or if they couldn't, then it would be up to us to try and talk 'em into just teaching a few people, or maybe . . . getting in with the kids as well.

In the beginning, Bellanger and other AIM organizers spent a lot of time "convincing some of these people who never felt that they had any talents to come in and help out." In the process, they helped parents discover that they did have something valuable to contribute:

> Well, you can be a janitor, can't you? And then find out, Well, you know how to do this and that, and, can you teach the *kids* how to do this and that? . . . and somebody that really liked geography, you know: Well, get a *map* out . . . let's show 'em what the world looks like.

Over time, Bellanger said, "the knowledge or the strength of a lot of people showed up." Some parents, inspired by their experience, decided to go back to school themselves. Some earned degrees in education, then returned to the survival schools as certified teachers.[32]

Empowering Indian parents brought great satisfaction to the AIM organizers who founded the survival schools. They had witnessed so much frustration and pain in Native families' interactions with Twin Cities educational institutions. Now, finally, something different was happening. Pat Bellanger remembers:

> here these kids are coming to school, and their parents—who have been so afraid of the PTA, and afraid of the teachers, and afraid of the courts—first wouldn't come near the school either. And they started coming.

For Bellanger, this process was "one of the biggest successes" that emerged from the survival school experiment:

> That whole idea of watching parents go from being afraid . . . and not participating—or, it's not just afraid, it was just unacceptable—again, because all of us had so many bad experiences in those schools . . . so, to see these parents come through, and all of a sudden volunteer to work in the kitchen, so the kids can have hot lunch.

Repeatedly in our interviews, Bellanger conveyed the joy of "watching that growth, right from the very beginning."[33]

The AIM survival schools contributed to a national movement for Native educational self-determination that already was under way by 1972. Like the AIM schools, earlier Indian schools also combined aspects of community school and open school models to create alternative educational experiences for Native students and foster Indian parental involvement and community control. In 1966, members of a Navajo reservation community near Chinle, Arizona, founded Rough Rock Demonstration School, which became the first successful experiment in Indian control over Indian education. A local Navajo corporation called DINE contracted with the Bureau of Indian Affairs to administer the school, and an all-Navajo school board had authority over staffing and curriculum. Educators at Rough Rock committed themselves to individualized education. They also cultivated parental and community input and involvement, recruiting parents and other community members to work as dormitory attendants, teach classes, and contribute to curriculum development projects.[34]

Similar goals inspired an Indian alternative elementary school in Minnesota. In 1970, Ojibwe people on the White Earth reservation created Pine Point Experimental Community School within the Park Rapids public school district. Seeking greater control over their children's education, Pine Point founders first lobbied for an independent local school board; when that proved impossible, they settled for an Indian advisory board to the Park Rapids school board. Like Rough Rock, Pine Point encouraged parental participation in school programs and engaged in community outreach efforts. Following the open school model, Pine Point abandoned conventional grade levels and took an individualized approach to instruction.[35]

Although they shared characteristics with these earlier Indian community schools, the AIM survival schools' degree of administrative independence also set them apart. At Rough Rock the school's status as a BIA contract school meant a level of federal oversight that led some to question the extent of true local control. Over the years, some community members also criticized the prevalence of non-Indian administrators and their dominance over administrative decisions. At Pine Point, local control also was compromised, especially in the school's early years. The community-based Indian advisory board had input but little real authority, while the non-Indian Park Rapids school board controlled financial decisions that also affected staffing choices. The situation improved in 1973 when the Indian community gained local autonomy over both finances and programs, but the school remained within the Park Rapids public school district. The survival schools, in contrast, existed outside of the Twin Cities public school systems throughout the 1970s and early 1980s, and their governing boards had complete control over finances, staffing, and programs.[36]

In their independence, the Twin Cities schools more closely resembled the Indian Community School, founded in Milwaukee in 1970. Building on the initiative of three Oneida mothers who began teaching their children at home in the fall of 1970, the Milwaukee school incorporated as a nonprofit educational institution in January 1971. Several of the founding women were affiliated with AIM, and after the Milwaukee AIM chapter took over an abandoned Coast Guard station near downtown, they moved the school there. By the end of November 1971 they had seventy Indian students enrolled. Rather than divide them into grades, they grouped them into four general levels: primary, middle elementary, junior high, and senior high.

The school remained an alternative, community-controlled institution, governed by an Indian board of directors, throughout the 1970s and 1980s. In 1980, it relocated to a site procured through an arrangement with the county and the Milwaukee Public Schools, but it remained administratively independent of the public school system.[37]

Family Schools: Environment and Student Relationships, 1972–82

The survival schools' organizers believed that the creation of an educational environment conducive to reaching alienated Indian youth required them to foster new kinds of relationships within school walls. In contrast to the adversarial relationships that so many young Indian people had experienced in the public schools, they encouraged more supportive interactions between their students and staff members. Throughout the 1970s, survival school people and outside observers alike described relations between students and staff as informal, close, caring, and based on mutual respect and responsibility. Visitors to the A.I.M. Survival School in Minneapolis in the spring of 1972 described the school's atmosphere as "relaxed . . . and friendly" and noted that "the teachers do not stand on ceremony and even the head administrator Chuck Robertson, is addressed by his first name by the children."[38]

A Red School House document from the late 1970s explained that "students and instructors regard one another . . . as brothers and sisters." At "the center of the Red School House philosophy" lay the concept of "mutual human respect." This concept also manifested itself physically in the classroom:

> All classes are conducted with students and instructors arranged in a circle. On many occasions, the instructor will take the center of the circle for teaching. But on many other occasions, students will occupy the center to present their ideas.

Students also had input into administrative decisions. At all-school assemblies and through student councils, students participated in discussions of school business. They voiced their opinions on staffing decisions, and helped plan the schedule for upcoming weeks.[39]

The survival schools also cultivated close bonds among students. Students were expected to watch out for one another like brothers and sisters and maintain cooperative, supportive relationships. In survival school classrooms, students with well-developed skills in particular subject areas helped those who struggled. Sometimes older students with free periods went into the classes of younger children to assist them. A researcher who spent a semester at Heart of the Earth in the late 1970s observed that when a teacher faced a discipline problem with the younger students, a senior high student often came in to reprimand them, to explain how important it was to get a good education, and to point out how fortunate they were to attend an Indian school.[40]

The survival schools functioned in many ways as extended families. Family members' involvement in school life meant that a remarkable number of students had relatives who worked at the school. Over time, life at Heart of the Earth and Red School House became defined by the presence of entire survival school families. The schools had begun with the members of two families, the Roys in Minneapolis and the Days in St. Paul. In the 1970s, the children of the schools' founders and volunteer teachers joined the schools' student bodies, including the daughters and sons of Clyde Bellecourt, Ona Kingbird, Pat Bellanger, and Eddie Benton-Banai. Increasingly through the years, the schools' hallways, classrooms, and offices became filled with the members of other survival school families. Members of these families attended as students, worked as staff, and served on governing boards. A typical survival school student moving through an average day might encounter a brother or sister at an all-school assembly, attend a class taught by a parent, eat a hot lunch cooked by an aunt, and ride a bus driven by an uncle. At Heart of the Earth, there were the Lussier, Beaulieu, Martin, Moose, Jones, Staples, Aubid, Benjamin, Ellis, and Sam families. At Red School House, there were Leiths, Havicans, Hermans, Quagons, Pettifords, Tall Bears, Morriseaus, Van Everys, Hunsuckers, Machgans, and Whites.[41]

At the survival schools, students tackled the challenges of learning secure in the knowledge that they were surrounded by their relations. They also were surrounded by other Indian students, and taught by a mostly Indian staff, which significantly increased their comfort level. Small class sizes and low student populations compared to the public schools, combined with the close quarters of survival school facilities, created a scale of human interaction that also contributed to a comfortable, intimate atmosphere. Staff members and volunteers sometimes brought their babies or toddlers to class with them, further shaping the schools into family-oriented, multi-generational spaces.[42] For young Indian people who had experienced profound alienation and pervasive hostility in the public schools, the survival schools' family atmosphere could make all the difference.

The multigenerational members of the Red School House "family" assemble for a school photo in the late 1970s. Many of those pictured here likely were related to one another. From "Heart Beat of Our Nation: Red School House Information Booklet," 1979, published by Indian Country Communications, Inc.; reprinted with permission.

Dorene Day, youngest daughter of survival school founder Charlotte Day, transferred from a public elementary school to begin high school at Red School House in the fall of 1972. At public school, the fierce protection of her older siblings had spared Day for the most part from harassment by non-Indian students, and she remembers one kind White teacher who encouraged her academically. Yet Day also recalls a palpable hostility toward Indian children from most teachers, and an ever-present potential threat from other students.

In contrast, transferring from public school to the survival school was "like going from one world to another." She remembers the Red School House as "a place where I didn't have to have my guard up all the time." In an interview, she elaborated on what that meant to her:

> once you know that you're unconditionally cared for, then you're in a totally safe place. So that feeling stays with you; the minute you come in the door, even after you go home, you still feel it. So that's the kind of environment it was: it was totally, totally conducive to learning.[43]

Heart of the Earth director Jim O'Brien described a similar sense of safety among his students when he told a researcher in 1978, "You see our children

Red School House director Eddie Benton-Banai sits in the school's "circle room." The words of welcome and belonging on the banner behind him signal a radically different environment from what some Native students had experienced in Twin Cities public schools. From "Heart Beat of Our Nation: Red School House Information Booklet," 1979, published by Indian Country Communications, Inc.; reprinted with permission.

The survival schools' small size, family environment, supportive relationships, and Indian staff and students provided many young Native people with a sense of safety that they had not found in public schools. From "Heart of the Earth Survival School Yearbook, 1979–80," published by Heart of the Earth Survival School, Inc.; reprinted with permission.

here, you see them comfortable and happy. Not being called 'dumb Indian.' They don't have that pressure where they have to watch their backs all the time." According to O'Brien, "that's one of the major reasons that we do have a successful program."[44]

Those who attended the survival schools especially appreciated the close, supportive relationships that staff members maintained with their students. In 1978, graduating senior Don Havlish (Ojibwe) reflected on his experience at Red School House:

> When I first attended the Red School House, I felt kind of skittish about the whole thing. I really didn't know too much about Indians although being of that heritage myself, but it didn't take me very long to see that I was in the right place. There was a friendly atmosphere around—everybody cared for one another, looked out for each other. You know, they made you feel like *someone*, instead of just another student.[45]

Looking back on her survival school years, fellow Red School House student Dorene Day remarked on the collective commitment it took to provide the feeling of security she so appreciated:

> I think what lends itself to that environment is, all the adults were teachers, whether they were secretaries, or janitors, or whatever. They knew they had the responsibility to lead you ...

Day recalled with deep fondness particular individuals' devoted encouragement of her intellectual and emotional development. She remained especially grateful to history and philosophy teacher Gabriel Horn, art instructor Joe Liles, community elder and Christmas party organizer Flo Bensrud, Red School House founder and director Eddie Benton-Banai, and longtime culture and language instructor Walter "Porky" White, whose abiding humor and years of cultural guidance shaped many young people's lives.[46]

As Dorene Day recognized, the maintenance of a tight-knit, family environment required the dedication of teachers and other staff members who went above and beyond the call of duty to provide support for their students. Vikki Howard, an Ojibwe woman from the Leech Lake reservation in northern Minnesota, taught at Heart of the Earth for twelve years, starting in the late 1970s at age twenty-five. She recalled how she and other survival school teachers filled multiple roles in their students' lives:

> you're not only the teacher, you're the counselor, you're the mother, you're the uncle, you're the auntie ... You're the confidante; they tell you things that they would never tell anybody else.

Teachers at both schools provided children with lodging for days or weeks at a time when their home lives became too chaotic. They also boarded students who came from outside of the Twin Cities or from other states. Staff members regularly advocated for their students and their families with social workers, probation officers, or the police.[47]

Survival school teachers' willingness to shoulder so many responsibilities on top of teaching several classes a day took tremendous commitment, especially because these schools paid significantly less than the public schools— that is, when they had the money to pay their teachers at all. Vikki Howard remembered responding to relatives who urged her to take a higher-paying position in the Minneapolis public school system: "No, I'm *not leaving these kids.*" Red School House director Eddie Benton-Banai told a reporter in 1978 that "very few teachers are here for salaries we pay." Rather, teachers stayed because "they believe in the school." Of himself, he explained, "I chose to be here. This is not a job. It's my cause."[48]

Conclusion

From 1972 to 1982, survival school educators built an educational system that combined elements of the international open school movement, the community school reforms that originated in urban African American neighborhoods, and the educational experiments initiated by earlier Indian community schools. Yet they did so to address their own local concerns and pursue their own goals. Throughout their first decade, Heart of the Earth and Red School House clearly reflected AIM's vision for changing the lives and conditions of Indian people. AIM founders and survival school organizers pursued that vision with an urgent sense of mission and with a firm belief in its critical importance for the survival of their people.

The survival schools furthered AIM's mission to reinvigorate Indigenous extended family relationships and rebuild community support systems around Native youth. They also embodied AIM organizers' commitment to restoring a sense of Indian identity within Native communities, particularly among urban youth. In their first ten years, the revitalization of precolonial cultural knowledge and Indigenous identity formed the foundation of the survival school curriculum. In this period, the schools' curriculum also cultivated a kind of political consciousness and nurtured a sort of community-mindedness that revealed AIM's strong influence in the schools' founding and early development. By the early 1980s, these aspects of the survival schools' curriculum would become their most defining characteristics.

CHAPTER 4

Building Our Own Communities:
Survival School Curriculum, 1972–1982

O N A MONDAY MORNING IN JANUARY, Heart of the Earth students and staff members began their school week with a ceremony called "circle time." In a blue-carpeted, first-floor communal gathering space, two adult men and several male students sat around a large drum. They drummed and sang as students of all ages filed into the room. The youngest children sat on the floor, older children sat in chairs at the back of the room, and high school students and staff members stood along the walls. Some of the older students stayed in the hallway outside the room, lounging against the door frame or sitting on the stairs leading to the second floor. Throughout the ceremony, they fidgeted, whispered, pestered each other, and generally made a point of not paying attention.

After everyone arrived, the singers played several more songs at the drum. Some of the youngest students—the five-, six-, and seven-year-olds— jumped up off the floor and danced. A serious-looking, bespectacled boy circled the room with a bowl of burning sage and a fan made of feathers. As he paused at each person, sweeping the fan forward over the bowl, students and staff members cupped their hands and pulled the fragrant smoke across their chests and over their heads. Later in the ceremony another student passed around a bowl of loose tobacco. People took a small amount to hold in their palms as language teachers Ona Kingbird and Velma LaFrambois said prayers in Ojibwe and Lakota.

During the assembly, two men addressed the gathering. Johnny Smith, longtime cultural instructor at Heart of the Earth and the school's current director, began by admonishing the high school students in the hallway for not participating in the ceremony. He reminded them of the years of struggle that had made their school possible and allowed them to carry out these cultural practices. He called on the older students to watch out for the younger ones, to set a good example for them.

When Johnny Smith finished speaking, he introduced Clyde Bellecourt. Bellecourt rose slowly from his seat along the wall, dressed in black pants, a red T-shirt, a half-zip pullover, and a dark wool coat. He wore his long black hair in a ponytail; it was streaked with gray. He was sixty-six years old.

Bellecourt told the students how he loved coming to the Monday morning ceremonies at the school, how good it made him feel to hear the drumming and watch the children dance. He urged them to embrace their Indian identity, to love who they were and to take pride in it. Turning to the high school students in the hall, he warned them to wise up and start taking advantage of what the school offered them. Here at Heart of the Earth, he reminded them, they had something important: a spiritual foundation. "We want to provide you with a good, sound education," he told the students. "But what good is it if you don't know who you are?"

In February 1976, St. Paul mayor George Latimer honored several Red School House people through the awarding of citations. Charlotte Day—founding parent, board member, and school cook—was named Indian Woman of the Year. Her daughter Dorene Day, then a junior at the school, won the honor of Indian Youth of the Year. Red School House founder and director Eddie Benton-Banai received recognition as Indian Man of the Year. Just five years earlier, a St. Paul public school principal and a Ramsey County social worker had called Charlotte Day an unfit mother and threatened to take her children away. Now, because of her work at Red School House, St. Paul's highest public official was honoring her. This sharp turnaround attested to the survival schools' growing reputation as innovative and successful experiments in Indian education.

By the mid-1970s, both survival schools received increased, and largely positive, local press coverage. In addition to their local accolades, the schools also garnered national recognition. In May 1976, the federal Office of Health, Education, and Welfare named the Red School House one of the top ten Indian education programs in the country. That summer the National Education Association honored Eddie Benton-Banai as its Indian Educator of the

Year. Heart of the Earth even captured the interest of a German Fulbright scholar, who spent a semester conducting research at the school.

In the fall of 1976, Red School House employees created an informational booklet that outlined their school's history, described its current programs, and expressed their hopes for its future. Reflecting on the hardships of the past and celebrating the relative stability of the present, the booklet's authors conveyed a sense of hopeful expectation. They wrote that "When we look back on how far we have come—from a one-room school house in a broken-down church, to a school that is well-rounded in terms of facilities and program—it tends to make us believe that we can accomplish most of the things that we set our hearts to."[1]

The schools' beginnings were humble and their survival in their first few years was uncertain. Given their tenacity and growth, and considering the recognition that Red School House recently had received from the city of St. Paul, such optimism seems well-founded. By the start of the 1976–77 academic year, school founders had built the framework for a viable alternative education, creatively combining elements of open school structure and instruction, community school governance and parental involvement, and Native self-determination and empowerment. Within this unconventional space, they believed that a new kind of Indian education could take place. But what, exactly, had the people of the survival schools set their hearts to? What kind of education did they provide for their students within this alternative space? From the mid-1970s to the early 1980s, as the survival schools flourished, the answers to these questions emerged.

While they crafted an alternative institutional structure, governing system, and environment, survival school people also created an innovative curriculum, one that was deeply embedded in AIM's founding mission and political philosophy and consciously departed from the public school model. The AIM organizers and Indian parents who created the survival schools, and those who shaped them most profoundly throughout the 1970s and early 1980s, all worked toward a central goal: to nurture the identity development of Native youth through an educational system grounded in traditional Indigenous knowledge, infused with a contemporary political consciousness, and anchored by a commitment to family and community. Over time, the survival schools themselves would become a center of Native community in the Twin Cities.

"A Life Source for Our Students": Cultural Knowledge and
Identity Development

When AIM organizers criticized the education of Indian children in the public schools, they returned again and again to the question of identity. They argued that anti-Indian hostility from teachers, administrators, and other students undermined Native students' self-confidence and sense of self-worth. The bias of most public school curriculum, which either ignored or denigrated Indigenous cultures, compounded the problem. In addition, survival school founders targeted a deeper issue. They believed in a fundamental, irreconcilable conflict between the values perpetuated by the mainstream educational system and those embedded within traditional Indian cultures. Native students whose families retained at least some of the knowledge of the old ways felt torn between the opposing social systems represented by school and home life. Other students, who lacked cultural grounding at home but remained alienated from the public school culture, simply felt a void. Either way, many young Native people struggled to develop a positive, integrated sense of self.

The survival school founders indicted the public schools for their failure to foster Indian students' identity development in appropriate, meaningful ways. This failure, they believed, condemned young Indian people to poor academic performance, behavioral problems, delinquency, truancy, and despair. As an alternative, the founders dedicated the survival schools to facilitating self-awareness, self-confidence, and feelings of self-worth among Indian youth. To fulfill this mission, they provided Indian students with a curriculum designed to foster an appreciation for their cultural heritage and an understanding of their identity as young Native people.

From the beginning, the creators of the survival schools offered their students instruction in Native languages. Although courses varied depending on teacher availability, both schools offered instruction in Ojibwe almost continuously throughout the 1970s and early 1980s. Students took daily language courses and staff members also spoke Ojibwe with students outside of class. Ojibwe teachers at Heart of the Earth during these years included Ona Kingbird and Rose Barstow, and William Bird taught Ojibwe at Red School House. Heart of the Earth also offered Lakota at various times, and the Red School House taught both Dakota and Ho-Chunk. For a small number of students, these courses reinforced languages still spoken at home by parents or grandparents. For most, they offered an introduction to languages that largely had been lost within their families, through generations of repression by missionaries, government agents, and boarding school teachers.[2]

In 1975, a visiting journalist recorded a scene from Ona Kingbird's Ojibwe classroom at Heart of the Earth:

> Ona tells one high school student, Katie Livingston, to count to 50 in Chippewa for the class. Katie counts softly and quickly, casting occasional questioning glances at Ona to make sure she pronounces particular numbers correctly. The students seem to respect Katie's skill, and one asks her as she sits down, "Hey, Katie, will ya teach me that sometime?" Katie asks Ona to write down the words for 51 to 100 so she can memorize them.

Small victories like this held profound significance for survival school educators. As Jon Reyhner has noted, "indigenous language revitalization is part of a larger attempt by indigenous peoples to retain their cultural strengths." For survival school educators, language instruction contributed to broader efforts to revitalize traditional cultures and to teach young Indian people

A Red School House instructor teaches students animal names in the Ojibwe language. From "We, Yesterday, Today, Tomorrow: Red School House Yearbook, 1977–78," published by Indian Country Communications, Inc.; reprinted with permission.

131

about the old ways of life. As former Heart of the Earth teacher and administrator Vikki Howard explained, "The language is the heart of our soul, the heart of our spirit, the heart of who we are, as Indian people. Within the language is the *culture*, and the *history*, and the *tradition*."[3]

Howard and her colleagues recognized in the 1970s what decades of work by linguists, educators, and community language activists has since confirmed: Native languages contain a wealth of irreplaceable cultural information. Through language, one gains insight into a culture's social structures, practices, values, philosophy, morality, and spirituality. Language expresses an entire way of looking at the world, and it contains the wisdom of past generations. As language activist Rosemary Christensen, a member of the Wisconsin Mole Lake band of Ojibwe, has written, "an understanding of language ... allows an understanding of culture."[4]

In addition to teaching Indigenous languages, the survival schools introduced students to the knowledge and skills used by Native people when they lived within fully functioning, precolonial, Indigenous societies. Students at Heart of the Earth and Red School House learned how their ancestors had organized subsistence activities around the cycle of the seasons and how they adapted to and used their natural environment. They learned how Native communities in the upper Midwest tracked and hunted various kinds of game; fished, gardened, and gathered berries in the summer; harvested wild rice in the fall; and tapped maple trees and made maple sugar in the spring. They discovered how Indian people prepared these traditional foods, and how they used the natural resources around them to make clothing, dwellings, tools, and medicines. They acquired craft skills such as beading and quill work and played traditional games. The schools also exposed students to the traditions and rituals of Indigenous spiritual life. Students were exposed to tribal drumming, singing, and dancing, discovered the importance of storytelling and oral tradition, and learned the significance of ceremonial objects like pipes, feathers, and drums.

Survival school organizers employed various methods to introduce their students to traditional Indigenous knowledge. They incorporated cultural instruction into the regular curriculum through daily or weekly culture classes with school staff members. They also brought in elders and other visiting Native people to share their cultural knowledge with students, and they brought students outside of school walls, taking them on day trips in or around the Twin Cities. Minneapolis and St. Paul's extensive city park systems and their proximity to state parks, nature preserves, and other undeveloped

Red School House director Eddie Benton-Banai teaches students about Native American history and philosophy, including the types and uses of ceremonial drums. From "We, Yesterday, Today, Tomorrow: Red School House Yearbook, 1977–78," published by Indian Country Communications, Inc.; reprinted with permission.

Red School House students watch a demonstration of ceremonial drumming and singing led by cultural instructor Walter "Porky" White. From "We, Yesterday, Today, Tomorrow: Red School House Yearbook, 1977–78," published by Indian Country Communications, Inc.; reprinted with permission.

areas offered multiple opportunities to get out into nature. There students could better grasp lessons about traditional subsistence practices and could try their hand at identifying plants, tracking animals, and recognizing signs of seasonal change. Throughout the cultural curriculum, instructors allowed students to observe the practice of the old ways and also encouraged them to participate actively in acquiring new skills.[5]

The survival schools also sent their students on more extended excursions out of the city and into reservation communities. While some students at HOTESS and Red School House had ties to nearby reservations, others lived far from their home reservations or knew little to nothing about their Native heritage. Some of them never had left the city. As Clyde Bellecourt remembered, school founders wanted to get these young people "out in the environment, to get them out of the urban setting, where they could get their feet back on the ground." Everyone from young children through high school seniors spent weekends and entire school weeks camping on Ojibwe land in Minnesota, Wisconsin, Michigan, and Canada. The survival schools organized fish camps in the summer and winter, wild rice camps in the fall, and sugar-bush camps in the spring. By the late 1970s, Heart of the Earth students also participated in a summer-long cultural program on the White Earth reservation in northwestern Minnesota. Through all of these reservation-based "survival camps," students learned firsthand how to start fires, make and paddle canoes, build teepees and wigwams, and gather medicinal and ceremonial plants. They planted trees, gardened, and cooked traditional foods. Local Native elders who had kept the old ways alive in remote places served as instructors, with survival school staff members offering additional guidance and supervision.[6]

Reservation-based "survival camps" provided intensive experiences that immersed young, urban Native people in the seasonal rhythms, physical activities, and conceptual framework of an Indigenous way of life. The authors of a 1975 Heart of the Earth funding proposal described their significance:

> We feel it necessary for our students' survival to experience the day-to-day personal living statement reflecting the unique body of knowledge that encompasses the values, traditions, and philosophies of their people. They learn of these things during the regular academic year. They need a time with traditional people to internalize these ways and to ultimately reflect them in their behavior.

A group from Red School House learns how to quarry pipestone at a site in southwestern Minnesota, a place with sacred significance for the Dakotas and other Native people of the upper Midwest. From "We, Yesterday, Today, Tomorrow: Red School House Yearbook, 1977–78," published by Indian Country Communications, Inc.; reprinted with permission.

Red School House students get out on the water to practice fishing skills during a visit to a Minnesota reservation. From "We, Yesterday, Today, Tomorrow: Red School House Yearbook, 1977–78," published by Indian Country Communications, Inc.; reprinted with permission.

A Red School House student boils sap while learning to make maple sugar. From "We, Yesterday, Today, Tomorrow: Red School House Yearbook, 1977–78," published by Indian Country Communications, Inc.; reprinted with permission.

As this statement reveals, survival school educators did not teach their students traditional knowledge, skills, and rituals simply for their own sake. Instead, they presented them as inextricably connected to an underlying system of values and beliefs. Rather than treating traditional cultural systems as relics of a long-ago past, the survival schools showed students that they still functioned, and offered them as a viable—indeed, necessary—foundation for their lives. As HOTESS proposal writers asserted, "Indian values are intact and can be a life source for our students if they can learn to identify them for themselves and consciously build upon them."[7] This was what it meant to be "survival" schools: providing a cultural grounding that their founders believed young people needed to survive and thrive in the modern world.

The commitment to providing a foundation of Indian identity through knowledge of traditional culture also characterized other Indian community schools in this period. The Rough Rock Demonstration School, founded on the Navajo reservation in 1966, taught Navajo language, history, and culture while also providing instruction in basic academic subjects. The school was designed to preserve Navajo values and economic practices, thus ensuring the survival of a distinct Navajo culture.[8]

In 1970, Ojibwe people on the White Earth reservation in Minnesota created Pine Point Experimental Community School. Like the AIM organizers who started the survival schools, Jerry Buckanaga and other Pine Point founders rejected the assimilationist agenda of the public schools in favor of a curriculum that would foster positive identity development and cultural pride among Native youth. They taught students Ojibwe history, language, traditions, music, and literature, and they encouraged them to live within an Ojibwe value system. In 1975, Ojibwe people on the Leech Lake reservation founded the Bug O Nay Ge Shig school (informally known as the Bug School) in order to incorporate more Native culture into their children's education. After efforts to start an Indian cultural program within the Cass Lake public school system failed, local Indian people had staged a walkout and created their own alternative school.[9]

The Indian Community School in Milwaukee, incorporated as a non-profit educational institution in early 1971, also combined academic and cultural instruction. This school's founders wanted to use alternative, community-controlled education "to restore American Indian dignity and pride in Indian youth through cultural education ... and through channeling the natural talents of Indian youth toward making contributions to their community." According to historian Susan Applegate Krouse, teachers worked to "relate academic subjects to Indian culture and history, creating an awareness in their students of their rich Indian heritage."[10]

At Heart of the Earth and Red School House, survival school educators introduced Indigenous values throughout the cultural curriculum. When students learned about the knowledge and skills that Native people used within traditional societies, they also absorbed a set of beliefs about the relationship between human beings and the natural world. Students learned about people's dependence on their natural environment and the need to live in balance with nature through environmental conservation and sustainability. They stressed the interconnection of all living things—human, animal, plant, and mineral—and the need to treat all forms of life with respect.

Through classes, visiting speakers, field trips, and survival camps, students also encountered cultural values about how to maintain proper relationships with other people. They learned to recognize their interconnection and interdependence with other human beings. They were encouraged to interact in cooperative rather than competitive ways, and to share what they had with others in need. They learned to make their responsibilities to their extended families their highest priority, and to respect the wisdom of their elders. Students absorbed lessons about women and men's social roles and responsibilities and learned to honor both the male and the female sides of life.[11]

```
THE DRUM IS ...
            SINGING SONGS,
            DANCING AROUND IT.
I RESPECT THE DRUM.
THE DRUM IS ...
            SONGS TO THE GREAT SPIRIT
            AND HONOR SONGS
            FOR SPECIAL OCCASIONS.
GIVE WELL SONGS TO THE SICK AND THE OLD.
                        SCOTT WRIGHT
```

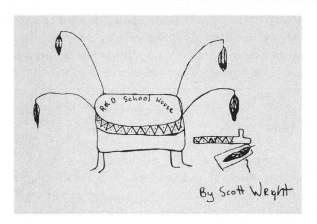

Survival school students' artwork and writing from the 1970s reveal the importance of the ceremonial drum to their developing cultural identities and its central place in school life. From "Heart Beat of Our Nation: Red School House Information Booklet"; "Three Fires: Voices from the Red School House"; and "We, Yesterday, Today, Tomorrow: Red School House Yearbook, 1977–78," published by Indian Country Communications, Inc.; reprinted with permission.

In their first ten years, survival school educators also worked to invest every component of the cultural curriculum at Heart of the Earth and Red School House with spiritual meaning. Lessons about traditional knowledge, skills, and practices explained them as part of a comprehensive philosophical and spiritual system, an entire way of looking at the world. When students learned about cultural traditions, rituals, and ceremonies, they also came to understand the spiritual significance of the pipe, the drum, the dance, and the song. The values and beliefs imparted to students reflected the spiritual foundation of traditional Native cultures, which regarded every aspect of life—including the natural, the supernatural, the material, and the social—as interconnected and infused with meaning.[12]

The prevalence of the circle as a philosophical and organizational concept demonstrates the survival schools' spiritual foundation. In many Native American and other Indigenous cultures, the idea of the circle anchors the traditional worldview. The circle represents a belief in the cyclical nature of life—the human life cycle, the cycle of the seasons, cycles of prophecy and history—rather than in linear development and progress. It conveys the conviction that all living things are interconnected and related to one another. At Red School House and Heart of the Earth, instructors and visiting speakers frequently spoke of the importance of the circle as a guiding philosophy. In classes and school assemblies, students, teachers, and visitors often sat in a circle. During the 1970s, both schools also began a practice called "circle time." On Monday mornings and again on Friday afternoons, all students and staff members gathered together in each school's "circle room" for ceremonies. Together they prayed, drummed, danced, sang, and performed the rituals of the pipe and tobacco.[13]

Tribal, Indian, and Indigenous Identities in Survival School Cultural Curriculum

In the Twin Cities survival schools, the cultural curriculum incorporated a complex mix of tribal, Indian, and Indigenous influences.[14] In terms of tribal education, Red School House and Heart of the Earth both provided a pervasive Ojibwe emphasis in their cultural programs. Most of the schools' founders, teachers, and administrators were Ojibwe, and most of their students' tribal affiliations included at least some Ojibwe heritage with connections to reservations in Minnesota, Wisconsin, and Michigan, as well as Canadian reserves. Because of their location, the schools also had access to the traditional knowledge of Ojibwe elders on Minnesota reservations.

139

I am an Ojibway Indian
                    Singing
                    Dancing
                    Drumming
Talking to Nokomis Moon
Listening to Migizi
Seeing Eagle feathers swinging
    around and they're dancing.

                    FRANK BUCK

Many survival school students had Ojibwe heritage. Red School House
students like Frank Buck explored and expressed this identity through
writing and visual art. From "We, Yesterday, Today, Tomorrow:
Red School House Yearbook, 1977–78," published by Indian Country
Communications, Inc.; reprinted with permission.

Thus, survival school programs exposed students to the seasonal round of subsistence activities that followed the patterns of traditional Ojibwe life, and provided instruction in Ojibwe craftwork and traditional medicine. The survival camps that immersed students in these activities took place primarily on Ojibwe reservations. Lessons about human beings' proper relationships to the natural world and to each other drew directly from Ojibwe teachings, and many of the rituals and ceremonies that students participated in also drew from the Ojibwe spiritual system.

The schools also introduced their students to a multitribal cultural education. While the survival schools' cultural curriculum was most firmly grounded in traditional Ojibwe culture, it also reflected the regional cultural traditions of other upper Midwestern tribal peoples. Significant numbers of staff and students had ties to Dakota, Lakota, and Ho-Chunk communities, and these traditions also influenced the survival school curriculum. Students also were exposed to the traditions of other tribes outside the upper Midwest, through activities such as drumming, singing, dancing, and tribal ceremonies.

While survival school educators sought to help their students develop as

The cover of a Heart of the Earth yearbook features cultural symbols relevant to the Dakotas, Lakotas, and other northern Plains tribes, reflecting the multitribal aspects of survival school curriculum. From "Heart of the Earth Yearbook, 1979–80," published by Heart of the Earth Survival School, Inc.; reprinted with permission.

members of specific tribal cultures, they also identified them more broadly as Native American people. The schools provided their students with an education that spoke of an *Indian* culture, distinct from Euro-American society but common across tribal groups in the United States. This approach had the practical advantage of incorporating the students whose tribal roots lay outside the upper Midwest. It also reflected a deliberate effort by survival school organizers to encourage young Indian people to understand their cultural identity, their collective history, and their contemporary political reality as connecting them to all other Native American people. The Heart of the Earth "Philosophy of Instruction" as articulated in 1975 stated that "the children become aware of tribal uniqueness but inter-tribal similarities are stressed." Pat Bellanger explained in an interview that the survival schools "always had the idea that . . . you have to look at all of the tribes—not just your own tribe, but all of the tribes." Thus, "It's not a Lakota school, and it's not an Ojibwe school. It's an Indian school, it's a survival school."[15]

The schools' approach to values and spirituality also reveals the cultivation of an even broader *Indigenous* identity. Survival school educators spoke of concepts like the circle, people's interdependence with nature, the interconnectedness of all living beings, and the infusion of spirituality into all areas of life as central not only to all American Indian cultures, but also to the world's Indigenous peoples. All Indigenous youth, they believed, needed to ground their identity development within a process of spiritual discovery and growth.

Negotiating among these levels of cultural identity was a complicated process on individual, collective, and curricular levels. This was especially true in the 1970s and early 1980s, when the effort to revive aspects of long-repressed cultural identities still was in its early stages, and postwar assimilationist policies and practices continued to exert powerful influence. Anthropologist Rachel Bonney has argued that in contrast to the National Indian Youth Council's emphasis on retaining tribal identities, in the 1970s AIM leaders mobilized a kind of "Indian nationalism" that subordinated or submerged tribal identities "in favor of a generalized sense of 'Indianness.'"[16] But Bonney's analysis oversimplifies the layers of identity negotiation evident in the curriculum at AIM's Twin Cities schools in this period.

Bonney's article, published in 1977, also lacks the larger historical context of Indian identity development as analyzed by scholars since the 1980s. North American Native identities always have been fluid, evolving through dynamic processes of change and exchange since before European contact.

Kinship systems, linguistic ties, geographic proximity, and exchange through trade, warfare, and intermarriage created shifting patterns of Indigenous relationships before contact with Europeans and the imposition of European and American political authority shaped Native peoples into modern tribal entities. In the twentieth century, boarding school experiences, urban migrations, and organized collective activism fostered intertribal connections and revealed shared historical experiences and common belief systems and worldviews, contributing to a sense of "Indianness" among Native people in the United States that AIM's activism both reflected and helped create. Yet, throughout these processes, many Native individuals and communities also retained a more tribally specific sense of self. Even in twentieth-century urban communities, where cross-tribal or, more broadly, "Indian" connections were particularly strong, people also held on to, sought out, rediscovered, and asserted their identities as Ojibwe, Dakota, Lakota, or Ho-Chunk, while also identifying as Indians.[17]

Survival school educators were developing their cultural curriculum during a time when the world's Indigenous peoples were beginning to build a global movement around common concerns that crossed tribal and national boundaries. As historian Susan Miller explains, in the 1970s Native peoples in North, Central, and South America, Hawaii, Australia, New Zealand, and Europe "found a collective voice to express a list of issues common to their communities." Efforts by members of the National Indian Brotherhood in Canada led to a meeting of global Indigenous leaders in 1974 and the first meeting of the World Council of Indigenous Peoples (WCIP) in British Columbia in 1975. The National Indian Brotherhood later was granted NGO status in the United Nations, while the WCIP gained observer status. In 1982, the United Nations formed the Working Group on Indigenous Populations, which began drafting a Declaration on the Rights of Indigenous Peoples in 1985.[18]

Survival school educators' multilayered approach to cultural instruction, while reflecting an increasingly expansive global Indigenous identity, also served practical local needs. Unlike reservation-based Indian community schools like Rough Rock in Arizona, Rocky Boy in Montana, and Pine Point and the Bug School in Minnesota, Heart of the Earth and Red School House served students within a large city. The Twin Cities Indian population included much more tribal and cultural diversity than the small, rural, relatively homogeneous reservation communities where other Indian community schools developed. Thus, while the other schools' curricula could

The cover of a Heart of the Earth yearbook reflects the challenge of creating a culturally grounded curriculum for students from multiple tribal backgrounds in the middle of a twentieth-century city. The eagle dancer poised between the Minneapolis skyline on the left and the trees on the right suggests urban Indian people's connection to their various homelands. This image also symbolizes the effort to help students find a balance between the traditional ways of their ancestors and the realities of modern life. From "Chimigezi Winage: Heart of the Earth Yearbook, 1983–84," published by Heart of the Earth Survival School, Inc.; reprinted with permission.

focus on single tribal cultures, the survival schools necessarily had to in-corporate multiple tribal perspectives. In these ways, the Twin Cities sur-vival schools bore a closer resemblance to the Indian Community School, founded in Milwaukee in 1971.

"To Train the Leaders": Political Consciousness and Social Action

The survival schools worked to instill a wide-ranging social and political consciousness in their students. They did so within the context of a cultur-ally defined, community-based process of identity formation. At Heart of the Earth and Red School House, educators intertwined historical, political, and social awareness with teachings about the traditional values of living as a community-minded individual, shouldering communal responsibilities, and working for the good of one's people.

As part of students' political education, survival school educators taught them U.S. history from a critical, Indian-centric perspective. Social studies and history teachers began their discussions of Native North American his-tory prior to European exploration. They emphasized Indian people's con-tributions to American culture and history and taught students about the accomplishments of "Native national leaders and heroes." Developed in re-action to the absence, distortion, or denigration of tribal histories in public school textbooks, this approach was meant to help students develop a posi-tive sense of Indian identity.[19]

Survival school educators also criticized the impact of Euro-American settlement and the actions of the U.S. government toward American Indian people. They wanted Indian youth to learn the darker truths about the treatment of Native peoples in America, truths that had been glossed over in standard public school curricula. In a grant proposal, Heart of the Earth spokespeople asserted their desire to give their students "a realis-tic and truthful account of history." In an interview, former Heart of the Earth social studies teacher and administrator Vikki Howard spoke force-fully about the "miseducation of young people" in the public schools and the need to uncover "the hidden history of America," including "the ugly, vindictive, genocidal practices of the United States government against American Indian people."[20]

The survival schools exposed their students to the histories of American Indian people throughout the United States. They encouraged students to see those histories as part of *their* story as Indian people, and to consider those struggles their own. Students were taught about the breaking of treaties by the federal government and tribal efforts to reestablish treaty rights across the United States. They commemorated the Wounded Knee massacre of 1890 and the occupation of Wounded Knee by AIM in 1973.

Survival school teachers also educated their students about contemporary social and political issues affecting Indian people. As German researcher Sonja Schierle discovered during a semester at Heart of the Earth, "according to the survival school concept, education can not be isolated from socio-economic . . . and legal conditions." Students learned about the socioeconomic disparities and political struggles within the Twin Cities Indian community and the political and economic conditions that shaped the lives of Native people on nearby reservations. Instructors encouraged students to understand their own legal rights and to apply their increasing political awareness to what they experienced in their families and saw in their communities. Students also learned about struggles over land and resources within the Mohawk nation in New York, on the Lac Courte Oreilles Ojibwe reservation in Wisconsin, and among the Lakota people of South Dakota.[21]

Throughout their education, survival school students heard about the meaning and importance of Native sovereignty. They discovered that Indian sovereignty derived from the government-to-government relationship established between tribes and the federal government through treaties. They learned that retaining tribal sovereignty meant maintaining control over reservation land and resources, and that it required the preservation of Native languages, belief systems, and traditions.[22]

The political awareness raised by the survival schools also included the history of other marginalized minority groups in America, as well as the struggles of Indigenous peoples in other parts of the world. Students learned about the African American civil rights movement and the work of Black Power and Chicano activists, as well as the struggles of Indigenous communities in Canada, Mexico, and Central and South America.[23]

Survival school students gained their wide-ranging political education in a variety of ways. They discussed Indian history, sovereignty, treaty rights, and global Indigenous issues during regularly scheduled class time with instructors, and they hosted presentations by visiting speakers. Local AIM organizers regularly spoke at both Heart of the Earth and Red School House, and other members of the Twin Cities Indian community came in to talk about their personal experiences and the social problems facing urban Indian people. Visitors also came to the schools from other nearby communities and from faraway places. They included residents of reservations in Minnesota and neighboring states, tribal leaders and activists from across the United States and Canada, Indigenous activists from other countries, and spokespeople for other minority rights movements in the United States. Students who attended the survival schools in the 1970s and early 1980s met American Indian leaders Janet McCloud (Tulalip) and Larry Anderson (Navajo), Guatemalan human rights activist and Nobel Peace Prize winner Rigoberto Menchú, singer-songwriters Floyd Red Crow Westerman (Dakota) and Buffy St. Marie (Cree), Black Power leader Stokely Carmichael, and members of the Chicago Brown Berets.[24]

Survival school educators also took students on field trips and other excursions to further their political education. Within the Twin Cities, students toured Indian-administered alcohol and drug rehabilitation programs and other urban Indian agencies. They visited city hall and observed local trials and court hearings. They also traveled to politically charged events in neighboring states and elsewhere in the country, such as the trial of AIM member Leonard Peltier in Milwaukee and commemoration ceremonies at Wounded Knee on the Pine Ridge Lakota reservation in South Dakota. They also attended AIM-organized national conferences addressing treaty rights, education, and other contemporary Native issues. As Heart of the Earth director Jim O'Brien told a reporter in 1978, "these kids are trucking around and picking up a lot of things."[25]

While teaching their students to be politically aware, the survival schools also encouraged them to become politically active. Students gained experiences and skills meant to help them become activists in their own right, not only later in adulthood, but also now as young people. The older students in particular participated in many local, AIM-organized protest actions. They marched to the federal building in downtown Minneapolis to demand the release of Leonard Peltier. They raised signs to protest a nuclear power plant located near the Prairie Island Dakota community in southeast Minnesota. At the state Capitol in St. Paul, they rallied to demand improvements in urban Indian housing, social services, and education.[26]

In 1978, survival school students participated in a national protest movement called the "Longest Walk." Concerned about pending federal legislation that threatened Indian self-determination, the American Indian Movement organized a chain of Native people to walk across the country from Alcatraz to Washington, D.C., educating tribal communities along the way. The walk culminated in the presentation of a set of demands to government officials

Heart of the Earth high school students protest the Prairie Island nuclear power plant in southeastern Minnesota and its impact on a nearby Dakota community. From "Heart of the Earth Survival School Yearbook, 1979–80," published by Heart of the Earth Survival School, Inc.; reprinted with permission.

in Washington. In April 1978, as the walk neared Lawrence, Kansas, AIM organized a group of Indian people from Minnesota and neighboring states into a "Run for Survival," which began at Fort Snelling in St. Paul and proceeded to meet the Longest Walk in Lawrence. Survival school students took part in the sunrise ceremonies that launched the Run for Survival at Fort Snelling the morning of April 16. They traveled eighty miles southwest to Mankato the next day to greet the runners and to commemorate the hanging of thirty-eight Dakota men by the state of Minnesota following the Dakota War of 1862. A few of the older students even joined the Run for Survival all the way to Lawrence.[27]

The teaching of a critical political awareness and the encouragement of student activism in the Twin Cities survival schools set them apart from most other Indian community schools of their time. These elements did not figure prominently in the curriculum of schools like the Rough Rock

Community School on the Navajo reservation in Arizona, or the Ojibwe schools on the White Earth and Leech Lake reservations in Minnesota. Other AIM-affiliated schools in this period did, however, have a similar political dimension to their curriculum, such as the AIM survival school in Rapid City, South Dakota, and the Indian Community School in Milwaukee.

In the more politicized elements of their curriculum, the Twin Cities survival schools resembled the alternative schools established by activists in the African American freedom struggle from the mid-1960s to the early 1970s. During the 1964 "Freedom Summer" in Mississippi, members of the Student Nonviolent Coordinating Committee (SNCC) started a network of "freedom schools" for Black youth. SNCC instructors taught students about African and African American history and culture and urged them to take pride in their heritage. Freedom school students also learned about the roots of socioeconomic oppression, discussing disparities between Blacks and Whites in housing, employment, and health care. SNCC activists led students to understand the workings of the racist power structure and encouraged them to imagine a different kind of world. SNCC members envisioned the freedom schools as a way to train African American youth to work for social change through nonviolent resistance.[28]

After the mid-1960s, some African American activists' ideologies shifted from integration and equality to nationalism and separatism, and their critiques of the status quo became more radical. During this Black Power period, the Black Panther Party established "liberation schools," with the first founded in Berkeley in 1969 and in Oakland in 1971. In these schools, students studied Black culture, history, and literature, and they learned to take pride in alternative values that challenged those of White mainstream society. Influenced by Marxist economic theories, liberation school instructors taught students to view the fight against inequality and oppression as part of a class struggle in which the current social structure must be destroyed. On field trips, students visited Black Panthers serving prison terms, and in class they sang revolutionary songs.[29]

The survival schools' political education, while comparable in some ways to the philosophy of the freedom schools and liberation schools, was grounded in a distinctive Indigenous educational philosophy. At Heart of the Earth and Red School House, students' social consciousness and political activism rested firmly on a cultural foundation of community responsibility. HOTESS and Red School House teachers, administrators, and visiting speakers all conveyed to students that they had the responsibility to work for the good of their families and communities and to fight for the rights of Indian people. As Vikki Howard, former social studies instructor and administrator at Heart of the Earth, explained in an interview:

> being a positive community member, contributing back to our own communities, building our own communities, and putting that in those young people—when they learn who they are, they know that it's their responsibility to build their own communities. What can I do for my own people? That's the teaching.[30]

This sense of collective responsibility was one of the core Indigenous values that survival school educators hoped to instill in young Indian people. As an integral part of their education, students learned "to contribute to this struggle of self determination and survival," a struggle that required both personal cultural grounding and collective political action.[31]

Many of the Native people who visited the schools and spoke with students in the first ten years intertwined political messages with cultural teachings. Visitors such as Janet McCloud (Tulalip), Larry Anderson (Navajo), Phillip Deere (Muskogee-Creek), Thomas Banyacya (Hopi), Oren Lyons (Onondaga), and Wallace "Mad Bear" Anderson (Tuscarora) exercised both spiritual and political leadership. They talked about their people's values, ceremonies, and prophecies as well as their political struggles. Local AIM leaders and school staff members also spoke in ways that tied students' growing political awareness to their emerging cultural identity. They attributed the erosion of traditional ways of life to the encroachment of Euro-American settlement and U.S. government policies. They called on students to resist political oppression in the same breath that they urged them to return to their traditional cultures. During circle time, prayers, drumming, and tobacco ceremonies combined with political discussions and history lessons. Rather than being treated as separate subjects, "culture" and "politics" were closely intertwined within the survival schools' curriculum and interconnected with teachings about community responsibility.[32]

School organizers saw the cultivation of community-mindedness within the next generation as necessary for their students' development into well-adjusted adults. They also considered it crucial for the future of all Native people. Pat Bellanger expressed school founders' belief "that the Indian children are *resources* of our tribes: they *are* the tribal chairmen, they're the tribal social workers, they're the tribal judges. The tribal attorneys, and the tribal

A Red School House instructor presents a lesson on Minnesota's Ojibwe reservations. While explaining Indian people's political status, he teaches his students words in the Ojibwe language. The class takes place in the "circle room," where the cultural, political, and community dimensions of the curriculum intertwined. From "We, Yesterday, Today, Tomorrow: Red School House Yearbook, 1977–78," published by Indian Country Communications, Inc.; reprinted with permission.

educators, are coming out of these schools. . . . So we looked at it that way: we had to train the leaders." A 1976 Red School House informational booklet stated that "We at the Red School House continue to press on for the education of our leaders of tomorrow."[33]

Political Curriculum: Challenges and Critiques

In the 1970s, the survival schools' political curriculum, and their affiliation with the American Indian Movement, generated some controversy. Critics raised questions about the schools' purposes and the politicization of their curriculum. At times, people within the schools also questioned the content and the potential consequences of the school's political programs.

The most extreme external criticisms condemned the schools as AIM

151

training camps intended to raise a new generation of Indian militants to overthrow the U.S. government. Politicians and other government officials made these charges in part as a reaction to AIM members' participation in the 1972 takeover of the BIA building in Washington and the 1973 Wounded Knee occupation. Thus, in the 1970s, AIM's growing national prominence complicated local people's efforts to sustain the schools.

As early as 1969, some AIM leaders began expanding the focus of their activities from local issues to assert a more national presence. Clyde Bellecourt and Dennis Banks began attending national Indian conferences, where they confronted the representatives of more established organizations like the National Congress of American Indians, criticized their approach as too conservative and conciliatory, and pushed them to pay more attention to urban Indian problems. Bellecourt and Banks also placed themselves on the agenda at non-Indian conferences during these years. At meetings of the National Council of Churches and other religious organizations, they sought financial support for the American Indian Movement while condemning the churches' historical suppression of Native religions. At gatherings of the National Conference of Welfare Workers, they castigated the discriminatory practices that damaged Indian families in cities and on reservations.[34]

While the in-your-face style and sharp rhetoric of AIM organizers alienated some of the Indian leaders they encountered, they inspired others to join their cause. At a conference in San Franscisco in 1969, Banks and Bellecourt met Russell Means, an Oglala Lakota living in Cleveland. Impressed with the AIM founders' passion and their imposing presence, Means aligned himself with them. Eventually, Means's own work in the Cleveland Indian community, his ties to Lakota reservations in South Dakota, and his charismatic leadership helped make AIM into a truly national movement. Within a few years of AIM's founding, a dozen local AIM chapters organized in cities outside of Minneapolis and St. Paul, including Denver, Cleveland, Milwaukee, and Ann Arbor. In 1971, AIM held its first national conference, at which Russell Means became the national coordinator.[35]

In addition to attending and hosting conferences, some AIM organizers began participating in and leading national protest actions. They joined in the occupation of Alcatraz from late 1969 to the summer of 1971, demonstrated against the representation of American Indians in the film *A Man Called Horse* in 1970, set up protest camps at Mount Rushmore in 1970 and 1971, and helped stage a Thanksgiving takeover of the *Mayflower II* at Plymouth Rock in 1971. By the early 1970s, AIM had emerged as the most visible national Indian organization, with a reputation as an outspoken advocate for Native people in Indian communities throughout the country.[36]

Late in 1972, AIM members staged their most ambitious national protest action yet, organizing Indian people from across the country to travel to Washington, D.C., and present a statement to the Nixon administration asserting treaty rights and demanding Indian policy reform. In what became known as the "Trail of Broken Treaties," two caravans of vehicles carrying Native activists followed a northern and a southern route until they met in St. Paul in October. There participants developed a twenty-point statement to present to the White House before continuing on. When the caravans arrived in Washington at the beginning of November, plans for a well-organized delegation to meet with top administration officials quickly broke down. Poor planning by Indian organizers and an overzealous D.C. riot police squad led to several hundred frustrated caravan participants taking over the headquarters of the Bureau of Indian Affairs. During a seven-day occupation, Indian protesters issued angry statements, trashed the building, garnered a lot of negative press, and alienated previously sympathetic government officials.[37]

AIM's participation in the BIA occupation and the leadership roles assumed there by Bellecourt and Banks brought negative consequences for the survival schools. Earlier in 1972, Red School House and Heart of the Earth each had won $20,000 grants from the Office of Economic Opportunity (OEO), their first major federal funding. After the BIA takeover, however, the OEO blocked distribution of the grant money, charging that AIM would use the money to fund its own operations and to train Indian militants in antigovernment protest tactics. Because the Indian Community School in Milwaukee had been affiliated with AIM, it also had previously granted OEO funds withheld during this period.[38]

Federal agencies' hostility toward the American Indian Movement and their suspicion of the AIM schools increased in 1973. In January and February of that year, AIM members led by Bellecourt, Banks, and Means joined Oglala Lakota people on the Pine Ridge reservation in South Dakota in protesting Dick Wilson's tribal government and violence against Indian people in nearby border towns. At the end of February, AIM members and supporters took over the village of Wounded Knee, site of an 1890 massacre of more than two hundred Lakotas by the U.S. Army. AIM's armed occupation of this symbolic site led to a seventy-one-day siege in which some three hundred federal troops and FBI agents surrounded the village, ending with the deaths of two Indian protesters in May. After Wounded Knee, the federal government launched a concerted effort to prosecute AIM leaders and shut down the organization. The occupation also gave federal officials more reason to maintain the blockade on OEO funding for the survival schools. Although an AIM lawsuit against the OEO eventually won a federal court order to release the money in 1974, these critical funds had been inaccessible for eighteen months.[39]

Charges that AIM was using the survival schools as revolutionary indoctrination camps are groundless. Survival school organizers refute them, former students and staff members laugh at them, and written documents do not support them. Fulbright researcher Sonja Schierle, who spent a semester immersed in school life at Heart of the Earth in 1978, also dismissed them. Although she acknowledged AIM's continuing influence on students, she concluded that "it goes too far to portray Heart of the Earth as an AIM training ground."[40]

Less extreme criticisms from outsiders that the schools promoted a general "anti-White" attitude among students prove more difficult to dismiss. Survival school educators certainly provided their students with a critical perspective on American history. They identified Euro-American colonization and U.S. government policies as a source of Indian people's geographic dislocations, cultural loss, and contemporary political struggles. According to Pat Bellanger, in order to understand the nature of AIM's work and the political content of survival school education, one must look carefully at those teachings characterized as "anti-White." Bellanger insisted in an interview that "the idea that White people are hated, hateful, is not true. It's the *government* that we're fighting, and *only* because they refused to listen to their own treaties." From the perspective of AIM organizers, she explained, perceptions of White people and criticisms of the U.S. government "are two separate issues."[41]

In the daily life of the schools, not everyone may have made such a fine distinction. School documents suggest that at times survival school educators conveyed negative generalizations about White people and Euro-American culture. After her semester at Heart of the Earth in 1978, Fulbright researcher Sonja Schierle described the message delivered by local AIM leaders who came in to talk to the students:

The speakers traced the loss of "Indian identity" to the negative influence of the "white man" and the "system." The students were encouraged to resist every oppression, to remember their Indiannness, and to avoid contact with whites, to be very mistrustful of them.[42]

Sally Thompson, a journalist who visited Heart of the Earth in 1975, documented a similar dynamic in classroom instruction, as teachers emphasized the differences "between values of white society and traditional Indian values":

> During a religion class Gabe [Horn] asked a student what he'd do if he killed a deer. "Would you eat it by yourself, or would you share it with us?" The boy answered he'd share it. "And what about the President of the United States?" Gabe asks. "What would he do?" He'd eat it himself, the students respond.

Gabe Horn offered this lesson to illustrate "an individual's obligation to work for the good of his people rather than for his own benefit."[43]

Some students do seem to have internalized anti-White attitudes while at the survival schools. In a 1976 Red School House informational booklet, student Lisa Davis imagined the thoughts of Mi-gi-zi, or Eagle, as he soared over a group of Ojibwe people gathered to give thanks for the wild rice harvest:

> I feel wonderful now. In times like this, when white people are polluting and mechanizing everything, it is a beautiful thing to see my people pray and take part in ceremonies just like their forefathers did.

In another Red School House publication, senior high student Sherry Blakey addressed these thoughts to her "White Brother":

> My people are hungry,
>   But you are full.
> Can you not hear the crying
>   Of those that are your brothers?
> Has your greed come to take your soul?

She concluded, "My White Brother, the time has come to pay your dues!"[44]

Teachings that contrasted White culture and history negatively with Native values and ways of life stemmed in part from the desire to affirm the positive elements of Indian culture and nurture students' pride in their Indian identity.

They also responded to the still widely used public school curriculum materials whose denigration of Native cultures and celebration of Euro-American "progress" and "civilization" damaged the self-esteem of Indian students. In these efforts, however, it seems that survival school educators sometimes swung to the opposite extreme. When they did, they undercut the schools' expressed goal of promoting understanding and brotherhood among Native Americans, Euro-Americans, and other peoples.[45]

The goal of fostering cross-cultural understanding was better served by survival school students' interpersonal engagement with local non-Indian people. Heart of the Earth students went out to speak at Twin Cities public schools, churches, universities, and community organizations about Indian history, cultures, and contemporary issues. A 1975 grant proposal explained the purpose of this program:

> Speaking engagements educate non-Indians to Native concepts, political and philosophical, that their education has denied them ... The Heart of the Earth students hope to create a bridge of understanding between two cultures, thus striving for a cooperative and better future for all People.[46]

Red School House students also educated non-Indian students around the Twin Cities about Native cultures, experiences, and perspectives. Dorene Day remembered speaking in public school classrooms as a Red School House student:

> I'd go into a school and have a bunch of fourth graders sit in a circle, and they'd say, "Well, where are your Indian clothes? Where are your feathers?" I said, "Well, I live in St. Paul; you do too. And to be a Native person, I don't wear feathers all the time. Or, if I do, my Native dress is for very specific purposes or reasons ... [and] we don't live in teepees anymore." And then, at the same time, as I'd tell them what my living situation was, I'd tell them, "But you know what? Before we got this house, we went to many houses where my mother wasn't allowed to rent there, because she was an Indian woman with children, and she was discriminated against. Do you know what that means?"

Reflecting on this cross-cultural dialogue, Day remarked, "We were little ambassadors."[47]

Survival school students found other creative ways to educate non-Indian people. The year of America's bicentennial sparked a flurry of activity at the

Red School House. In May 1976, Red School House students and staff staged a public performance of a one-act play called *Our Brothers' Keeper* at St. Luke's school in St. Paul. Written by school director Eddie Benton-Banai, the play offered "a truthful look into the life and function of Native American medicine people of yesterday and today." That same year, students and staff created a multimedia presentation "emphasizing the Native American's viewpoint on America's 200th birthday." They also produced a half-hour television program for a local public station called *The Bicentennial—White Man's Birthday, Will It Be Red Man's Wake?* As described in school documents, the program "emphasized the fact that while many Americans are celebrating their freedom in 1976, there are many others who are living in oppression."[48]

Sometimes the politicized nature of survival school education created conflicts within school walls. When she conducted research at Heart of the Earth in 1978, German Fulbright scholar Sonja Schierle found that the more political aspects of the curriculum posed both practical and ideological challenges for some teachers. In her interactions with school staff, she found that "a few teachers complained about the frequent gatherings for political speeches." Instructors became especially frustrated when "unanticipated school assemblies" forced them to postpone or eliminate significant portions of their lesson plans. These teachers experienced a conflict between school-organized political gatherings and their efforts to provide students with basic academic skills as well as "the activities that try to teach students about Indian culture and Indian life." At times, they found it impossible to give equal attention to all three components.[49]

According to Schierle, while some teachers complained on practical grounds, some objected on principle. She wrote that Heart of the Earth teachers "are not necessarily ... AIM supporters, just because they support survival school education." In her conversations with school staff, some "said that they would give everything for a good education for the children, including a political education, but sometimes they had the feeling of being used for goals ... that had little to do with the pedagogical mission." In one instance, AIM leaders offered the school gym to a group of Iranian protesters so that they could stage a hunger strike against the shah's government. "This decision," Schierle reported, "called down harsh criticism on school administration, and above all on Clyde Bellecourt, who ... wanted to demonstrate solidarity with the oppressed ... people." Fearing a police raid or other retaliation, some teachers also objected to the potential endangerment of their students.[50]

Front cover of the program for Our Brothers' Keeper, *a play performed by Red School House students and staff during the 1976 bicentennial to educate non-Native Americans about Indian history and culture. Published by Indian Country Communications, Inc.; reprinted with permission.*

OUR BROTHERS' KEEPER

... A TRUTHFUL LOOK INTO THE LIFE AND FUNCTION OF NATIVE AMERICAN MEDICINE PEOPLE OF YESTERDAY AND TODAY... WITH A MESSAGE FOR AMERICA'S BICENTENNIAL. ...A ONE ACT PLAY BY EDWARD BENTON BANAI PERFORMED BY THE STUDENTS AND STAFF FROM THE THREE FIRES PROGRAM OF THE RED SCHOOL HOUSE, ST. PAUL, MN.

MAY 14, 1976

ST. LUKE'S SCHOOL AUDITORIUM

1065 SUMMIT AVE., ST. PAUL, MINNESOTA

"To Achieve Every Goal": Balancing Academic, Cultural, and Political Curriculum

Survival school organizers set ambitious goals for their students. They wanted to provide them with basic academic skills. At the same time, they wanted to give them a distinctly culture-based education, grounded in traditional values and ways of life. They also politicized their students, and encouraged them to become socially aware and politically active community members. As they created their alternative system, survival school educators had to decide how to balance all of these elements.

Perhaps most fundamentally, school organizers had to define the proper relationship between the culturally driven components of their curriculum and more basic academic instruction in skills such as reading, writing, and mathematics. Throughout this period, survival school people conveyed a desire to provide students with *both* kinds of instruction—culture-specific as well as academic—in order to help students make their way in modern American society. German researcher Sonja Schierle concluded this from her semester-long ethnographic study at Heart of the Earth:

> the survival school concept strives for a bicultural education ... Indian children grow up in two "worlds." The task of Indian education lies in enabling the children to find the right way in both worlds. The parents consider it absolutely necessary that their children learn the standard subjects at the same time that they learn about Indian history and culture.[51]

Red School House educators expressed a similar commitment to "developing the student as a whole and complete person, to help him bridge the chasm between functioning in a modern and complex world and keeping his cultural traditions secure."[52]

School founders, teachers, and administrators wanted to give their students a good basic education. As articulated in a 1975 grant proposal, Heart of the Earth's objectives included providing "the basic academic skills which

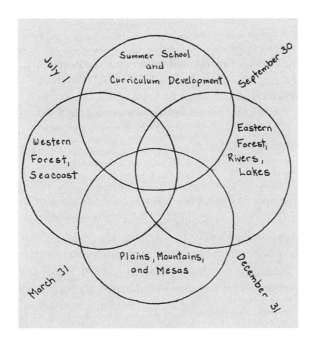

This diagram from a Heart of the Earth funding proposal in 1975 reveals how survival school educators conceptualized their curriculum through Indigenous cultural symbols such as the circle. It illustrates how learning about the Indigenous people of various geographic regions would correspond to the seasons of the school year.

159

are essential for taking control of one's life, preparing for future education, and for jobs." A Red School House document from 1979 lists a similar objective: "To graduate students who are prepared for higher education, advanced vocational training, or productive employment." Yet survival school organizers also believed that to teach their students even the most basic skills, they had to present them within a cultural context. For the troubled, alienated Indian youth who came to these schools, cultural knowledge and identity development were seen as the necessary foundation for all other types of learning and growth. In an interview, Pat Bellanger explained the founders' belief that "the more you know about yourself and your own culture, . . . the easier it is to understand other things beyond that." As Clyde Bellecourt said, "We knew that . . . a standard curriculum was important, but we had to base it around Indian culture."[53]

Many survival school people, in fact, considered cultural education the most important part of their mission, especially in the schools' first decade. Sonja Schierle concluded that "the transmission of factual knowledge is not the primary goal of survival school education."[54] Rather, the emphasis lay on students' discovery of their cultural identity and their development of self-confidence and self-respect. Survival school founder and longtime HOTESS board chairman Clyde Bellecourt explained his priorities for Native students:

> Their whole foundation is their language and their culture, and without that, we might as well forget it. I want them to have a good education; I want them to be doctors, I want them to be lawyers, teachers. I want them to achieve every goal that they set out for themselves, but I tell them every chance I get: What good is it going to be if you're not going to be an Indian? It's as simple as that.[55]

In a 1975 visit to Heart of the Earth, journalist Sally Thompson recorded a similar sentiment written on a classroom blackboard: "If we do not survive as a People following the instruction and purpose of the Creation—then we must ask, what is the purpose of survival?"[56]

Ideally, the survival schools sought to create a curriculum that was thoroughly permeated by cultural instruction. Students learned basic reading and writing skills through exercises that incorporated Native history, values, and spiritual concepts. In literature classes, students read fiction, poetry, essays, and speeches by American Indian authors and orators. They played Indian games that required them to add, subtract, and multiply. In art class, students used colors and symbols with cultural significance for Native people. Instructors with knowledge of Indigenous languages incorporated Ojibwe, Dakota, Lakota, or Ho-Chunk into their lessons whenever they could.[57]

While seeking a balance between teaching basic skills and conveying cultural knowledge, survival school educators also had to decide how to incorporate their students' political education. As with the relationship between basic skills and cultural instruction, here the more academic aspects of the curriculum did not hold top priority for some school founders. In a 2002 interview, Pat Bellanger remarked that "whether or not you're good in math doesn't mean whether or not you're gonna be a good leader. We had to look beyond how they did in school to what their talents may actually be."[58]

Both survival schools sought to integrate all three components of academic, cultural, and political curriculum into a comprehensive educational system. In practice, there were differences between the two institutions.

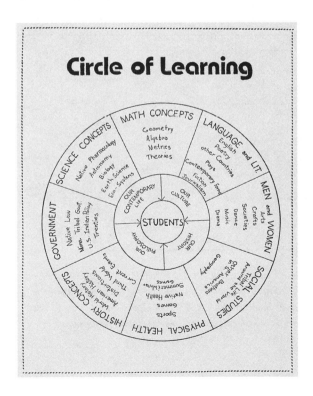

The Red School House "Circle of Learning" demonstrates the integration of the academic, cultural, and political components of the curriculum, as well as the importance of the circle within Indigenous educational philosophies. From "Heart Beat of Our Nation: Red School House Information Booklet," 1979, published by Indian Country Communications, Inc.; reprinted with permission.

161

TIME & PLACE	MONDAY	TUESDAY	WEDNESDAY	THURSDAY	FRIDAY
9:00 - 9:45 a.m.	ASSEMBLY ELOIE	ASSEMBLY JOE	ASSEMBLY BILL	ASSEMBLY RON	STUDENTS' ASSEMBLY
9:45 - 10:30 ANGIE-SHOP	MATH WITH ANGIE	MATH WITH ANGIE	MATH WITH ANGIE	MATH WITH ANGIE	N.A. HISTORY
10:35 - 11:20 RON-LIBRARY	ENGLISH	WORLD HISTORY	ENGLISH	WORLD HISTORY	OJIBWAY HISTORY WITH EDDIE OR ASTRONOMY WITH MIKE
11:25 - 12:00 N	LANGUAGE LAB LIBRARY	MUSIC WITH SHANNON IN THE SHOP	LANGUAGE LAB LIBRARY	LANGUAGE LAB LIBRARY	
12:00 - 12:45 p.m.	LUNCH	LUNCH	LUNCH	LUNCH	LUNCH
12:45 - 1:00	ASSEMBLY	ASSEMBLY	ASSEMBLY	ASSEMBLY	ASSEMBLY
1:00 - 1:45 p.m.	STUDENT COUNCIL MEETING	N.A. LITERATURE AND PHILOSOPHY WITH BILL	N.A. LITERATURE AND PHILOSOPHY WITH BILL	N.A. HISTORY WITH BILL	FIELD TRIP OR STUDY AFTER-NOON
1:50 - 2:35	GYM	N.A. LAW WITH LARRY LIBRARY	MEN'S AND WOMEN'S HOUR WITH ANGIE AND JIM	MEN'S AND WOMEN'S HOUR WITH ANGIE AND JIM	
2:40 - 3:25		DANCE AND DRAMA WITH SHANNON	BASIC SKILLS WITH BILL	MUSIC/SHANNON IN THE SHOP	

TIME & PLACE	MONDAY	TUESDAY	WEDNESDAY	THURSDAY	FRIDAY
9:00 - 9:45 a.m.	ASSEMBLY EDDIE	ASSEMBLY JOE	ASSEMBLY BILL	ASSEMBLY RON	STUDENTS' ASSEMBLY
9:45 - 10:30 RON-RON'S ROOM	ENGLISH	WORLD HISTORY	ENGLISH	WORLD HISTORY	MATH
10:35 - 11:20 BILL-ASSEMBLY	N.A. HISTORY	N.A. LITERATURE AND PHILOSOPHY	N.A. HISTORY	N.A. LITERATURE AND PHILOSOPHY	OJIBWAY HISTORY WITH EDDIE OR ASTRONOMY WITH MIKE
11:25 - 12:00 N FORRY-RON'S ROOM	LANGUAGE LAB	LANGUAGE LAB	LANGUAGE LAB	MUSIC/SHANNON IN THE SHOP	
12:00 - 12:45 p.m.	LUNCH	LUNCH	LUNCH	LUNCH	LUNCH
12:45 - 1:00	ASSEMBLY	ASSEMBLY	ASSEMBLY	ASSEMBLY	ASSEMBLY
1:00 - 1:45 p.m.	STUDENT COUNCIL MEETING	MATH/ANGIE IN THE SHOP	MATH/ANGIE IN THE SHOP	MATH/ANGIE IN THE SHOP	FIELD TRIP OR STUDY AFTER-NOON
1:50 - 2:35	GYM	N.A. LAW WITH LARRY	MEN'S AND WOMEN'S HOUR WITH ANGIE AND JIM	MEN'S AND WOMEN'S HOUR WITH ANGIE AND JIM	
2:40 - 3:25		DANCE & DRAMA SHANNON	MUSIC/SHANNON IN THE SHOP	BASIC SKILLS/BILL IN RON'S ROOM	

Daily schedules for Area III and Area V students at Red School House from 1976 show the integration of the academic, cultural, and political components of the curriculum. From "Knowledge through Cultural Understanding: Red School House Information Booklet," published by Indian Country Communications, Inc.; reprinted with permission.

From the mid-1970s through the early 1980s, Red School House and Heart of the Earth developed distinct identities, reflecting how each school balanced the components of its curriculum and what its programs emphasized.

During this period, Red School House proved more successful at creating and maintaining a consistently culturally grounded curriculum. Laura Waterman Wittstock worked with both schools in the early 1970s as a staff member of the National Indian Education Association, writing grants and developing curriculum. Later she was employed as an administrator at both schools, serving at Red School House in the mid-1970s and at Heart of the Earth in the early 1980s. Looking back on this period twenty years later, Wittstock observed that "Red School House did better with integrating traditional Ojibwe culture and language in the curriculum."[59]

Lisa Bellanger, the daughter of AIM organizer and survival school founder Pat Bellanger, agreed with Wittstock's assessment. Lisa attended high school and later worked at Heart of the Earth, and she also was familiar with Red School House programs, students, and staff because of her mother's involvement there. Like Wittstock, Lisa Bellanger saw a more successful integration of culture and academics at the St. Paul school:

> It always seems to me like Red School House had it together, for the way culture and education blended. For Heart of the Earth, it had a sense of traditionalized school setup: you'd go to math, you'd go to English, social studies, science, dot dot dot, right in a row. And then you would have a language class, there might be tanning hides, preparing wild rice . . . you would go to drum and dance, so it was all separated out. And it seemed like Red School House had it more immersed, academics immersed in the cultural content.[60]

Written documents also indicate that Red School House developed its cultural and spiritual foundation more fully and maintained it more consistently than Heart of the Earth did in this period. Concrete examples of a culturally integrated curriculum are more easily found in documents from the Red School House. More kinds of cultural outreach also emanated from the St. Paul school.[61]

In contrast, according to Wittstock, Heart of the Earth "did better with integrating . . . American Indian history and political science into the curriculum." The Minneapolis school, she said, "was much more dedicated to contemporary affairs and teaching students how to understand the systems that

functioned in the city." Wittstock's assessment also is reflected in school documents from the 1970s and early 1980s. Politicized objectives receive more
emphasis in Heart of the Earth mission statements and other descriptions
of the school's philosophy and programs than they do in similar statements
from Red School House. Overtly political activities, such as participation in
protests and other demonstrations and visits from Indigenous activists, also
appear more frequently in Heart of the Earth materials.[62]

The difference in emphasis between cultural and political elements at
Heart of the Earth and Red School House reflected the influence of leading figures at the two schools. AIM cofounder Clyde Bellecourt had a significant presence at Heart of the Earth throughout the 1970s and early
1980s, acting as chairman of the school board and frequently coming in
to talk to the students. His confrontational political style, his participation in local and national protests, and his fierce fighting spirit certainly
influenced Heart of the Earth curriculum in this period. At Red School
House, founder and director Eddie Benton-Banai provided a constant guiding force. Although he also worked as an AIM organizer and supported the
struggle for Native self-determination, he practiced a less publicly confrontational kind of politics, and he seldom appeared in the national limelight.
He exerted more personal leadership in the realm of cultural and spiritual
revitalization, and his work in that area shaped the emphasis of Red School
House programs.

The Three Fires group at Red School House also provided a source
of cultural education and outreach that set the St. Paul school apart from
Heart of the Earth. Staff and students formed the group in the mid-1970s to
encourage young Indian people "to rediscover and to gain spiritual power
from their heritage." Led by Benton-Banai and guided by cultural instructors Walter "Porky" White (Ojibwe), Ron Leith (Dakota), and Jerry Dearly
(Lakota), Three Fires members learned traditional drumming, singing, and
dancing and participated in spiritual ceremonies. They also organized cultural activities such as gathering maple sugar, quarrying pipestone, tanning
deer hides, and making pipes and drums. The group also traveled to reservations, high schools, colleges, and universities throughout the United States
and Canada, where they spoke, conducted workshops, and performed music,
poetry, and drama for both Indian and non-Indian audiences. Through such
outreach efforts the Three Fires hoped to foster "an understanding and insight into Native American cultures and brotherhood amongst people of
all nations."[63]

A series of ambitious curriculum development projects also bolstered the cultural content of Red School House education and extended the school's cultural influence. By the fall of 1975, the school housed an all-Indian printing operation called Red School House Graphics. From their boiler room–turned–print shop, students and staff created informational booklets, brochures, and posters publicizing Red School House programs. They also designed and printed student newsletters and promotional materials for other Twin Cities Indian organizations. Red School House Graphics was envisioned as a way to train young Indian people in graphic design, art layout, offset printing, screen printing, and photography.[64]

The school's printing operation also had another mission: the creation and publication of culture-specific curriculum materials. A Red School House informational booklet from 1979 described such materials as vital to the construction of a culturally integrated educational system:

> encompassed in the structure of Red School House as an Indian-initiated, Indian-controlled, and Indian-oriented "survival school" has been the dire need for Indian developed and produced curriculum materials which reflect a valid and undistorted content and approach in Indian history, culture, art, religion, and philosophy, and Indian-centered perspectives to mathematics, science, environmental studies, and English language skills. Thus curriculum development has been a necessary ongoing activity since the outset of program operations.

Staff members wrote and designed the materials and students and staff printed them at the school. In a series of coloring books called the *Mishomis Books*, Eddie Benton-Banai drew from both oral tradition and written sources in order to teach young people about Anishinaabe history, philosophy, and spiritual teachings. Illustrated by Joe Liles, a Red School House art instructor, the series grew to five books by the fall of 1979.[65]

Eventually, Red School House Graphics evolved into a comprehensive printing operation called Indian Country Press, which published materials for use at the Red School House and for distribution to other schools. In 1979, the press published a single-volume, noncoloring book version of *The Mishomis Book*. In the late 1970s and early 1980s, it also published several poetry and prose collections written by Red School House students and staff. At the time, Indian educators faced a dearth of curriculum materials that treated Native cultures with respect, incorporated Indian historical

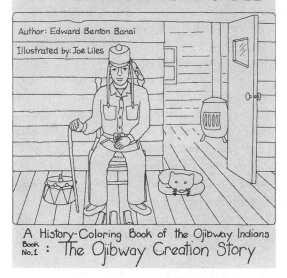

A MISHOMIS BOOK

Author: Edward Benton Banai

Illustrated by: Joe Liles

A History-Coloring Book of the Ojibway Indians
Book No.1 : The Ojibway Creation Story

Mishomis in his Cabin

The production of a series of "Mishomis Book" coloring books helped Red School House educators teach the cultural components of their curriculum. The books were published by staff and students through the school's graphic design program and in-house printing press in the late 1970s and early 1980s. From A Mishomis Book: A History-Coloring Book of the Ojibway Indians, Book 1 and Book 3, *published by Indian Country Communications, Inc.; reprinted with permission.*

Vocabulary

Draw a line from the words to the picture

Ma-en-gun   Moose

Mi-gi-zi   Food

Moonze   Bone

A-mik   Eagle

We-sin-ni-win   Wolf

O-kun   Beaver

Singular — Plural

In the Ojibway language when you are talking about one thing and you switch to talking about more than one, you must change the form of the word. Practice saying each of these words in the singular and in the plural.

Ah-ni-moosh (dog)   Ah-ni-moosh-shug (dogs)
Gee-zhi-gad (day)   Gee-zhi-gad-doon (days)
Dee-bee-kad (night)   Dee-bee-kad-doon (nights)
O-way-see (animal)   O-way-se-ug (animals)
O-kun (bone)   O-kun-nug (bones)
O-gee-bic (root)   O-gee-bic-coon (roots)

Definitions

Teachings - stories handed down by Indian people that tell of their history and religion. Teachings also give directions as to how people should live.

Cycle - something that happens the same way over and over again. An example would be the traveling of the Sun accross the sky. See how many kinds of cycles you can think of.

Clan System - division of a tribe into large family groups. Each group or clan had an important part to play in everyday life.

Vanishing American - a phrase that was applied to Native Americans because it was thought that Indians were disappearing from the Earth.

Creation - the act of making something. Can refer to everything that the Grandfather made on this Earth. Everything that He made can be grouped together in "the Creation."

Destruction - the tearing apart of something. Opposite of Creation. Can refer to what some people are doing to the Earth today.

Ceremony - a sacred meeting of people meant to draw them closer to the Creator. Prayers can be used in ceremonies for giving thanks, for curing, and for helping people with their problems. These ways, sometimes called "rituals" were given to Indian people in their Original teachings. They were meant to guide people in their lives.

Red School House educators used the "Mishomis Book" coloring book series to teach students about Ojibwe history and traditions and provide instruction in the Ojibwe language. From A Mishomis Book: A History-Coloring Book of the Ojibway Indians, Book 2, published by Indian Country Communications, Inc.; reprinted with permission.

perspectives, or reflected traditional spirituality. Thus the work of Red School House Graphics and Indian Country Press was crucial to the ability of Red School House educators to teach from within an Indigenous cultural context.[66]

While Heart of the Earth and Red School House struck different balances within their curriculum, in both schools' first decade there was considerable consensus around their educational priorities. Most survival school staff in these years supported the schools' core mission of nurturing young Indian people's identity development and their commitment to community-mindedness. From the early 1970s through the early 1980s, survival school administrators and teachers worked to develop their students' identities through a curriculum that provided cultural knowledge, fostered political awareness, and encouraged social action while also teaching academic subjects and skills.

"Pillar of Strength": Community Education and Family Services

Most of the survival school founders' concern and their schools' educational programs focused on young people. Indian youth were the most vulnerable to what AIM organizers and parents considered the dangers of assimilationist mainstream institutions. They also embodied the most potential for change, and they represented the greatest hopes for the future. Yet the survival school experience was not limited to K–12 students; it also was offered to students' families and other community members. Pat Bellanger recalled in an interview that "We wanted to look at, how do we get kids interested in education and learning, and then how do we build their confidence in themselves, and how do we involve the parents—the *family*, not the parents, the *family?*" A Heart of the Earth funding proposal from 1975 further explained the importance of family within the survival school system:

> The process of education is open-ended and in an Indian sense, has a dual direction. First, it is oriented to the student to provide awareness, understanding, and self-discipline necessary for proper growth and maturity. Secondly, it is oriented to the family to increase communication, knowledge, and preserve the present integrity of Indian culture intact for the benefit of all Indian people.

Thus, a survival school education, Bellanger insisted, "is not just about kids . . . it's about *families.*"[67]

The reach of the survival schools also extended beyond blood relatives to embrace members of the broader Twin Cities Indian community. Certainly, those whose children, grandchildren, nieces, nephews, cousins, or siblings attended the schools had the deepest connections. Over time, though, increasing numbers of other Native adults and youth became involved with the schools and benefited from their programs.

The survival schools welcomed students' families, friends, and other community members into the process of cultural discovery, introducing or reintroducing them to traditional practices, beliefs, and values. Family and community members came in to the schools to listen to visitors share cultural teachings and learn traditional skills. They accompanied students on cultural field trips and they participated in school-sponsored ceremonies. As a result of all of these activities, Pat Bellanger recalled, "families actually began developing as their child was going through this particular school system, and getting involved made a difference in their lives as well." Adults from the community "became more and more attuned to their culture, as well as the children."[68]

Families and community members also became connected to the schools through social gatherings. The schools hosted powwows and seasonal feasts with drumming, dancing, traditional foods, and prayers spoken in Native languages. Former Heart of the Earth student Lisa Bellanger recalled the joy of Red School House feasts:

> I remember bringing my friends along, and we'd go there, and we'd eat, and it was a chance to get together and see people from the neighborhood. And not even just a geographic neighborhood, but, some of the students lived in West St. Paul, some of them lived on East Side, some of them lived right near the school, some of them lived in Midway area, so it drew in Native people from a broader community, or it broadened the term "neighborhood" for the school. . . . And people would bring their prized dishes, and share them with the whole community.[69]

Red School House also organized the 49 Club, which brought together staff, students, families, and other interested young people and adults for weekly Native social dancing, drumming, and singing. Both schools invited people from the community to attend students' birthday and graduation celebrations.

By the mid-1970s, both Heart of the Earth and Red School House offered adult education classes. A 1975 HOTESS funding proposal described the adult education program:

The philosophy underlying this instruction reflects that of the school....
[B]asic academic skills, consumer education, as well as Indian history
and literature and language and culture classes are all taught, emanating
from the circle of traditional values and traditions.

Red School House, too, offered adults courses in reading, writing, and math,
as well as American Indian history, culture, and religion. In the late 1970s,
both schools extended their educational outreach to Native juveniles and
adult Indian inmates at St. Cloud Reformatory, Stillwater State Prison, and
Shakopee Women's Prison.[70]

Along with the students, adults also were encouraged to become more
socially aware and politically involved. They met tribal leaders and community activists who came to speak at the schools, traveled to conferences, and

In 1978, Heart of the Earth began administering an Adult Education Prison Program for Indian men and women incarcerated in Twin Cities prisons. From "Heart of the Earth Yearbook, 1987–88," published by Heart of the Earth Survival School, Inc.; reprinted with permission.

joined students at local protests and rallies. Because the schools remained closely affiliated with the American Indian Movement in these years, anyone who attended school-sponsored events encountered AIM organizers and ideas. For those who had little or no previous relationship with AIM, such exposure could spark further involvement. For those who already actively supported AIM, the schools became centers for gathering with like-minded people to share information and organize for social change.[71]

By the early 1980s, Red School House was offering a broad array of social services to Twin Cities Indian families. In conjunction with St. Paul AIM, the school provided a drop-in center offering after-school recreation activities for Native youth. Red School House also ran the Parole and Probation Project, organized "to help Indian youth in Ramsey County with problems concerning police, probation officers, and the legal system." At their shared location on Virginia Street, Red School House and St. Paul AIM also hosted a medical center and operated the Abenugee Day Care Center, which provided free child care for working mothers.[72]

In 1980, Heart of the Earth administrator Elaine Salinas asserted that "Heart of the Earth exists as a pulse beat of the Minneapolis community." Around the same time, a visitor to Red School House observed that the St. Paul school "serves not only as a schoolhouse, but, also as a community center." As Lisa Bellanger explained, for survival school people, being an Indian community school in an urban environment required attention to more than pedagogy:

> A school has to be connected with community, and has to be able to function within that community, and address all those issues that are important . . . Economic issues, legal issues—you know, sometimes we had parents or families that were being torn apart by the system, and children taken out of homes, and the school had to be the pillar of strength for that family. That was the one place that that family could count on for support or assistance. And even though it wasn't designed to be a social-service agency, in order to serve the child well, in a Native community, we believe that you have to serve the family, you have to be available for the family.

In the process of supporting students and their families and addressing community needs, the schools themselves became, in Bellanger's words, a "center and foundation for community."[73]

Conclusion

By the mid-1970s, the Twin Cities survival schools had established themselves as sustainable educational systems. They offered alternative institutional environments, governing models, curricula, and programs that made a positive difference in the lives of Indian students and their families. By the late 1970s, the schools also had emerged as important community resources for Native people in Minneapolis and St. Paul. For Charlotte Day and her children, and for other Twin Cities Indian families, the survival schools had become "a powerful educational force."[74]

Even in the schools' most vital decade, however, balancing the various components of the curriculum and achieving their founders' ambitious goals proved challenging. School organizers' idealistic vision for an alternative Indian education came up against the reality of providing daily instruction for dozens of students of all ages, many of them socially and academically troubled, across a range of subjects. Founders, administrators, staff, and parents had various, sometimes competing, perspectives on how best to balance and implement school curriculum. The more politicized elements of the curriculum caused some internal conflicts; over time, as the American Indian Movement's national influence grew, they also fed external criticism.

Both internal and external challenges would become more acute in the following decades. Any community, particularly one that is intensely close-knit and driven by an urgent sense of mission, can be contentious as well as cooperative. After the mid-1980s, the survival school community would become increasingly divided, as shifts in federal policy and in American political culture undermined their efforts to keep survival school programs strong.

CHAPTER 5

Conflict, Adaptation, Continuity, and Closure, 1982–2008

Early on a september morning, I met Heart of the Earth executive director and culture instructor Johnny Smith for an interview. As we talked, Smith expressed thoughts of leaving the school and retiring. After fourteen years, he thought this might be his last year at the school, that he might leave Minneapolis and go back to Red Lake, his home reservation in northern Minnesota.

Making plans to leave seemed to be Johnny Smith's perpetual state; this was the third time I had met him over a three-month period, and each time he talked as if he were about to pack it in and move on to the next thing. But on this day, he did seem to be reaching some sort of breaking point, and he looked especially tired. The reason, he told me, was his frustration with school politics. He did love teaching, and interacting with the kids; that was the joy of his work, and what had kept him at the school for so long. "The only bad thing about the job," he said, "is the political climate." Whether he would stay or leave depended on the outcome of the upcoming school board elections: if "good" people were chosen, he would stay; if not, he was done.

Many of Smith's frustrations centered on Clyde Bellecourt, then chairman of the school board. Bellecourt had become too controlling, Smith said. He had become a "liability" to the school. This surprised me, because when I interviewed Smith two months previously, he had defended Bellecourt against his detractors and asserted that although they had different approaches, in the end they were fighting for the same thing. Smith also criticized previous directors for their administrative and financial incompetence. When he became director, he said, he had started making people accountable, which had created some resentment. In the past, Smith said, some administrators had treated the survival schools as "their own personal pocketbook."

In the middle of this troubling conversation, Smith suddenly switched gears. "You know, my wife works here too," he told me. Without his knowledge, a former director had hired her to make powwow dance regalia for the students. One day she showed up at his office, for what he assumed was a friendly visit. As she got ready to leave, she said, "Well, I have to go to work." "Oh, where are you working?" Smith asked. "Here," she replied. "Since when??" he demanded. "Two days ago," she said.

Smith told the story with humor, and it lightened his dark mood. It also spoke to the complexity of the school's internal dynamics. Even as Smith clashed with those who once had been allies, and though institutional finances had deteriorated, aspects of the school's identity persisted. Smith's office still was lined with fancy-dance bustles, ceremonial staffs, and drums. Now that his wife had joined the staff, she also would contribute to the school's cultural curriculum, and their relationship would expand the Heart of the Earth family circle.

THE PERIOD from the mid-1980s through the mid-1990s became one of increasing struggle and conflict for the people of the survival schools. Internal disagreements divided administrators, teachers, families, and community members at the same time that external forces undermined their ability to maintain the schools. The troubles did not begin entirely in this period; some of their roots lay in earlier years. Other conflicts resulted from more recent changes that took place in the 1980s. Whatever their origins, the problems became more acute and more compounded over time, building to a head in the mid-1990s. The two schools emerged differently from this turbulent period: Heart of the Earth survived as an institution, while Red School House did not. Despite devoted efforts to save it, the St. Paul school closed at the end of the 1994–95 school year, and it did not reopen. Heart of the Earth remained open until 2008, when it also closed amid controversy over administrative misconduct. Compared to earlier years, in many ways this was a time of deep crisis.

Yet, even as survival school educators struggled with internal conflicts and external challenges, they continued to provide a distinctive educational experience for their students and critical resources for Native families and community members, and they still functioned as extended families. The schools also changed in response to shifting sociopolitical conditions. In the years from 1982 until Heart of the Earth closed in 2008, in addition to experiencing crisis, the people of the survival schools also maintained some continuity and practiced creative adaptation to their changing circumstances.

Internal Conflicts, 1982–94

The survival schools sprang from a well of deep emotion, passionate commitment, and farsighted vision. For many years, a set of shared experiences and beliefs knit the people of the survival schools together into a common purpose that transcended differences. To be sure, there were differences, even in the schools' most cohesive period. Some teachers who worked at the schools in the 1970s criticized their colleagues' approach to discipline and academic achievement; others disagreed with the more political aspects of school curriculum. For the most part, though, those most responsible for setting school policies, directing curriculum, nurturing students, and interacting with the community worked toward the same goals and largely agreed about the best ways to reach them.

In the 1980s and 1990s, this consensus eroded. Serious internal conflicts appeared and widened over time, developing into increasingly divisive rifts. There were growing conflicts over the schools' mission and identity, their educational priorities, and how best to balance the various components of school curriculum. Some survival school people in these years remained fully committed to reviving traditional Indigenous knowledge and ways of life, while others approached this issue with more ambivalence. There were questions of whether to follow a more conventional academic structure and curriculum or maintain a more fully alternative school structure, and how much to emphasize the mastery of basic skills.[1]

Staff, administrators, and board members also diverged over the schools' commitment to engaging students in social issues and political activism. Documents from the early 1980s through the mid-1990s show less evidence of the political aspects of survival school education than those from earlier years. The political curriculum is not entirely absent; records still show efforts to cultivate political awareness and activism among students and community members. Students attending Heart of the Earth during the 1985–86 school year, for example, rallied for Indian education at the state Capitol in

St. Paul and listened to visiting Navajo elders speak about legislation threatening to remove them from their homelands in Arizona. The program for a 1991 Heart of the Earth powwow included statements from AIM members commemorating the Wounded Knee Massacre of 1890 and calling the impending quincentenary of Columbus's arrival in North America a "Legacy of Genocide." In an interview, former Heart of the Earth teacher and administrator Vikki Howard described taking the school's drum and dance group to Twin Cities high schools in the early 1990s to educate non-Indian students about Indian culture. Overall, however, there are fewer references to political activities in school documents from these years.[2]

Declining evidence of a politicized education in the survival schools speaks to a larger trend that developed in the 1980s and 1990s. As the years passed and as some founding figures distanced themselves from the schools, as new influences moved in, and as ideological conflicts played themselves out, the balance among the academic, cultural, and political elements of school programs changed. In this later period, both the desire and the ability of school leaders to integrate all three curricular components within a comprehensive educational experience waxed and waned. The relative scarcity of documentation for the 1980s and 1990s and survival school people's reluctance to discuss these years in detail made it difficult to get a comprehensive picture of school programs or trace them consistently from year to year. Heart of the Earth yearbooks, however, do offer one window into school life during these years.

Yearbooks for the 1983–84 and 1984–85 school years document no overtly political activities and make no mention of the American Indian Movement. This differs strikingly from the school's 1979–80 yearbook, which features photographs of students protesting against nuclear power at Prairie Island, attending a performance by Dakota protest singer Floyd Red Crow Westerman, and visiting Wounded Knee, and also includes a dedication to murdered AIM activist Anna Mae Aquash. Among examples of poetry by adult education students at Minnesota correctional facilities a caption proclaims, "Freedom and Justice for Leonard Peltier and All Native Political Prisoners." A time line of the school's history and statements of its mission and philosophy include specific references to AIM's influence. If one pages through the 1979–80 yearbook, there is no doubt that this is an AIM school. In contrast, a reading of Heart of the Earth yearbooks from 1983 to 1985 reveals no ties to AIM.

The cultural curriculum also has a less obvious presence in the Heart of the Earth yearbooks from 1983–84 and 1984–85 than it does in school documents from earlier years. The difference is not as dramatic as with the political curriculum; there still is evidence of students learning Native languages, practicing cultural skills, and absorbing traditional beliefs and values. Compared to 1979–80, however, there are fewer photos and descriptions of cultural activities, and elements of Indigenous spirituality appear less pervasive.

An analysis of Heart of the Earth yearbooks suggests that in the mid-1980s and early 1990s, the balance of programs at Heart of the Earth shifted once again. In 1985–86, students again are portrayed participating in politicized activities, references to AIM reappear, and Indigenous culture appears more central. The 1993–94 yearbook also explicitly acknowledges AIM's influence at the school, both past and present, though it does not document any overt examples of political education at the school that year. In the 1993–94 yearbook, cultural and spiritual activities and values also are featured more prominently than in 1983–84 or 1984–85.[3]

Of course, one cannot reach definitive conclusions about school programs based on yearbooks, which provide only incomplete records of school life. Those who created the yearbooks for 1983–84 and 1984–85 might not have had the resources or documentation necessary to portray all of the political or cultural activities that students actually engaged in. Yet yearbooks do offer a glimpse into school life at Heart of the Earth, and they reflect staff members' choices about how to represent the school year.

The varying content of Heart of the Earth yearbooks suggests the influence of individual staff members over both the content and the representation of school programs. During the years when Heart of the Earth yearbooks display the most cultural and political content (1979–80, 1985–86, and 1993–94), Vikki Howard worked at the school as a teacher or administrator. In each of those years, Howard, an Ojibwe from Leech Lake, also either advised or directed the creation of the yearbook. In 1983–84 and 1984–85, she was not employed at Heart of the Earth and in those years the school's yearbooks seem less influenced by traditional culture and make no mention of AIM. Howard's family had a long history of leadership in the preservation of traditional culture and spirituality. As a high school student in Minneapolis and a college student at Macalester College in St. Paul in the early 1970s, Howard "grew into an adult . . . with the American Indian Movement," aligning herself with other AIM youth and participating in protest actions.[4]

While working at Heart of the Earth, Howard was committed to the values of extended family and community responsibility and to the struggle for Native self-determination. Howard's personal priorities likely guided the selection of yearbook content during the years she worked at the school. Surely they also shaped school programs in significant ways. As a teacher and eventually as elementary principal at Heart of the Earth, Howard infused survival school education with her own cultural and political commitments.

Survival school directors also played a significant role in shaping the orientation of school programs. Eddie Benton-Banai, early AIM organizer, Midewiwin spiritual leader, and Red School House founder, served as Heart of the Earth director in 1993–94, when the school's yearbook reflects a strong cultural orientation and a clearly politicized identity. During her years as a student, staff member, parent, and board member at Heart of the Earth, Lisa Bellanger noticed how the priorities of individual directors shaped the school's direction. In her experience, Heart of the Earth's commitment to the cultural and political mission of the American Indian Movement fluctuated, depending on the director at the time:

> When I went to the school [as a student], the director had a big part in the movement, or really supported the movement, and so we did a lot of movement activities: we were able to do the Run for Survival, the Longest Walk, going to Peltier's trial in Milwaukee, going to the Treaty Council; there was different things that happened at the school that were supported because the director believed in the movement.... And then I remember working at the school as a staff person, and the director was *not* a movement person, you know, she was a church person. She *knew* her own language, and she *knew* her own traditional lodge and stuff, but she ... didn't see academics and the movement as being in the same room.

Bellanger also noted how the shifting priorities of successive directors either facilitated or hindered the efforts of instructors to teach their students from a more politicized perspective. In an interview, she recalled that at one point she "almost got fired" for taking Heart of the Earth students to protests surrounding Native spearfishing rights in Wisconsin. Former Red School House student and administrator Gabrielle Strong also noted that Heart of the Earth programs changed over time as the school was led by different directors, "some stronger with AIM roots than others."[5]

In addition to differences over curriculum, interpersonal conflicts also increased in this period. Latent resentments, some of them with origins in the 1970s, built over time, then erupted into full-blown power struggles in the mid-1990s. Many of these struggles centered on the leading figures of Clyde Bellecourt and Eddie Benton-Banai. Although many people had contributed to the founding and early success of the two schools, Bellecourt and Benton-Banai garnered most of the public attention and much of the credit. Reporters and researchers singled these men out for information and quotes, in part because of Benton-Banai's long-held position as Red School House executive director and Bellecourt's equally long tenure as chairman of the Heart of the Earth school board. Bellecourt's prominence as a national AIM leader, his outspokenness, and the relatively frequent turnover of Heart of the Earth directors also led outsiders to treat him as the school's natural spokesperson. Some people close to the survival schools criticized what they perceived as Bellecourt's love of the limelight and charged that he claimed more credit than he deserved for the school's existence and success, when so many others had worked behind the scenes.[6]

In the opinion of longtime AIM organizer and survival school founder Pat Bellanger, Bellecourt and Benton-Banai were "extremely powerful, charismatic leaders" whose vision was not always understood or appreciated by those around them. Born into the Ojibwe crane clan, Bellecourt's inherited cultural roles included political leadership and stirring oratory. Benton-Banai's fish clan traditionally exercised intellectual leadership and functioned as "stargazers," looking far ahead to guide the future of the community. According to Bellanger, "in the old times, they would have been the chief council, and nobody would have questioned them." In modern times, not everyone accepted their leadership without criticism.[7]

By the early 1980s, some individuals at both schools believed that too much power and control had become concentrated in the hands of these two men, especially when it came to money. Over time people in the community charged Benton-Banai and Bellecourt with everything from mismanaging school funds to outright stealing them. Like other conflicts of this period, such financial accusations created sometimes irreparable divisions among people who once had worked collectively for a common purpose.

From the beginning, the biggest challenge for school leaders had been finding, procuring, and maintaining sufficient funding. Thus it is no surprise that in the 1980s and 1990s, many of the schools' problems revolved around money. Survival school administrators always had struggled to bring their expansive vision for alternative Indian education in line with the bureaucratic requirements of federal and state funding sources. For many years the schools derived much of their budgets from government grants intended for such disparate purposes as improving the academic performance of Indian children, teaching Native culture, reducing poverty, alleviating chemical dependency, providing social services to minority youth and families, and developing community institutions in inner-city neighborhoods. Every grant the schools' leaders received included a daunting array of regulations governing where, when, and how they could spend the money and how to report its use.

In an interview Pat Bellanger pointed out that when AIM organizers founded the schools, few of them had relevant practical experience for the task of running a school:

> We weren't people that were administratively trained. So you've got people that are charismatic, maybe—leaders in another way—that really can't function on an administrative level, and might screw things up. And it happened several times, you know: things wouldn't get written on time, proposals wouldn't get written, federal reports and things that needed numbers. I learned fast, about the whole statistics thing, and how you evaluate something by numbers—which is not our way of evaluating anything—but how many you say you're gonna do this for, how many actually do it, how it failed, what were the successes, kind of thing. And that was a type of vision that Indians don't have, mostly.

As Bellanger concluded, "Trying to be a round peg in a square hole is *really* hard to do. And that's basically what we're forced to do."[8]

Being "a round peg in a square hole" created multiple difficulties for survival school leaders. In some cases, as Pat Bellanger suggested, people with great cultural knowledge and innovative ideas for reforming Indian education lacked the skills to negotiate bureaucratic requirements or manage mountains of paperwork. The need for administrative expertise sometimes led survival school people to hire directors who had more formal education and more experience managing grants and budgets in the non-Indian world. This strategy sometimes backfired, as Pat Bellanger recalled:

> And then you'd have people that would come in, as a director, who were educated, and who we *hired* because they were educated, who would

then see math and English as the top [priority] . . . and kind of down-grading the cultural side of the education. And then pretty soon there'd be the turmoil again.[9]

Administrative and financial challenges, then, exacerbated existing peda-gogical and ideological differences, further destabilizing the schools.

In some cases, school leaders fully understood the restrictions attached to federal and state grant money, but chose to ignore them. They sometimes spent grant money on cultural events like powwows, feasts, ceremonies, and survival camps, even though it was earmarked for more conventional types of curriculum development. To many survival school people, culture *was* the curriculum, and fulfilling the schools' cultural and spiritual mission was more important than strict compliance with grant stipulations. Over the years, money also moved back and forth between the schools and other Indian programs, agencies, and events that were more or less connected to the schools. From the perspective of some school leaders, community cul-tural gatherings and political actions always had been an integral part of the survival school system. Thus they constituted a legitimate use of school funds, especially when students and their families participated.

Although school leaders felt justified in their unconventional use of funds, it did not always sit well with granting agencies. Over the years, such practices contributed to inconsistencies in record keeping and reporting that made federal agencies and other grantors increasingly reluctant to pro-vide funds. Such methods also generated criticism within the schools and among members of the broader Indian community. Some people close to the schools disagreed with leaders' management of grant money on prin-ciple; others objected because it threatened future sources of funding. Still others—those who already harbored resentments against leading figures for more personal or political reasons—used accusations of mismanagement in their attempts to unseat administrators from positions of power. In the 1980s and 1990s, other survival school directors and administrators besides Bellecourt and Benton-Banai also were accused of mismanaging or stealing school funds by school staff or community members.

Accusations of cronyism and nepotism also undermined the survival school community in this period. Some close to the schools believed that too often directors and administrators hired friends or family members to fill staff positions. If these people lacked the necessary skills or credentials to perform their jobs successfully, it could threaten the integrity of school programs. Perceptions of shortsighted favoritism also created resentment among other survival school people and others in the community.[10]

The financial, bureaucratic, administrative, and interpersonal challenges that destabilized the survival schools in these years have affected other Native communities' efforts to exercise educational self-determination. Education scholar Teresa McCarty describes similar dynamics at Rough Rock Demonstration School (later renamed Rough Rock Community School) on the Navajo reservation in Arizona in the 1980s and 1990s. Such problems continue to trouble the operation of Indian community schools in the United States and elsewhere. In a 2000 essay, Mi'kmaq educator Marie Battiste called for more educational leadership in Canada that is both Indigenous and qualified, arguing that "The First Nations must allow their own educated Aboriginal people to assume responsible positions in their community development . . . instead of passing these jobs to non-Aboriginal people or to family members with lesser qualifications." Battiste also asserted that "The strength of tribalism lies in our collective values, which must be fostered toward a collective consciousness as opposed to individual gain." Although a commitment to community well-being motivated survival school founders and influenced their curriculum, as in any human community some of those associated with the schools over the years also acted out of individual interests, and some sought personal gain.[11]

External Challenges, 1982–94

Escalating conflicts in the Twin Cities survival schools in the 1980s and early 1990s, while related to internal issues, also reflected the pressures imposed by changing external circumstances. During the survival schools' first ten years, federal policies and programs provided sources of both financial and ideological support for community-controlled, culture-based Indian education. By the mid-1980s, changes in the national political context constrained the schools' ability to sustain themselves, thus intensifying internal conflicts.

In the late 1960s and early 1970s, federal Indian policy had shifted away from the postwar attempt to terminate tribal status and the persistent push for assimilation toward a policy of "self-determination without termination." As formulated under President Lyndon Johnson, formalized by the Nixon administration, and slowly adopted within the Bureau of Indian Affairs, this new policy encouraged Indian communities to create and manage their own programs, agencies, and institutions, while promising that the federal government would not abrogate its treaty-based, government-to-government relationship or its trust responsibility to Indian tribes. Policies during these years included self-determination over education and encouraged community control over Indian schools.[12]

Federal antipoverty programs launched during President Johnson's War on Poverty also had facilitated the development of Indian-controlled educational programs. The Equal Opportunity Act of 1964 created the Office of Economic Opportunity (OEO), which worked to eradicate poverty by empowering poor communities to determine their own needs and manage their own social programs. The money provided by the OEO and its flagship program, the Community Action Program (CAP), was extended to Indian communities through CAP grants to reservation agencies and through urban programs made available to Indian people living in cities such as Minneapolis and St. Paul. Both Heart of the Earth and Red School House received funding through OEO grants in the 1970s. They also benefited from the precedent set by the OEO, and later adopted by other federal agencies, of providing direct grants to Indian communities without going through the Bureau of Indian Affairs. This proved especially valuable in an urban context, where Indian community institutions remained largely ineligible for BIA funds. Both Twin Cities survival schools, for instance, received money directly from the Department of Health, Education, and Welfare during the 1970s.[13]

Support for educational self-determination became enacted into key pieces of federal legislation that also provided structural and financial support for Indian community schools. The 1972 Indian Education Act, also known as Title IV, provided funds to develop culture-based and bilingual curriculum materials and encouraged parental and community participation and control. Importantly for the urban survival schools, it also extended federal educational aid to Native people living off reservations. After funds for the Indian Education Act were allocated in 1974, both Red School House and Heart of the Earth received substantial grants from Title IV programs throughout the rest of the decade. The Indian Education Act also established the Office of Indian Education within the Department of Health, Education, and Welfare to administer Title IV grants, thus creating another source of support for urban Indian education outside of the BIA. In 1975, the Indian Self-Determination and Educational Assistance Act solidified the federal government's ideological and financial commitment to community control over Indian education.[14]

Other developments within educational theory and policy also had fostered Indian people's efforts to create and sustain culturally relevant, community-controlled schools. Educational scholar Teresa McCarty characterizes the late 1960s and early 1970s as "periods of incredible activity in bilingual and bicultural education," during which innovations in the field received "a good measure of political support," including the appropriation of federal funds. The 1968 Bilingual Education Act, also known as Title VII, reflected this trend.[15]

In the early 1980s, however, much of the federal support for Indian educational programs like those of the survival schools evaporated. As early as 1974, one important source of support disappeared when the Nixon administration shut down the Office of Economic Opportunity, replacing it with the far less expansive Community Services Administration. With the election of Ronald Reagan as president in 1980, federal Indian policy underwent a fundamental shift, with negative consequences for Heart of the Earth, Red School House, and other Indian community schools. While maintaining the rhetoric of Indian self-determination, the Reagan administration initiated sweeping budget cuts to federal Indian programs that undermined the viability of community-controlled institutions. This resulted in what the editors of a Native newspaper called "termination by accountants."[16]

The Reagan administration also renounced the federal trust responsibility for Indian education, a policy that one historian has characterized as "a wholesale assault" on Indian educational programs. It drastically cut funding for the Title IV grants established by the Indian Education Act of 1972, which had anchored federal support for educational self-determination. Reagan also targeted programs that provided human services to Indian communities, both reservation and urban. One casualty of his administration, the Comprehensive Employment and Training Act (CETA), had helped pay for the salaries of Red School House staff members in the 1970s. Besides its cuts to Indian education, the Reagan administration also withdrew support from other funding sources for bilingual and multicultural education.[17]

Even in the 1970s, the survival schools' financial stability had been tenuous. School administrators had to piece together budgets from disparate funding sources with multiple goals, guidelines, and underlying philosophies. Federal programs rarely awarded grants with more than a few years' life cycle, forcing school leaders to expend tremendous amounts of time and energy applying, reapplying, and negotiating assessment requirements. But substantial amounts of money had been available to those with the perseverance to seek it out and the creativity to find ways to use it. In the 1980s, the policies of the Reagan administration made far less federal money available. Both survival schools had depended on funding from federal programs, especially Title IV, for the majority of their budgets throughout the 1970s. As these sources dried up, and the schools' financial stability became increasingly uncertain, internal struggles also intensified.[18]

Other Indian community schools experienced similar dynamics over time. In the 1970s, building on the example of the Twin Cities schools, a network of Indian survival schools had developed across the country. The passage of the Indian Education Act in 1972 encouraged Native communities to found these schools, and they relied primarily on federal money, especially Title IV grants, to fund their programs. They also received logistical, curricular, and philosophical support from the Federation of Native American Controlled Survival Schools, established under AIM leadership in 1975. In the late 1970s, some sixteen survival schools in the United States and Canada belonged to the Federation, including schools in Ohio, Wisconsin, South Dakota, Montana, Colorado, Manitoba, and Ontario. By the mid-1980s, however, the Federation had disbanded, and only a handful of its schools survived the decade. When reflecting on the fate of the survival school network, leaders of the Twin Cities schools targeted the search for funding sources and the maintenance of financial stability as the most serious challenges faced by all of these community institutions.[19]

The history of the nation's first community-controlled Indian school, Rough Rock Demonstration School, echoes the survival schools' struggles in transitioning from the policy context of the 1970s to that of later decades. Rough Rock was founded on the Navajo reservation in Arizona in 1966 through a combination of BIA financial support and OEO grant money. School founders' efforts to teach Navajo language and culture and foster community participation also benefited from the funding provided by the 1968 Bilingual Education Act, the Indian Education Act of 1972, and other federal programs. From a period of creativity, excitement, and growth in the 1970s, Rough Rock experienced the Reagan years as a time of increasing hardship. In her history of Rough Rock, Teresa McCarty describes the 1980s as "years of explosive internal turmoil—of continuing financial uncertainty, curricular instability, and incredibly high staff turnover—as the school struggled constantly with a conservative new federal administration intent on downsizing bilingual and Indian education." The divisions that developed in these years over finances, management, and pedagogy erupted in a 1996 protest and boycott that split the community apart and nearly shut the school down.[20]

Crisis and Closure, 1994–2008

In the Twin Cities, as at Rough Rock, the combination of internal conflicts and external pressures brought the survival schools to a crisis point in the mid-1990s. At Red School House, struggles over money influenced founder and longtime director Eddie Benton-Banai's decision to leave the school in the mid-1980s. Benton-Banai was, as Pat Bellanger has said, "the *heart* of Red School House." His commitment to cultural revitalization, his work in curriculum development, his knowledge of Anishinaabe history and spiritual traditions, and his vision for a different kind of education had provided the guiding force behind Red School House ever since the school's founding. Over the years, however, his strong leadership also created resentment, and his use of funds raised questions. By the end of the 1984–85 school year, Benton-Banai had resigned as director within an atmosphere of scandal that included accusations of embezzlement.[21]

After Benton-Banai stepped down, Red School House cycled through a series of directors; though many cared deeply about the school, none stayed for more than a few years, making it difficult to develop a long-term plan or sustain program continuity. Some of those close to Red School House since the early years also maintain that, in Benton-Banai's absence, the school's cultural and spiritual core, its family atmosphere, and its role as a community center for St. Paul's Indian people were diminished. By the mid-1980s, because of health problems and for other personal reasons, Pat Bellanger and several other influential and dedicated people also had ended their active involvement with the school, further contributing to institutional instability.

From the mid-1980s to the early 1990s, the financial situation at Red School House also worsened, as the school lost its federal funding and suffered from inadequate fiscal management. In 1993, Dorene Day, her brother Eddie, and her sisters Charlene, Janet, and Sharon—all former Red School House students and/or staff members—stepped in to run the school, hoping to recover its former strength. The Day siblings knew that they needed federal funding to support the cultural and community programs that they wanted to revive. Unfortunately, previous administrations had not kept the records or made the reports necessary for them to write successful grant applications. After a year and a half of struggling to pull together the necessary materials, they conceded defeat. At the conclusion of the spring semester in 1995, Red School House closed its doors. Students, staff members, families, and others in the St. Paul Indian community mourned its loss.[22]

After Red School House closed, its sister school carried on alone. Heart of the Earth became a charter school within the Minneapolis public school system in 1999, which brought increased access to state funds. Still, the period from 1994 to 1996 was a very troubled time for those close to the school. One executive director resigned amid questions over his use of grant money; another clashed with other administrators over his allocation of funds as well as staffing decisions and control over curriculum. These years also included an intense conflict between staff members and their families over an incident of student discipline that left former close allies irreconcilably opposed. By the end of the 1995–96 academic year, more than 80 percent of the staff who had been at the school in 1994 had left their positions, many of them under duress. The staff members who remained connected to Heart of the Earth and other members of the Twin Cities Indian community had become deeply divided over what had happened in the school. Although the school survived these difficult years, they left lasting scars, and many of those who had left the school did not return.[23]

In the late 1990s and into the early 2000s, Heart of the Earth people wrestled with many familiar challenges. Internal ideological and personal conflicts persisted, punctuated by personnel shakedowns that exacerbated an already high staff turnover rate and opened additional rifts among staff members. Accusations of financial mismanagement and corruption resurfaced, and budget cuts threatened to close the school down. School leaders continued to face the difficult question of how to balance basic skills, political awareness, and an Indigenous cultural curriculum within an integrated educational program. Critics decried students' lack of discipline and their poor performance on standardized tests. After Heart of the Earth became a charter school in 1999, administrators came under more pressure to meet state standards. This pressure intensified after No Child Left Behind legislation passed in 2001.[24]

By 2003, the school, now known as Oh Day Aki (Ojibwe for "Heart of the Earth"), was in serious financial trouble. The school board hired Joel Pourier as executive director to try to turn things around. Pourier had been working as the school's finance director since 2002, and his impressive résumé indicated that he was a good man for the job. In the next five years, however, Pourier would bring the school to ruin.

In 2007, a routine audit revealed irregularities involving invoices, money transfers, and undocumented expenses. In July 2008, the school's book-keeper voiced suspicions about Pourier, which launched a criminal inves-tigation for suspected fraud. In early August 2008, another audit, filed six months late, found $160,000 in school funds unaccounted for. Further inves-tigation suggested that up to $238,000 had been mishandled. The Minnesota Department of Education froze the school's assets and the Minneapolis School District revoked its charter a month before classes were scheduled to resume. Oh Day Aki closed late in the summer of 2008, leaving the fami-lies of more than two hundred enrolled students scrambling to find other schools and stranding twenty-five staff members without work.

The school did not reopen. After nearly a year's investigation, in late May 2009, Joel Pourier was charged with embezzling $1.38 million from Oh Day Aki during his five years as executive director. Principal Darlene Leiding expressed shock at the extent of the damage. Pourier had forged signatures, including that of school board chair John Plunkett, transferred money to personal bank accounts, and written checks out to himself for spu-rious expenses. His embezzlement bought him a lavish lifestyle; he owned an Escalade, a Hummer, and three houses ranging in value from $200,000 to more than $650,000. Meanwhile, according to the criminal complaint filed against him, the school "routinely did not have enough money to finance field trips, supplies, computers or textbooks." Employees' checks bounced and their medical insurance premiums were not being paid.

When asked how he afforded his lifestyle, Pourier attributed it to the casino payments he received as a member of the Shakopee Mdewakanton Sioux Community and to family wealth. But, as it turned out, he was not an enrolled Shakopee member, and he had grown up poor on the Pine Ridge reservation. Pourier's academic credentials proved equally spurious. Despite what his résumé said, he had earned neither a B.A. nor an M.A. in business administration, nor even the associate degree in accounting that he claimed. Everything about Pourier, it seemed, was a lie. When he was hired as finance director in 2002, school board members had not performed a background check on his résumé. During his time as executive director, the board had not reviewed the checks that returned from the bank, and they saw only general monthly summary statements of school finances.

In July 2009, a local paper reported that Pourier also had been charged with criminal vehicular operation for a hit-and-run, as well as domestic as-sault. Finally, in July 2010, he pleaded guilty to the embezzlement charges, and in August he was sentenced to ten years in prison. The same week, the building that had housed the Oh Day Aki school for more than thirty years was demolished to make way for new apartments.[25]

Continuity and Adaptation, 1982–2008

The period from the mid-1980s to the mid-1990s was a difficult one for the survival schools. The bright hope, common purpose, and vibrant creativity that had characterized the preceding decade faded in the shadow of internal dissension and financial crisis. The retrenchment of federal funding and policy support for community-controlled Indian education further compromised the schools' ability to provide an alternative education for Indian students. The closing of Red School House in 1995 left a void in St. Paul's Indian community that would not easily be filled, and its absence offered a painful reminder of the troubles of the preceding years. Although Heart of the Earth managed to stay open through the difficult years of the mid-1990s, it did not entirely escape the problems that had plagued its sister school, and eventually corrupt leadership and financial crisis led to its closure.

Despite the struggles of these years, it would be wrong to see the period as one of inexorable decline or to conclude that the survival school experiment had failed. Throughout the 1980s and early 1990s, school administrators, staff members, and parents at both schools worked hard to maintain them as viable community institutions. Their efforts kept alive key aspects of the schools' founding mission, alternative structure and environment, innovative curriculum, and community programs. Even in the midst of conflict, Heart of the Earth/Oh Day Aki and Red School House continued to provide positive educational experiences and needed services to students, their families, and other members of the Twin Cities Indian community.

As in earlier years, a large percentage of survival school students in this period were at-risk Indian youth: refugees from the public school system, veterans of the juvenile courts, survivors of troubled family histories. Many survival school leaders continued to see culture-based identity development within a supportive, family school environment as the key to these students' educational success. Johnny Smith, an Ojibwe from the Red Lake reservation in northern Minnesota, was hired to teach traditional singing, drumming, and dancing at Heart of the Earth in 1988. Although he intended to remain for only a year, he stayed for twenty, working as a cultural instructor, history teacher, and administrator until the school's closing in 2008.

189

Asked to reflect on the school's purpose, Smith answered firmly, "Identity. Teaching these kids identity. That's what it's about. Make 'em feel good about themselves; when they feel good about themselves, they can do anything they want."[26]

To foster those feelings of self-worth, teachers and administrators at Heart of the Earth and Red School House still worked to ground young Native people's identity development in Indigenous knowledge. They introduced students to Native languages and taught them skills like drumming, singing, dancing, beading, constructing teepees and lodges, tapping maple trees, making maple sugar, and harvesting and parching wild rice. Survival school students continued to attend reservation-based survival camps as well as feasts, powwows, and ceremonies. As in earlier years, participation in these cultural activities also taught students about Native values and incorporated spiritual teachings from multiple tribal and Indigenous traditions.[27]

In addition to cultural and spiritual grounding, survival school educators continued to provide an alternative institutional structure and environment that featured flexibility and multifaceted support. A Red School House promotional document from 1989 highlighted the school's individualized educational approach, its open school grade model, and its caring environment. Interviews with Heart of the Earth and Red School House teachers and administrators from these years show that staff members such as Vikki Howard, Johnny Smith, Walter "Porky" White, and others continued to give deeply of themselves, both in and out of the classroom, in order to understand and care for their students.[28]

Johnny Smith, a Heart of the Earth staff member since 1988, regularly shared cash from his own pocket with young people from poor homes and gave students rides home from school. He gave his home phone number to students and told them to call him, day or night, whenever they needed someone to talk to or had a problem that he might help them solve. As a teacher, Smith recognized how conditions at home affected his pupils' academic performance, and he often worked one-on-one with students who were struggling with their schoolwork. Smith explained the motive behind these efforts as a continuance of the commitments of the past: "This is what I want our school to be, and this is what our school has been since I've been here, and before I started here: it's *always* been a second home for these kids."[29]

Johnny Smith and others who worked at the survival schools in the 1980s and 1990s maintained the family atmosphere that had permeated Heart of the Earth and Red School House in their earlier years. In this later period, too, many of those involved with the schools actually were related to each other. Parents, grandparents, siblings, cousins, aunts, uncles, nieces, nephews, husbands, and wives came together in the schools as students, staff members, and volunteers. School documents from these years still feature the frequently repeated surnames of multigenerational survival school families: Beaulieu, Benjamin, Benton, Cloud, Cook, Eagle, Goose, Graves, Lussier, Kingbird, Means, Mountain, Powers, Roberts, Sam, Staples, Sutten, Thunder, and White. For those students not surrounded by blood relations, the survival schools offered comfort through the traditional concept of an expansive, extended-family kinship. Clyde Bellecourt, Heart of the Earth founder and school board chair throughout most of the 1980s and 1990s, noted in an interview how many of the school's students had grown up without a father in the home: "So, I feel it's a responsibility of people like myself to be the father, to be the uncle, be the grandpa, if that's what they want."[30]

As in earlier years, the survival schools' mission still extended beyond nurturing and educating Indian youth, as they continued to offer cultural knowledge, academic instruction, and vocational skills to students' parents, their extended families, and other community members through adult education courses, including programs that served inmates at local prisons. The schools also provided social services to American Indian people in Minneapolis and St. Paul. In the mid-1980s, for example, Heart of the Earth administered the Young Warriors Program, in which students performed chores and organized social and cultural activities for community elders. At Red School House, the Abenugee Day Care Center continued to provide services, and in 1984 school leaders founded the Ain Dah Yung (Our Home) shelter, which provided emergency housing, counseling, and other services for homeless and runaway Indian youth. The schools also maintained their commitment to parental and community involvement in decisions about school structure, programs, and personnel.[31]

While functioning as community centers, the survival schools continued to inculcate in students their cultural responsibility to contribute to their communities and work for the good of their people. A Red School House document from 1989 offered this statement of the school's purpose:

> Red School House provides a supportive environment for promoting and developing Native American cultural knowledge and understanding, personal growth, and academic excellence so all students can learn in

191

preparation for leading good lives and strengthening our community in a changing world. With yesterday, we learn for tomorrow.[32]

As in the earlier period, the "tomorrow" envisioned by survival school leaders was a future in which traditional Native cultures would provide direction for modern Indian lives. Johnny Smith explained his vision of the Heart of the Earth mission:

> I see this school as not only educating our children, but as keeping some of our old ways of life alive, and one of the main things is our values. We have a value system—all people of this earth, from their own background, have their certain values, but a lot of them push them aside. You keep those values alive, and keep that language alive, keep those songs alive, and those dances alive, that gives you a certain identity, a certain good feeling about yourself.

Smith concluded, "I think that's the main reason for our school is, our culture's dying. We need to keep it alive."[33]

While maintaining continuity with the past, survival school educators also introduced new elements into the curriculum. By the mid-1980s, leaders at both schools had introduced computer classes into the regular curriculum, and in the subsequent decade computer instruction and technical education both expanded. Heart of the Earth students also began taking Spanish-language classes in addition to Ojibwe and Lakota.[34]

After the Red School House closed in 1995, Heart of the Earth survived as an institution. School leaders kept it open by adapting and evolving, and to some degree by strategically compromising aspects of its founding goals and priorities. In an effort to secure a more stable source of funding, they applied for charter school status, and in May 1999, Heart of the Earth administrators received approval from the Minnesota State Board of Education for the school to become a charter school within the Minneapolis public school system. Charter status brought substantially increased financial support from the state, which meant less reliance on short-term, competitive federal grants. Yet it also brought some negative consequences. School leaders had to tolerate more state oversight and conform to more externally imposed rules and regulations. State charter laws also required that teachers fill a majority of the school board positions, which compromised the survival school's commitment to parental control. Because of the ongoing scarcity of Native teachers, it also reduced the number of Indian people on the school board. In the early 2000s, school leaders placed increasing emphasis on teaching basic academic skills and improving students' performance on standardized tests. They did so in response to internal and external criticisms, the requirements of charter status, and national trends in educational policy and practice, including No Child Left Behind legislation.[35]

While making these changes, Heart of the Earth administrators and staff members continued to embrace much of the mission that had guided the school during its founding and early years. In the late 1990s and early 2000s, they still encouraged culture-based identity development for young Native people, especially those who had floundered in the city's public school systems. They emphasized individualized instruction, family and community involvement, and a holistic educational approach. Students still learned traditional languages, skills, and values. The school also continued to provide an extended family environment for its students. While educating Native students, Heart of the Earth people also worked for the survival of Indian ways of life.[36]

In the early 2000s, Heart of the Earth leaders were developing an ambitious new direction for the school, making plans and raising money to expand into a larger facility on a new campus and to create a research and resource center for culture-based Indian education. They were using their charter school status within the Minneapolis public school system to try to attain greater financial stability and additional resources for their programs. In 2008, the school claimed an 80 percent graduation rate, far higher than the national average of 54 percent for Native students and the Minnesota rate of 36 percent. Unfortunately, during this same period, the school's director, Joel Pourier, was exploiting school funds for his personal gain, destabilizing its educational programming, and ultimately triggering its closure in August 2008.[37]

Conclusion

When Heart of the Earth/Oh Day Aki closed in the summer of 2008, the story of the survival schools came, in one sense, to a close. By the time both schools closed, their finances were in shambles. Interpersonal conflicts had created bitter divisions among people who once had worked closely together in solidarity for the cause of students' cultural development and the survival of community-controlled education. The community forged through the practice of self-determination, cultural reclamation, language revitalization, and political action lost some of its vitality and much of its cohesiveness. Red School House people grieved the loss of their school when it closed in 1995. Oh Day Aki's sudden closure and the investigation launched against Pourier in 2008 proved a blow from which the school could not recover. Revelations of the extent of Pourier's corruption and the depth of his betrayal left the Twin Cities Indian community reeling.

Yet, even during these most difficult years, an alternative narrative was unfolding. As the first survival school students graduated and began their adult lives, it became apparent that for many of them, the schools' teachings had taken firm hold. Some of them remained closely connected to the schools, and when they had their own children, they sent them there. By the turn of the twenty-first century, a second and even a third generation of survival school families had been profoundly influenced by their survival school education, and hundreds of other Twin Cities Indian people also had their lives changed for the better. Even while the schools, as institutions, were nearing the end of their existence, their long-term outcomes and their deeper meanings were becoming clear.

CHAPTER 6

The Meanings of Survival School Education:
Identity, Self-Determination, and Decolonization

O<small>N AN UNSEASONABLY COLD WEEKEND IN</small> O<small>CTOBER,</small> several hundred Indian people gathered near the Bad River reservation in northern Wisconsin for the fall ceremonies of the Midewiwin lodge. Although mostly Anishinaabeg from Minnesota and elsewhere in the upper Midwest, they also came from other Native nations across the United States as well as Indigenous communities in Canada, Mexico, and Central America. The three-day ceremonies took place in a long structure constructed of maple saplings, curved overhead, tied with twine, and covered with tarps. More than a hundred feet long and twenty feet wide, the lodge stood in an open field along Highway 2, backed by pine woods and the south shore of Lake Superior.

Over the course of a day spent at the ceremonies, I lost all normal sense of time. Low-hanging clouds and intermittent rain and snow outside made it impossible to track the path of the sun across the sky. Inside, the lodge was a dusky, timeless space. The low illumination provided by the central fire, a hole in the ceiling above the fire pit, and strings of small lightbulbs varied little from morning to evening. There were no clocks and the day's events followed no hourly schedule; they began when people were ready, lasted however long was necessary, and ended when they were finished. Each part of the day's proceedings—from the teachings delivered to the Midewiwin initiates by Grand Chief Eddie Benton-Banai, to the many dances, to the jingle dress healing ceremony, to the afternoon and evening feasts—took hours to complete.

Within this self-contained world, past and present merged. The smell of wood smoke, cedar, tobacco, and sage; the feel of the earth underneath; the sounds of the Ojibwe language and the drumming and singing; the rituals of water, fire, and food; and the pervasive communality of the space, all evoked the traditional Anishinaabe life of three hundred years ago. Yet they coexisted with the trappings of modern American society: winter jackets and boots, baseball hats and stocking caps, plastic lawn chairs, and English spoken in thick Midwestern accents.

From an outsider's perspective, the day contained elements of powwow, religious revival meeting, hunting camp, training seminar, small-town high school basketball game, and family reunion. Stretches of great seriousness and deep focus alternated with moments of joyous abandon. Traditional teachings about how to live a good life were interspersed with wry inside jokes. Babies slept on blankets and toddlers trundled around inside the lodge, while outside the older children ran and roughhoused. Old friends met with hugs, tears, and teasing.

Above all, the lodge was a place of palpable spiritual vitality. Those gathered here were not just a few die-hard traditionalists clinging to the almost-forgotten, irrelevant ways of the distant past. This was a well-organized, humming, intergenerational event, run by cultural experts who managed the complex logistics of the dawn-to-midnight ceremonies with competence. Common human beings rose to their responsibilities as caretakers and culture bearers for their people. Together they worked as fire keepers, feast preparers, pipe carriers, water carriers, smudgers, drummers, singers, dancers, teachers, and healers. This was a strong, thriving, spiritual community, ready to continue on for the coming generations.

AT ITS HEART, the survival school system worked to provide students with meaning for their lives. That meaning developed from young people's discovery and acceptance of their cultural identity, the revival of Indigenous value systems, the strengthening of extended family support networks, and the infusion of daily life with a sense of interconnectedness and belonging. It also derived from the cultivation of political awareness and community-mindedness and the encouragement of active work for the good of Indian people and the survival of ancestral knowledge. In this way, the people of Heart of the Earth and Red School House sought to help students find their place in the world, and to uncover their life's purpose.

How, then, did students respond to this alternative educational system? What meanings did they find within it and how did it influence their development into young adults? What did the schools mean to students' families, and how did they shape Indian communities?

The survival schools' impact was most ambiguous in terms of academic outcomes. Over the life of the schools, they received their most consistent criticisms in the area of academic achievement and accomplished their least obvious successes. Neither Heart of the Earth nor Red School House ever provided an exceptional academic education as calculated by most standard measures of achievement, and at times they performed quite poorly in comparison to other schools. In the late 1990s and early 2000s, Heart of the Earth leaders placed more emphasis on raising test scores and producing other quantifiable improvements in students' mastery of basic academic skills, with some success.

Survival school founders have challenged negative assessments of their schools by standard measures of academic achievement. They have emphasized the results of studies that demonstrated individual students' improvement on basic skills rather than school-wide statistics. They also have pointed out the exceptionally high concentration of low-income, high-risk pupils in their student body, many of whom already had struggled and failed in the public school system. Certainly, one could argue that by attending one of the survival schools, some students simply *got* a basic education who otherwise would not have done so, given their past experience in public schools. This seems as true in Oh Day Aki's last years as it was when the A.I.M. Survival School first opened in 1972.

Some survival school educators—and particularly their founders—also have maintained that, while necessary and important, proficiency in basic academic skills was not their highest priority, nor has it been the purpose of this book to assess the schools in terms of academic achievement. I had neither the desire nor the expertise to engage in such analysis, even if there had been enough data to do so effectively. While decisions about how to balance instruction in basic skills with the cultural and political curriculum posed challenges that contributed to internal divisions within the schools, most of those I interviewed—whether founders, teachers, administrators, parents, or former students—prioritized other goals and emphasized other outcomes than academic achievement. As a historian interested in understanding Native people's experiences from their perspectives, I also looked elsewhere for the schools' most significant outcomes and meanings.

One of the survival schools' most significant outcomes was their influence on the identity development of students and their families, as they grew to understand themselves as Native people and become leaders in their communities. For those who founded and worked in the schools, they provided a way for Indian people to practice self-determination over their children's education. Over time, the survival schools also became centers for the rebuilding of Indigenous community in the Twin Cities and in the upper Midwest region. The members of what linguist Joshua Fishman might call this "community of belief" came together to ensure the survival of Indigenous difference in American society. Thus they worked against settler colonialism's persistent "logic of elimination" and furthered Indigenous decolonization in ways that have continued after Red School House and Oh Day Aki closed their doors.[1]

"She Found Out Who She Is": Student Experiences of Cultural Education

The cultural components of the survival schools' curriculum had the most profound and far-reaching impact on their students. School organizers had set out to help students discover and embrace their tribal, Indian, and Indigenous identities within an educational environment grounded in ancestral cultural knowledge. Many young Native people responded positively to this effort, and it shaped their lives in powerful and lasting ways.

Some students were drawn to Heart of the Earth and Red School House by an already-existing desire to learn about their cultures and a need to understand who they were as Indian people. In 1978, Tom King, then a ninth grader at Heart of the Earth, explained to a reporter why he "eagerly" had put his name on the school's waiting list five years earlier. "I didn't know my culture, and I wanted to," King said. "That's why I came here."[2]

Once they spent time in the schools, many students experienced the kind of self-awakening that school organizers had hoped to provide for them. Red School House graduating senior Don Havlish reflected on this process in 1978:

> Within the three years I was there, I really feel I learned a lot, academically and culturally speaking. I felt like a new person. I learned about the ways of our people, the traditions—the religion—I had finally discovered my real identity and I feel that's important to every individual, regardless of what your ethnic background may be.[3]

In the mid-1970s, Heart of the Earth student Leona Flores also discovered a new sense of self through her survival school education. After bouncing from one Minneapolis public school to another in the early 1970s, Flores landed at South High, where she continued to feel out of place and came into conflict with other students. When a fight led to her suspension from South, she transferred to Heart of the Earth. Once there, she embraced her Indian identity in a way she never had before. Flores was sixteen in 1975 when her mother, Harriet Heisler, told a journalist, "That school is the most important thing in her life. She found out who she is."[4]

The survival schools created a space in which young Indian people could feel safe in the process of exploring who they were and begin to feel good about themselves, without prejudice or hostility and without feeling the pressure to change themselves to conform to dominant social norms. Early in 1978, Betsee Knox, a health teacher and counselor at Heart of the Earth, explained to a reporter that in contrast to the public schools, "Here kids can feel more comfortable to be what they are and to believe what they believe." Lisa Bellanger, then a junior at Heart of the Earth, further explained that "In other schools, they put you on the spot and expect you to be the Indian that they made up for you. Here you can be the Indian that you are."[5]

Evidence suggests that for those survival school students who had struggled the most painfully in the public schools, entering that alternative, culturally defined space improved their attitudes toward school and enabled greater academic success. In early March 1972, psychologist Dr. Norman Silverberg tested students at the two-month-old A.I.M. Survival School (later Heart of the Earth) in Minneapolis in reading, spelling, and mathematics. Late in May he returned to repeat the tests. In the eleven weeks between testing sessions, Silverberg found that students had increased their grade level equivalencies across all three skill areas. In a written evaluation of the school and its curriculum, Silverberg stated:

> I was very favorably impressed, not only with the results of the quantitative evaluation, but also in terms of my observation of the children. They are happier and interested in learning.... It would appear to me ... that the AIM Survival School is meeting the needs of many children of the Indian community and is therefore successful.[6]

According to Clyde Bellecourt, this improvement was a direct result of the school's emphasis on culture and identity. In a later interview, Bellecourt recalled the Silverberg tests:

> Sometimes our kids that come to us were three or four years behind in reading, they're behind in math, and they're behind in different subjects. They all have special learning [and] behavioral problems ... But they found out, with the introduction of Indian language, with culture, tradition, starting to instill some pride in these kids, that these kids were running anywhere from one-half grade to one and a half grade levels *higher*.[7]

The work of psychologist Dr. Margaret Silverberg corroborated Bellecourt's attribution of students' improved academic performance to the survival schools' cultural context. Silverberg also conducted academic testing at the Minneapolis survival school in the early 1970s and she maintained ongoing contact with Heart of the Earth students through her work as a psychological consultant for a local Indian advocacy agency. In a 1975 interview, she condemned the public schools for imposing a culturally hostile environment on Indian children. In contrast, she praised the survival schools for encouraging Indian youth to explore their cultural identities. In such an atmosphere, she asserted, Native students "can develop a stronger concept of self-esteem and self-worth than would be possible in public schools." As a result, "kids can be more relaxed and able to apply themselves to learning."[8]

Staff and students at Heart of the Earth also attested to the positive impact of the school's cultural environment on students' educational development in the 1970s. In 1978, Heart of the Earth director Jim O'Brien told a journalist that "children at Heart of the Earth are learning more than they would in a public school" and that "they also have better attitudes." The experience of eleventh grader Jolene Bounds supported O'Brien's assertions:

> She was expelled from Marshall–University High School three years ago because, she said, "I didn't get along with the white kids or the teachers and I wasn't learning anything." Now, at the survival school, her attitude has noticeably changed. She has regained an interest in school, she said, and has decided to pursue a career in law.[9]

In a survival school, O'Brien explained, "Native American children ... do not feel caught between cultures as they do in public schools." As Eddie Benton-Banai argued, once Indian students develop a positive Indian identity and build up their self-esteem, "then you'll see the academic rise and their ability and their striving and their drive. That's what culture-based education is."[10]

1. Red School House is a place where people gather together.

2. The Red School House teaches respect.

3. The Red School House is a place where I learn to speak Ojibway.

4. The Red School House has showed me the Indian ways.

5. The Red School House makes me feel smart.

STEVE QUAGON

Yesterday we were talking about how Come the new kids came to this School. Well I'll Tell you why I came. Since the first week I came here I Understood a lot about This School. This School has a lot of Pride And Understanding. IT IS Not like any Public School. in a Public School they're mean to you just because of your Color. Well thats not right! I guess These Indians, at Red School house are not like that anyhow. this School has respect and they know what the Sacred Circle means. the other Schools I went to Don't make you feel AT Home. This one does. All the people Are Bright here.
Maryanne Smith

Red School House student writing from the 1970s reveals how the survival schools' supportive, culturally relevant environment helped students develop positive attitudes toward education and facilitated their learning. From "We, Yesterday, Today, Tomorrow: Red School House Yearbook, 1977–78" and "Knowledge through Cultural Understanding: Red School House Information Booklet," published by Indian Country Communications, Inc.; reprinted with permission.

Beyond their impact on academic progress, the survival schools reached some young people on an intensely personal level, touching a spiritual core that they had not known they even had. Lisa Bellanger had attended the St. Paul Open School, cofounded by her mother Pat, through the ninth grade. At that point she considered transferring to Red School House, but found her mother's heavy involvement there a bit too close for comfort. She was interested in attending Heart of the Earth in Minneapolis, but because

201

they lived in St. Paul, her mother didn't want her to take the city bus that far every day. So Lisa chose to transfer to Central High School in St. Paul, where many friends from her neighborhood attended. Although Central was a large, mainstream, public school, Pat agreed to let Lisa try it. As Lisa remembered in an interview, the experiment did not last long:

> On my first day of school, I walked in the first set of doors, and after going from a small school . . . to going to this school where there was a thousand kids, I never made it through the second set of doors at Central; I turned around and went home. And never, ever went back there.[11]

Rather than admit to her mother what had happened, Lisa pretended for weeks that she was attending Central, when in fact she was spending her days at home.

Eventually, Lisa got bored at home, and so her friend Susan Bellecourt, daughter of Clyde and Peggy Bellecourt and a student at Heart of the Earth, suggested that Lisa come to school with her. Lisa laughingly recounted what happened after several weeks of tagging along with Susan:

> One day the principal or one of the counselors cornered me and they said, "You know, you're here every day. And we've let you sit in the classes, and hang out; you might as well just enroll." So, then I had to go back, 'cause my mom had to sign papers, and tell her I had not gone to school at Central! I had to 'fess up. . . . So she said, "Yeah, all right, as long as you're in school!" So she signed the papers, and I started attending at Heart of the Earth.[12]

Lisa stayed at Heart of the Earth for the rest of her high school years until her graduation in 1979.

From her first days at Heart of the Earth, Lisa Bellanger had felt comfortable there, for reasons that did not become clear until years later:

> At that time, I couldn't tell you why I liked Heart of the Earth . . . I just liked it. There were other Indian students there, we learned, we had our culture classes, we had language classes, we had circle time, and I just knew that it felt good there. . . . And now, as an adult, I can think back and look at the elements of what it was that drew me there; now I know about that. I believe it has to do with ancestral memory—blood memory, it's sometimes referred to as—where the smell of smudging the sage

and the cedar connected with something inside of me that I didn't realize was there until I was older.

Bellanger believes that the educational environment at Heart of the Earth tapped into that "conceptual or ancestral memory that we know that we have, everybody has." Her sense of belonging within that cultural space happened because "when you go home to your original home, you feel it; you feel something there, but you can't describe it. And that's when I think that you've touched that place in your heart or in your memory where it's stored."[13]

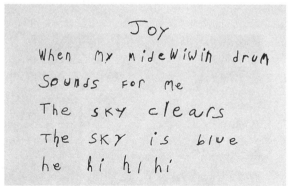

Red School House students' creative work from the 1970s demonstrates how the survival schools' cultural curriculum shaped young people's developing sense of self. From "We, Yesterday, Today, Tomorrow: Red School House Yearbook, 1977–78," published by Indian Country Communications, Inc.; reprinted with permission.

For Dorene Day, entering the survival school environment also felt like coming home. By the time she completed sixth grade, Day had attended three public schools, one in northern Minnesota and two in the Twin Cities. In the fall of 1972, she began seventh grade at the newly founded Red School House in St. Paul. Compared to the public schools, Day remembered Red School House as "this really wonderful place." The biggest difference for her was the "ever-present" spiritual atmosphere and the introduction to Indigenous values and beliefs. As she described it, when she entered the survival school, "I was like a sponge." She soaked up everything she learned about her culture, and it nourished her. As she put it, "I was fed spiritually."[14]

Within the cultural environment of the Red School House, Day flourished, growing into a strong, centered, creative young woman:

Red School House student Dorene Day, youngest daughter of founding parent Charlotte Day, soaked up the school's cultural teachings and thrived in its spiritual environment in the 1970s. From "Knowledge through Cultural Understanding: Red School House Information Booklet," published by Indian Country Communications, Inc.; reprinted with permission.

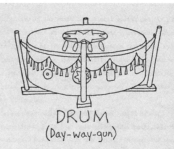

DRUM
(Day-way-gun)

BOOSHOO, I HAVE A CHANCE TO TELL YOU ABOUT MYSELF. I AM A TRADITIONAL DRUM. THESE MEN THAT MAKE MUSIC THROUGH ME ARE SINGERS.

ONE THING I WANT TO SAY IS THAT I WAS CREATED FROM THE MOTHER OF ALL THINGS AND THIS IS WHAT I STAND FOR. I STAND FOR HER. I WAS CREATED TO HONOR HER AND ALL WOMEN.

I AM ROUND LIKE THE CIRCLE OF LIFE.

THE WAY I SPEAK STANDS FOR THE HEART BEAT OF ALL LIVING THINGS. I WAS CREATED FROM OTHER LIVING THINGS IN ORDER THAT I MIGHT BE HEARD, THAT I WOULD BE A PART OF THE VOICES OF MANY.

I HAVE THE FEELINGS OF THE SOFT, SWIFT DEER THAT IS MY SKIN. I HAVE THE FEELINGS OF THE OAK TREE THAT IS MY BODY. I HAVE THE FEELINGS OF YOU PEOPLE THAT I HONOR. THAT IS WHO MY VOICE IS FOR.

THE MEN ARE ONLY ALLOWED TO SOUND ME FOR I AM THE KEEPER OF SONGS THAT WOMEN ONLY SING HALF-WAY THROUGH. WHEN THE MEN SOUND ME THEY KNOW THAT IT IS THE YOUNG ONES THAT HAVE TO LEARN TO RESPECT ME AND NOT TO ABUSE ME. THE YOUNG ONES HAVE TO LEARN THE SONGS TO CARRY THEM ON. FOR IF THEY DON'T, I WILL NOT LIVE.   DORENE DAY

That's really where I excelled in all of my writing and singing and every-thing else that I became interested in, because basically, they were teach-ing us how to express ourselves, from that cultural context, which could kind of go on forever. You know, once you have some of the principles—some of the teachings, or ideals—then you can do art forever, or you can write forever, or you can sing forever. So, that was a big deal for me . . . Once I got into that environment, where I felt safe and loved and cared for, and I had all these beautiful things around me, I just excelled.[15]

Throughout her high school years, Day wrote poetry and stories, and she became one of the school's leading traditional dancers and singers. While she explored her artistic talents, she also struggled with family tragedy and loss. Her father was killed when she was sixteen, and she also lost her grand-mother during her teenage years. Day credits the Red School House with providing the cultural and spiritual grounding she needed to survive those difficult times.

"The Youth Need a Voice": Student Experiences of Political Education

The political education provided by the survival schools worked differently for different students. At their best, Heart of the Earth and Red School House offered young Indian people a set of integrated, relevant experiences that helped them become more socially aware and more politically empowered. Former Heart of the Earth student Lisa Bellanger recalled in a 2002 interview:

I don't know how many protests and rallies I was at! You know, *learning* about Native rights, *learning* about human rights, *learning* about fairness, and equality, [and] justice.

Although many of those learning opportunities took place outside of the regular school day, Bellanger remembers them as well-connected to the gen-eral curriculum. As she put it, "There were many times that we were out of school doing things, but then we had to relate back to education."[16]

Some of the survival school students' most transformative political ex-periences occurred at national conferences. Throughout the 1970s, students traveled across the country to multitribal gatherings of Indian people spon-sored by the American Indian Movement and other intertribal organiza-tions. They attended meetings of the International Indian Treaty Council and the Federation of Native American Controlled Survival Schools, participated in youth and elders gatherings, and attended annual conferences of the National Indian Education Association. At these meetings, survival school students listened to elders, tribal leaders, and community activists discuss the most pressing concerns of contemporary Indian people: treaty rights, sovereignty, and self-determination; land, water, and mineral resources; health, housing, employment, and education. They also absorbed teachings about cultural values, beliefs, and prophecies and the importance of preserving traditional ways of life.[17]

At these gatherings, students also spoke out about their own concerns and their vision for the future of Indian people, as Lisa Bellanger remembered:

> Students from the survival schools would stand up and say, "You know, the *youth* need a voice in these issues; this is *our* issue, this is what *we* want to talk about." And you would hear young people talking about the responsibilities and rights of sovereignty, and as applied to treaty rights, and as applied to protecting land and natural resources ... [W]e were out there telling people, "You know, you *are*, this *is* a sovereign nation. We have, and should have, the right to government-to-government relationships and negotiations."[18]

Some of these students used their emerging sense of justice to push the adults further along the path to self-determination. At times they also led the call to revive their ancestral knowledge and return to traditional ways of life. According to a report from a 1975 education conference:

> [Survival school] students present at the conference reminded their elders that there were things more important than money and political power. "We never came together before to learn from each other," Sherri Blakey, co-chairman of the Red School House student council said. "Our orientation is spiritual and cultural, as well. A lot of learning can take place in a sweat lodge."[19]

While they spoke to the adults at national conferences, these young leaders also inspired their fellow students. Dorene Day attended many such gatherings while a student at Red School House, and the youth activism she witnessed made an impression:

There was a bunch of young people, that we went to every AIM conference and convention. And we were always doing work, I mean we
were always trying to do stuff—I was probably less active than some of
the other ones. . . . But I remember their actions, their faces, you know,
people that were involved in stuff like that. . . . [S]ome of them, like Lisa
[Bellanger] and Ingrid [Washinawatok], had been at it for a few years by
the time I started going. So I started to watch everything they did.

Before long, Day moved from watching and learning to speaking out and
leading in her own right.[20]

Both Lisa Bellanger and Dorene Day were galvanized by the political
education they received at Heart of the Earth and Red School House. They
cannot, however, give the survival schools the entire credit for their politicization. Both of these young women had family backgrounds that pre-
disposed them to political awareness and activism. Lisa Bellanger's mother
Pat was a longtime community activist, an American Indian Movement
founder, and a survival school organizer. Lisa already had attended many
AIM rallies and conferences by the time she enrolled at Heart of the Earth.
Both of Dorene Day's parents encouraged social awareness in their children from a young age. When Charlotte Day attended AIM protests in the
early 1970s, she often brought her children along. Day's older siblings also
set an activist example. Her brothers and sisters participated in the Trail of
Broken Treaties, the Wounded Knee occupation, and the Longest Walk, and
her older sister Sharon protested against the Vietnam War. The older Day
children also attended Red School House, so that their home and school
environments became mutually reinforcing influences on their developing
political consciousness.[21]

Red School House student Gabrielle Strong also came from a politically
oriented family. A Sisseton-Wahpeton Dakota from South Dakota, Strong
transferred to the St. Paul school for her senior year when the BIA closed the
boarding school she attended in Fort Sill, Oklahoma. Strong's mother, an
AIM supporter, sent her daughter to the survival school in part because of
its AIM affiliation and its politicized curriculum. Although Strong arrived
with a preexisting social awareness, she appreciated the opportunity to exercise it actively as part of her education. Looking back, the marches, protests,
and conferences stood out as highlights of her year at Red School House
and as key contributors to her developing sense of identity.[22]

Not all survival school students experienced their political awakenings as an integrated component of a broader educational curriculum. Rick Powers attended Red School House briefly in 1972. Raised by a non-Indian adoptive family, Powers had grown up knowing little about his Indian heritage. As a teenager, he became a chronic runaway, until he was sent to the juvenile correctional facility at Lino Lakes north of St. Paul. While there he was approached by AIM organizers Billy Blackwell and Butch Old Shield, who offered to help him out of Lino Lakes and get him reconnected to his Native identity. They got Powers released into Old Shield's custody, and within a few days Blackwell, Old Shield, and Eddie Benton-Banai had taken him to a sweat lodge, enrolled him in the Red School House, and helped him take his "first step . . . from the White world into the Indian world."

Powers subsequently embarked on an intense journey of cultural and political awakening. The Red School House, however, contributed little to this process. Drawn to the AIM community in Minneapolis, he began cutting classes to spend time along Franklin Avenue getting to know young Indian people and community activists. When the Trail of Broken Treaties organized in the fall of 1972, Powers joined the caravan, traveled to Washington, D.C., and participated in the occupation of the BIA building. Then, instead of returning to school, he accompanied other AIM members to the Pine Ridge reservation in South Dakota, where he became embroiled in the Lakota community's conflicts with tribal chairman Dick Wilson, their struggle for fair treatment within the justice system, the occupation of Wounded Knee, and its divisive and violent aftermath. Powers eventually retreated from frontline activism, but he never returned to Red School House. In the late 1970s, he earned his high school diploma through the GED program in the St. Paul public school system. For Powers, then, his political development diverged from his formal education—though as an adult, he did return to the survival school system to work at Heart of the Earth in the 1990s.[23]

"It Really Does Extend Itself": Strengthening Native Families

For some of those who completed their education at Red School House or Heart of the Earth, the survival schools shaped their lives in lasting ways. By the turn of the twenty-first century, the schools' influence had extended into the second and third generations of Indian families who had been involved with the schools as founders, administrators, staff members, or students. The first and second generations of survival school families were founders such as Jerry and Pat Roy, Charlotte Day, Pat Bellanger, Clyde and Peggy Bellecourt, and Eddie Benton-Banai, and their children who attended the schools in the 1970s. As these children and other former students grew up, graduated, and began raising families of their own, some of them also sent *their* children to the survival schools for their education, creating a third generation of Indian families whose lives became closely connected to the schools. Pat Bellanger's daughter Lisa, a 1979 Heart of the Earth graduate, had three children attend the school before it closed in 2008: her daughter Binaishi, her younger son Mukwah, and her oldest son Jacob. Charlotte Day's youngest daughter Dorene, who graduated from Red School House in 1977, had four children—Ariana, Bud, Alyssa, and Alana—attend Red School House prior to its closure in 1995.

As parents, these former students wanted their children to experience the kind of educational environment they had loved and be influenced in similarly positive ways. Lisa Bellanger sent her children to Heart of the Earth in order to provide them with the same foundation of cultural practices, symbols, and meanings that had supported her as a teenager. "I wanted them to go to Heart of the Earth," she said, "because I wanted them to experience circle time." Because of the school's grounding in traditional Native culture, "it's helping to instill values that I want instilled in them." Bellanger saw the school environment and the home as mutually reinforcing: "the values that I want my children to learn, are upheld and they're validated at school. And then I, in turn, validate what the school teaches my children; they come home and they ask me about this or that, and we'll talk about it." In the 1960s and 1970s, educational reformers had targeted the dissonance between home and school cultures as one of the most serious problems for Indian public school students. As a three-generation survival school family, the Bellangers stopped the cycle of education-induced cultural alienation and replaced it with one of school-supported cultural reinforcement.[24]

Like Lisa Bellanger, Dorene Day has described the survival school as a place that felt comfortable, safe, and deeply relevant, like a cultural homecoming. She credited that environment with nurturing her intellectual, emotional, and spiritual development. As evidence of her devotion to Red School House, which she attended throughout high school, Day pointed out that though she could have graduated a year early at age seventeen, she chose not to do so. "I loved the place so much," she explained, "that I went to school for another year." When she became a parent, she said, "I wanted that same kind of education for the kids." She wanted them in a small Indian school. She wanted to send them to "a place that will really love kids, and embrace kids, even when they're bad, and they do stuff wrong . . . a place where they know people care about them, 24–7."

More than anything, Day wanted her children in a culturally supportive educational environment. As a young child, Day's daughter Alana was "the kind of kid that danced down the hallway singing Indian songs." Day feared that in a public school, Alana would learn that "artistically or spiritually expressing yourself was wrong." Instead, Day explained, "I want my kids to know that they're respected for their culture, who they are, they're respected for their spirituality." For all of these reasons, Day sent her four oldest children to Red School House until it closed. Then she chose a multicultural alternative high school in St. Paul called Guadalupe Alternative Programs (GAP). Although not exclusively an Indian school, Day described GAP as "the closest thing that I can find to Red School House."[25]

Dorene Day and Lisa Bellanger could not, and did not, rely entirely on these educational institutions to direct their own children's development. But, as they worked to guide their children's lives in positive, meaningful directions, they drew from their experiences at Heart of the Earth and Red School House. By enrolling their children in survival schools when possible, and by passing on the values nurtured by a survival school education, they have raised the next generation of their families to be both culturally grounded and politically engaged.

Lisa's son Mukwah and her daughter Binaishi both were very active in traditional cultural activities as young people. As members of the drum and dance club at Heart of the Earth, they performed regularly at powwows, feasts, graduation ceremonies, and other community events. They faithfully participated in Midewiwin ceremonies and other seasonal gatherings. Lisa's mother Pat Bellanger, survival school founder and proud grandmother, praised Mukwah's affinity for traditional ways of life, even at a young age. In an interview, she gleefully recounted how he had cooked wild rice for the guests at a recent traditional funeral. "You should have seen the elders!" she exclaimed. She also delighted in describing Mukwah's tenth birthday party, where he invited elders as well as children and led his young friends in a traditional honor song for his grandmother.[26]

Like Lisa Bellanger, Dorene Day also raised her children with an Indigenous cultural orientation. As a Red School House graduate, Day attributed her family's solid cultural grounding to the spiritual nourishment she received during her years in the survival school system:

If someone never took me to ceremonies, if someone never took me on a sweat lodge, if someone never took me out in the woods to fast, I wouldn't be the person that I am today. If someone didn't put that kind of energy into me, and didn't tell me all of our history and culture and stories—philosophy, traditions, everything—I wouldn't be the person I am today, and my kids wouldn't be the people *they* are. So, it really does extend itself.

With the birth of her grandson, Omashkoonce (Little Elk), Dorene and her family began encouraging a fourth generation of Days to grow into maturity from a firm cultural foundation. As Day said proudly, "My grandson is already a little Midewiwin boy." This gave her great hope for the future:

My grandson sings at the top of his lungs, with the drum . . . He plays about ceremonies, that's how he plays. He wants to sing, he wants to replicate those things in the lodge that he sees, he wants to dance, he wants to sit by the drum, he wants to do all that. So, he's gonna have those memories *well* before I did; I didn't have those memories till I was twelve, thirteen years old. He has them from birth. And that's going to make a difference.

Because of her grandson's early exposure to traditional culture, Day believes, "he is going to be so far ahead of all of us that he will have some kind of impact."[27]

Survival school graduates also are grooming their children and grandchildren to have an impact on the world by raising them to be socially aware and politically active. Dorene Day educated her family about contemporary Native struggles, such as the fight to save Coldwater Springs, a sacred site in Minneapolis, from destruction during the reroute of Highway 55, and the resistance of the Qwich'in people in Alaska to oil drilling in the Arctic National Wildlife Refuge. Day characterized these efforts as an extension of the political education she received as a young person, from her parents and from the survival schools:

They are having the same kinds of experiences that I had, which hopefully will give them . . . the motivation to stay socially and politically knowledgeable about what happens to them, the environment, to people. 'Cause that's really how I was raised: I was raised going to protests, and I learned early what those fights were about, so I understood that. And so that's how my kids are. My kids, I take them to the American Indian Movement conferences, I take them to protests.

Lisa Bellanger also has continued the legacy of political activism within her family, talking to her children about many of the same issues and bringing them to the same events as Dorene Day.[28]

The children of these multigenerational survival school families have proven relatively resistant to the problems that continue to plague young Native people in the United States, such as high dropout, suicide, and teen pregnancy rates; widespread substance abuse; and entanglement in the juvenile justice and child welfare systems. Lisa Bellanger's oldest child Jacob received most of his education at Heart of the Earth and graduated there in 2002, and she credited the school with helping him avoid destructive life patterns:

> We went through our hard times with him. But, you know what, he's gonna be twenty years old and he's not a father yet. You know, he understands that responsibility. And going into his adult life, he's never been sentenced to serve any time in any correctional facility.

Although Jake had not avoided trouble entirely, his mother was proud of the young man he had become. For Dorene Day, her grandson represented the third generation of Days who might grow up "chemical-free." This is a significant achievement in a family, and a community, with a history of alcohol addiction.[29]

Certainly, there were other influences besides the survival schools that shaped how Dorene Day and Lisa Bellanger raised their children. Both had culturally oriented, politically conscious parents, and both of them had formative experiences at home that influenced their choices as adults. But both Day and Bellanger insisted that without their years in the survival schools, their own families' trajectories would have been drastically different. As Day explained:

> I firmly believe that my kids were exposed to various things all of their lives because of my education. And now my kids are the way they are because of that exposure. And they will do even more with it than I did, you know what I'm saying? . . . [T]he fact that they are starting out way younger, it's gonna make them that much stronger. And it all

comes from that education I got. That's where it all comes from. I'm sure it came from my mother, and from my ancestors as well, but that's where I was able to see the connection; that's where I was able to have it flourish.[30]

Rather than losing more cultural knowledge with each new generation, survival school families like the Days and Bellangers are gaining it. By weaving survival school teachings into their adult lives, they are strengthening the social fabric of Indian families that had been weakened by American colonial policies and assimilationist institutions.

"I Want to Give Back": Rebuilding Native Community

The survival schools' long-term impact also extended beyond the circle of family to influence a broader Indian community. The schools had cultivated a spirit of community-mindedness among young Indian people, encouraging them to work for the collective good of their communities, their tribes, and other Indian and Indigenous people. Over the decades, these teachings bore fruit as Native people nurtured within the survival school system became community workers and cultural leaders, in the Twin Cities and beyond.[31]

Some of the students inspired by the survival schools' lessons about collective responsibility and community commitment returned to work in the schools as teachers, administrators, staff members, or volunteers. After graduating from Heart of the Earth in 1979, Lisa Bellanger worked off and on at the school for a total of ten years, holding positions as a secretary, administrative assistant, computer instructor, adult education tutor, student services coordinator, and career counselor. She also served many years as a school board member. In addition, she spent hundreds of hours volunteering for the school, helping with the drum and dance club, acting as a cheerleading adviser, organizing and chaperoning school events, and shuttling students to powwows, ceremonies, conferences, and protests.[32]

Former Red School House students also returned to work within the survival school system. After graduating from Red School House in 1981, Gabrielle Strong worked at the school as a receptionist, teacher aide, and drug and alcohol counselor before leaving to attend Macalester College in St. Paul. After receiving her bachelor's degree, Strong returned to work as a youth counselor at Ain Dah Yung, a student housing facility and shelter for runaway and homeless Indian youth that was founded and administered by Red School House. Within a year, she became the director at Ain Dah Yung, where she stayed for the next fifteen years. Red School House graduate Sherry Blakey, who had been a student leader in cultural and spiritual activities, also worked at the school after graduating in 1978. Another early student, Keith Herman, returned to Red School House to work as a teacher, counselor, and coach. Five of Charlotte Day's children who attended Red School House in the 1970s—Sharon, Cheryl, Charlene, Janet, and Dorene—worked at the school in some capacity in the years before it closed.[33]

In addition to former students, adults with connections to the survival school community also returned to give something back. Many parents and other relatives of survival school students received GEDs and job training through survival school adult education programs or the American Indian Opportunities Industrialization Center (AIOIC), an AIM-founded vocational training center in Minneapolis. Over the years, some of these family members came back to the schools to share their new skills, often as computer teachers or administrative support staff.[34]

Those whose lives were shaped by the survival schools also have provided educational leadership in other Twin Cities schools. Former Red School House student and employee Keith Herman moved on to work with Indian students at South High School in Minneapolis. Gabrielle Strong, a 1981 Red School House graduate and later an employee, has been a leader in Indian educational reform in St. Paul. In 2002, she was serving her eleventh term as an elected member of the parent committee on Indian education in the St. Paul public school system. Frustrated with the persistent achievement gap and the ongoing alienation of Indian children in the public schools, she also was seeking innovative ways to teach Indian children. In conversations with people in several Dakota communities, she was exploring the possibility of establishing a network of Native home schools focused on language revitalization and grounded in traditional Dakota culture.[35]

Former Heart of the Earth teacher and administrator Vikki Howard also maintained her commitment to improving Indian education in the Twin Cities. After leaving employment at Heart of the Earth in 1995, she helped a Minneapolis Indian agency develop a family education center. She went on to a position as education director at Nawayee Center School, an alternative Indian school founded in Minneapolis in the 1970s and accredited in 1981. In 1998, Howard began working as a community relations coordinator in the Indian studies department at the University of Minnesota. There she engaged in outreach efforts to reservations and the Twin Cities Indian population and acted as an advocate and community builder for Native university students and their families.[36]

Former survival school staff members also have applied the experience gained at Heart of the Earth and Red School House to their work in Indian education outside of the Twin Cities. Vikki Howard worked as education director for the Leech Lake band of Ojibwe on her home reservation in north-central Minnesota. Laura Waterman Wittstock, a Seneca woman who worked as an administrator at both survival schools, helped write funding proposals for the Circle of Life, an Indian community school on the White Earth Ojibwe reservation in northwestern Minnesota. By spring 2012, the Circle of Life school had expanded into a new building, where it delivered a curriculum that followed the survival school model, providing an "individualized, quality, culturally based education that emphasizes maximum academic, emotional, social, spiritual, and physical development for all individuals in a safe and productive environment." Elaine Salinas, a White Earth Ojibwe, served as a program developer and administrator at Heart of the Earth for many years in the 1970s and 1980s. Subsequently, she continued to work for reforms in Indian education through her involvement with the Urban Coalition in Minneapolis and the Rural School and Community Trust on the Oneida reservation in Wisconsin. Rosalie Brown Thunder, a Ho-Chunk from Wisconsin, worked as the elementary principal at Heart of the Earth from the mid-1980s to the early 1990s. In 1993, she left to take a position as tribal education director on her home reservation.[37]

The Day and Bellanger families have made ongoing commitments to work in Indian education, outside of the survival schools as well as in them. In 2002, Red School House graduates Sharon and Dorene Day and Heart of the Earth graduate Lisa Bellanger founded a new alternative Indian school in Minneapolis called Native Arts High School (NAHS). Dorene Day left the project after a year to work as a teacher at Guadalupe Alternative Programs (GAP) high school in St. Paul, where the diverse student body included many Native students. In 2010, Lisa earned an masters in education from the University of Minnesota Duluth and in 2012 she was working as dean of students at Multicultural Indigenous Academy, a charter school in St. Paul.[38]

In their work as educators, Lisa Bellanger and the Day sisters have re-created many aspects of the survival schools. Native Arts High School followed the survival school model of immersing academics within a comprehensive cultural framework based on traditional Native practices, beliefs, and values. NAHS students applied math and physics concepts to the construction of model sweat lodges and a full-sized birch-bark lodge. They learned about science and nutrition by planting and harvesting traditional foods and using them to prepare a meal. Like the Red School House, NAHS also encouraged students' creative expression through journal writing and visual art projects. As a small, mostly Indian school, NAHS also had the intimate family atmosphere and supportive student–staff relationships that characterized the survival schools.[39]

At Guadalupe Alternative Programs high school in St. Paul, Dorene Day worked in a larger and significantly more diverse institution than NAHS. Even so, Day was drawn to GAP because of the ways in which it resembled Red School House. She liked the fact that educators at GAP provided a supportive, loving environment for students, even those branded "troublemakers" by other schools. She appreciated that the educational philosophy at GAP encouraged a holistic approach to learning that integrated intellectual, emotional, and spiritual development. In an interview, she contrasted this environment with the typical public school, where "you're supposed to do everything with your brain." Gesturing back and forth between her head and her heart, she continued:

> [In a public school] you're not supposed to connect the two. Well, how I learned everything I learned is by connecting the two. So, that's why I try to re-create that for kids, because they need to know that that's how they're going to live life anyway. If they're gonna make good, responsible . . . healthy choices, they're gonna have to have those two things working together. They're gonna have to have their mind and their emotions *intact* enough so they can navigate [those decisions].

As a teacher, Day felt comfortable at GAP because the school valued all dimensions of a child's development, "whether it's math, or writing, or the sweat lodge."[40]

Day remained at GAP in large part because of the school's commitment to providing students with spiritually meaningful experiences. On a regular basis, she said, "something is taking place that's getting them connected" to "things of a spiritual nature." Some of those spiritual experiences, like time in the sweat lodge, came from American Indian traditions, while some reflected the other cultural backgrounds of GAP students. The survival school philosophy, especially as it developed at Red School House, had promoted understanding of Indian culture among non-Indian people. As a Red School House student, Day participated in cultural outreach efforts within Twin Cities public schools. As a teacher at GAP, she facilitated an exchange of cultural perspectives among a diverse student population. For her, this multicultural, spiritually grounded quality of GAP education made the school a "cultural oasis" in the city.[41]

No school has replaced Red School House in the hearts of the Days and the other Indian families whose lives were centered there. As Dorene Day said, "There'll never be another Red School House." Yet she has learned to live with its loss by recognizing its lasting legacy:

> I used to be really sad about it being gone. . . . And now I've sort of had this healing process over the years, that this is always going to be here, as long as I'm alive and I'm teaching it. And as long as someone else after me picks it up and teaches it, it's still going to be alive.[42]

Thus the spirit of Red School House lives on, in the community leadership and cultural work of people like Dorene Day and those whose lives she influences.

In their work at GAP and NAHS, Dorene Day and Lisa Bellanger also perpetuated the survival school practice of cultivating political awareness and action among their students. Both brought students to protests and demonstrations related to contemporary Indian issues. In the fall of 2002, Day educated GAP staff members and students about the University of Minnesota's plans to participate in the building of a telescope on Mount Graham in Arizona, a site considered sacred by the Apache people. Day and other Twin Cities Indian activists had been protesting the university's involvement in the project, and she encouraged like-minded GAP students to register their concerns with the Board of Regents.[43]

Besides their work in education, survival school people have labored in other ways to improve the lives and conditions of Indian people. Some are former staff members whose time at the schools inspired a commitment to community-based work. Jeannette "Poncho" Jones, a former Red School House parent and employee, went on to work as a youth counselor at the Upper Midwest American Indian Center in Minneapolis. Pat Bellanger credited Jones's involvement at Red School House for giving her the training and confidence to become an active community worker. A former Heart of the Earth bus driver named Arnold Stands continued to act on the schools' teachings by providing services to needy Indian elders in Minneapolis.[44]

Former survival school students also have worked for their communities in a variety of agencies and institutions. One of the first Heart of the Earth students became an attorney and a tribal council member on the Flandreau reservation in South Dakota. Lisa Bellanger remembered her speaking at the 2001 graduation ceremonies "about how Heart of the Earth had changed her life" and "broadened her whole sense of . . . who she is as a Native woman." Red School House graduate and former Ain Dah Yung director Gabrielle Strong went on to become a program officer at the Grotto Foundation. There she administered grant programs supporting Native families, communities, languages, and cultures. Former Red School House student and employee Charlene Day worked as a family advocate for the Minnesota Chippewa Tribe at its urban office in Minneapolis. A few blocks down Franklin Avenue, her sister Sharon, also a former Red School House student and staff member, served as director of the Indigenous People's Task Force, providing social and spiritual services to Native people living with HIV and AIDS. Walter Pederford, another early Red School House student, joined the St. Paul police force. As an officer, Pederford encouraged Indian youth to stay in school, avoid drugs and alcohol, and become involved in drum groups and other cultural activities.[45]

Certainly, the schools could not inspire everyone who encountered them to make the world a better place for Indian people. In some cases, the schools were unable to prevent troubled Indian youth from continuing along a self-destructive path. Although Dorene Day asserted that "we left those schools knowing that we could do whatever it is we wanted to do," she also acknowledged that "there were kids that really grasped on to that, and worked that well, and there were other kids that still fell into things":

> I have friends that I graduated with that drank themselves to death. I have friends that I grew up with in the Red School House that have as many kids as me, but don't have a financial means to take care of them the way I do. So, I've seen a lot of different things. And I think what it breaks down to is, on an individual basis, what you do with what you carry, how you live out those teachings in your life. Some of us did it to the fullest, like myself, and some of us didn't.[46]

Lisa Bellanger reflected, "I know there's some students that went to Heart of the Earth that never got it. And I don't know if they ever will, because their family environment might not support those same values." In her own experience, she found that "being part of a family where I hear it outside of school and in school makes a difference for me." Not all survival school students experienced the same sort of reinforcement in the home.[47]

Yet Bellanger expressed hope, even for those who did not recognize the benefits of a survival school education in their youth:

> I know that there are some that never got it early on, but as adults now, are starting to look back and realize what it is that made a difference in their life. You know, maybe they have sobered up or maybe they have had some kind of a change of experience, where they realize how important it is to think about their traditions, and they go back: "I remember at Heart of the Earth, we used to do it like this." And if it's one memory that helps them to change or to grow in a good, positive, strong way as an adult, I think that's really important.

She concluded, "I think what Heart of the Earth planted was seeds."[48]

Even for those who committed themselves to community work as adults, the survival schools provided just one influence among many. Students like Lisa Bellanger, Gabrielle Strong, and the Day siblings came from families that encouraged their children to live within their cultural traditions and carry collective responsibility for community well-being. These families also cultivated a wide-ranging political consciousness that motivated their children to become activists as adults. Survival school employees like Vikki Howard, Laura Waterman Wittstock, and Elaine Salinas also had engaged in community activism prior to their time at Red School House and Heart of the Earth.

Although the survival schools were not the only influence on these individuals' community leadership, they were *an* influence. Many Native people became drawn into the orbit of the schools and the work of the American Indian Movement over time as students, family members, employees, and volunteers. For at least some of these people, their time in the schools influenced their future paths in significant ways. At the very least, the schools encouraged a preexisting community orientation. Gabrielle Strong was careful to point out in an interview that "I always knew, and felt, that I didn't want to work anywhere else but for and within my own community; that's just something that I always had within me." At the same time, she acknowledged, "that was nurtured at Red School House."[49]

As a place of employment, the survival schools provided a system in which Native people could practice their commitment to community-based work. Strong, whose very first job out of high school was working for Red School House, said of her experience:

> I was happy to come back, I was really thrilled. I thought, Yeah, I'm going back to work, and giving back to the school. That was really good for me, I really liked that idea. I felt really good about that.

In her time as a Red School House employee, Strong worked her way up from a receptionist position to become the director of Ain Dah Yung, a Red School House–affiliated housing facility for homeless and runaway Indian youth. Under her leadership, Ain Dah Yung split off from the school to become an independent, $1.6-million agency providing culture-specific social services to Indian youth and families in the Twin Cities. During her years at Red School House and Ain Dah Yung, Strong gained valuable skills in working with Indian families, administering community programs, and managing a complex service organization. Those experiences helped shape her into a compassionate, clear-eyed community leader.[50]

Having the opportunity to work for their own communities through programs, services, and institutions of their own making and under their own control had tremendous significance for Native people, particularly in the 1970s and 1980s. For nearly two hundred years, federal Indian policy had limited Indigenous sovereignty and eroded Native people's ability to determine their own futures. In the post–World War II period, federal and state policies, as well as local institutional practices, intruded deeply into Native families and exerted significant control over the social reality of Indian communities. The practice of self-determination, through the survival schools and other community-controlled, Indian-led programs, thus altered long-standing, powerful historical patterns.

Some of what Indian people learned through their involvement with the survival schools was lessons about how *not* to operate community institutions. In interviews, Gabrielle Strong credited Red School House leaders with creating an inspirational model for culture-based Indian education, and she expressed gratitude for her many positive experiences during her year as a student there. Yet she also asked, "From those painful experiences that we all had there—and there *were* painful experiences—what did we learn from that? And how could we do it better?" During her time as a student and employee and in her years working for an affiliated agency, Strong learned the necessity of hiring people for their ability to teach well, provide effective services, and ensure a safe environment for children, rather than out of loyalty to relatives or friends. At Red School House, she says, this was not always the case. Former Red School House student Rick Powers, who worked at Heart of the Earth in the mid-1990s, also criticized the practice of hiring or retaining employees for reasons of personal loyalty rather than merit. Such staffing decisions had negative consequences during his time at the school, weakening educational programming and escalating inter-personal conflicts in ways that undermined the cohesion of the survival school community.[51]

From her experiences at the St. Paul survival school, Gabrielle Strong also came to believe in the critical importance of hiring staff members who would provide good role models for Indian youth and whose actions con-sistently embodied the values they taught. Among some Red School House teachers and administrators, she said, "there was a disparity sometimes, in what people talked, and how they walked." Strong knows that in the early years of running their own school, "people did the best they could, the best they knew how." Yet the hypocrisy of some Red School House staff mem-bers around issues such as alcohol and drug use had a "detrimental effect" on Strong and other students. Learning from those experiences later shaped her priorities as an educational leader.[52]

Strong learned other lessons from her involvement with Red School House. She came to believe that building successful community institutions requires leadership from people who can translate an inspiring vision into sustainable practice:

> I think it did boil down to, how do we manage resources, and *did* we know how to manage resources back then? . . . Because everything be-gins with a vision, and a concept, but along with that you need a plan, right? You need a good plan to enact it. And you need people with integ-rity to caretake the resources that go along with putting that plan into action, whether it's money, or space, or staff. And I don't know that we knew all that then. And that's where things broke down, in the carrying out of that vision.

Strong also asserted that while Red School House had some "dynamic, vi-sionary leaders," too many of them "were very territorial, or very dictato-rial." Healthy institutions, she maintained, need leaders who cultivate future leaders among the youth and within their communities, rather than trying to control everything themselves.[53]

At their best, the survival schools offered a positive model for those who wanted to create change for Indian people through community-controlled institutions. While expressing some sharp criticisms, Gabrielle Strong also acknowledged that the survival schools stood on the cutting edge of Indian self-determination, and that they set a precedent for others to follow. "This was an era," she pointed out, "when Indian people were in charge for the very first time." The people of the survival schools provided inspiration for those of younger generations, even though they made mistakes along the way.[54]

For some young Indian people, their time at the schools guided their development into cultural workers and community leaders in absolutely critical ways. Both Lisa Bellanger and Dorene Day spoke frequently in interviews of the internal drive to "give something back" that has motivated their seemingly tireless community work, and both gave the survival schools credit for feeding the force that has driven them all their adult lives. In conversations about her work as a spiritual leader, Dorene Day consistently traced it back to her time at Red School House:

> That's important to me, to be able to give back something, 'cause I have received so much ... as a result of my cultural and spiritual education.... To me, that deserves a really big celebration. So, part of how I celebrate is to do what I do, you know? I sing, take kids to the sweat lodge—I really, really wanted this really simplistic life, and it's probably never gonna be that way, 'cause I always feel like there's lots of work to do.[55]

Lisa Bellanger spoke in similar ways about her decision as a young adult to accept a job offer at Heart of the Earth:

> I want to give back. I want to do that, and that was done for me, and that was why I went back to work at Heart of the Earth.... And people said, "How come you left your job at the city to work at Heart of the Earth, you know, there's *no* job security. You never know if you're gonna have a job the next year or not, you never know if the school's gonna be there the next year." And I just said, "Well, I want to give back to the school and to the kids, what the school gave to me."

The example set by survival school founders and teachers, Bellanger said, was the reason "why I wanted to give back: I wanted to be that person that helped me. I wanted to be like [Ojibwe language and culture teacher] Ona Kingbird, I want to be like [Heart of the Earth principal] Chuck Robertson, I want to be like Clyde Bellecourt . . . I want to be like my mom." Of her deeply ingrained "community sense" Bellanger said: "I really owe that to the survival schools." She insisted that "what Heart of the Earth gave me really did form and give me a foundation of who I am today. I didn't get that at [the St. Paul] Open School, I didn't get that at public school; I *know* I got it at Heart of the Earth."[56]

In Bellanger's opinion, her experience is not unique. Although she acknowledged that her mother's cultural orientation and community activism gave her "more of an opportunity . . . than the other students," she believes that other young Indian people also left Heart of the Earth and Red School House with comparable experiences and similar commitments to community work. As survival school educators involved students in feasts, powwows, ceremonies, and other communal gatherings, "that became a part of our life and a part of things that we liked to do. So, now that we're older, most of the students that *I* remember from Red School House and from Heart of the Earth, some of the longer-term students, still have a really strong foundation, or sense of community." That foundation comes from "the schools' emphasis on culture and traditions and teachings." It was because of these teachings, Lisa Bellanger said, that Dorene Day now "works in the heart of the community." Because of Dorene, her sisters, and other former students, Bellanger said, "I think that the biggest thing that I've seen the survival schools do is create a level of individuals that have a sense of community and culture." Those individuals have become "the pillar of culture, and a pillar of community-centeredness."[57]

"Bringing Back" Indigenousness: Cultural Revitalization and Indigenous Decolonization

From their founding in 1972, the survival schools strengthened Native families, built Indian community, and reclaimed Indigenous knowledge and identities. They helped Native youth and adults discover and reconnect to their tribal heritage and expand their political consciousness, and they furthered the practice of Indian self-determination through community-controlled institutions. Taken together, these processes represent a kind of Indigenous decolonization. The AIM survival schools furthered social, cultural, and psychological decolonization for Native people in the Twin Cities and elsewhere in the upper Midwest. This outcome of the survival school system has outlasted the schools themselves.

The historical process of European and Euro-American colonialism in North America had material and physical consequences for the Native people whose lands became occupied and exploited, including territorial dispossession, resource depletion, economic dependence, military conquest, epidemic disease, and unprecedented depopulation. For Native North Americans, as for other colonized peoples, there also were less tangible consequences. Land loss, military conflict, and competition over diminishing resources disrupted subsistence patterns that had defined Indigenous societies and anchored their worldviews for centuries. European and American explorers, missionaries, traders, negotiators, and military and government agents dealt with Native people in ways that undermined traditional political leadership, kinship networks, gender roles, and family relationships. With U.S. territorial expansion and the implementation of removal and reservation policies in the eighteenth and nineteenth centuries, tribal people lost control over nearly every aspect of their lives.

As Native people were alienated from their homelands and the U.S. government extended its authority over their communities, the psychological, social, cultural, and spiritual consequences of American colonialism became increasingly severe. They included the loss of language, songs, and ceremonies; the erosion of spiritual beliefs; the weakening of value systems; and the unraveling of collective identities that had developed over centuries of people's adaptation to and identification with the places where they dwelled. Intrusive federal policies also deliberately destabilized family and community structures and disrupted the passing of cultural knowledge from generation to generation.

The sociopsychological effects of what Mi'kmaq education scholar Marie Battiste terms "cognitive imperialism" and what Chickasaw legal philosopher James Youngblood Henderson calls "the cognitive legacy of colonization" were devastating for Indigenous individuals and communities, and their legacy has persisted over multiple generations. Battiste defines cognitive imperialism as "the imposition of one worldview on a people who have an alternative worldview, with the implication that the imposed worldview is superior," thus working to "disclaim other knowledge bases and values" in a way that "denies people their language and cultural integrity by maintaining the legitimacy of only one language, one culture, and one frame of reference." Thus, colonialism creates an entire cognitive system that, according to Henderson, "explicitly and implicitly confirms Aboriginal inadequacy and asserts a negative image of Aboriginal heritage and identity." For generations of Native people living within such a system, this has resulted in a kind of "cognitive imprisonment." Ultimately, Battiste argues, cognitive colonialism becomes "the means by which whole groups of people have been denied existence"—an outcome that, not incidentally, also "has been used . . . as the means of confiscating" their land and resources.[58]

From this perspective, the work of Indigenous decolonization must go beyond the restoration of the land base, the reclamation of resources, and the reassertion of political sovereignty. It also must address what human rights scholar Erica-Irene Daes calls the "subjective, social, and spiritual" effects of colonialism and their ongoing manifestations in contemporary Native societies. Seminole historian Susan Miller writes that through this work, "Indigenous communities and nations decolonize their collective identities and their institutions, and individuals decolonize their minds and their ways of interacting and participating in institutions." She also describes a process of "bringing back," a "movement to revitalize Indigenous languages and recover lapsed Indigenous practices" as well as "ancestral skills and concepts," thus "reclaiming the knowledge" and restoring the "lost heritage" that U.S. policies suppressed. Marie Battiste defines decolonization as "a source of deconstruction and reconstruction" that rejects colonial categories and dismantles Eurocentric cognitive systems while restoring "Indigenous knowledge and heritage." Thus, decolonization is a process of "healing and rebuilding" Indigenous "nations . . . communities, and selves."[59]

The AIM survival schools contributed to these processes of social, cultural, and cognitive decolonization for American Indigenous people. They furthered sociocultural decolonization in part through the rebuilding of traditional extended family structures. The schools brought siblings, parents, grandparents, aunts, and uncles together in their classrooms, offices, and programs and at their social gatherings. They fostered familial relationships among their students and staff members and encouraged students' parents and other family members to become closely integrated into the life of the schools. By involving students' relatives and other community members in their programs, the survival schools reinvigorated the commitment to extended family that had anchored traditional Native cultures. Parents, other relations, friends, neighbors, and anyone else interested in students' lives and invested in their well-being—all were considered essential partici-pants in their education and valuable contributors to their process of intel-lectual, emotional, and spiritual growth.

From the beginning, the schools also were built on a model of parental and community control over staffing, structure, curriculum, and pedagogy. For Twin Cities Indian people, involvement in their children's education and community control over school governance had profound historical and political significance. Since the mid-nineteenth century, Native people's experiences with formal schooling in the United States had been defined by the *loss* of control. Within the federal boarding school system, Indian families and communities lost influence not only over their children's edu-cation but over their entire social and cultural development. In the public schools of the post–World War II period, Indian parents felt alienated from the mainstream educational system, and many retained traumatic personal and familial memories from the boarding schools. Some responded by dis-investing themselves from their children's education. Others tried to en-gage with it but struggled to navigate what they experienced as a hostile environment.

The commitment of survival school founders to involve families di-rectly in their children's education, and their efforts to knit community members closely into the fabric of school life, represented a seismic shift in Twin Cities Indian people's relationships to schooling. Because Heart of the Earth and Red School House enrolled mostly Native students, parental control over school governance also meant *Indian* control over Indian edu-cation. Instead of non-Indian people setting the parameters for their experi-ence, Native people were creating an alternative social reality, constructed through a system of their own making. This made the survival schools sites where Indian people practiced the decolonization of their children's edu-cation. They worked to repair the social and psychological damage caused by the mission school and boarding school education of earlier decades. They also resisted the assimilationist imperative operating in postwar public schools, which worked more subtly to neutralize or eliminate the Indigenous alternative in modern American life. Thus they furthered what Mi'kmaq scholar Marie Battiste has identified as the "deconstruction" work of decolonization, by exposing the fallacies of colonial education systems and challenging their hegemony over Native people's mental universes.[60]

The survival schools also revived aspects of traditional Indigenous peda-gogical practices. According to Gregory Cajete:

> Indigenous education is, in its truest form, about learning relationships in context. This context begins with family. It extends to the clan, to the community and tribe, and to all of the world. The goal is completeness. . . . Our idea of education is a reflection of that social ecology.[61]

Marie Battiste describes an Indigenous education as one that furthers young people's "development as human beings" in ways that "involve the elders and our life ways" throughout the development process. The survival schools did this by incorporating extended family and community members into their students' learning and personal development; involving elders as teachers of traditional knowledge and skills; instructing students in cultural values through observation and experiential practice; and approaching education as a holistic, integrated process with intellectual, physical, emotional, social, and spiritual dimensions. In these ways, they reinvigorated Indigenous models for nurturing the next generation into adulthood.[62]

In many ways, the schools functioned as extended family and community structures would have in traditional Indigenous society, but in a form adapted to twentieth-century urban circumstances. Thus they contributed to what Marie Battiste has identified as the "reconstruction" work of decolonization, repairing some of the damage inflicted by generations of social disruption and rebuilding a version of precolonial Indigenous societies. Through their multidimensional community presence, the schools also embodied key values they hoped to instill in their students: the acceptance of responsibility to one's community and the willingness to work collectively for the good of Indian people. As the survival school system fostered these values, it protected Indigenous ways of being. To survival school educators, community-mindedness was a fundamental component of Indigenous identity. Within the schools, lessons about community responsibility and social activism were taught within a traditional cultural context. Those who spent time at Heart of the Earth and Red School House learned that the work of preserving Native languages and restoring ancestral knowledge was critical to the survival of their people.[63]

The most powerful kind of decolonization practiced by the survival schools was their contribution to the revitalization of Indigenous knowledge and identity. Heart of the Earth and Red School House taught Native languages and encouraged their use in daily school life, and they involved students in the practice of traditional subsistence skills. They taught students tribal and intertribal dances, songs, and ceremonies and introduced them to Native values and belief systems. They encouraged students to discover who they were as Indian people, and within that process of discovery to find a sense of self-worth. In all these ways, survival school educators helped build what Hawaiian Indigenous rights activist Poka Laenui has described as "the foundation" of Indigenous decolonization: the individual and collective process of "rediscovery and recovery," of language, identity, and pride.[64]

Some of those nurtured within the survival schools went on to become local and regional leaders in the process of Indigenous cultural and spiritual revitalization, becoming the "pillar of culture" to which Lisa Bellanger referred. Vikki Howard, who worked at Heart of the Earth as a teacher and school principal, credits the survival school environment for reconnecting her with her cultural identity and practice:

> Through the movement I was exposed to . . . spirituality, different elders. All this came about as I started working at Heart of the Earth. And that's when I began my journey to find my way and that's where I found my way back to the Anishinaabe way of life.[65]

Howard's family had been oriented toward their traditional culture and she had been engaged in political activism and aligned with AIM since her high school years in Minneapolis in the early 1970s. Yet she locates her personal cultural awakening during her time at Heart of the Earth. Since then, Howard has carried her commitment to Indigenous cultural and spiritual practice into her work as an educator and community advocate, in the Twin Cities and on her home reservation in northern Minnesota.

Many of the survival school people who became community leaders have incorporated cultural revitalization into their work as educators, counselors, community advocates, and administrators of service agencies, while others have made cultural work their primary focus. Ron Leith, a former student and then a teacher at Red School House, went on to run cultural and spiritual programs for the Lower Sioux Dakota community in southern Minnesota and helped organize sun dance ceremonies. Red School House Lakota teacher Jerry Dearly became a fixture at Twin Cities area powwows and other cultural gatherings as a master of ceremonies, storyteller, and respected traditional singer. Former Red School House student Paula Horn organized annual spiritual gatherings held in sacred places around the world.[66]

Since the early 1980s, survival school people have led a modern revitalization movement dedicated to restoring the practice of traditional Anishinaabe culture and spirituality in the upper Midwest and the transnational Great Lakes region. Called the Three Fires Society, this movement works to maintain and strengthen the Ojibwe language as well as the ancestral teachings and spiritual ceremonies of the Anishinaabe people, as practiced through the Midewiwin lodge. The Anishinaabeg are linguistically and culturally related peoples whose ancestors migrated over hundreds of years from the East Coast, along the St. Lawrence River, and westward through the Great Lakes. According to oral tradition, they were fulfilling a prophecy, on a journey in search of the place "where food grows on water," which they found in wild rice. Various groups of Anishinaabeg settled at different points along the migration route, eventually coalescing into the Ojibwe, Odawa, and Potawatomi peoples. During the colonial period, these three tribes maintained cultural, political, and military ties through the Three Fires confederacy and through their common history.[67]

The ancestors of those Anishinaabeg who became the Ojibwe people eventually settled along the south shore of Lake Superior in present-day Wisconsin. There they established their cultural homeland and built a way of life spiritually centered on an island that they called Moningwunakawning. French explorers renamed it LaPointe; later it was called Madeline Island, and it now forms part of the Apostle Islands. At the core of this way of life, for the Ojibwes as for other Anishinaabe people, was a seasonal round of communal subsistence activities in which small bands of people worked together to hunt, gather, and cultivate the land. In the winter, multiple extended families lived together in a village settlement where they hunted, maintained trap lines, and made and repaired clothing and tools. During the spring, summer, and fall, smaller groups of families set up seasonal camps in different parts of their homeland to tap maple trees, gather berries and medicinal plants, fish, garden, hunt, trap, and harvest wild rice. This seasonal round, while defining the people's economy, also ordered the maintenance of social relationships through collective gatherings for feasts, dances, giveaways, and ceremonies. Social roles and responsibilities were based in the clan system and individuals understood their collective identities through a kinship network of extended families and bands.[68]

The most important seasonal gatherings were for the Midewiwin ceremonies, which were the spiritual heart of the Anishinaabe people. The Midewiwin lodge, also known as the Grand Medicine Society, was based on principles of physical and spiritual healing and the maintenance of harmony and balance among people and between human beings and the rest of the creation. Mide priests were respected healers and spiritual leaders who guided the people down the path of living a good life. Periodically, people from scattered camps and villages came together on Moningwunakawning for several days of Midewiwin ceremonies. There they listened to the teachings of Mide leaders; performed rituals and prayers of thanksgiving, honor, and respect for the creation; contemplated their place in the universe; and reaffirmed their collective commitment to what Ojibwe historian Paulette Fairbanks Molin has called their "philosophy of living."[69]

In the early 1980s, Red School House founder Eddie Benton-Banai and other survival school people revived the Midewiwin lodge as a center for Indigenous spiritual practice and Anishinaabe identity, through the formation of the Three Fires Society. Since then, Mide followers have gathered for seasonal ceremonies at various sites in the upper Midwest and the Great Lakes region of the United States and Canada. In recent years, they have met most frequently near the Bad River reservation along the south shore of Lake Superior in Wisconsin, not far from Madeline Island and in the heart of the Anishinaabe homeland. Members of the Three Fires Society also hold Ojibwe-language immersion camps for Native youth and travel to Indigenous communities in the United States and Canada to facilitate workshops, deliver lectures, share their drum and dance groups, and perform healing ceremonies. Through all of these activities, the Three Fires Society promotes the traditional Anishinaabe value and belief system as a means to "spiritual, physical, emotional, and mental well-being." They offer Midewiwin teachings and ceremonial practices as an antidote to alcohol and drug abuse, family violence, self-loathing, hopelessness, and social disintegration.[70]

By the early twenty-first century, the Three Fires Midewiwin Society had grown into a multitribal, international community, with a membership of more than two thousand people from Indigenous communities in the United States, Canada, Mexico, and Central America. Yet it has remained rooted in Anishinaabe culture and centered on Midewiwin teachings. Geographically as well as spiritually, it has been grounded in Ojibwe communities in northern Wisconsin, particularly at the Lac Courte Oreilles and Bad River reservations. Much of the leadership within the Three Fires Society has come from people who spent years within the survival school system. Eddie Benton-Banai, founder and longtime director of Red School

House, was and still is the movement's spiritual leader, serving as the Grand Chief of the Midewiwin lodge. Former Red School House cultural instructor Walter "Porky" White was the president of the Three Fires board of directors until his death in November 2001. Other members of the board have included Lisa Bellanger, Dorene Day, and Ramon Benton, the son of Eddie Benton-Banai and a former Red School House student.[71]

Seasonal Midewiwin ceremonies held near the Bad River reservation in northern Wisconsin hold particular significance. It is here that, in anthropological terms, the ethnogenesis of the Anishinaabe people occurred, long before European contact. Those who revived the Midewiwin lodge through the Three Fires Society thus have returned Anishinaabe spiritual practices to the place where they began. This is where Anishinaabe culture first developed, and where it flourished for generations before the first contacts

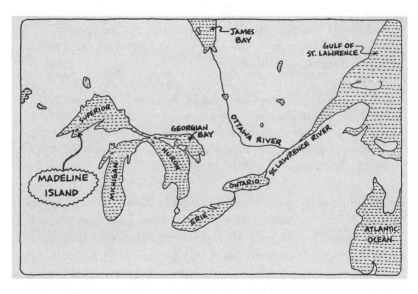

In Book 1 of the "Mishomis Book" coloring book series, The Ojibway Creation Story, *Eddie Benton-Banai traced the historical migration of the Anishinaabe people west through the Great Lakes to Moningwunakawning (Madeline Island), the center of the Ojibwe people's traditional homeland. Since the 1980s, Benton-Banai and other survival school people have held seasonal Midewiwin ceremonies near this sacred island, along the south shore of Lake Superior in northern Wisconsin. From* A Mishomis Book: A History-Coloring Book of the Ojibway Indians, Book 1, *illustration by Joe Liles, published by Indian Country Communications, Inc.; reprinted with permission.*

with French explorers, fur traders, and missionaries in the early seventeenth century. Through the seventeenth and eighteenth centuries, Anishinaabe people had successfully negotiated the French, British, and then American presence in the western Great Lakes region. Until the War of 1812 solidified American control of the upper Midwest, they had participated fully in the creation of a dynamic mixed society. They also maintained a distinctive transnational identity as Anishinaabe people, whose economic and cultural orientation to the Great Lakes crossed the border imposed by the creation of the U.S. and Canadian nation-states.[72]

Reconnecting Native people to their homelands and restoring an Indigenous relationship to place are essential components of decolonization. In this context, survival school people's revival of seasonal Midewiwin ceremonies on the south shore of Lake Superior, near Moningwunakawning (Madeline Island)—the place where the Anishinaabe people have their cultural origins—becomes especially meaningful. Maintaining their interdependent relationships with all beings in the context of a particular place provides the essential grounding for an Indigenous identity. As James Youngblood Henderson describes it:

> Aboriginal understandings, languages, teachings, and practices developed through direct interaction with the forces of the natural order of ecology. This experience intimately connects their worldviews and knowledge with a certain space. This is more than mere ecological awareness; it is a living relationship with a specific environment.

According to Henderson, "Aboriginal worldviews are empirical relationships with local ecosystems, and Aboriginal languages are an expression of these relationships." Blackfoot Native studies scholar Leroy Little Bear describes "Aboriginal philosophy" as "firmly grounded in a particular place," while Susan Miller has defined Indigenousness as "a way of relating to everything else in the cosmos," in which "human communities are bound to the land in an intimate and committed relationship," guided by principles and ritual practices of "reciprocity (or balance) and respect." Thus "the well-being of Indigenous communities" depends on the maintenance of an "ongoing integrated relationship" with the land and all the other beings of a particular place.[73]

As Little Bear describes Indigenous philosophy, upholding these place-based, reciprocal relationships not only ensures Native people's survival; it keeps the world intact. He writes that "the function of Aboriginal values and customs is to maintain the relationships that hold creation together." According to this worldview, "if creation is to continue, then it must be renewed. Renewal ceremonies, the telling and retelling of creation stories, the singing and resinging of the songs, are all humans' part in the maintenance of creation." For Indigenous people, as Susan Miller explains, their "relation to the sacred is encoded in the language."[74] Thus it is critical that the stories be told, the songs sung, and the ceremonies conducted in the people's Native language.

By building a seasonal Midewiwin lodge at the site of the Anishinaabe people's cultural origins, and by reclaiming that space for songs, dances, teachings, and ceremonies conducted in the Ojibwe language, the Three Fires Society has restored what American colonialism worked to destroy: a distinctly Indigenous, sacred relationship to creation, grounded in its proper place. This has powerful meaning for individual psychologies and personal identity development. As James Youngblood Henderson explains, in order to "understand the meaning of life," Indigenous people must "re-establish a relationship with their local ecological order." Midewiwin ceremonies also rebuild a collective Anishinaabe identity, as participants carry out communal cultural practices necessary to fulfilling their people's role within the interdependent web of living beings, thus doing their part to maintain the balance of the universe.[75]

Arguing that survival school people worked as agents of Indigenous decolonization does not mean that they always did so effectively, nor would I claim that everything AIM people did, locally or nationally, furthered the process of decolonization. Some AIM leaders and some survival school educators made choices and engaged in behaviors that contradicted their own profession of Indigenous beliefs and values. Some took actions that undermined the schools' founding ideals, hurt Indian families, and compromised the well-being of Native communities. Even at their best, the people of Heart of the Earth and Red School House made mistakes, and sometimes their work fell short of their own expansive vision for Indigenous education.

Following Marie Battiste's definition of decolonization as involving both the "deconstruction" of the colonial paradigm and the "reconstruction" of Indigenous consciousness, one might argue that the cognitive *de*construction that took place in the survival schools, particularly in the more political components of their curriculum, was oversimplified and at times heavy-handed. Their efforts at cultural *re*construction were complicated by their

The Midewiwin Lodge

The Lodge is the center of all thought, planning and action. The lodge structure and all that flows from it is based upon the natural laws of creation, for example: traditional forms of government, societal framework, communication, relationship with the land, health, law, and artistic expression, peace and freedom.

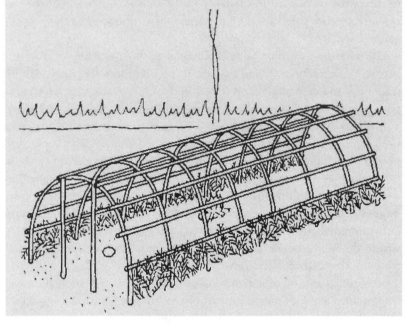

The Three Fires Society, led by Eddie Benton-Banai and other survival school people, has helped restore the teachings, traditions, and seasonal ceremonies of the Midewiwin lodge, the spiritual heart of traditional Anishinaabe life. The people of the Three Fires Society have practiced Indigenous decolonization for Anishinaabe and other Native people in the western Great Lakes region and provided a foundation for a modern Anishinaabe identity. They contribute to the revitalization of the Ojibwe language through lodge ceremonies, immersion education, and other language initiatives. From a 2003 Three Fires Society brochure; illustration by Joe Liles.

urban location, multitribal student population, and financial instability, and undermined by the mid-1970s federal backlash against AIM, inexpert and at times corrupt management, and internal ideological conflicts. It seems possible—from an outsider's perspective and in theoretical hindsight— that some of the schools' interpersonal conflicts, especially at their most intense in the 1980s and 1990s, might have been in part disagreements about whether and to what degree individual administrators and teachers were committed to the project of decolonization and whether they wanted the schools to function as decolonizing institutions.[76]

Although in some ways troubling, the messier dimensions of survival school history and the unevenness with which the schools practiced Indigenous decolonization are not surprising when considered in their historical context. From the schools' founding in 1972 through the 1980s, they were on the experimental edge of alternative, community-controlled, culture-based Indian education, particularly in urban areas. They had few models and little to draw from for appropriate curriculum materials. Most of their people lacked relevant training to carry out the responsibilities they took on.

Although the AIM organizers who founded and staffed the survival schools developed a creative educational philosophy, they were not intellectuals; few of them even had college degrees. Even if they had been academically oriented, in the 1970s the field of postcolonial theory was in its infancy. Moreover, it was not until the late 1990s that scholars began to develop decolonization theories from distinctly Indigenous perspectives and analyze the dynamics of settler colonialism and the place of Native peoples in contemporary settler societies. It is only in the last decade that scholars have begun systematically to apply these theoretical insights to Indigenous people in the United States. Still, these schools helped pave the way for others to practice culture-based, community-controlled Indian education. They made something new seem possible.

Maori scholar Linda Tuhiwai Te Rina Smith has written about what happens when Indigenous communities put decolonization theory into practice. Drawing from her experience with community-controlled Maori immersion schools in Aotearoa/New Zealand, she observes that when Indigenous people "take hold of the project of emancipation and attempt to make it reality ... [t]he end result cannot be predetermined. The means to the end involves human agency in ways that are complex and contradictory." One can try to contain, but cannot entirely avoid, "the unevenness and unpredictability, under stress, of people engaged in emancipatory struggles."

While "Western academics" might "quibble about the success or failure of the emancipatory project and question the idealism that lies behind it . . . this stance assumes that oppression has universal characteristics that are independent of history, context, and agency. At the level of abstraction, this is what has to be argued, in a sense, but it can never be so on the ground."[77]

Within decolonizing projects like the survival schools, carried out by common human beings in particular historical circumstances, visionary ideals and daily realities do not always match up. And all the while, those engaged in this work struggle with the destructive legacy left by the historical experience of colonization, as well as the ongoing efforts of the settler society to eradicate their Indigenousness.

Conclusion

Heart of the Earth and Red School House helped nurture hundreds of young Indian people through their childhood and adolescent years. The word *adolescence* has Latin roots meaning "to come to maturity, be kindled, burn" and "to feed, sustain." This captures what the survival schools did for at least some of their students. They helped them develop into maturity, secure in their Indian identity and aware of their responsibilities to their communities and nations. They kindled a cultural and political awakening in young Indian people and fed them spiritually in ways that would sustain them into adulthood. The long-term consequences of this process would become apparent in the 1990s and 2000s, in the lives and families of former survival school students.

The survival schools also functioned as vital community centers for many Indian people in Minneapolis and St. Paul. The processes of identity development and personal growth provided for local Native youth also extended to adult family and community members. The schools provided social services and support networks that helped families navigate city life and negotiate the consequences of federal, state, and local policies and institutional practices. Through parental and community involvement, Red School House and Heart of the Earth also facilitated the American Indian Movement's effort to provide local Indian people with community-controlled institutions that met their needs and respected their cultural perspectives. Thus they contributed to the movement for Native American self-determination—political, social, and cultural—that began in the 1960s and has gathered strength ever since.

The survival schools also furthered the movement to reclaim Indigenous knowledge and revitalize Indigenous identities. Through this work the schools became centers of a distinctly Indigenous community in the Twin Cities. They also helped create a transnational community of Anishinaabe cultural and spiritual revitalization in the upper Midwest and Great Lakes regions.

From this perspective, the survival schools' founding and development must be understood as part of the transnational history of global Indigenous decolonization movements since the 1960s. Just as the reach of European colonialism was global in scope, so the movements for Indigenous decolonization have crossed national borders and connected Native peoples from across the globe through common purpose in the work of decolonizing projects. Many of these projects have incorporated or been centered in the practice of community-based education. In the United States, as in other settler societies shaped by the persistent desire to eliminate Indigenous ways of being, educational initiatives like the survival schools have nurtured communities of difference, thus ensuring the survival of Indigenousness in the modern world.

The Global Importance of Indigenous Education

ON A COLD, RAINY AFTERNOON IN LATE NOVEMBER, I met a man named Jake MacSiacais in the An Cultúrlann café on the Falls Road in West Belfast. I'd come to Belfast to research interactions between AIM organizers and Irish nationalists in the early 1980s when Sinn Fein contacted AIM to learn about the survival schools. After meeting with two community education activists in their home in West Belfast, one of them brought me to An Cultúrlann. This multipurpose cultural center with a book shop, art galleries, theater, radio station, classrooms, meeting spaces, and a busy café has been the hub of Belfast's Irish-language community since 1991. As we walked into the café, my host scanned the room, looking for people who might shed light on my research. Suddenly, she grabbed my arm. "There," she said. "There's the man you need to meet." She marched me over to a table where a middle-aged man in a sharp-looking suit was finishing a late lunch. She introduced us, said something vague about my purpose, and left.

Jake MacSiacais had a round, pleasant face, close-cropped hair, and the quiet confidence of a man who felt entirely at home in his surroundings. He invited me to sit down, then listened as I explained why I was there. MacSiacais had no personal knowledge of the communication between AIM organizers and Irish nationalists that had taken place thirty years earlier. He did have a lot to reveal about the resonance between the survival schools' history and the Irish activism that had created the space in which we now sat. MacSiacais, as it turned out, had been part of a movement to revitalize Irish language and identity in Northern Ireland since the 1970s, a movement now anchored at An Cultúrlann and in other agencies with nearby offices along this stretch of the Falls Road.

For Jake MacSiacais, as for Dennis Banks and Clyde Bellecourt, the story began in prison. While serving time in Long Kesh prison in the 1970s with other Irish Republicans, he had participated in efforts to study and speak the Irish language and to learn more about precolonial Irish history. After their release from prison, these young nationalists had pursued a project of linguistic and cultural revival as part of their resistance to British hegemony in Northern Ireland. In the early 1980s, they began supporting Irish-language schools in Belfast and pursuing other educational projects to further cultural revitalization and resistance.

MacSiacais spoke eloquently of the importance of the Irish language to what he and other nationalists had worked to reclaim from the legacy of British colonialism in the north of Ireland. Language, he argued, was essential to the social structures and spiritual philosophy that defined a people's culture. It anchored an understanding of the world and one's place in it, and it provided the necessary foundation for both individual and communal identity. A people's native language contained essential cultural knowledge that could not otherwise be expressed or translated; once lost, it could not be recovered.

As I listened to MacSiacais, I marveled at how closely his arguments echoed those made by Indigenous language activists since the 1960s about the importance of Native language reclamation. I also heard the voices of AIM organizers who had explained to me in interviews the reasons why they had founded the American Indian Movement and the survival schools. When I said this to MacSiacais, he shrugged, unsurprised. "Well," he said, "we consider ourselves to be an Indigenous people."

As I conclude my history of the Twin Cities survival schools, I have found at least some answers to the questions that started this project. My research also has sparked new questions and led me in unexpected directions. When I first read that brief, tantalizing reference to the survival schools and decided to find out more about them, I could not have anticipated that my curiosity would lead me to a conversation with a former Irish Republican prisoner in a Belfast café. There are things that I have not been able to explain in the kind of depth I had hoped, and there are people essential to the history of the schools who I unfortunately was not able to interview. Yet, thanks to the generosity of those who did spend time talking to me, I have been able to tell a version of the survival schools' story. That story gives human shape and historical specificity to the abstractions of postcolonial and decolonization theory. It grounds the Indigenous experience in a particular local place, while also revealing its global dimensions.

AIM organizers and other Twin Cities Indian parents created the survival schools in response to a local crisis in Indian education and in resistance to the child welfare and juvenile justice systems that, in Clyde Bellecourt's words, were "sweeping our children up" and removing them from Indian families at panic-inducing rates. Desperate to help families that did not want to lose their children, and seeking to help Native students who were struggling in the public school systems, they created an educational alternative so that at-risk youth could stay in school, get an education, stay out of juvenile court, avoid incarceration, and remain with their families.[1]

The survival schools' mission also went beyond crisis management. School founders set out to provide an entirely different kind of education than the public schools. They wanted to help Native youth discover and take pride in their tribal, Indian, and Indigenous identities, as a foundation for personal development and as a source for a new sense of self-worth. The schools taught students Native languages as well as ancestral knowledge, skills, values, and beliefs. School founders educated their youth to become community-minded, spiritually grounded leaders for their people. They also incorporated students' families and other community members into the processes of cultural discovery, community building, identity development, and personal growth. Ultimately, survival school organizers worked to repair the cultural losses of the past and regain the ability to determine their own future.

Survival school educators asserted the right to difference in modern American society. They insisted on living by Indigenous values and priorities and within an alternative social structure that diverged significantly from the Euro-American norm. They also reclaimed the possibility of raising their children and future generations within an Indigenous social and cultural system. This was the schools' truly subversive potential. They were not training Indian youth to overthrow the U.S. government; they were educating them to resist American settler colonialism's logic of elimination. They were refusing to be replaced.

Chickasaw scholar James Youngblood Henderson has written that one of the assumptions underpinning European colonialism was the insistence that European cultures and value systems were universal and absolute;

therefore, any peoples who did not share them were deficient and inferior. Colonialism worked in part by "elevating some kinds of knowledge and suppressing others." Henderson has called this the "strategy of differences," through which European peoples ensured a perpetual position of superiority and privilege. In settler colonial societies, this logic supported the construction of an entire social and political system:

> Colonial law made the idea of the universal central to the legal order under the guise of impartiality and equality. Equality was identified with sameness, and difference was identified with deviance or devaluation. These universal norms provided an assimilative template for the denial of the value of Aboriginal people.

Survival school education rejected Eurocentric universalism and challenged the "strategy of differences" that either required them to assimilate or relegated them to a perpetual state of diminished humanity. This was an anticolonial project. It furthered what Mi'kmaq educator Marie Battiste calls the "deconstruction" work of decolonization, by refusing to accept the categories assigned to Native people.[2]

The AIM survival schools also have furthered the "reconstruction" necessary to Indigenous decolonization by creating powerful "places of difference" in American society. Indigenous education scholars K. Tsianina Lomawaima and Teresa McCarty have written that "American Indian survival—of peoples, cultural practices, and languages—constitutes real and meaningful diversity at the heart of our nation." Yet, for many Americans, that diversity seems to pose "a threat to the national fabric," especially when Indian people "insist on surviving on their own terms." According to Lomawaima and McCarty, "critical democracy demands that the United States be a nation of educational opportunity for all, not merely a homogenizing and standardizing machine." This requires "more than a benignly neutral diversity that 'celebrates' cultural differences while muting the ideological forces that privilege certain differences and marginalize others." In order to thrive, "individual human beings as well as social groups need room—and opportunity and resources—to develop and implement their values, philosophies, and beliefs. They need places where difference is not perceived as a threat, even as the pressures for standardization gather momentum across the United States and, indeed, across the globe."[3]

The assertion of the right to difference, and the creation of physical, psychological, and social spaces in which to *be* different, in safety and in community, connect the AIM survival schools to the transnational decolonization and cultural revitalization movements that have developed in settler societies around the world since the 1960s. Within settler states like those that emerged from the British Empire in the United States, Canada, Australia, New Zealand, and Northern Ireland, colonized peoples practice decolonization when they subvert the logic of elimination and resist the power of the assimilationist imperative. They do this most defiantly by reclaiming their ancestral knowledge, including their native languages, and reasserting their unique ways of being in the world. Colonized peoples also further decolonization when they empower communities previously destabilized by the colonial process and marginalized within contemporary polities and economies, and when they challenge the structures of power and privilege that underpin the settler state. Decolonization also happens when the peoples once displaced and replaced by settler populations re-create viable alternative societies within the settler nation.

Approaching the history of the survival schools from this transnational perspective explains why Northern Ireland language activist Jake MacSiacais talked a lot like AIM organizers. Considering the seventeenth century "plantation" policy that displaced the native Irish-speaking Catholics and replaced them with English-speaking, Protestant settlers helps make sense of his statement that members of the Irish nationalist community would "consider ourselves to be an Indigenous people." When MacSiacais told me, "We believe that what we are doing is a global project," he was expressing a collective refusal by colonized peoples to be replaced—physically, linguistically, socially, spiritually, economically, and politically—by the settler state.[4]

The people of the American Indian Movement largely have not been acknowledged for their place in the transnational history of Indigenous decolonization or their contributions to Native cultural revitalization in the United States. Since the late 1960s, the reclamation of Indigenous identities and social and spiritual systems has been a predominant theme in Native American history, and this work continues to mobilize Indian people in reservation and urban communities today. AIM has been part of this movement since its founding in 1968. Some have criticized AIM's leaders for promoting a superficial, insincere Indian identity and characterized the movement as a militant urban organization with no authentic connections to reservation communities or tribal traditions. The AIM survival schools reveal a very different story.

In 1996, White Earth Ojibwe activist Winona LaDuke told a reporter that "the Indian community nationally and in Minnesota owes a great deal" to the AIM organizers of the 1960s and 1970s:

> They started the survival schools. They were part of the cultural renaissance here at White Earth. I was pretty much raised by this movement, and I know I am able to do the work that I do because people before me busted down some doors.

LaDuke serves as director of the White Earth Land Recovery Project (WELRP), whose mission is to "facilitate recovery of the original land base of the White Earth Indian Reservation, while preserving and restoring traditional practices of sound land stewardship, language fluency, community development, and strengthening our spiritual and cultural heritage." WELRP projects include reclaiming reservation land, growing and harvesting traditional foods, supporting traditional arts and crafts production, running an independent Anishinaabe radio station, starting a wind farm, and promoting the Ojibwe language. This is the kind of decolonizing work that AIM has enabled LaDuke to do.[5]

As LaDuke reminds us, AIM has blazed a trail for Indigenous decolonization specifically through the practice of educational self-determination. Heart of the Earth and Red School House were among the first Indian-controlled community schools. They helped pave the way for other urban and reservation Indian schools, as well as cultural programs in public school systems, and they helped lay the groundwork for the network of tribal colleges that has grown across the country since the 1970s. A century before AIM's founding, federal policy makers made Native children the prime target for assimilation and used schools as their primary weapon against Indigenous ways of life. Over the past four decades, Indian educators, parents, and community leaders have used alternative education and community-controlled schools as powerful tools for their own opposite purposes. The people of the survival schools played no small part in this remarkable turnaround.

No good historian would leave this story without asking the "so what?" question. Why does this history matter to those of us who did not live it and have not personally been affected by it? Why should we care? One reason we should care is that the destructive consequences of American settler colonialism and the persistent power of the assimilationist imperative continue to break the hearts of young Indian people. As I was working on this book in the winter of 2012, I learned of a recent incident at a Wisconsin middle school in which a twelve-year-old Menominee girl was punished for speaking her native language at school. Miranda Washinawatok was a seventh grader at Sacred Heart, a Catholic school near the Menominee reservation in eastern Wisconsin with more than 60 percent Native students. According to news reports, she had exchanged a few words in Menominee with two friends while sitting in her homeroom classroom. The supervising teacher, Julie Gurta, approached the girls and told them to stop speaking their language. She was angry because she could not understand them. How did she know they weren't saying something "bad"? Gurta demanded. The words that the girls spoke in Menominee were "hello," "I love you," and "thank you."[6]

Although Miranda insisted that she gave her teacher no trouble, and said that she and her friends "would have translated what the words meant if she asked," Gurta told Miranda's basketball coach that the girl had an "attitude issue," and the coach benched her from that night's game. Miranda told a reporter, "I want to be able to talk in Menominee because it's part of my culture; I like to express that." At the time, Miranda's maternal grandmother was the director of the Menominee tribe's Language and Culture Commission.[7]

The logic of elimination is alive and well in Wisconsin, and the expression of Indigenous difference remains threatening to some non-Native Americans. Telling the history of the survival schools might not prevent something like this from happening to Native students in American schools, but it does help explain why it happens, and it might help those of us who find it unacceptable to think about how to respond. As K. Tsianina Lomawaima and Teresa McCarty remind us, Indian self-determination can come to full fruition only if "the ideologies that have motivated federal repression of tribal sovereignty and cultural/linguistic difference are exposed and transformed."[8] If we are to expose these colonialist ideologies, first we must understand where they came from and why they are still around. If we hope to transform our societies to make space for Indigenous persistence, we might learn something from the successes, failures, and dreams of those who have been doing this work for decades.

Those who support Indigenous revitalization through language reclamation and community education also argue that this work, while good for Native people, benefits all of us. Lomawaima and McCarty assert that "nurturing 'places of difference' within American society is a necessary component of a fully functional democracy." If schools can become places "where children are free to learn, question, and grow from a position that affirms who they are," this is a "vision of critical democracy" that "has the power to create a more just and equitable educational system for all."[9] Marie Battiste argues that "Western education has much to gain by viewing the world through the eyes and languages of Aboriginal peoples":

> To allow tribal epistemology to die through the loss of the Aboriginal languages is to allow another world of knowledge to die, one that could help to sustain us. As Aboriginal peoples of this land, we have the knowledge to enable us to survive and flourish in our own homeland. Our stories of ancient times tell us how. Our languages provide those instructions.[10]

From this perspective, preserving Indigenous knowledge could help us all learn how to live more sustainably on the Earth.

Linguist Joshua Fishman has counted the collective social costs of the losses suffered by Indigenous people over generations of cultural repression. "What does the country lose," Fishman asks, "when it loses individuals who are comfortable with themselves, cultures that are authentic to themselves, the capacity to pursue sensitivity, wisdom, and some kind of recognition that one has a purpose in life?"[11] One also might ask, what does the country—or a community, or humanity—*gain* when it recovers these things, when we provide spaces for them to thrive? For Indigenous places of difference to survive in settler societies like the United States, in the words of Ojibwe educator David Beaulieu, there is still "a great deal of work to do."[12] Let us all do what we can to support this work. May this book prove useful to those who carry it out.

Acknowledgments

Writing may be a solitary enterprise, but many people contributed to the completion of this book. First and foremost, I must thank the people of the survival schools who spoke with me in oral history interviews and informal conversations. I am indebted to them for sharing their knowledge, experiences, stories, and dreams. Pat Bellanger was especially generous with her time; she provided invaluable insights as an AIM organizer and survival school founder and parent, and she helped me secure other important interviews. The hours I spent in her company were delightful and transformative. Pat's daughter Lisa Bellanger and Dorene Day provided crucial perspective on how the survival schools influenced students' lives. Dorene spent considerable time talking to me and shared deeply personal stories, and Lisa invited me to community gatherings, school events, and the Midewiwin ceremonies in northern Wisconsin, where I witnessed the schools' powerful contribution to Indigenous cultural revitalization. These three women profoundly shaped my understanding of the survival schools; without them, it simply would not have been possible for me to write this book. *Miigwech.*

My editor at the University of Minnesota Press, Jason Weidemann, has been patient beyond measure as I inched my way toward the completion of the final manuscript. I appreciate his enthusiasm for the project and his encouragement throughout the process. Our mutual commitment to crafting a narrative that would engage general readers as well as enlighten scholars, and his understanding of the survival schools' historical significance for the

Twin Cities Indian community, made it possible for me to write the kind of book I had hoped to write.

The College of St. Benedict and St. John's University, where I have taught history for the past six years, provided multidimensional institutional support. The most coveted and elusive treasure for an assistant professor on the tenure track is time, and my department colleagues and academic administrators granted me a reduction in teaching duties during two semesters so that I could devote more time to research and writing. I received generous financial support for travel to conferences, where I worked through ideas with colleagues in Native studies, Native American and Indigenous history, settler colonial studies, and postcolonial theory. Throughout my time at CSB/SJU, our departmental office manager Norma Koetter has provided cheerful and efficient administrative support for my teaching, research, and writing.

In June 2010, my institution provided funding for me to present on the AIM survival schools at the Sixth Galway Conference on Colonialism in Ireland. Attending that provocative and convivial international conference expanded my thinking about the transnationality of colonialism and its ongoing consequences for Indigenous peoples within settler societies like the United States.

While teaching at CSB/SJU, I also had the opportunity to spend a semester directing our study abroad program near Galway, where I had enlightening conversations with Dr. Laurence Marley about the resonance between Irish and Native American historical experiences and the patterns of colonization and decolonization in Northern Ireland. While directing the study abroad program, I also made my first visit to Belfast, and another round of institutional funding enabled me to return there for field research the following summer. Exploring the convergences and divergences between Northern Irish and Native American histories and puzzling over the nature of the Irish Indigenous identity enriched my analysis of the survival schools as decolonizing projects.

My students on the Ireland study abroad program and in my courses back at home helped me work through ideas for this book. Confronting the complexity and violence of Northern Irish history and experiencing the intensity of historical memory in Derry and Belfast with my study-abroad students in fall 2009 clarified the persistence of settler colonial dynamics in the supposedly "postcolonial" period. The students in my historiography course at CSB/SJU the next semester helped me process the insights gained during my time in Ireland and apply them in a comparative context. Sixteen brave souls in my American Indian history course in spring 2012 read a partial draft of the book manuscript, and their analysis and feedback assisted me with final revisions.

Colleagues and friends at CSB/SJU provided essential intellectual and emotional support while I labored to turn my dissertation into a book manuscript and sweated through several stages of revisions. Annette Atkins, Steven Thomas, Rachel Melis, Kate Costello, and Nina Kollars engaged in conversations about our work, shared food and drink, talked me down from various ledges, cared about my research, cared about me, and generally were good comrades in the creative struggle to make sense of the human experience through words, ideas, and principled action. Kelly Berg did all of these things and more; her committed, compassionate, loving friendship has been essential to my well-being and my ability to do this work. For many of us in the local academic community, the owners and baristas of the Local Blend coffee shop in St. Joseph, Minnesota, have provided a productive communal space in which to think and write.

My friendship with Vicki Farden was forged years ago in a narrative nonfiction class, and she has supported my writing ever since. Nikki James encouraged me from both sides of the Atlantic Ocean. Other friends in my Facebook community (and they really are true friends) followed my progress and provided virtual shouts of encouragement, as well as the occasional digital kick in the ass. The members of my neighborhood gardening collective cheered me on and covered for me when the writing kept me away from the vegetable beds. Ho-Chunk scholar Amy Lonetree was my soul sister in book writing, and she helped me overcome challenges of theoretical analysis, structure, and narrative voice. I have so much respect for Amy's work in Indigenous history, public history, and Native studies, and her unshakable belief in the value of what I was doing and in my ability to tell this story meant the world to me. *Pinagigi*, Amy.

For most of my adult life, I have been blessed with the steadfast friendship of Cindy Miller, with whom I share a love for the well-written word. She and Sean Beaton ground me, and their children Gus and Susanna remind me that it is far more important to be a beloved auntie than a brilliant scholar (though one can strive to be both). The blessed members of my biological family have been my loudest cheerleaders and longest-suffering champions. With all my love and gratitude, I thank my mother Sandy, my father Muryl, and my sister Cindy for their unconditional support.

My maternal grandmother Eleanor, whom we called Muga, told me practically from birth that I could accomplish anything I wanted to do. She was impatient for me to finish "The Book," even when it was just a dissertation. Her voracious curiosity, her delight in intellectual inquiry, her unwavering commitment to education, and her conviction that I was going to do something meaningful in the world, remain with me always. *Tusen takk, Muga. Jeg savner deg.*

Notes

Preface

1. I personally conducted, recorded, and transcribed all of the oral history interviews that I use in this book, in accordance with the professional guidelines developed by the Oral History Association, of which I am a member. As is the norm among oral historians, I use the names of narrators I quote, with their permission. Everyone whose interviews I draw from signed a release form granting permission to use my transcriptions of their interviews in the writing of my Ph.D. dissertation and for subsequent publications resulting from that research. At times, when individuals discussed particularly personal, painful, or volatile subjects, though I had permission to use their names, I wrote about these subjects in more general and anonymous terms, without attributing the information to a specific narrator. When transcribing the interviews, I adhered closely to the original content as well as to the narrators' habitual patterns of speech. When selecting quotes I edited slightly for clarity, eliminating most repetitious phrases and conversation fillers while retaining something of the individuals' characteristic cadences of expression.

2. My approach to oral history has been influenced by Thompson, *The Voice of the Past;* Frisch, *A Shared Authority;* Portelli, *The Death of Luigi Trastulli and Other Stories;* and Portelli, *The Battle of Valle Giulia.*

3. Jones, "The Etymology of Anishinaabe," 48. Indigenous scholars have called for the use of oral history as necessary to conducting ethical research on Native people and writing history from indigenous perspectives. See, for example, Fixico, "Ethics and Responsibilities in Writing American Indian History"; Wilson, "American Indian History or Non-Indian Perceptions of American

Indian History?"; Wilson, "Grandmother to Granddaughter"; and Wilson, "Power of the Spoken Word."

4. Patrick Wolfe describes the goals of Indigenous "displacement and re-placement" as the fundamental imperative underlying all settler colonial proj-ects, and argues that rather than disappearing in the supposedly "postcolonial" period, they take on new forms. Wolfe has articulated his analysis in "Land, Labor, and Difference"; "Logics of Elimination"; *Settler Colonialism and the Trans-formation of Anthropology;* and "Structure and Event." I first encountered Wolfe's ideas in a talk he delivered on the topic "Imperialism in Theory and Practice" at the Moore Institute, in conjunction with the Sixth Galway Conference on Colo-nialism, National University of Ireland, Galway, June 23, 2010.

5. See Miller, "Native America Writes Back" and "Native Historians Write Back."

6. Broker, *Night Flying Woman,* 21; Chamberlin, "From Hand to Mouth," 136; Lomawaima, "Tribal Sovereigns," 14–15.

7. Miller, "Native Historians Write Back," 38; Johnny Smith, interview, July 10, 2002.

Introduction

1. Different accounts recalled by multiple people at various points in time diverge on the details of this founding meeting, including who organized it and where it was held. My account of AIM's organizing meeting is compiled from reading and comparative analysis of the following sources: Banks, "Background of the American Indian Movement," http://members.aol.com/Nowacumig/ backgrnd.html (August 26, 2002); Banks, "The Black Scholar Interviews," 29; Banks, *Ojibwa Warrior;* Bonney, "The Role of AIM Leaders in Indian National-ism," 209, 212; Cohen, "The Indian Patrol in Minneapolis"; Hayes, "Blood Broth-ers"; Mosedale, "Bury My Heart," 14; Smith and Warrior, *Like a Hurricane,* 128, 136; and Vick, "The Press and Wounded Knee, 1973," 7; and interviews with Clyde Bellecourt and Pat Bellanger.

2. According to various accounts, in addition to Banks, Bellecourt, and Mitchell, attendees of AIM's founding meeting included Alberta Atkin, Audrey Banks, Ellie Banks, Jeanette Banks, Pat Bellanger, Peggy Bellecourt, Eddie Benton-Banai, Pearl Brandon, Polly Chabwa, Arlene Dakota, Charles Deegan, Caroline Dickenson, Roberta Downwind, Francis Fairbanks, Harold Good Sky, Bobby Jo Graves, Ron Libertus, George Mellessey, John Red Horse, Rita Rogers, Annette Sargent, Ervin Sargent, Elaine M. Stately, Joanne Strong, Melissa Tapio, Darcy Truax, Gerald Vizenor, and Mary Jane Wilson.

3. Banks, *Ojibwa Warrior,* 62.

4. Clyde Bellecourt, interview, January 21, 2003; "Deegan, a Founding Member of AIM, Dies at 67," 3.

5. Banks, *Ojibwa Warrior*, 63.

6. Ibid., 58–61.

7. Narrative from Clyde Bellecourt, interview, January 21, 2003; Banks, *Ojibwa Warrior*, 62; quote from Mosedale, "Bury My Heart," 12.

8. In *Ojibwe Warrior*, his memoir of the American Indian Movement, Dennis Banks devotes just four of 362 pages to AIM's local work in the Twin Cities, all of it prior to 1970. He barely mentions the survival schools, and then only specifically names one, the Red School House. Szasz provides only a brief mention of the AIM survival schools in *Education and the American Indian: The Road to Self-Determination since 1928*, focusing instead on reservation-based Indian community schools. In *To Remain an Indian*, Lomawaima and McCarty give no attention to the survival schools in their chapters on educational self-determination and bilingual and bicultural education projects in the postwar period.

9. Child, *Holding Our World Together*, 156, 160. In *Keeping the Campfires Going*, Susan Applegate Krouse and Heather A. Howard edited a collection of essays on women's activism within urban Indian communities in the United States and Canada. Applegate Krouse's essay in chapter 9, "What Came Out of the Takeovers," focuses on the educational activism of women in the Milwaukee chapter of AIM in the 1970s and 1980s.

10. Miller, "Native America Writes Back," 18; Clyde Bellecourt, interview, January 21, 2003.

1. The Origins of the Twin Cities Indian Community and the American Indian Movement

1. Wolfe to Joanne Barker, "A Note from Patrick Wolfe (Reprinted with Permission)," Tequila Sovereign blog, April 26, 2011; Wolfe, "Settler Colonialism and the Elimination of the Native," 388.

2. For analyses of settler colonialism in British North America, the development of the U.S. settler state, and their impact on Indigenous people, see Bruyneel, *The Third Space of Sovereignty;* Byrd, *The Transit of Empire;* Ford, *Settler Sovereignty;* Jacobs, *White Mother to a Dark Race;* Janiewski, "Gendering, Racializing, and Classifying"; Tyrell, "Beyond the View from Euro-America"; Wolfe, "Land, Labor, and Difference"; Wolfe, "Logics of Elimination"; Wolfe, "Structure and Event"; and the settler colonial studies blog created by Edward Cavanagh and Lorenzo Veracini in 2010, http://settlercolonialstudies.org/. According to Mark Rifkin, the concept of settler colonialism is most analytically useful when

used to describe the formation of settler states, to discuss "the kinds of jurisdiction and sovereignty exercised by such states over Indigenous peoples and possibly as a retrospective way of characterizing those forms of colonization that eventuated in the creation of settler states" (Mark Rifkin, "A Note to Patrick Wolfe," Tequila Sovereign blog, May 2, 2011).

3. Child, *Boarding School Seasons*, 9.

4. Discussions of the deterioration of reservation economies and subsequent migrations to off-reservation towns and cities can be found in Meyer, *The White Earth Tragedy*; Child, *Boarding School Seasons*; Broker, *Night Flying Woman*; and Beaulieu, "A Place among Nations," 403–4. Information on the Twin Cities Indian community in the early twentieth century comes from Shoemaker, "Urban Indians and Ethnic Choices," and Brunette, "The Minneapolis Urban Indian Community."

5. Shoemaker ("Urban Indians and Ethnic Choices") emphasizes the economic advantages of urban relocation for Twin Cities Indian people in this period, as does Brunette ("The Minneapolis Urban Indian Community").

6. Pejsa, *The Life of Emily Peake*.

7. Paul Levy, "Winnie Jourdain: The Spirit of White Earth," *Minneapolis Star Tribune*, November 9, 2001; Jackie Crosby, "Celebrating a Century: Winnie Jourdain Turns 100," *Minneapolis Star Tribune*, August 1, 2000; Brunette, "The Minneapolis Urban Indian Community," 8; Pejsa, *The Life of Emily Peake*, 87.

8. Shoemaker, "Urban Indians and Ethnic Choices."

9. Levy, "Winnie Jourdain"; Crosby, "Celebrating a Century"; Pejsa, *The Life of Emily Peake*; Brunette, "The Minneapolis Urban Indian Community," 7–8.

10. Brunette, "The Minneapolis Urban Indian Community," Shoemaker, "Urban Indians and Ethnic Choices."

11. Bernstein, *American Indians and World War II*, 40, 68.

12. Buff, *Immigration and the Political Economy of Home*, 196; Brunette, "The Minneapolis Urban Indian Community," 7–8; Pejsa, *The Life of Emily Peake*, 90; Shoemaker, "Urban Indians and Ethnic Choices," 434.

13. Shoemaker, "Urban Indians and Ethnic Choices," 434; Brunette, "The Minneapolis Urban Indian Community," 8; Bernstein, *American Indians and World War II*.

14. Statistics from Fixico, *The Urban Indian Experience*, 10–25, 71, 76. Fixico also discusses the program, its promises, and its influence on Indian urban migration in *Termination and Relocation*. LaGrand also provides a useful overview of the relocation program in *Indian Metropolis* (see especially chapter 2). Twin Cities information from Shoemaker, "Urban Indians and Ethnic Choices," 443, and Brunette, "The Minneapolis Urban Indian Community," 8–9.

15. Demographics of the postwar Indian community come from Shoemaker, "Urban Indians and Ethnic Choices," 443; Brunette, "The Minneapolis

Urban Indian Community," 8–9; League of Women Voters of Minneapolis, *Indians in Minneapolis*, 2; Woods and Harkins, *A Review of Recent Research on Minneapolis Indians: 1968–1969*, 1; Harkins and Woods, *Indian Americans in St. Paul*, 1–2, 5; U.S. Commission on Civil Rights, *Bridging the Gap: The Twin Cities Native American Community*, 13.

16. U.S. Commission on Civil Rights, *Bridging the Gap: The Twin Cities Native American Community*, 14; League of Women Voters of Minneapolis, *Indians in Minneapolis*, 96; Harkins and Woods, *Indian Americans in St. Paul*, 12; Harkins, Sherarts, and Woods, *The Elementary Education of Saint Paul Indian Children*, 2; Pat Bellanger, interview, December 3, 2002.

17. Reasons for postwar Indian migration to the Twin Cities are discussed in League of Women Voters of Minnesota, *Indians in Minnesota* (1971), 39; Woods and Harkins, *A Review of Recent Research on Minneapolis Indians*, 3; U.S. Commission on Civil Rights, *Bridging the Gap: The Twin Cities Native American Community*, 14.

18. Shoemaker, "Urban Indians and Ethnic Choices," 433.

19. Harkins and Woods, *Indian Americans in St. Paul*, 5; Miller and Wittstock, *American Indian Alcoholism in St. Paul*, 6; U.S. Commission on Civil Rights, *Bridging the Gap: The Twin Cities Native American Community*, 90; Woods and Harkins, *A Review of Recent Research on Minneapolis Indians*, 9.

20. Pat Bellanger, interview, June 20, 2002; U.S. Commission on Civil Rights, *Bridging the Gap: The Twin Cities Native American Community*; Woods and Harkins, *A Review of Recent Research on Minneapolis Indians*, 12.

21. Brunette, "The Minneapolis Urban Indian Community," 11; League of Women Voters of Minnesota, *Indians in Minnesota* (1971), 39, 103.

22. Woods and Harkins, *A Review of Recent Research on Minneapolis Indians*, 15; Craig, Harkins, and Woods, *Indian Housing in Minneapolis and St. Paul*, 3–5; League of Women Voters of Minnesota, *Indians in Minnesota* (1971), 109.

23. Brunette, "The Minneapolis Urban Indian Community," 434; League of Women Voters of Minneapolis, *Indians in Minneapolis*, 42; Rich Antell, interview, September 20, 2002; Tom Sorensen, "East Franklin Av.: There Are Dreams despite Vacant Stores, Broken Glass and Poverty," *Minneapolis Tribune*, October 22, 1977.

24. Harkins and Woods, *Indian Americans in St. Paul*, 28, 1; Dorene Day, interview, March 14, 2003.

25. U.S. Commission on Civil Rights, *Bridging the Gap: The Twin Cities Native American Community*, 77–78, 83.

26. Ibid., 60–61.

27. League of Women Voters of Minneapolis, *Indians in Minneapolis*, 49–54; League of Women Voters of Minnesota, *Indians in Minnesota* (1971), 137.

28. Woods and Harkins, *A Review of Recent Research on Minneapolis Indians*,

11; League of Women Voters of Minneapolis, *Indians in Minneapolis*, 16–17, 44; U.S. Commission on Civil Rights, *Bridging the Gap: The Twin Cities Native American Community*, 14; League of Women Voters of Minnesota, *Indians in Minnesota* (1971), 39.

29. Donald Fixico outlines the common problems shared by urban Indian people across the country in *The Urban Indian Experience in America* (see especially 11–24 and 55). See also Amerman, *Urban Indians in Phoenix Schools*; Carpio, *Indigenous Albuquerque*; Danziger, *Survival and Regeneration*; Lobo and Peters, *American Indians and the Urban Experience*; Sorkin, *The Urban American Indian*; and Weible-Orlando, *Indian Country, L.A.* LaGrand describes the particular experiences of Indian people in Chicago in *Indian Metropolis* (see especially 98–122, 165).

30. Pejsa, *The Life of Emily Peake*.

31. For descriptions of the founding and services of the Department/Division of Indian Works, see League of Women Voters of Minneapolis, *Indians in Minneapolis*; League of Women Voters of Minnesota, *Indians in Minnesota* (1971); and Harkins and Woods, *Indian Americans in St. Paul*. For descriptions of other cooperative efforts, see Brunette, "The Minneapolis Urban Indian Community," 10; Beaulieu, "A Place among Nations," 411; and Pejsa, *The Life of Emily Peake*.

32. Pejsa, *The Life of Emily Peake*, 138; Beaulieu, "A Place among Nations," 412.

33. Brunette, "The Minneapolis Urban Indian Community," 10; Buff, *Immigration and the Political Economy of Home*, 42, 88–90; Pejsa, *The Life of Emily Peake*, 138, 145; Beaulieu, "A Place among Nations," 411; "City Natives Find a Connection," *The Circle* (January 1997); League of Women Voters of Minneapolis, *Indians in Minneapolis*; and League of Women Voters of Minnesota, *Indians in Minnesota* (1971).

34. Rachel Buff has commented on how contact with people from diverse tribal backgrounds and the shared struggles of city life shaped urban Indian identity in the Twin Cities in the 1950s and 1960s (Buff, *Immigration and the Political Economy of Home*, 12, 79). In *Indian Metropolis*, James LaGrand stressed how the socioeconomic and cultural conditions of city life fashioned a distinctly urban Indian identity among Native people in Chicago, and how that identity became increasingly pan-tribal. Donald Fixico discusses a similar process among urban Indian people generally in *The Urban Indian Experience in America*.

35. Banks, "The Black Scholar Interviews," 29; Banks, *Ojibwa Warrior*, 59. For other accounts of AIM organizers' grievances against the police, see Bonney, "The Role of AIM Leaders in Indian Nationalism," 214; and Cohen, "The Indian Patrol in Minneapolis." Clyde Bellecourt and Pat Bellanger also spoke in interviews about discriminatory arrests in Phillips, police officers' targeting of Indian

bars on Franklin Avenue, and the calculated and disproportionate use of Indian men by the corrections system for unpaid labor.

36. For accounts of the activities of the Indian Patrol, see Banks, *Ojibwa Warrior*, 63–64; Bonney, "The Role of AIM Leaders in Indian Nationalism," 214; Cohen, "The Indian Patrol in Minneapolis"; and Smith and Warrior, *Like a Hurricane*, 128.

37. My sense of the scope of AIM's early activities comes from Pat Bellanger, interviews, May 30, 2002; June 13, 2002; June 20, 2002; October 17, 2002; and December 3, 2002; Clyde Bellecourt, interview, January 21, 2003; and Dorene Day, interview, November 5, 2002. For published accounts of AIM's early concerns and activities, see "Deegan, a Founding Member of AIM, Dies at 67"; League of Women Voters of Minnesota, *Indians in Minnesota* (1971), 42; Banks, "The Black Scholar Interviews," 29–30; Banks, *Ojibwa Warrior*, 63–64; and Smith and Warrior, *Like a Hurricane*, 131–35.

38. The St. Paul chapter of AIM is dated to 1970 in "AIM Opens St. Paul Office," *St. Paul Pioneer Press*, June 6, 1970, 1. Pat Bellanger, interview, May 30, 2002.

39. Fay Cohen describes early AIM activities as characteristic of a mutual aid society in "The Indian Patrol in Minneapolis." Accounts of AIM's mutual assistance activities also are found in Banks, *Ojibwa Warrior*, 64, and Smith and Warrior, *Like a Hurricane*, 132.

40. Banks, *Ojibwa Warrior*, 60.

41. Mosedale, "Bury My Heart," 14.

42. Clyde Bellecourt, interview, January 21, 2003.

43. Buff, *Immigration and the Political Economy of Home*, 98.

44. Information on alternative urban institutions founded by AIM comes from U.S. Commission on Civil Rights, *Bridging the Gap: The Twin Cities Native American Community*; Banks, "The Black Scholar Interviews"; Brunette, "The Minneapolis Urban Indian Community"; "Deegan, a Founding Member of AIM, Dies at 67"; League of Women Voters of Minneapolis, *Indians in Minneapolis*; League of Women Voters of Minnesota, *Indians in Minnesota* (1971); League of Women Voters of Minnesota, *Indians in Minnesota* (1974); and Thompson, "Survival Schools."

45. Means, quoted in Mosedale, "Bury My Heart," 14.

46. Pejsa, *The Life of Emily Peake*, 152–65.

47. Wolfe, quoted from an e-mail communication to Joanne Barker, posted as a blog entry under "A Note from Patrick Wolfe (Reprinted with Permission)," Tequila Sovereign blog, April 26, 2011.

48. Overviews of federal assimilation policy and the key role of the off-reservation boarding school system in carrying it out can be found in Hoxie, *A Final Promise*, and Adams, *Education for Extinction*.

49. Child, *Boarding School Seasons*, 14, Appendix 1.

50. Brenda Child describes the hardships that the boarding schools imposed on Minnesota Ojibwe families in ibid.

51. Ibid., 277, 11.

52. Peacock and Wisuri, Ojibe: *Waasa Inaabidaa*, 57, 81; Kugel, *To Be the Main Leaders of Our People*, 144; Broker, *Night Flying Woman*.

53. Residents of the Red Lake reservation in northern Minnesota, for example, resisted land cession and allotment, thus retaining a relatively intact land and resource base.

54. Child, *Boarding School Seasons*, 17; Broker, *Night Flying Woman*, 125.

55. Bonney, "The Role of AIM Leaders in Indian Nationalism," 213–14.

56. Banks, *Ojibwa Warrior*, 12–30.

57. Ibid., 28.

58. Ibid., 30–60.

59. Hayes, "Blood Brothers," 4; Clyde Bellecourt, interview, January 21, 2003.

60. Clyde Bellecourt, interview, January 21, 2003. Bellecourt has told versions of this story many times in public speeches and in interviews; see, for instance, the accounts in Mosedale, "Bury My Heart at Wounded Knee," and Hayes, "Blood Brothers."

61. Clyde Bellecourt, interview, January 21, 2003. See also Mosedale, "Bury My Heart at Wounded Knee"; Hayes, "Blood Brothers."

62. Clyde Bellecourt, interview, January 21, 2003.

63. Benton-Banai has described his childhood and upbringing in public speeches and interviews; for a particularly comprehensive and insightful account that includes his explanation of the Midewiwin tradition, see Martin, "Thoughts from a Born-Again Pagan."

64. Martin, "Thoughts from a Born-Again Pagan"; Clyde Bellecourt, interview, January 21, 2003.

65. Clyde Bellecourt, interview, January 21, 2003. See also Wittstock, Salinas, and Aasen, "Russell Means."

66. Clyde Bellecourt, interview, January 21, 2003.

67. Clyde Bellecourt, interview, January 21, 2003; Martin, "Thoughts from a Born-Again Pagan."

68. Clyde Bellecourt, interview, January 21, 2003.

69. Pat Bellanger, interview, May 30, 2002.

70. Clyde Bellecourt, interview, January 21, 2003; Pat Bellanger, interview, December 3, 2002; Benton-Banai quoted in Lounberg, "The New Face of the American Indian Movement," 463.

71. Pat Bellanger, interview, December 3, 2002. Information on AIM's early commitment to cultural and spiritual revitalization also taken from Pat Bellanger, interviews, June 20, 2002, and September 30, 2004; and Clyde Bellecourt,

interview, January 21, 2003. See also Buff, *Immigration and the Political Economy of Home*, 42, 97.

72. Clyde Bellecourt, interview, January 21, 2003.

73. Martin, "Thoughts from a Born-Again Pagan."

2. Keeping Ourselves Together

1. Child, *Boarding School Seasons*, 17.

2. Child, *Boarding School Seasons;* Peacock and Wisuri, *Ojibwe: Waasa Inaabidaa*, 82; Broker, *Night Flying Woman*, 33, 130–31.

3. Pat Bellanger, interviews, May 30, 2002, and June 20, 2002; Hayes, "Blood Brothers," 4.

4. Hayes, "Blood Brothers," 4.

5. Pat Bellanger, interview, May 30, 2002.

6. Hayes, "Blood Brothers," 4; Banks, *Ojibwa Warrior*, 12–23; Buff, *Immigration and the Political Economy of Home*, 96.

7. Horne and McBeth, *Essie's Story*, 129.

8. Fixico, *Urban Indian Experience*, 44; Buff, *Immigration and the Political Economy of Home*, 96. For similar dynamics in other cities, see Carpio, *Indigenous Albuquerque*, and Danziger, *Survival and Regeneration*.

9. Pat Bellanger, interviews, May 30, 2002, and June 7, 2002. Donald Fixico also notes this experience among Indian migrants to cities across the country during this period (*Urban Indian Experience*, 4, 14, 141–42).

10. Dorene Day, interview, March 14, 2003.

11. Dorene Day, interview, December 10, 2002. In *Urban Indian Experience in America*, Donald Fixico has cited the separation from nature and the unfamiliarity of the physical environment as significant contributors to the culture shock initially experienced by urban Indian migrants across the country (11–24).

12. Dorene Day, interview, December 10, 2002.

13. Ibid.

14. My understanding of the values and social orientation that set more traditionally minded Indian people apart in the Twin Cities during this period has been shaped by my interviews with Pat Bellanger and Dorene Day, as well as with Clyde Bellecourt, January 21, 2003; my analysis of contemporary research studies in the Twin Cities; and the insights of Ojibwe educator Rosemary Christensen as quoted in League of Women Voters of Minnesota, *Indians in Minnesota* (1971), 23. Donald Fixico notes that in the postwar period, similar differences in cultural values and social structures distinguished urban Indian people from the dominant White, middle-class society in cities across the country (*Urban Indian Experience*, 43–60).

15. Harkins et al., *Junior High Indian Children in Minneapolis*, 49; U.S. Commission on Civil Rights, *Bridging the Gap: The Twin Cities Native American Community*, iii. Economist Alan Sorkin also found a conflict in cultural values to be a significant problem for Indian people living in cities in the 1970s, including Minneapolis (*The Urban American Indian*, 76, 125).

16. U.S. Commission on Civil Rights, *Bridging the Gap: The Twin Cities Native American Community*, 16, 17; Woods and Harkins, *A Review of Recent Research on Minneapolis Indians*, 12.

17. Pierce, "From the Reservation, to the City and Back," 33; U.S. Commission on Civil Rights, *Bridging the Gap: The Twin Cities Native American Community*.

18. League of Women Voters of Minnesota, *Indians in Minnesota* (1971), 76; League of Women Voters of Minneapolis, *Indians in Minneapolis*, 93; U.S. Commission on Civil Rights, *Bridging the Gap: The Twin Cities Native American Community*, 2–3, 62; Westermeyer, "Indian Powerlessness in Minnesota," 49.

19. Wolfe, quoted from an e-mail communication to Joanne Barker, posted as a blog entry under "A Note from Patrick Wolfe (Reprinted with Permission)," Tequila Sovereign blog, April 26, 2011; Lorenzo Veracini, "Lorenzo Veracini's Response to the Skepticism of Tequila Sovereign," Settler Colonial Studies blog, April 20, 2011; Edward Cavanagh and Lorenzo Veracini, "Definitions," Settler Colonial Studies blog, 2010 (http://settlercolonialstudies.org/about-this-blog/).

20. LaGrand provides a brief but useful summary of the postwar social and political forces that converged to push for assimilation in this period, particularly as expressed in federal termination and relocation policies, in *Indian Metropolis*, 46–47. Buff ties these developments in Indian policy to the broader context of postwar ethnicity theory in *Immigration and the Political Economy of Home*, 45–73. Other discussions of assimilationist policies and their underpinnings in this period can be found in Bernstein, *American Indians and World War II*; Fixico, *Termination and Relocation*; Philp, *Termination Revisited*; and Prucha, *The Great Father*, 340–56.

21. Westermeyer, "Indian Powerlessness in Minnesota," 45, 51.

22. Brunette, "The Minneapolis Urban Indian Community," 10; U.S. Commission on Civil Rights, *Bridging the Gap: The Twin Cities Native American Community*, iii.

23. This assumption is particularly clear in League of Women Voters of Minneapolis, *Indians in Minneapolis*, 108, 93, and Harkins et al., *Junior High Indian Children in Minneapolis*, 1. On the trend in studies of urban Indians in the 1960s, see Krouse and Howard, "Introduction," and Lobo, "Urban Clan Mothers."

24. Quoted in U.S. Commission on Civil Rights, *Bridging the Gap: The Twin Cities Native American Community*, 89–90.

25. League of Women Voters of Minnesota, *Indians in Minnesota* (1971), 145.

26. Brunette, "The Minneapolis Urban Indian Community," 13, 10. James

LaGrand found a similar range of perspectives within the postwar Indian community in Chicago (*Indian Metropolis*, 74–93). Donald Fixico has made similar observations about urban Indian experiences in general (*The Urban Indian Experience in America*, 43–60).

27. Vernon Bellecourt quoted in Bonney, "The Role of AIM Leaders in Indian Nationalism," 213–14; Brunette, "The Minneapolis Urban Indian Community," 10.

28. Shoemaker outlines the purposes and activities of these organizations and profiles their leadership and membership in "Urban Indians and Ethnic Choices."

29. Buff reveals these dynamics at work within Twin Cities Indian organizations in *Immigration and the Political Economy of Home*, 94–96; see also Pejsa, *The Life of Emily Peake*, 137. Donald Fixico discusses how urban Indian people in other cities negotiated between assimilation and the preservation of traditional cultures in *The Urban Indian Experience in America*, 34, 44–45, 162–63.

30. Szasz, *Education and the American Indian*, 89.

31. Woods and Harkins, *A Review of Recent Research on Minneapolis Indians*, 3. See also Harkins and Woods, *Indian Americans in St. Paul*, 11; League of Women Voters of Minnesota, *Indians in Minnesota* (1971), 56; Harkins, Woods, and Sherarts, *Indian Education in Minneapolis*, 1.

32. League of Women Voters of Minneapolis, *Indians in Minneapolis*, 29; League of Women Voters of Minnesota, *Indians in Minnesota* (1971), 56; Harkins and Woods, *Indian Americans in St. Paul*, 5; Sorkin, *The Urban Indian American*, 100.

33. Sorkin, *The Urban Indian American*, 100; League of Women Voters of Minnesota, *Indians in Minnesota* (1971), 56; U.S. Commission on Civil Rights, *Bridging the Gap: The Twin Cities Indian Community.*

34. Harkins, Woods, and Sherarts, *Indian Education in Minneapolis*, 5, 10. See also League of Women Voters of Minneapolis, *Indians in Minneapolis*, 35; U.S. Commission on Civil Rights, *Bridging the Gap: The Twin Cities Indian Community.*

35. U.S. Commission on Civil Rights, *Bridging the Gap: A Reassessment*, 22. See also Harkins, Woods, and Sherarts, *Indian Education in Minneapolis*, 7; Harkins and Woods, *Indian Americans in St. Paul*, 3; Harkins, Sherarts, and Woods, *Attitudes of St. Paul Indian Parents and Influential Persons toward Formal Education.*

36. Harkins, Woods, and Sherarts, *Indian Education in Minneapolis*, 8; Harkins, Sherarts, and Woods, *Attitudes of St. Paul Indian Parents and Influential Persons toward Formal Education*, 30–31; Anderson and Eglitis, "Public Schools Link Indian, White Cultures," 11–15; Pat Bellanger, interview, May 30, 2002; U.S. Commission on Civil Rights, *Bridging the Gap: A Reassessment*, 34.

37. Harkins, Woods, and Sherarts, *Indian Education in Minneapolis*, 8; U.S. Commission on Civil Rights, *Bridging the Gap: The Twin Cities Indian Community*,

34; Harkins, Sherarts, and Woods, *Attitudes of St. Paul Indian Parents and Influential Persons toward Formal Education;* Harkins, Sherarts, and Woods, *Teachers of Minneapolis Elementary Indian Children,* 24; Harkins et al., *Junior High Indian Children in Minneapolis,* 44; Harkins, Sherarts, and Woods, *Teachers of St. Paul Elementary Indian Children,* 3; League of Women Voters of Minnesota, *Indians in Minnesota* (1971).

38. Harkins, Woods, and Sherarts, *Indian Education in Minneapolis,* 8, 10; Anderson and Eglitis, "Public Schools Link Indian, White Cultures," 11–15; Dorene Day, interview, November 5, 2002.

39. Dorene Day, interviews, November 5, 2002, and December 10, 2002.

40. Dorene Day, interviews, March 14, 2003, and November 5, 2002.

41. Dorene Day, interviews, December 10, 2002, and November 5, 2002.

42. Harkins, Woods, and Sherarts, *Indian Education in Minneapolis,* 1; Harkins et al., *Junior High Indian Children in Minneapolis,* 50. For examples of such opinions among public school educators, see Harkins, Sherarts, and Woods, *Teachers of Minneapolis Elementary Indian Children,* 24; Harkins et al., *Junior High Indian Children in Minneapolis,* 20; and Harkins, Sherarts, and Woods, *Urban Indian Education in Minneapolis,* 5. For conclusions drawn by researchers about Indian home life based on these findings, see Harkins, Woods, and Sherarts, *Indian Education in Minneapolis,* 5, 16; League of Women Voters of Minnesota, *Indians in Minnesota* (1971); Harkins, Sherarts, and Woods, *Teachers of St. Paul Elementary Indian Children,* *The Elementary Education of St. Paul Indian Children,* and *Attitudes of St. Paul Indian Parents and Influential Persons toward Formal Education.*

43. Harkins, Woods, and Sherarts, *Indian Education in Minneapolis,* 8. See also League of Women Voters of Minnesota, *Indians in Minnesota* (1971); Harkins, Sherarts, and Woods, *Teachers of Minneapolis Elementary Indian Children,* 24; Harkins, Sherarts, and Woods, *Urban Indian Education in Minneapolis,* 5.

44. Harkins, Sherarts, and Woods, *Teachers of Minneapolis Elementary Indian Children,* 24; Harkins, Sherarts, and Woods, *Teachers of St. Paul Elementary Indian Children,* 7.

45. Harkins, Sherarts, and Woods, *Teachers of St. Paul Elementary Indian Children,* 4; Harkins, Sherarts, and Woods, *Urban Indian Education in Minneapolis,* 3–4.

46. Journalist Catherine Watson made this suggestion in "Indian School Classrooms," Special Report on Indian Education in Minnesota (Part 2), Sunday Picture Magazine, *Minneapolis Tribune,* March 1969.

47. Szasz summarizes some of the problems of Indian education in this period in *Education and the American Indian,* 150–51, 187. For contemporary observations and criticisms, see Fuchs and Havighurst, *To Live on This Earth;* Henry, *The American Indian Reader;* Convocation of American Indian Scholars, *Indian Voices;* and U.S. Senate Committee on Labor and Public Welfare, *Indian Education.*

48. Pejsa, *The Life of Emily Peake;* U.S. Commission on Civil Rights, *Bridging the Gap: The Twin Cities Indian Community;* League of Women Voters of Minnesota, *Indians in Minnesota* (1971); Harkins and Woods, *Indian Americans in St. Paul;* Harkins, Woods, and Sherarts, *Indian Education in Minneapolis;* and League of Women Voters of Minneapolis, *American Indians and Minneapolis Public Services.*

49. Peacock and Wisuri, *Ojibwe: Waasa Inaabidaa,* 85–86; Beaulieu, "A Place among Nations," 424; Antell, "National Indian Education Association," 373; National Indian Education Association, "Call to Convention," 4–5.

50. The results of the National Study of American Education were published as Fuchs and Havighurst, *To Live on This Earth.* See also U.S. Senate Committee on Labor and Welfare, *Indian Education.*

51. Pat Bellanger, interviews, May 30, 2002, and June 13, 2002; Clyde Bellecourt, interview, January 21, 2003.

52. Pat Bellanger, interviews, May 30, 2002, and June 7, 2002; Banks, *Ojibwa Warrior,* 33.

53. Recorded conversation with Greg Bellanger, May 30, 2002.

54. Pat Bellanger, interviews, May 30, 2002, and June 7, 2002.

55. Information on reforms in Indian education in Minnesota and the Twin Cities comes from U.S. Commission on Civil Rights, *Bridging the Gap: The Twin Cities Indian Community;* League of Women Voters of Minnesota, *Indians in Minnesota* (1971); League of Women Voters of Minneapolis, *American Indians and Minneapolis Public Services;* Harkins and Woods, *Indian Americans in St. Paul;* and Harkins, Woods, and Sherarts, *Indian Education in Minneapolis.*

56. League of Women Voters of Minnesota, *Indians in Minnesota* (1971), 56; League of Women Voters of Minneapolis, *American Indians and Minneapolis Public Services;* Westermeyer, "Indian Powerlessness in Minnesota," 45.

57. Quoted in Harkins, Sherarts, and Woods, *Urban Indian Education in Minneapolis,* 7.

58. Both Clyde Bellecourt and Pat Bellanger discussed the frustrations of AIM members with efforts to reform Indian education from within the public educational system (Bellecourt, interview, January 21, 2003; Pat Bellanger, interviews, May 30, 2002, and June 7, 2002). Information on the St. Paul Open School comes from Pat Bellanger, interview, May 30, 2002. For an overview of the open education philosophy, see Barth, *Open Education and the American School.* For a discussion of how to practice open education by a leading contemporary proponent, see Kohl, *The Open Classroom.*

59. Pat Bellanger, interview, May 30, 2002.

60. Benton-Banai, quoted in Martin, "Thoughts from a Born-Again Pagan."

61. Pat Bellanger, interview, June 7, 2002.

62. Benton-Banai, quoted in Mary Jane Saunders, "Indian Students Learning

to Succeed," *St. Paul Dispatch*, October 31, 1978. Similarly, in a Heart of the Earth funding proposal from 1975, the grant writers stated that the Indian parents who started Heart of the Earth "wanted their children to be proud—to feel good about themselves and their heritage" (Martin, "Heart of the Earth Survival School," 11).

63. Jack Miller, "AIM Leader Asks School of, by, for Indians," *Minneapolis Tribune*, October 13, 1970.

64. Ibid.; Deborah Howell, "Indian 'Jury' Takes No Action on Bias Charge in City Schools," *Minneapolis Star*, October 22, 1969.

65. Miller, "AIM Leader Asks School of, by, for Indians"; Clyde Bellecourt, interview, January 21, 2003.

66. Westermeyer, "Indian Powerlessness in Minnesota," 49.

67. Ibid.; Holt, *Indian Orphanages*, 4; Mindell and Gurwitt, "The Placement of American Indian Children," 61–62; League of Women Voters of Minneapolis, *Indians in Minneapolis*, 51–53.

68. As reported by Mannes in "Factors and Events Leading to the Passage of the Indian Child Welfare Act," 269; Westermeyer, "Indian Powerlessness in Minnesota," 50; Bensen, "Introduction," 13; Byler, "The Destruction of American Indian Families," 1; League of Women Voters of Minneapolis, *Indians in Minneapolis*, 64.

69. Westermeyer, "Indian Powerlessness in Minnesota," 50; Byler, "The Destruction of American Indian Families," 2.

70. Mannes, "Factors and Events Leading to the Passage of the Indian Child Welfare Act," 267; Holt, *Indian Orphanages*, 4–5; Matheson, "The Politics of the Indian Child Welfare Act," 233; Byler, "The Destruction of American Indian Families," 1.

71. Quoted in Farley, *Women of the Native Struggle*, 81.

72. Peacock and Wisuri, *Ojibwe: Waasa Inaabidaa*, 81. Holt has outlined the impact of government policies, including the boarding school system, on Native family and social structures in *Indian Orphanages*, 13–15.

73. Such arguments have been made by Delaware-Cherokee psychologist Carolyn Attneave and historian Marilyn Irvin Holt. See Attneave, "The Wasted Strength of Indian Families," 30; and Holt, *Indian Orphanages*, 13–15.

74. Byler, "The Destruction of American Indian Families," 2–3; Blanchard, "The Question of Best Interest," 11–12.

75. Byler, "The Destruction of American Indian Families," 3. See also Red Horse, "American Indian Elders," 490–91; Sorkin, *The Urban American Indian*, 82. For other discussions of the misunderstanding of American Indian extended families and kinship networks by child-care workers, see Holt, *Indian Orphanages*, 10; and Halverson, Puig, and Byers, "Culture Loss," 322.

76. Byler, "The Destruction of American Indian Families," 3; Abourezk, "The Role of the Federal Government," 12.

77. Byler, "The Destruction of American Indian Families," 4, 5; Unger, "Preface," iii; Mindell and Gurwitt, "The Placement of American Indian Children," 63; Jimson, "Parent and Child Relationships in Law and in Navajo Custom," 68.

78. Armitage, *Comparing the Policy of Aboriginal Assimilation*, 209.

79. Ibid., 192.

80. Ibid., 193; Mark Rifkin, "A Note to Patrick Wolfe," comment on Tequila Sovereign blog, April 28, 2011.

81. Armitage, *Comparing the Policy of Aboriginal Assimilation*, 240, xii.

82. Dorene Day, interview, March 14, 2003.

83. Ibid.

84. Ibid.

85. Clyde Bellecourt, interview, January 21, 2003; Pat Bellanger, interview, December 3, 2002.

86. Pat Bellanger, interviews, May 30, 2002, and December 3, 2002; Clyde Bellecourt, interview, January 21, 2003; League of Women Voters of Minnesota, *Indians in Minnesota* (1971), 134.

87. Dorene Day, interview, March 14, 2003.

88. Dating this sequence of events accurately is difficult, as written and oral sources provide conflicting information, diverging by as much as two years. I have constructed my chronology of events by comparing many different accounts and creating a timeline that the most reliable sources support. Information in this paragraph comes from Clyde Bellecourt, interview, January 21, 2003; Pat Bellanger, interview, May 23, 2002; Vikki Howard, interview, May 9, 2002; Jim O'Brien as reported in Fife, *Indian Education*, 9.

89. Martin, "Heart of the Earth Survival School," states that at Christmas in 1971, "A parent is threatened with jail if his children do not attend public school" (2). Based on an interview with Clyde Bellecourt conducted in September 1974, U.S. Commission on Civil Rights, *Bridging the Gap: The Twin Cities Indian Community*, states that it was in 1971 that a judge "threatened to sentence an Indian couple to the workhouse if they did not enroll their children in school" (52). Thompson writes in "Survival Schools" that the Roys "faced workhouse sentences if they didn't comply with a court order to return their sons to public schools" (23). Clyde Bellecourt told me that the Roys "came and told us the courts sentenced them to six months in the workhouse, and they were going to take their children away from them, for contributing to the delinquency of minors." Bellecourt also said the Roys had been homeschooling for "a couple of months before they got caught" (Clyde Bellecourt, interview, January 21, 2003).

90. Clyde Bellecourt, interview, January 21, 2003.

91. Pat Bellanger, interview, May 30, 2002; Clyde Bellecourt, interview,

January 21, 2003. Bellecourt recalled that the school was founded in February 1971. A timeline in Martin, "Heart of the Earth Survival School," however, states that the school opened on January 3, 1972 (2). In "Survival Schools," Thompson says that the school opened in 1972 (23), as do Fife, *Indian Education* (9), and "The Heart of the Earth Survival School," *Akwesasne Notes.* The Articles of Incorporation of A.I.M. Survival School, Inc., were signed and notarized April 10, 1972.

92. Thompson, "Survival Schools," 23; Martin, "Heart of the Earth Survival School," 2; Clyde Bellecourt, interview, January 21, 2003.

93. Dorene Day, interview, November 5, 2002.

94. Ibid.

95. Dorene Day, interviews, November 5, 2002, and March 14, 2003.

96. Pat Bellanger, interview, June 13, 2003.

97. Clyde Bellecourt, interview, January 21, 2003; Pat Bellanger, interviews, May 23, 2002, and May 30, 2002.

98. Dorene Day, interviews, March 14, 2003, and September 27, 2004.

3. From One World to Another

1. This portrait of survival school students comes from Heart of the Earth Survival School, "The Heart of the Earth Survival School," 1979–80, 14; Schierle, *Funktion einer Survival School für städtische Indianer,* 93, 159; Martin, "Heart of the Earth Survival School," 6, 8, 48; Thompson, "Survival Schools," 22; Honor the Earth Committee, "Program"; Lounberg, "The New Face of the American Indian Movement," 464; Clyde Bellecourt, interview, January 21, 2003; Pat Bellanger, interviews, June 7, 2002, June 13, 2002, and June 20, 2002; and Johnny Smith, interview, July 10. 2002.

2. Clyde Bellecourt, interview, January 21, 2003; Pat Bellanger, interview, June 7, 2002; Martin, "Heart of the Earth Survival School," 2–3; U.S. Commission on Civil Rights, *Bridging the Gap,* 52; Schierle, *Funktion einer Survival School für städtische Indianer,* 95; Red School House, "Heart Beat of Our Nation," 12–13.

3. Clyde Bellecourt, interview, January 21, 2003; Fife, *Indian Education,* 9; Martin, "Heart of the Earth Survival School," 3, 52; Thompson, "Survival Schools," 18, 23; Martin, "Heart of the Earth Survival School"; Honor the Earth Committee, "Program."

4. Red School House, "Knowledge through Cultural Understanding," 7, 19–20; Red School House, "Heart Beat of Our Nation," 11; Dorothy Lewis, "Indian School Has Direction," *St. Paul Dispatch,* September 6, 1976; Dorothy Lewis, "Indian School Fights for Survival," *St. Paul Dispatch,* October 3, 1974.

5. Pat Bellanger, interview, May 30, 2002; Red School House, "Heart Beat

of Our Nation," 12; U.S. Commission on Civil Rights, *Bridging the Gap: The Twin Cities Indian Community,* 52; Heart of the Earth Survival School, "The Heart of the Earth Survival School," Heart of the Earth yearbook, 1979–80, 14; Pat Bellanger, interviews, June 7, 2002, June 20, 2002.

6. Pat Bellanger, interviews, June 7, 2002, June 20, 2002, and October 17, 2002.

7. Thompson, "Survival Schools," 23; Fife, *Indian Education,* 9; Martin, "Heart of the Earth Survival School," 2–3, 35; Clyde Bellecourt, interview, January 21, 2003; Heart of the Earth Survival School, "The Heart of the Earth Survival School," 1979–80, 14; U.S. Commission on Civil Rights, *Bridging the Gap: The Twin Cities Indian Community,* 52.

8. Red School House, "Red School House: Information Packet," 1–2; Red School House, "Heart Beat of Our Nation," 12; Lewis, "Indian School Has Direction"; Rachelle Crow, "Students Help at Red School," *St. Paul Dispatch,* August 4, 1978; Heart of the Earth Survival School, "The Heart of the Earth Survival School," 1979–80, 14; Lewis, "Indian School Fights for Survival."

9. The schools' procurement of permanent facilities is documented in Lewis, "Indian School Fights for Survival"; Red School House, "Knowledge through Cultural Understanding," 7–10; Red School House, "Heart Beat of Our Nation," 14; Clyde Bellecourt, interview, January 21, 2003; Heart of the Earth Survival School, "The Heart of the Earth Survival School," 1979–80, 14; Honor the Earth Committee, "Program"; Schierle, *Funktion einer Survival School für städtische Indianer,* 95; and "The Heart of the Earth Survival School," *Akwesasne Notes.* Quotes from Schierle, *Funktion einer Survival School für städtische Indianer,* 95, and Red School House, "Knowledge through Cultural Understanding," 9–10.

10. Funding information for Heart of the Earth comes from U.S. Commission on Civil Rights, *Bridging the Gap: The Twin Cities Indian Community,* 52; Schierle, *Funktion einer Survival School für städtische Indianer,* 95; "The Heart of the Earth Survival School," *Akwesasne Notes;* and Fife, *Indian Education,* 11–12. For the Red School House, funding history comes from Red School House, "Knowledge through Cultural Understanding," 1, 21; Red School House, "Heart Beat of Our Nation," 12–13; Bourman, "The Red School House of St. Paul," 5–6; and Red School House, *The Seventh Fire.* The receipt of OEO funds is documented in U.S. Commission on Civil Rights, *Bridging the Gap: The Twin Cities Indian Community,* 52; and Schierle, *Funktion einer Survival School für städtische Indianer,* 94. The growth enabled by increased funding during these years is reflected in Red School House, "Heart Beat of Our Nation," 13; Lewis, "Indian School Has Direction"; and Heart of the Earth Survival School, "The Heart of the Earth Survival School," 1979–80, 14–15.

11. A sense of the survival schools' changing relationship to the public

schools comes from U.S. Commission on Civil Rights, *Bridging the Gap: A Reassessment*, 13; Fife, *Indian Education*, 10–12; and Red School House, "Red School House: Information Packet," 3. Information on the schools' first graduates comes from Heart of the Earth Survival School, "The Heart of the Earth Survival School," 1979–80, 14; and Red School House, "Heart Beat of Our Nation," 12.

12. The founding of the Federation is covered in "The Heart of the Earth Survival School," *Akwesasne Notes*.

13. The theory and practice of dividing survival school students into modules and areas rather than grades is addressed in Thompson, "Survival Schools," 19; Schierle, *Funktion einer Survival School für städtische Indianer*, 109; Red School House, "Knowledge through Cultural Understanding," 11; Red School House, "Heart Beat of Our Nation," 20; and Bourman, "The Red School House of St. Paul," 2.

14. The emphasis on individualized learning is highlighted in Schierle, *Funktion einer Survival School für städtische Indianer*, 109–10, 159; Red School House, "Knowledge through Cultural Understanding," 11; and Red School House, "Heart Beat of Our Nation," 20.

15. Interview with Eddie Benton-Banai reported in Mary Jane Saunders, "Indian Students Learning to Succeed," *St. Paul Dispatch*, October 31, 1978; "The Red School House Philosophy" from Red School House, "We, Yesterday, Today, Tomorrow." Benton-Banai expressed a similar commitment to individualized education in a statement in Red School House, "Knowledge through Cultural Understanding," 2–3.

16. Barth provides a theoretical overview of the characteristics of open education in *Open Education and the American School*; see especially 3–58. For another contemporary perspective by a leading practitioner of open education, see Kohl, *The Open Classroom*.

17. Evidence of group learning is found in Martin, "Heart of the Earth Survival School," 47; Schierle, *Funktion einer Survival School für städtische Indianer*, 101; Fife, *Indian Education*, 10; Red School House, "Knowledge through Cultural Understanding," 11; and Red School House, "Heart Beat of Our Nation," 20.

18. Lounberg, "The New Face of the American Indian Movement," 464–66.

19. "An Indian School," *Focus: Indian Education* 3, no. 5 (1972): 16–17.

20. Schierle, *Funktion einer Survival School für städtische Indianer*, 108, 112 (my translation).

21. Thompson, "Survival Schools," 23.

22. Schierle, *Funktion einer Survival School für städtische Indianer*, 112–13, 104, 137; Pat Bellanger, interview, June 7, 2002.

23. Thompson, "Survival Schools," 23.

24. Schierle, *Funktion einer Survival School für städtische Indianer*, 135, 138 (my translation). Former Heart of the Earth teachers and administrators Vikki

Howard and Johnny Smith also spoke in interviews about the problem of high teacher turnover, though they attributed it primarily to the lower pay scale than in the public school system (Vikki Howard, interview, May 9, 2002; Johnny Smith, interview, July 10, 2002).

25. Pat Bellanger, interviews, May 30, 2002, June 7, 2002, and October 17, 2002.

26. Clyde Bellecourt, interview, January 21, 2003; Benton-Banai quoted in Red School House, "Knowledge through Cultural Understanding," 2–3.

27. Clyde Bellecourt, interview, January 21, 2003; Pat Bellanger, interviews, June 7, 2002, June 20, 2002, October 17, 2002. The dedication of the volunteers who staffed and otherwise supported the survival schools in the beginning also figures prominently in every written account of the schools' founding and early years.

28. Pat Bellanger, interview, June 13, 2002. References to parental participation at the survival schools are also found in Pat Bellanger, interviews, June 7, 2002, June 20, 2002, and October 17, 2002; Martin, "Heart of the Earth Survival School"; Red School House, "Red School House: Information Packet"; Honor the Earth Committee, "Program"; statement of "The Red School House Philosophy," in Red School House, "We, Yesterday, Today, Tomorrow"; "An Indian School," 17; and Schierle, *Funktion einer Survival School für städtische Indianer*, 105.

29. Schierle, *Funktion einer Survival School für städtische Indianer*, 104 (my translation); statement of "The Red School House Philosophy," in Red School House, "We, Yesterday, Today, Tomorrow."

30. Information about HOTESS governing structure comes from Martin, "Heart of the Earth Survival School," 54, appendix 1. Red School House information comes from Red School House, "Knowledge through Cultural Understanding," 2, and Red School House, "Heart Beat of Our Nation," 19.

31. For a description of the community control movement in urban public schools, see Gittel, "Urban School Reform in the 1970s," 295–303.

32. Pat Bellanger, interviews, June 13, 2002, and June 20, 2002.

33. Pat Bellanger, interview, June 7, 2002.

34. Information on Rough Rock Demonstration School comes from Castile, "The Community School at Rough Rock"; Dunlap, *The Educational Process of Rough Rock Community High School;* Iverson, *Diné,* 235; Johnson, *Navaho Education at Rough Rock;* Lomawaima and McCarty, "When Tribal Sovereignty Challenges Democracy," 279–305; McCarty, *A Place to Be Navajo;* Roessel, *Navajo Education in Action;* Rosenfelt, "Indian Schools and Community Control"; and Szasz, *Education and the American Indian,* 170–76.

35. Information on Pine Point comes from Buckanaga, "Pine Point School"; Pine Point Elementary School, "Pine Point School"; and Pine Point Experimental School, "Pine Point Experimental School."

36. Iverson, *Diné*, 235; McCarty, *A Place to Be Navajo*, 132–50; Buckanaga, "Pine Point School"; Pine Point Elementary School, "Pine Point School"; and Pine Point Experimental School, "Pine Point Experimental School."

37. Krouse, "What Came Out of the Takeovers," 146–59.

38. "An Indian School," 17. Other comments on student–staff relationships are found in Peggy Gislason, "School Stresses Cultural Survival," *Minnesota Daily*, January 26, 1978; Heart of the Earth Survival School, "The Heart of the Earth Survival School," 1979–80, 17; Martin, "Heart of the Earth Survival School," 60; and Bourman, "The Red School House of St. Paul," 3–4.

39. Red School House, "We, Yesterday, Today, Tomorrow." Red School House founder and director Eddie Benton-Banai also expressed commitment to fostering close, supportive relationships between staff and students in a statement in Red School House, "Knowledge through Cultural Understanding," 2–3.

40. Descriptions of the relationships fostered among students come from Martin, "Heart of the Earth Survival School," 12, 29, 37; Red School House, "Knowledge through Cultural Understanding," 2–3, 11; Bourman, "The Red School House of St. Paul," 3; and Schierle, *Funktion einer Survival School für städtische Indianer*, 109, 113.

41. Reflections on the family environment created by the survival schools come from Gislason, "School Stresses Cultural Survival"; Schierle, *Funktion einer Survival School für städtische Indianer*, 159; and Johnny Smith, interview, July 10, 2002. Evidence of the widespread blood ties among survival school students and staff is gleaned from "An Indian School"; Heart of the Earth Survival School, "The Heart of the Earth Survival School," 1979–80; Red School House, "Red School House: Information Packet"; Red School House, "Knowledge through Cultural Understanding"; Red School House, "We, Yesterday, Today, Tomorrow"; and Clyde Bellecourt, interview, January 21, 2003.

42. Dr. Margaret Silverberg, a psychologist who worked with HOTESS students, commented on the importance of having Indian teachers for Indian students in an interview with journalist Sally Thompson (Thompson, "Survival Schools," 22). HOTESS director Jim O'Brien emphasized the comfort level created by having mostly Indian students in small classrooms in Fife, *Indian Education*, 10. In a December 10, 2002, interview, former Red School House student Dorene Day spoke of her appreciation for the school's small size and intimate atmosphere. The presence of staff members' babies and toddlers in the survival schools is addressed in Lounberg, "The New Face of the American Indian Movement," 465, and Heart of the Earth Survival School, "The Heart of the Earth Survival School," 1979–80.

43. Dorene Day, interview, December 10, 2002.

44. Quoted in Fife, *Indian Education*, 12.

45. Quoted in Red School House, *The Seventh Fire*, 6.

46. Dorene Day, interview, December 10, 2002.

47. Vikki Howard, interview, May 9, 2002. The similarly multifaceted responsibilities and deep personal commitment of teachers at the Red School House is described by Joni Bourman in "The Red School House of St. Paul," 3. Bourman visited Red School House in the fall of 1978.

48. Vikki Howard, interview, May 9, 2002; Eddie Benton-Banai quoted in Saunders, "Indian Students Learning to Succeed."

4. Building Our Own Communities

1. Red School House, "Knowledge through Cultural Understanding," 15.

2. Information on language courses and instructors comes from Thompson, "Survival Schools," 20; Schierle, *Funktion einer Survival School für städtische Indianer*, 114; Red School House, "Red School House: Information Packet," 11; Red School House, "Heart Beat of Our Nation," 20; Leslie Scanlon, "A Matter of Pride and Culture," *Minnesota Daily*, November 17, 1977; Red School House, *The Seventh Fire*, 30–32.

3. Thompson, "Survival Schools," 20; Reyhner, "Some Basics of Indigenous Language Revitalization," v–vi; Vikki Howard, interview, May 9, 2002.

4. Christensen, "Written Statement," 101. See also Littlebear, "Preface"; Reyhner, "Rationale and Needs for Stabilizing Indigenous Languages"; Krauss, "Status of Native American Language Endangerment"; and Fishman, "What Do You Lose When You Lose Your Language?" I also have drawn from Reyhner, "Some Basics of Indigenous Language Revitalization," and Kawagley, "Nurturing Native Languages."

5. Information about the traditional knowledge, skills, traditions, and rituals taught to survival school students in this period comes from Martin, "Heart of the Earth Survival School"; Schierle, *Funktion einer Survival School für städtische Indianer;* Heart of the Earth Survival School, "The Heart of the Earth Survival School," 1979–80; Red School House, "Red School House: Information Packet"; Red School House, "Heart Beat of Our Nation"; Red School House, "We, Yesterday, Today, Tomorrow"; Red School House, *The Seventh Fire;* Thompson, "Survival Schools"; Pat Bellanger, interviews, May 30, 2002; June 7, 2002; June 13, 2002; June 20, 2002; October 17, 2002; and December 3, 2002; Clyde Bellecourt, interview, January 21, 2002; Lisa Bellanger, interviews, August 27, 2002, and November 4, 2002; and Gabriel Strong, interviews, December 11, 2002, and January 7, 2003. Descriptions of school field trips are found in Thompson, "Survival Schools," 21–22, and Schierle, *Funktion einer Survival School für städtische Indianer,* 116.

6. Clyde Bellecourt, interview, January 21, 2003. Information on reservation visits and seasonal camps also comes from Pat Bellanger, interviews, May 30, 2002, and June 7, 2002; Martin, "Heart of the Earth Survival School"; Heart of

the Earth Survival School, "The Heart of the Earth Survival School," 1979–80; Red School House, "Heart Beat of Our Nation"; and Red School House, "We, Yesterday, Today, Tomorrow."

7. Martin, "Heart of the Earth Survival School," 18, 16.

8. Information on Rough Rock Demonstration School comes from Castile, *The Community School at Rough Rock;* Dunlap, *The Educational Process of Rough Rock Community High School;* Iverson, *Diné,* 235; Johnson, *Navaho Education at Rough Rock;* Lomawaima and McCarty, "When Tribal Sovereignty Challenges Democracy"; McCarty, *A Place to Be Navajo;* Roessel, *Navajo Education in Action;* Rosenfelt, "Indian Schools and Community Control"; and Szasz, *Education and the American Indian,* 170–76.

9. Information on Pine Point comes from Buckanaga, "Pine Point School"; Pine Point Elementary School, "Pine Point School"; and Pine Point Experimental School, "Pine Point Experimental School."

10. Krouse, "What Came Out of the Takeovers," 148, 151.

11. Information about the traditional values taught in the survival schools comes from Martin, "Heart of the Earth Survival School"; Heart of the Earth Survival School, "The Heart of the Earth Survival School," 1979–80; Schierle, *Funktion einer Survival School für städtische Indianer;* Thompson, "Survival Schools"; Red School House, "Knowledge through Cultural Understanding"; Red School House, "Heart Beat of Our Nation"; Red School House, "We, Yesterday, Today, Tomorrow"; Red School House, "Indian Student Motivational Posters"; and three coloring books written by Eddie Benton-Banai and published as cultural curriculum materials by the Red School House: *A Mishomis Book, Book One: The Ojibway Creation Story, Book Two: Original Man Walks the Earth,* and *Book Three: Original Man and His Grandmother No-ko-mis.* I also have drawn from interviews with Lisa Bellanger, Pat Bellanger, Clyde Bellecourt, Dorene Day, Vikki Howard, and Gabrielle Strong.

12. The spiritual dimension of survival school education permeates school documents and other primary texts. It also emerged in interviews with Lisa Bellanger, Pat Bellanger, Clyde Bellecourt, Dorene Day, Vikki Howard, Johnny Smith, and Gabrielle Strong.

13. The prevalence of the circle in the schools during this period emerged from Red School House, "Heart Beat of Our Nation," 20; Fife, *Indian Education,* 14; Mary Jane Saunders, "One Day at School," *St. Paul Dispatch,* November 7, 1978; and interviews with Pat Bellanger, Clyde Bellecourt, Dorene Day, and Vikki Howard.

14. It is difficult to tease out of school documents exactly which kinds of identities were incorporated into what parts of school curriculum, how they were taught, and what students took away from them. Interviews with survival school educators and former students did not entirely clarify things. Some people

seemed reluctant to talk about this issue, and some did not seem to think it was important enough to discuss in depth. What follows is an explanation of what I was able to glean from interviews and document research, also analyzed in a broader historical and theoretical context.

15. Heart of the Earth "Philosophy of Instruction" as stated in Martin, "Heart of the Earth Survival School"; Pat Bellanger, interview, June 7, 2002.

16. Bonney, "The Role of AIM Leaders in Indian Nationalism," 210–11.

17. The persistence and rediscovery of tribal identities in twentieth-century urban Indian communities is emphasized in Straus and Valentino, "Retribalization in Urban Indian Communities," and Carpio, *Indigenous Albuquerque.*

18. Miller, "Native America Writes Back," 10, 22–24; Battiste, "Maintaining Aboriginal Identity, Language, and Culture in Modern Society," 192.

19. Quote from Martin, "Heart of the Earth Survival School," 27. Tribal leaders, accomplishments, and contributions also are emphasized in teacher's manuals produced by a South Dakota curriculum project and used at Heart of the Earth in 1977–78: Allery, *The Indians Speak for Themselves,* and Palm, *Government of the Indian People.*

20. Martin, "Heart of the Earth Survival School," 27; Vikki Howard, interview, May 9, 2002. Teacher's manuals for a set of curriculum materials used at HOTESS in the late 1970s take a critical approach to the history of Indian–white relations in the United States. See Allery, *The Indians Speak for Themselves;* Palm, *Government of the Indian People;* and Bublitz, *Indian Memories.*

21. Schierle, *Funktion einer Survival School für städtische Indianer,* 88 (my translation). Schierle's study devotes considerable attention to the political component of the educational philosophy and curriculum at Heart of the Earth.

22. Information about the political awareness cultivated at the survival schools comes from ibid.; Martin, "Heart of the Earth Survival School"; Thompson, "Survival Schools"; Heart of the Earth Survival School, "The Heart of the Earth Survival School," 1979–80; Red School House, "Red School House: Information Packet"; Red School House, "Heart Beat of Our Nation"; Red School House, *The Seventh Fire;* and interviews with Lisa Bellanger, Pat Bellanger, Dorene Day, and Vikki Howard.

23. The schools' concern with other minority and Indigenous struggles emerged primarily from interviews with Lisa Bellanger, Pat Bellanger, Dorene Day, and Vikki Howard.

24. This account of the political education that took place within the survival schools comes from Schierle, *Funktion einer Survival School für städtische Indianer;* Heart of the Earth Survival School, "The Heart of the Earth Survival School," 1979–80; Martin, "Heart of the Earth Survival School"; Red School House, "Heart Beat of Our Nation"; and interviews with Lisa Bellanger, Pat Bellanger, Dorene Day, and Vikki Howard.

25. Quoted in Gislason, "School Stresses Cultural Survival." Accounts of political excursions come from Schierle, *Funktion einer Survival School für städtische Indianer;* Heart of the Earth Survival School, "The Heart of the Earth Survival School," 1979–80; Martin, "Heart of the Earth Survival School"; and interviews with Lisa Bellanger, Pat Bellanger, and Dorene Day.

26. Accounts of students' participation in political actions within the Twin Cities come from Schierle, *Funktion einer Survival School für städtische Indianer;* Heart of the Earth Survival School, "The Heart of the Earth Survival School," 1979–80; and interviews with Lisa Bellanger, Dorene Day, and Gabrielle Strong.

27. Schierle, *Funktion einer Survival School für städtische Indianer,* 131–32.

28. Information on the freedom schools comes from Adickes, *The Legacy of a Freedom School;* McAdam, *Freedom Summer;* Payne, *I've Got the Light of Freedom;* Perlstein, "Minds Stayed on Freedom" and "Teaching Freedom"; and Van Deburg, *New Day in Babylon,* 49–51.

29. Information on the Black Panther schools comes from Perlstein, "Minds Stayed on Freedom."

30. Vikki Howard, interview, May 9, 2002.

31. Heart of the Earth Survival School, "The Heart of the Earth Survival School," 1979–80, 62. An emphasis on cultural teachings regarding community responsibility and working for one's people also surfaced in Martin, "Heart of the Earth Survival School," 23–26, 37; Red School House, "Heart Beat of Our Nation," 31; and interviews with Pat Bellanger.

32. The messages of visiting speakers comes from Schierle, *Funktion einer Survival School für städtische Indianer,* and from interviews with Lisa Bellanger, Pat Bellanger, Clyde Bellecourt, and Dorene Day. Descriptions of circle time come from Red School House, "Heart Beat of Our Nation," 20; Saunders, "One Day at School"; and interviews with Pat Bellanger, Clyde Bellecourt, Dorene Day, and Vikki Howard.

33. Pat Bellanger, interviews, May 30, 2002, and June 20, 2002; Red School House, "Knowledge through Cultural Understanding."

34. Smith and Warrior, *Like a Hurricane,* 132.

35. Ibid., 99, 132; Vick, "The Press and Wounded Knee, 1976," 7; League of Women Voters of Minnesota, *Indians in Minnesota* (1971), 42.

36. Smith and Warrior, *Like a Hurricane,* 135–36, 115; Laura Waterman Wittstock and Elaine J. Salinas, "A Brief History of the American Indian Movement," American Indian Movement Web site, accessed August 26, 2002, http://www.aimovement.org/ggc/history.html.

37. Smith and Warrior provide an extensive account of the Trail of Broken Treaties and the BIA occupation in *Like a Hurricane,* 139–68.

38. U.S. Commission on Civil Rights, *Bridging the Gap: The Twin Cities Indian Community,* 52; Fife, *Indian Education,* 10; Heart of the Earth Survival

School, "The Heart of the Earth Survival School," 1979–80, 14; Schierle, *Funktion einer Survival School für städtische Indianer*, 94; Krouse, "What Came Out of the Takeovers," 150.

39. AIM's activities on the Pine Ridge reservation and the Wounded Knee occupation are described in Smith and Warrior, *Like a Hurricane*, 177–268. AIM's lawsuit against the OEO and the federal court ruling are documented in Martin, "Heart of the Earth Survival School," 3, appendix 1; Heart of the Earth Survival School, "The Heart of the Earth Survival School," 1979–80, 14; Fife, *Indian Education*, 10. Clyde Bellecourt also discussed them in an interview on January 21, 2003. The case represented Heart of the Earth, the Red School House, and the Indian Community School of Milwaukee, and it was decided by Judge Miles W. Lord of U.S. District Court, District of Minnesota 4-73 Civ. 197, on November 7, 1973.

40. Fife, *Indian Education*, 10; Heart of the Earth Survival School, "The Heart of the Earth Survival School," 1979–80, 14; Clyde Bellecourt, interview, January 21, 2003; Pat Bellanger, interview, June 7, 2002; Schierle, *Funktion einer Survival School für städtische Indianer*, 139 (my translation).

41. Pat Bellanger, interview, June 7, 2002.

42. Schierle, *Funktion einer Survival School für städtische Indianer*, 131 (my translation).

43. Thompson, "Survival Schools," 20–21.

44. Red School House, "Knowledge through Cultural Understanding"; Blakey and Benton-Banai, *The Sounding Voice*, 14.

45. The goal of cross-cultural understanding is especially prominent in Red School House, "Heart Beat of Our Nation"; Red School House, "Knowledge through Cultural Understanding"; and Benton-Banai, *The Mishomis Book*. It also is reflected in Dorene Day's recollections of the Red School House cultural outreach program (interview, December 10, 2002) and in an interview with Eddie Benton-Banai in Dorothy Lewis, "Indian School Has Direction," *St. Paul Dispatch*, October 3, 1974. Similar goals at Heart of the Earth are expressed in Martin, "Heart of the Earth Survival School," 28, and in an interview with HOTESS director Jim O'Brien in U.S. Commission on Civil Rights, *Bridging the Gap: The Twin Cities Indian Community*, 53.

46. Martin, "Heart of the Earth Survival School," 28.

47. Dorene Day, interview, December 10, 2002.

48. Red School House, *Our Brothers' Keeper*; Red School House, "Knowledge through Cultural Understanding."

49. Schierle, *Funktion einer Survival School für städtische Indianer*, 138 (my translation).

50. Ibid., 139, 133 (my translation).

51. Ibid., 129 (my translation).

52. Red School House, "Heart Beat of Our Nation," 8.

53. Martin, "Heart of the Earth Survival School," 22; Red School House, "Heart Beat of Our Nation," 6; Pat Bellanger, interview, June 13, 2002; Clyde Bellecourt, interview, January 21, 2003.

54. Schierle, *Funktion einer Survival School für städtische Indianer,* 101 (my translation), 94.

55. Clyde Bellecourt, interview, January 21, 2003.

56. Thompson, "Survival Schools," 23.

57. Examples of culturally integrated curriculum come from Martin, "Heart of the Earth Survival School," 28–29; Schierle, *Funktion einer Survival School für städtische Indianer,* 124; and Fife, *Indian Education,* 10–11.

58. Pat Bellanger, interview, June 20, 2002.

59. Laura Waterman Wittstock, e-mails to author, September 24, 2002, and February 26, 2003.

60. Lisa Bellanger, interview, November 4, 2002.

61. Laura Waterman Wittstock, e-mails to author, September 24, 2002, and February 26, 2003.

62. Ibid.

63. Red School House, "Heart Beat of Our Nation," 31. Three Fires activities also are described in Red School House, "Knowledge through Cultural Understanding"; Red School House, *The Seventh Fire,* 7; Lounberg, "The New Face of the American Indian Movement," 463; Red School House, *Our Brothers' Keeper;* and Red School House, "Three Fires: St. Paul, Minn." The group's name alludes to a historical alliance among the Ojibwe, Odawa, and Potawatomi nations.

64. The beginnings of Red School House Graphics are narrated in Red School House, "Knowledge through Cultural Understanding," 13.

65. Red School House, "Heart Beat of Our Nation," 32. The *Mishomis Book* coloring book series, written by Eddie Benton-Banai, included "Book One: The Ojibway Creation Story"; "Book Two: Original Man Walks the Earth"; "Book Three: Original Man and His Grandmother No-ko-mis"; "Book Four: The Earth's First People"; and "Book Five: The Great Flood."

66. The noncoloring book version of the *Mishomis Book* series was written by Eddie Benton-Banai and published as *The Mishomis Book: The Voice of the Ojibway* in 1979. Collections of student and staff writings published by Indian Country Press include Blakey and Benton-Banai, *The Sounding Voice,* and Neima, *We Learn about Ourselves Now.*

67. Pat Bellanger, interviews, June 7, 2002, and May 30, 2002; Martin, "Heart of the Earth Survival School," 57.

68. Pat Bellanger, interview, June 7, 2002. Examples of family and community involvement in survival school cultural programs are found in Red School House, "Knowledge through Cultural Understanding"; Red School House,

"Heart Beat of Our Nation"; Red School House, "We, Yesterday, Today, Tomorrow"; Bourman, "The Red School House of St. Paul"; Heart of the Earth Survival School, "The Heart of the Earth Survival School," 1979–80; Schierle, *Funktion einer Survival School für städtische Indianer*, 105, 126; and interviews with Lisa Bellanger, Pat Bellanger, Clyde Bellecourt, Dorene Day, and Vikki Howard.

69. Lisa Bellanger, interview, November 4, 2002.

70. Martin, "Heart of the Earth Survival School," 16–17. The schools' adult education programs also are described in Heart of the Earth Survival School, "The Heart of the Earth Survival School," 1979–80; Schierle, *Funktion einer Survival School für städtische Indianer*, 105; Fife, *Indian Education*, 11; Red School House, "Knowledge through Cultural Understanding"; and Red School House, *The Seventh Fire*, 29.

71. Evidence of family and community members' political involvement comes from Schierle, *Funktion einer Survival School für städtische Indianer*, 126; Bourman, "The Red School House of St. Paul"; and interviews with Lisa Bellanger, Pat Bellanger, Clyde Bellecourt, Dorene Day, and Vikki Howard.

72. Description of Red School House social-service programs comes from Red School House, "Knowledge through Cultural Understanding," 12–14.

73. Elaine Martin Salinas, quoted in Heart of the Earth Survival School, "The Heart of the Earth Survival School," 1979–80, 59; Bourman, "The Red School House of St. Paul," 5; Lisa Bellanger, interview, November 4, 2002.

74. Honor the Earth Committee, "Program."

5. Conflict, Adaptation, Continuity, and Closure, 1982–2008

1. My understanding of the kinds of conflicts that developed at the survival schools in this period, as discussed here in and in the following paragraphs, draws from interviews with Lisa Bellanger, Pat Bellanger, Clyde Bellecourt, Dorene Day, Rick Powers, Johnny Smith, and Gabrielle Strong.

2. Heart of the Earth Survival School, "The Heart of the Earth Survival School," 1985–86; Heart of the Earth Survival School, "Welcome to the 6th Annual Heart of the Earth Contest Pow Wow"; Vikki Howard, interview, May 9, 2002.

3. Heart of the Earth Survival School, "The Heart of the Earth Survival School," 1979–80, 1985–86, and 1993–94; Heart of the Earth Survival School, "Chimigezi Winage," 1983–84 and 1984–85.

4. This analysis draws from Heart of the Earth Survival School, "The Heart of the Earth Survival School," 1979–80, 1985–86, and 1993–94; Heart of the Earth Survival School, "Chimigezi Winage," 1983–84 and 1984–85; Heart of the Earth Survival School, "Welcome to the 6th Annual Heart of the Earth Contest Pow Wow"; Vikki Howard, interview, May 9, 2002; Pat Bellanger, interview,

June 13, 2002; and Child, *Holding Our World Together*, 157–58; Howard quoted in Child, *Holding Our World Together*, 157.

5. Lisa Bellanger, interview, November 4, 2002; Gabrielle Strong, interview, January 7, 2003.

6. My understanding of the interpersonal conflicts that developed at the survival schools in this period, as discussed here in and in the following paragraphs, draws from interviews with Lisa Bellanger, Pat Bellanger, Clyde Bellecourt, Dorene Day, Rick Powers, Johnny Smith, and Gabrielle Strong.

7. Pat Bellanger, interview, June 13, 2002.

8. Ibid.

9. Ibid.

10. Gabrielle Strong, interviews, December 11, 2002, and January 7, 2003; Rick Powers, interview, August 8, 2002.

11. McCarty, *A Place to Be Navajo*, chapters 9, 10, and 12; Battiste, "Maintaining Aboriginal Identity," 207.

12. President Nixon used the phrase "self-determination without termination" in his Special Message to Congress on Indian Affairs, delivered on July 8, 1970. But the foundations of a federal Indian policy of self-determination were laid during Johnson's presidency. For discussions of the roots of self-determination policy, see Castille, *To Show Heart*, and Cobb, "Philosophy of an Indian War."

13. For OEO programs and Indian communities, see Castille, *To Show Heart*, and Cobb, "Philosophy of an Indian War." Information on survival school funding comes from U.S. Commission on Civil Rights, *Bridging the Gap: The Twin Cities Indian Community*; Fife, *Indian Education*; Schierle, *Funktion einer Survival School für städtische Indianer*; Dorothy Lewis, "Indian School Fights for Survival," *St. Paul Dispatch*, October 3, 1974; Red School House, "Knowledge through Cultural Understanding"; Red School House, "Heart Beat of Our Nation"; Bourman, "The Red School House of St. Paul"; and Red School House, *The Seventh Fire*.

14. For discussions of the provisions and importance of these pieces of legislation, see Szasz, *Education and the American Indian*, 197–200; Reyhner and Eder, *American Indian Education*; Castille, *To Show Heart*; and McCarty, *A Place to Be Navajo*, 114–20.

15. McCarty, *A Place to Be Navajo*, 114.

16. Morris, "Termination by Accountants," 65.

17. Ibid. See also McCarty, *A Place to Be Navajo*, 142.

18. McCarty illuminates the shifting political and financial context for Indian-controlled, culture-based, community schools from the late 1960s through the 1980s and examines their impact on internal school politics at the Rough Rock Demonstration School in *A Place to Be Navajo*. My sense of how these

dynamics played out in the survival schools comes from interviews with Pat Bellanger, Lisa Bellanger, Dorene Day, and Gabrielle Strong.

19. Pat Bellanger, interview, October 17, 2002; Lisa Bellanger, interview, November 4, 2002; Vikki Howard, interview, May 9, 2002. Information on the other survival schools and the Federation also comes from Schierle, *Funktion einer Survival School für städtische Indianer,* 97–98; Lounberg, "The New Face of the American Indian Movement," 464; Peggy Gislason, "School Stresses Cultural Survival," *Minnesota Daily,* January 26, 1978; and Red School House, *The Seventh Fire,* 21.

20. McCarty, *A Place to Be Navajo,* 132; see also chapter 12, "Protest."

21. Pat Bellanger, interview, June 20, 2002. My sense of the circumstances surrounding Benton-Banai's departure from Red School House and its consequences also comes from other interviews with Pat Bellanger as well as Dorene Day and Gabrielle Strong.

22. This account is drawn from interviews with Dorene Day, Gabrielle Strong, and Pat Bellanger.

23. This account comes primarily from Rick Powers, interview, August 8, 2002. Powers began employment at Heart of the Earth in the mid-1980s and worked as a reading tutor, home-school liaison, counselor, and court advocate. Between 1994 and 1996, he served as high school principal, then resigned amid the conflicts of this period. I have helped establish the time line of Powers's account with Vikki Howard, interview, May 9, 2002, and Heart of the Earth Survival School, "The Heart of the Earth Survival School," 1993–94.

24. Johnny Smith, interviews, July 10, 2002, September 24, 2002, and October 28, 2002; Anthony Lonetree, "Fiscal Woes Still Plague Charter Schools, Entenza Says," *Minneapolis Star Tribune,* May 11, 2003; Allie Shah, "School Revival Is at the Heart of Test Success," *Minneapolis Star Tribune,* May 1, 1999; Duane Stinson, "Heart of the Earth School Restructures in the Face of Financial Woes," *The Circle: Native American News and Arts,* May 2002.

25. My summary of the Pourier case in this chapter comes from Tim Nelson, "American Indian Charter School Faces Closure," mprnews.org, August 8, 2008, accessed January 10, 2012, http://minnesota.publicradio.org/display/web/2008/08/08/charter_school_close/; Jenna Ross, "Minneapolis Charter School Director Allegedly Embezzled $1.38 Million," StarTribune.com, June 1, 2009, accessed January 10, 2012, http://www.startribune.com/local/minneapolis/46627937.html?page=1&c=y; Trisha Volpe, "Pourier Sentenced to 10 Years in Jail for Stealing from School," Kare11.com, August 31, 2011, accessed January 10, 2012, http://www.kare11.com/news/news_article.aspx?storyid=869015.

26. Johnny Smith, interview, July 10, 2002. References to survival school students' troubled backgrounds in this period also come from League of Women Voters of Minneapolis, *American Indians of Minneapolis;* and Clyde Bellecourt, interview, January 21, 2003.

27. Evidence of a continuing emphasis on identity development and traditional culture and spirituality comes from Heart of the Earth Survival School, "Chimigezi Winage," 1983–84 and 1984–85; Heart of the Earth Survival School, "The Heart of the Earth Survival School," 1985–86 and 1993–94; Heart of the Earth Survival School, "Welcome to the 6th Annual Heart of the Earth Contest Pow Wow"; segment on Heart of the Earth in *First Americans Today*, prod. Mary Jo Meagher; League of Women Voters of Minneapolis, *American Indians of Minneapolis*; Red School House, "Red School House," brochure; Vikki Howard, interview, May 9, 2002; Johnny Smith, interview, July 10, 2002; Clyde Bellecourt, interview, January 21, 2003; Lisa Bellanger, interviews, August 27, 2002, and November 4, 2002; and Pat Bellanger, interviews, May 23, 2002; May 30, 2002; June 7, 2002; June 20, 2002; October 17, 2002; December 3, 2002; and September 30, 2004.

28. Red School House, "Red School House: A Native American School." Evidence of survival school educators' continuing commitment to providing multifaceted support for their students also comes from Vikki Howard, interview, May 9, 2002, and Johnny Smith, interview, July 10, 2002."

29. Johnny Smith, interview, July 10, 2002.

30. Clyde Bellecourt, interview, January 21, 2003. Family names come from Heart of the Earth Survival School, "Chimigezi Winage," 1983–84 and 1984–85; Heart of the Earth Survival School, "The Heart of the Earth Survival School," 1985–86 and 1993–94; and Red School House, "Wahbung Ogi Chi Daw Ikway (Tomorrow's Leader, Woman)."

31. References to parental and community involvement in running the schools come from Heart of the Earth Survival School, "The Heart of the Earth Survival School," 1985–86; and Red School House, "Red School House: A Native American School." Evidence of community programs comes from Heart of the Earth Survival School, "Chimigezi Winage," 1983–84 and 1984–85; Heart of the Earth Survival School, "The Heart of the Earth Survival School," 1985–86; Red School House, "The American Indian Adult Education Program"; Red School House, "Red School House," brochure; and Red School House, "Red School House: A Native American School."

32. Red School House, "Red School House: A Native American School."

33. Johnny Smith, interview, July 10, 2002. See also Heart of the Earth Survival School, "The Heart of the Earth Survival School," 1985–86 and 1993–94.

34. Evidence of expanded technical training comes from Heart of the Earth, "Chimigezi Winage," 1983–84 and 1984–85; Red School House, "The American Indian Adult Education Program"; Red School House, "Red School House," brochure; Red School House, "Red School House: A Native American School"; and Pat Bellanger, interview, June 20, 2002. Spanish-language instruction appears in Heart of the Earth, "Chimigezi Winage," 1983–84 and 1984–85, and Heart of the Earth Survival School, "The Heart of the Earth Survival School," 1985–86.

35. Lisa Bellanger, interview, November 4, 2002; Johnny Smith, interview, July 10, 2002; Heart of the Earth Survival School, "Heart of the Earth Center for American Indian Education"; Allie Shah, "School Revival Is at the Heart of Test Success," *Minneapolis Star Tribune*, May 1, 1999; Stinson, "Heart of the Earth School Restructures in the Face of Financial Woes."

36. My sense of the continuity at Heart of the Earth in this period comes from interviews with Lisa Bellanger, Pat Bellanger, Clyde Bellecourt, and Johnny Smith, as well as Heart of the Earth Survival School, "Center for American Indian Education" and Shah, "School Revival Is at the Heart of Test Success."

37. Volpe, "Pourier Sentenced to 10 Years in Jail for Stealing from School."

6. The Meanings of Survival School Education

1. Joshua Fishman has written that those who commit themselves to revitalizing indigenous languages and cultures become "members of the community of belief" (Fishman, "What Do You Lose When You Lose Your Language?" 90).

2. Tom King quoted in Peggy Gislason, "School Stresses Cultural Survival," *Minnesota Daily*, January 26, 1978.

3. Don Havlish's statement from Red School House, *The Seventh Fire*, 6.

4. Harriet Heisler, quoted in Thompson, "Survival Schools," 22.

5. Gislason, "School Stresses Cultural Survival."

6. Dr. Norman Silverberg, quoted in U.S. Commission on Civil Rights, *Bridging the Gap*, 54. Results of 1972 tests reported in U.S. Commission on Civil Rights, *Bridging the Gap*, 54, and Martin, "Heart of the Earth Survival School," appendix 6.

7. Clyde Bellecourt, interview, January 21, 2003.

8. Dr. Margaret Silverberg, quoted in Thompson, "Survival Schools," 22.

9. Gislason, "School Stresses Cultural Survival."

10. O'Brien, quoted in ibid.; Benton-Banai, quoted in Martin, "Thoughts from a Born-Again Pagan."

11. Lisa Bellanger, interview, August 27, 2002.

12. Ibid.

13. Ibid.

14. Dorene Day, interviews, November 5, 2002, and December 10, 2002.

15. Ibid.

16. Lisa Bellanger, interview, November 4, 2002.

17. Descriptions of the conferences attended by survival school students come from "Heart of the Earth Survival School," *Akwesasne Notes;* and interviews with Lisa Bellanger, Pat Bellanger, Dorene Day, and Vikki Howard.

18. Lisa Bellanger, interview, 4 November 2002.

19. "Heart of the Earth Survival School," *Akwesasne Notes.*

20. Dorene Day, interview, December 10, 2002.

21. Lisa Bellanger, interview, August 27, 2002; Dorene Day, interviews, November 5, 2002, and December 10, 2002.

22. Gabrielle Strong, interview, December 11, 2002.

23. Rick Powers, interview, August 8, 2002.

24. Lisa Bellanger, interview, August 27, 2002.

25. Dorene Day, interviews, November 5, 2002, December 10, 2002, and March 14, 2003.

26. Lisa Bellanger, interviews, August 27, 2002, and November 4, 2002; Pat Bellanger, interviews, June 7, 2002, June 20, 2002, and December 3, 2002.

27. Dorene Day, interviews, November 5, 2002, and December 10, 2002.

28. Dorene Day, interview, December 10, 2002; Lisa Bellanger, interviews, August 27, 2002, and November 4, 2002.

29. Lisa Bellanger, interview, August 27, 2002; Dorene Day, interview, December 10, 2002.

30. Dorene Day, interview, November 5, 2002.

31. It is difficult to quantify the numbers of survival school people who have gone on to work for Indian communities, cultures, or causes. Neither Heart of the Earth nor Red School House has tracked the paths of former students consistently. What data has been recorded over the years has not remained in any central repository, much of it scattering into the private possession of former administrators or other unknown locations in the wake of periodic institutional shake-ups. Information about former students and employees gleaned from interviews is incomplete. What follows is an attempt to sketch the outlines of at least some survival school people's community work, drawn from interviews and available documents.

32. Lisa Bellanger, interview, August 27, 2002.

33. Gabrielle Strong, interview, December 11, 2002; Dorene Day, interviews, December 10, 2002, March 14, 2003, and September 27, 2004; Red School House, "Heart Beat of Our Nation"; Heart of the Earth Survival School, "The Heart of the Earth Survival School," 1993–94.

34. Pat Bellanger, interview, June 13, 2002.

35. Gabrielle Strong, interview, December 11, 2002. Information on Keith Herman is drawn from Pat Bellanger, interview, September 30, 2004; Dorene Day, interview, September 27, 2004; and Red School House, "Heart Beat of Our Nation."

36. Vikki Howard, interview, May 9, 2002.

37. Laura Waterman Wittstock, telephone conversation with author, August 12, 2002; Circle of Life Academy, "Circle of Life Academy: Home of the Warriors," accessed May 11, 2012, http://www.col.bie.edu/; Martin, "Heart of the Earth Survival School"; Elaine Salinas, e-mail to author, February 22, 2003; Heart

of the Earth Survival School, "The Heart of the Earth Survival School," 1985–86 and 1993–94.

38. Lisa Bellanger, interview, November 4, 2002; Dorene Day, interview, November 5, 2002.

39. Lisa Bellanger, interview, November 4, 2002.

40. Dorene Day, interview, November 5, 2002.

41. Ibid.

42. Dorene Day, interviews, November 5, 2002, March 14, 2003, and September 27, 2004.

43. Dorene Day, interviews, November 5, 2002, and December 10, 2002.

44. Pat Bellanger, interview, September 30, 2004.

45. Lisa Bellanger, interview, November 4, 2002; Gabrielle Strong, interview, December 11, 2002; Strong, "AIFEP Changes Focus of Grantgiving"; Dorene Day, interview, September 27, 2004; Pat Bellanger, interview, September 30, 2004.

46. Dorene Day, interview, December 10, 2002.

47. Lisa Bellanger, interview, August 27, 2002.

48. Ibid.

49. Gabrielle Strong, interview, December 11, 2002.

50. Ibid.

51. Gabrielle Strong, interviews, December 11, 2002, and January 7, 2003; Rick Powers, interview, August 8, 2002.

52. Gabrielle Strong, interviews, December 11, 2002, and January 7, 2003.

53. Ibid.

54. Gabrielle Strong, unrecorded telephone conversation, November 23, 2004.

55. Dorene Day, interview, December 10, 2002.

56. Lisa Bellanger, interviews, August 27, 2002, and November 4, 2002.

57. Lisa Bellanger, interview, November 4, 2002.

58. Battiste, "Maintaining Aboriginal Identity," 193, 198; Henderson, "Postcolonial Ghost Dancing," 58–59; Henderson, "Postcolonial Ledger Drawing," 162; Battiste, "Animating Sites of Postcolonial Education," 10–11.

59. Daes, "Prologue," 7; Miller, "Native America Writes Back," 15; Miller, "Native Historians Write Back," 35; Battiste, "Animating Sites of Postcolonial Education," 10; Battiste, "Introduction," xvii, xxi. My perspective on Indigenous decolonization also has been shaped by all of the essays in Battiste, *Reclaiming Indigenous Voice and Vision,* as well as Alfred, *Wasáse;* Alfred, *Peace, Power Righteousness;* Grande, *Red Pedagogy;* Smith, *Decolonizing Methodologies;* Wilson, *Remember This!;* and Wilson and Yellow Bird, *For Indigenous Eyes Only.*

60. Battiste, "Introduction," xvii.

61. Cajete, "Indigenous Knowledge," 183.

62. Battiste, "Maintaining Aboriginal Identity," 202. The survival schools

also clearly embodied aspects of traditional Ojibwe or Anishinaabe education, as described in Peacock and Wisuri, *Ojibwe*, 68–77; Broker, *Night Flying Woman;* Kegg, *Portage Lake;* Child, *Boarding School Seasons;* and a course on Ojibwe culture and history taught by Dennis Jones at the University of Minnesota in the summer of 1996.

63. Lobo writes about women's activism as creating "nodes" of Indian community in the San Francisco Bay area in "Urban Clan Mothers."

64. Laenui, "Processes of Decolonization," 152–53.

65. Vikki Howard quoted in Child, *Holding Our World Together*, 158.

66. Dorene Day, interview, September 27, 2004.

67. In *The Mishomis Book,* Eddie Benton-Banai estimates that the westward migration that brought the Ojibwe people's ancestors west through the Great Lakes began around AD 900 and lasted about five hundred years, placing the Ojibwes at Madeline Island by the early 1400s. The first European accounts reveal that the Ojibwe settlement there was well established by the early seventeenth century. For accounts of these early Ojibwe migrations, see Benton-Banai, *The Mishomis Book,* 94–102; Peacock and Wisuri, *Ojibwe*, 22–27; and Meyer, *The White Earth Tragedy*, 16–17.

68. Meyer emphasizes the centrality of the seasonal round of activities to Ojibwe people in this period and describes their approach to the land in *The White Earth Tragedy*, 20–27. The seasonal round and land use also are highlighted as key components of the traditional way of life in two accounts drawn from Ojibwe oral history: Broker, *Night Flying Woman*, and Kegg, *Portage Lake.*

69. Molin, "Foreword to *Night Flying Woman*," xiii. Descriptions of the Midewiwin as it functioned in traditional Ojibwe life are found in Benton-Banai, *The Mishomis Book,* 67–73, 103; Meyer, *The White Earth Tragedy*, 16–17, 111; and Johnston, *Ojibway Heritage*, 83–93.

70. Information on the Three Fires Society comes from the Three Fires Culture and Education Society, "Three Fires Society: 'Our Story,'" and the group's Web site, Three Fires Midewiwin Lodge, http://www.three-fires.net/tfn/.

71. Ibid.

72. My thinking about Anishinaabe people's place in the transnational Great Lakes economy and society has been influenced by two papers presented at the Organization of American Historians/National Council on Public History annual meeting in Milwaukee on April 21, 2012: Ann Keating, "John Kinzie and the Indian Country of the Western Great Lakes, 1789–1828," and Karen Marrero, "Making New Nations: Natives, Euro-Americans and the Reconfiguration of the Midwest Region in the Nineteenth Century."

73. Henderson, *"Ayukpachi,"* 259–60; Little Bear, "Jagged Worldviews Colliding," 78; Miller, "Native America Writes Back," 11, 13.

74. Little Bear, "Jagged Worldviews Colliding," 81, 78; Miller, "Native Historians Write Back," 29.

75. Henderson, "*Ayukpachi*," 257; Battiste, "Introduction," xvii.

76. Battiste, "Introduction," xvii.

77. Smith, "Kaupapa Maori Research," 229.

Conclusion

1. Clyde Bellecourt, interview, January 21, 2003.

2. Henderson, "Postcolonial Ghost Dancing," 70, 66; Henderson, "*Ayukpachi*," 267; Battiste, "Animating Sites of Postcolonial Education," 10.

3. Battiste, "Animating Sites of Postcolonial Education," 10; Lomawaima and McCarty, "When Tribal Sovereignty Challenges Democracy," 280–81.

4. My thinking about the connections between American Indigenous decolonization and Irish nationalism, particularly on the issue of language revitalization and in relation to education, has been influenced by Coleman, *American Indians, the Irish, and Government Schooling*; Kachuk, "A Resistance to British Cultural Hegemony"; Kachuk, "Irish Language Activism in West Belfast"; Ó Maolchluiche, "The Language and the State in Colonial Ireland"; conversations with Laurence Marley, a Belfast native and an Irish historian at the National University of Ireland, Galway; conversations with Jake MacSiacais and other Irish-language activists in West Belfast; and interviews with Pat Bellanger and Clyde Bellecourt.

5. Winona LaDuke quoted in Hayes, "Blood Brothers," 13.

6. Tiffany Wilbert, "Using Menominee Words at School Gets Girl Benched," *Shawano Leader*, January 26, 2012; Levi Rickert, "Menominee Seventh Grader Suspended for Saying 'I Love You' in Her Native Language," Native News Network Web site, accessed February 3, 2012, http://www.nativenewsnetwork.com.

7. Wilbert, "Using Menominee Words at School Gets Girl Benched."

8. Lomawaima and McCarty, "When Tribal Sovereignty Challenges Democracy," 283.

9. Ibid., 280, 299–300.

10. Battiste, "Maintaining Aboriginal Identity, Language, and Culture in Modern Society," 202.

11. Fishman, "What Do You Lose When You Lose Your Language?" 80–81.

12. Beaulieu, "A Place among Nations," 429.

Bibliography

Many primary documents listed here are in the collections of the Minnesota Historical Society in St. Paul. Others can be found in the collections of the Labriola National American Indian Data Center in the Charles Trumbull Hayden Library at Arizona State University in Tempe and in the University of Minnesota Libraries.

Abourezk, James. "The Role of the Federal Government: A Congressional View." In *The Destruction of American Indian Families,* edited by Steven Unger, 12–13. New York: Association on American Indian Affairs, 1977.

Adams, David Wallace. *Education for Extinction: American Indians and the Boarding School Experience, 1875–1928.* Lawrence: University Press of Kansas, 1995.

Adickes, Sandra. *The Legacy of a Freedom School.* New York: Palgrave Macmillan, 2005.

Akard, William Keith. "Wocante Tinza: A History of the American Indian Movement." Ph.D. diss., Ball State University, 1987.

Alfred, Taiaiake. *Peace, Power, Righteousness: An Indigenous Manifesto.* 2d ed. Toronto: Oxford University Press, 2009.

———. *Wasáse: Indigenous Pathways of Action and Freedom.* Toronto: University of Toronto Press, 2009.

Allery, Alan J. *The Indians Speak for Themselves: Literature Booklet.* Pierre: Indian Ethnic Heritage Studies Curriculum Development Project, South Dakota Department of Education and Cultural Affairs, 1974–75.

Amerman, Stephen Kent. *Urban Indians in Phoenix Schools, 1940–2000.* Lincoln: University of Nebraska Press, 2010.

Anderson, Meredith, and Ilga Eglitis. "Public Schools Link Indian, White Cultures." In *Closing the Circle: The Indian in Minneapolis: A New Era*, edited by Betty Binkard, 11–15. Minneapolis: University of Minnesota School of Journalism and Mass Communication, 1975.

Antell, Will D. "National Indian Education Association." In *Native America in the Twentieth Century: An Encyclopedia*, edited by Mary B. Davis. New York: Garland Publishing, 1994.

Armitage, Andrew. *Comparing the Policy of Aboriginal Assimilation: Australia, Canada, and New Zealand.* Vancouver: University of British Columbia Press, 1995.

Attneave, Carolyn. "The Wasted Strength of Indian Families." In *The Destruction of American Indian Families*, edited by Steven Unger, 29–33. New York: Association on American Indian Affairs, 1977.

Banks, Dennis. "The Black Scholar Interviews: Dennis Banks." Interview by William H. McClendon. *Black Scholar* 7, no. 9 (1976): 29–36.

Banks, Dennis, with Richard Erdoes. *Ojibwa Warrior: Dennis Banks and the Rise of the American Indian Movement.* Norman: University of Oklahoma Press, 2004.

Barth, Roland. *Open Education and the American School.* New York: Agathon Press, 1972.

Battiste, Marie. "Animating Sites of Postcolonial Education: Indigenous Knowledge and the Humanities." CSSE Plenary Address, University of Saskatchewan, Manitoba, May 2004.

———. "Introduction: Unfolding the Lessons of Colonization." In *Reclaiming Indigenous Voice and Vision*, edited by Marie Battiste, xvi–xxx. Vancouver: University of British Columbia Press, 2009.

———. "Maintaining Aboriginal Identity, Language, and Culture in Modern Society." In *Reclaiming Indigenous Voice and Vision*, edited by Marie Battiste, 192–208. Vancouver: University of British Columbia Press, 2009.

Beaulieu, David. "A Place among Nations: Experiences of Indian People." In *Minnesota in a Century of Change: The State and Its People since 1900*, edited by Clifford E. Clark Jr., 397–432. St. Paul: Minnesota Historical Society Press, 1989.

Bensen, Robert. "Introduction." *Children of the Dragonfly: Native American Voices on Child Custody and Education*, 3–15. Tucson: University of Arizona Press, 2001.

Benton-Banai, Edward. *A Mishomis Book: A History-Coloring Book of the Ojibway Indians. Book One: The Ojibway Creation Story.* St. Paul: Red School House Graphics, 1975.

———. *A Mishomis Book: A History-Coloring Book of the Ojibway Indians. Book Two: Original Man Walks the Earth.* St. Paul: Red School House Graphics, 1976.

———. *A Mishomis Book: A History-Coloring Book of the Ojibway Indians. Book Three: Original Man and His Grandmother No-ko-mis.* St. Paul: Red School House Graphics, 1976.

———. *The Mishomis Book: The Voice of the Ojibway.* Hayward, Wis.: Indian Country Communications, 1988.

Bernstein, Alison R. *American Indians and World War II: Toward a New Era in Indian Affairs.* Norman: University of Oklahoma Press, 1991.

Blakey, Sherry, and Edward Benton-Banai. *The Sounding Voice: A Collection of Poetry and Writings.* St. Paul: Indian Country Press, [1978?].

Blanchard, Evelyn. "The Question of Best Interest." In *The Destruction of American Indian Families,* edited by Steven Unger, 57–60. New York: Association on American Indian Affairs, 1977.

Bonney, Rachel A. "The Role of AIM Leaders in Indian Nationalism." *American Indian Quarterly* 3, no. 3 (1977): 209–24.

Bourman, Joni. "The Red School House of St. Paul, Minnesota and Other Indian Organizations and Activities in or near the Minneapolis–St. Paul Area." Paper written for course IED 411 at Arizona State University, fall semester 1978.

Broker, Ignatia. *Night Flying Woman: An Ojibway Narrative.* St. Paul: Minnesota Historical Society Press, 1983.

Brunette, Pauline. "The Minneapolis Urban Indian Community." *Hennepin County History* 49, no. 1 (1989–90): 4–15.

Bruyneel, Kevin. *The Third Space of Sovereignty: The Postcolonial Politics of U.S.–Indigenous Relations.* Minneapolis: University of Minnesota Press, 2007.

Bublitz, Mona. *Indian Memories: The Elderlies Were Wise and Knowledgeable.* Pierre: Indian Ethnic Heritage Studies Curriculum Development Project, South Dakota Department of Education and Cultural Affairs, 1974–75.

Buckanaga, Jerry. "Pine Point School: 'The Sky Is Our Limit.'" Statement presented to the Minnesota Indian Affairs Commission, December 1968.

Buff, Rachel. *Immigration and the Political Economy of Home: West Indian Brooklyn and American Indian Minneapolis, 1945–1992.* Berkeley: University of California Press, 2001.

Byler, William. "The Destruction of American Indian Families." In *The Destruction of American Indian Families,* edited by Steven Unger, 1–11. New York: Association on American Indian Affairs, 1977.

Byrd, Jodi A. *The Transit of Empire: Indigenous Critiques of Colonialism.* Minneapolis: University of Minnesota Press, 2011.

Cajete, Gregory. "Indigenous Knowledge: The Pueblo Metaphor of Indigenous Education." In *Reclaiming Indigenous Voice and Vision,* edited by Marie Battiste, 181–91. Vancouver: University of British Columbia Press, 2009.

Carpio, Myla Vicenti. *Indigenous Albuquerque.* Lubbock: Texas Tech University Press, 2011.

Castile, George. "The Community School at Rough Rock." Master's thesis, University of Arizona, 1968.

Castile, George Pierre. *To Show Heart: Native American Self-Determination and Federal Indian Policy, 1960–1975.* Tucson: University of Arizona Press, 1998.

Chamberlin, J. Edward. "From Hand to Mouth: The Postcolonial Politics of Oral and Written Traditions." In *Reclaiming Indigenous Voice and Vision*, edited by Marie Battiste, 124–41. Vancouver: University of British Columbia Press, 2009.

Child, Brenda J. *Boarding School Seasons: American Indian Families, 1900–1940.* Lincoln: University of Nebraska Press, 1998.

———. *Holding Our World Together: Ojibwe Women and the Survival of Community.* New York: Viking, 2012.

Christensen, Rosemary. "Written Statement." In *Stabilizing Indigenous Languages*, edited by Gina Cantoni, 101–2. Flagstaff: Northern Arizona University, 1996.

Cobb, Daniel M. "Philosophy of an Indian War: Indian Community Action in the Johnson Administration's War on Poverty, 1964–1968." *American Indian Culture and Research Journal* 22, no. 2 (1998): 71–102.

Cohen, Fay G. "The Indian Patrol in Minneapolis: Social Control and Social Change in an Urban Context." Ph.D. diss., University of Minnesota, 1973.

Coleman, Michael C. *American Indians, the Irish, and Government Schooling: A Comparative Study.* Lincoln: University of Nebraska Press, 2007.

Convocation of American Indian Scholars. *Indian Voices: The First Convocation of American Indian Scholars.* San Francisco: Indian Historian Press, 1970.

Couture, Steven L. "The American Indian Movement: A Historical Perspective." Ed.D. diss., University of St. Thomas, 1996.

Craig, Gregory W., Arthur M. Harkins, and Richard G. Woods. *Indian Housing in Minneapolis and St. Paul.* Minneapolis: Training Center for Community Programs, University of Minnesota, 1969.

Daes, Erica-Irene. "Prologue: The Experience of Colonization around the World." In *Reclaiming Indigenous Voice and Vision*, edited by Marie Battiste, 3–10. Vancouver: University of British Columbia Press, 2009.

Danziger, Edmund Jefferson, Jr. *Survival and Regeneration: Detroit's American Indian Community.* Detroit: Wayne State University Press, 1991.

"Deegan, a Founding Member of AIM, Dies at 67." *Native American Press/Ojibwe News*, April 18, 2003.

Dunlap, Douglas. *The Educational Process of Rough Rock Community High School: A Program for Community and School.* Chinle, Ariz.: Rough Rock Community High School, 1972.

Farley, Ronney, ed. *Women of the Native Struggle: Portraits and Testimony of Native American Women.* New York: Orion Books, 1993.

Fife, Gary. *Indian Education: An Examination of Issues. The Ford Fellows in Educational Journalism Report.* Washington, D.C.: Institute for Educational Leadership, George Washington University, 1979.

Fishman, Joshua. "What Do You Lose When You Lose Your Language?" In *Stabi-*

lizing Indigenous Languages, edited by Gina Cantoni, 80–91. Flagstaff: Northern Arizona University, 1996.

Fixico, Donald L. "Ethics and Responsibilities in Writing American Indian History." In *Natives and Academics: Researching and Writing about American Indians,* edited by Devon A. Mihesuah, 84–99. Lincoln: University of Nebraska Press, 1998.

———. *Termination and Relocation: Federal Indian Policy, 1945–1960.* Albuquerque: University of New Mexico Press, 1986.

———. *The Urban Indian Experience in America.* Albuquerque: University of New Mexico Press, 2000.

Ford, Lisa. *Settler Sovereignty: Jurisdiction and Indigenous People in America and Australia, 1788–1836.* Cambridge: Harvard University Press, 2010.

Frisch, Michael. *A Shared Authority: Essays on the Craft and Meaning of Oral History and Public History.* Albany: State University of New York Press, 1990.

Fuchs, Estelle, and Robert J. Havighurst. *To Live on This Earth: American Indian Education.* New York: Doubleday, 1972.

Gittel, Marilyn. "Urban School Reform in the 1970s." In *School Reform: Past and Present,* edited by Michael B. Katz, 295–303. Boston: Little, Brown, 1971. First published in *Education and Urban Society* 1, no. 1 (1968): 9–20.

Grande, Sandy. *Red Pedagogy: Native American Social and Political Thought.* Lanham, Md.: Rowman and Littlefield, 2004.

Halverson, Kelly, Maria Elena Puig, and Steven R. Byers. "Culture Loss: American Indian Family Disruption, Urbanization, and the Indian Child Welfare Act." *Child Welfare* 81, no. 2 (2002): 319–36.

Harkins, Arthur M., and Richard G. Woods. *Indian Americans in St. Paul: An Interim Report.* National Study of American Indian Education. Minneapolis: Training Center for Community Programs, University of Minnesota, 1970.

Harkins, Arthur M., et al. *Junior High Indian Children in Minneapolis: A Study of One Problem School.* National Study of American Indian Education. Minneapolis: Training Center for Community Programs, University of Minnesota, 1970.

Harkins, Arthur M., I. Karon Sherarts, and Richard G. Woods. *Attitudes of St. Paul Indian Parents and Influential Persons toward Formal Education.* National Study of American Indian Education. Minneapolis: Training Center for Community Programs, University of Minnesota, 1970.

———. *The Elementary Education of St. Paul Indian Children: A Study of One Inner-City School.* National Study of American Indian Education. Minneapolis: Training Center for Community Programs, University of Minnesota, 1970.

———. *Teachers of Minneapolis Elementary Indian Children: 1969 Survey Results.* National Study of American Indian Education. Minneapolis: Training Center for Community Programs, University of Minnesota, 1970.

———. *Teachers of St. Paul Elementary Indian Children: 1969 Survey Results.* National Study of American Indian Education. Minneapolis: Training Center for Community Programs, University of Minnesota, 1970.

———. *Urban Indian Education in Minneapolis: An Interim Analysis of Survey Materials Gathered from School Officials and Influential Persons.* National Study of American Indian Education. Minneapolis: Training Center for Community Programs, University of Minnesota, 1970.

Harkins, Arthur M., Richard G. Woods, and I. Karon Sherarts. *Indian Education in Minneapolis: An Interim Report.* National Study of American Indian Education. Minneapolis: Training Center for Community Programs, University of Minnesota, 1969.

Hayes, Jack. "Blood Brothers." *Minneapolis–St. Paul Magazine,* March 1996.

Heart of the Earth Survival School. "Chimigezi Winage." Heart of the Earth yearbook, 1983–84 and 1984–85.

———. "Heart of the Earth Center for American Indian Education: A K–12 Culture Specific Charter School." Brochure, [1999?].

———. "The Heart of the Earth Survival School." Heart of the Earth yearbook, 1979–80, 1985–86, and 1993–94.

———. "Welcome to the 6th Annual Heart of the Earth Contest Pow Wow." Program for a powwow held at the Minneapolis Convention Center, February 22–24, 1991.

"The Heart of the Earth Survival School." *Akwesasne Notes.* Early autumn 1975.

Henderson, James (Sákéj) Youngblood. "*Ayukpachi:* Empowering Aboriginal Thought." In *Reclaiming Indigenous Voice and Vision,* edited by Marie Battiste, 248–78. Vancouver: University of British Columbia Press, 2009.

———. "Postcolonial Ghost Dancing: Diagnosing European Colonialism." In *Reclaiming Indigenous Voice and Vision,* edited by Marie Battiste, 57–76. Vancouver: University of British Columbia Press, 2009.

———. "Postcolonial Ledger Drawing: Legal Reform." In *Reclaiming Indigenous Voice and Vision,* edited by Marie Battiste, 161–71. Vancouver: University of British Columbia Press, 2009.

Henry, Jeannette, ed. *The American Indian Reader: Education.* San Francisco: Indian Historian Press, 1972.

Hoikkala, Paivi Helena. "Native American Women and Community Work in Phoenix, 1965–1980." Ph.D. diss., Arizona State University, 1995.

Holt, Marilyn Irvin. *Indian Orphanages.* Lawrence: University Press of Kansas, 2001.

Honor the Earth Committee. "Program: A Benefit Concert Supporting American Indian Social Change." Program for a concert held at Northrup Auditorium, University of Minnesota, May 15, 1975.

Horne, Esther Burnett, and Sally McBeth. *Essie's Story: The Life and Legacy of a Shoshone Teacher.* Lincoln: University of Nebraska Press, 1998.

Hoxie, Frederick E. *A Final Promise: The Campaign to Assimilate the Indians, 1880–1920.* New York: Cambridge University Press, 1989.

Indergaard, Michael Leroy. "Urban Renewal and the American Indian Movement in Minneapolis: A Case Study in Political Economy and the Urban Indian." Master's thesis, Michigan State University, 1983.

"An Indian School." *Focus: Indian Education* 3, no. 5 (1972): 16–17.

Iverson, Peter. *Diné: A History of the Navajos.* Albuquerque: University of New Mexico Press, 2002.

Jacobs, Margaret D., *White Mother to a Dark Race: Settler Colonialism, Maternalism, and the Removal of Indigenous Children in the American West and Australia, 1880–1940.* Lincoln: University of Nebraska Press, 2009.

Janiewski, Dolores. "Gendering, Racializing, and Classifying: Settler Colonization in the United States, 1590–1990." In *Unsettling Settler Societies: Articulations of Gender, Race, Ethnicity and Class,* edited by Daiva Stasiulis and Nira Yuval-Davis, 132–60. Thousand Oaks, Calif.: Sage Publications, 1995.

Jimson, Leonard B. "Parent and Child Relationships in Law and in Navajo Custom." In *The Destruction of American Indian Families,* edited by Steven Unger, 67–78. New York: Association on American Indian Affairs, 1977.

Johnson, Broderick H. *Navaho Education at Rough Rock.* Rough Rock, Ariz: Rough Rock Demonstration School, 1968.

Johnson, Troy. *The Occupation of Alcatraz Island: Indian Self-Determination and the Rise of Indian Activism.* Urbana: University of Illinois Press, 1996.

Johnson, Troy, Joane Nagel, and Duane Champagne, eds. *American Indian Activism: Alcatraz to the Longest Walk.* Urbana: University of Illinois Press, 1997.

Johnston, Basil. *Ojibway Heritage.* Toronto: McClelland and Stewart, 1976; reprint, Lincoln: University of Nebraska Press, 1990.

Jones, Dennis. "The Etymology of Anishinaabe." *Oshkaabewis Native Journal* 2, no. 1 (1995): 43–48.

Kachuk, Patricia. "A Resistance to British Cultural Hegemony: Irish-Language Activism in West Belfast." *Anthropologica* 36:2 (1994): 135–54.

Kachuk, Patricia Mary Catherine. "Irish Language Activism in West Belfast: A Resistance to British Cultural Hegemony." Ph.D. diss., University of British Columbia, 1993.

Kawagley, Angayuquq Oscar. "Nurturing Native Languages." In *Nurturing Native Languages,* edited by Jon Reyhner et al., vii–x. Flagstaff: Northern Arizona University, 2003.

Kegg, Maude. *Portage Lake: Memories of an Ojibwe Childhood.* Edited by John D. Nichols. Minneapolis: University of Minnesota Press, 1993.

Kohl, Herbert. *The Open Classroom*. New York: Vintage Books, 1970.

Krauss, Michael. "Status of Native American Language Endangerment." In *Stabilizing Indigenous Languages*, edited by Gina Cantoni, 16–21. Flagstaff: Northern Arizona University, 1996.

Krouse, Susan Applegate. "What Came Out of the Takeovers: Women's Activism and the Indian Community School of Milwaukee." In *Keeping the Campfires Going: Native Women's Activism in Urban Communities*, edited by Susan Applegate Krouse and Heather A. Howard, 146–62. Lincoln: University of Nebraska Press, 2009.

Krouse, Susan Applegate, and Heather A. Howard. "Introduction." In *Keeping the Campfires Going: Native Women's Activism in Urban Communities*, edited by Susan Applegate Krouse and Heather A. Howard, ix–xxv. Lincoln: University of Nebraska Press, 2009.

Kugel, Rebecca. *To Be the Main Leaders of Our People: A History of Minnesota Ojibwe Politics, 1825–1898*. East Lansing: Michigan State University Press, 1998.

Laenui, Poka [Hayden F. Burgess]. "Processes of Decolonization." In *Reclaiming Indigenous Voice and Vision*, edited by Marie Battiste, 150–60. Vancouver: University of British Columbia Press, 2009.

LaGrand, James B. *Indian Metropolis: Native Americans in Chicago, 1945–1975*. Urbana: University of Illinois Press, 2002.

League of Women Voters of Minneapolis. *American Indians and Minneapolis Public Services*. Minneapolis: League of Women Voters of Minneapolis, 1971.

———. *American Indians of Minneapolis: An Update*. Minneapolis: League of Women Voters of Minneapolis, 1984.

———. *Indians in Minneapolis*. Minneapolis: League of Women Voters of Minneapolis, 1968.

League of Women Voters of Minnesota. *Indians in Minnesota*. 2d ed. St. Paul: League of Women Voters of Minnesota, 1971.

———. *Indians in Minnesota*. 3d rev. ed. St. Paul: League of Women Voters of Minnesota, 1974.

Little Bear, Leroy. "Jagged Worldviews Colliding." In *Reclaiming Indigenous Voice and Vision*, edited by Marie Battiste, 77–85. Vancouver: University of British Columbia Press, 2009.

Littlebear, Richard E. "Preface." In *Stabilizing Indigenous Languages*, edited by Gina Cantoni, xiii–xv. Flagstaff: Northern Arizona University, 1996.

Lobo, Susan. "Urban Clan Mothers: Key Households in Cities." In *Keeping the Campfires Going: Native Women's Activism in Urban Communities*, edited by Susan Applegate Krouse and Heather A. Howard, 1–21. Lincoln: University of Nebraska Press, 2009.

Lobo, Susan, and Kurt Peters, eds. *American Indians and the Urban Experience*. Lanham, Md.: Rowman and Littlefield, 2001.

Lomawaima, K. Tsianina. *They Called It Prairie Light: The Story of Chilocco Indian School.* Lincoln: University of Nebraska Press, 1994.

———. "Tribal Sovereigns: Reframing Research in American Indian Education." *Harvard Educational Review* 70, no. 1 (2000): 1–21.

Lomawaima, K. Tsianina, and Teresa L. McCarty. *To Remain an Indian: Lessons in Democracy from a Century of Native American Education.* New York: Teacher's College, Columbia University, 2006.

———. "When Tribal Sovereignty Challenges Democracy: American Indian Education and the Democratic Ideal." *American Educational Research Journal* 39, no. 2 (2002): 279–305.

Lounberg, Dan. "The New Face of the American Indian Movement." *Crisis* 84, no. 10 (1977): 463–66.

Mannes, Marc. "Factors and Events Leading to the Passage of the Indian Child Welfare Act." *Child Welfare* 74, no. 1 (1995): 264–82.

Martin, Carol. "Thoughts from a Born-Again Pagan." Soo Today.com, September 13, 2009. http://www.sootoday.com.

Martin, Elaine. "Heart of the Earth Survival School: An Alternative for Native American Youth: Part B." Funding proposal to the United States Office of Education, 1975–76.

Matheson, Lou. "The Politics of the Indian Child Welfare Act." *Social Work* 41, no. 2 (1996): 232–35.

McAdam, Doug. *Freedom Summer.* New York: Oxford University Press, 1988.

McCarty, Teresa L. *A Place to Be Navajo: Rough Rock and the Struggle for Self-Determination in Indigenous Schooling.* Mahwah, N.J.: Lawrence Erlbaum, 2002.

Meagher, Mary Jo, producer and scriptwriter. *First Americans Today.* 60 min. Bloomington Community Education, 1993. Videocassette.

Meyer, Melissa L. *The White Earth Tragedy: Ethnicity and Dispossession at a Minnesota Anishinaabe Reservation.* Lincoln: University of Nebraska Press, 1994.

Miller, Michael, and Laura Waterman Wittstock. *American Indian Alcoholism in St. Paul: A Needs Assessment.* Edited by Judith H. Weir. Minneapolis: Center for Urban and Regional Affairs, University of Minnesota; St. Paul: Community Planning Organization, 1981.

Miller, Susan. "Native America Writes Back: The Origin of the Indigenous Paradigm in Historiography." *Wicazo Sa Review* 23, no. 2 (fall 2008): 9–28.

———. "Native Historians Write Back: The Indigenous Paradigm in American Indian Historiography." *Wicazo Sa Review* 24, no.1 (spring 2009): 25–45.

Mindell, Carl, and Alan Gurwitt. "The Placement of American Indian Children— The Need for Change." In *The Destruction of American Indian Families,* edited by Steven Unger, 61–66. New York: Association on American Indian Affairs, 1977.

Molin, Paulette Fairbanks. "Foreword." In Ignatia Broker, *Night Flying Woman: An Ojibway Narrative*. St. Paul: Minnesota Historical Society Press, 1983.

Morris, Patrick C. "Termination by Accountants: The Reagan Indian Policy." In *Native Americans and Public Policy*, edited by Fremount J. Lyden and Lyman H. Letgers, 63–84. Pittsburgh: University of Pennsylvania Press, 1992.

Mosedale, Mike. "Bury My Heart." *City Pages: The News and Arts Weekly of the Twin Cities*, February 16, 2000.

Nagel, Joane. *American Indian Ethnic Renewal: Red Power and the Resurgence of Identity and Culture*. New York: Oxford University Press, 1996.

National Indian Education Association. "Call to Convention: National Indian Education Association: Silver Anniversary Year, 1969–1994." Program for NIEA Convention, held in St. Paul, Minnesota, October 15–19, 1994.

Neima, Cherie, ed. *We Learn about Ourselves Now: Voices from the Red School House*. St. Paul: Indian Country Press, 1980.

Ó Maolchluiche, Liam. "The Language and the State in Colonial Ireland: The Growth of Irish Medium Schools in the North of Ireland since 1981." Master's thesis, National University of Ireland, Galway, 1995.

Palm, Sister Charles. *Government of the Indian People*. Pierre: Indian Ethnic Heritage Studies Curriculum Development Project, South Dakota Department of Education and Cultural Affairs, 1974–75.

Payne, Charles M. *I've Got the Light of Freedom: The Organizing Tradition and the Mississippi Freedom Struggle*. Berkeley: University of California Press, 1995.

Peacock, Thomas, and Marlene Wisuri. *Ojibwe: Waasa Inaabidaa: We Look in All Directions*. Afton, Minn.: Afton Historical Society Press, 2002.

Pejsa, Jane. *The Life of Emily Peake: One Dedicated Ojibwe*. Minneapolis: Nodin Press, 2003.

Perlstein, Daniel. "Minds Stayed on Freedom: Politics and Pedagogy in the African-American Freedom Struggle." *American Educational Research Journal* 39, no. 2 (2002): 249–77.

———. "Teaching Freedom: SNCC and the Creation of the Mississippi Freedom Schools." *History of Education Quarterly* 30 (1990): 297–324.

Philp, Kenneth R. *John Collier's Crusade for Indian Reform, 1920–1954*. Tucson: University of Arizona Press, 1977.

———. *Termination Revisited: American Indians on the Trail to Self-Determination, 1933–1953*. Lincoln: University of Nebraska Press, 1999.

Pierce, Nancy. "From the Reservation, to the City and Back: A Search for Self-Sufficiency." In *Closing the Circle: The Indian in Minneapolis: A New Era*, edited by Betty Binkard, 31–34. Minneapolis: University of Minnesota School of Journalism and Mass Communication, 1975.

Pine Point Elementary School. "Pine Point School: It's History, It's Purpose, It's Preservation *[sic]*." [1978?].

Pine Point Experimental School. "Pine Point Experimental School: For E-quay-zance and Gwi-we-zance." November 1975.

Portelli, Alessandro. *The Battle of Valle Giulia: Oral History and the Art of Dialogue.* Madison: University of Wisconsin Press, 1997.

———. *The Death of Luigi Trastulli and Other Stories: Form and Meaning in Oral History.* Albany: State University of New York Press, 1991.

Prucha, Francis Paul. *The Great Father: The United States Government and the American Indians.* Abr. ed. Lincoln: University of Nebraska Press, 1986.

Red Horse, John G. "American Indian Elders: Unifiers of Indian Families." *Social Casework* 61, no. 8 (1980): 491–93.

Red School House. "The American Indian Adult Education Program: A Project of the Red School House." Brochure, [1985?].

———. "Heart Beat of Our Nation: Red School House Information Booklet." 1979.

———. "Indian Student Motivational Posters." Red School House Instructional Materials Development Project, 1980.

———. "Knowledge through Cultural Understanding: Red School House Information Booklet." [1976].

———. *Our Brother's Keeper.* Program for a one-act play by Edward Benton-Banai, performed at St. Luke's School auditorium, St. Paul, May 14, 1976.

———. "Red School House." Brochure, [1989?].

———. "Red School House: A Native American School." Brochure, [1989?].

———. "Red School House: Information Packet." 1974.

———. *The Seventh Fire* 3, no. 2 (summer 1978).

———. "Three Fires: St. Paul, Minn." Brochure, n.d.

———. "Wahbung Ogi Chi Daw Ikway (Tomorrow's Leader, Woman)" 1, no. 2 (September 1984); 3, no. 4 (January 1986); and 3, no. 7 (May 1986).

———. "We, Yesterday, Today, Tomorrow. Red School House Yearbook, 1977–78."

Reyhner, Jon. "Rationale and Needs for Stabilizing Indigenous Languages." In *Stabilizing Indigenous Languages,* edited by Gina Cantoni, 3–15. Flagstaff: Northern Arizona University, 1996.

———. "Introduction: Some Basics of Indigenous Language Revitalization." In *Revitalizing Indigenous Languages,* edited by Jon Reyhner et al., v–xx. Flagstaff: Northern Arizona University, 1999.

Reyhner, Jon, and Jeanne Eder. *American Indian Education: A History.* Norman: University of Oklahoma Press, 2004.

Roessel, Robert A., Jr. *Navajo Education in Action: The Rough Rock Demonstration School.* Chinle: Navajo Curriculum Center, Rough Rock Demonstration School, 1977.

Rosenfelt, Daniel. "Indian Schools and Community Control." *Stanford Law Review* 25, no. 4 (1973): 489–550.

Schierle, Sonja. *Funktion einer Survival School für städtische Indianer: Heart of the Earth Survival School: Indianische Alternativschule in Minneapolis, Minnesota.* Wiesbaden: Franz Steiner Verlag, 1981.

Shoemaker, Nancy. "Urban Indians and Ethnic Choices: American Indian Organizations in Minneapolis, 1920–1950." *Western Historical Quarterly* 19, no. 4 (1988): 431–47.

Smith, Linda Tuhiwai. *Decolonizing Methodologies: Research and Indigenous Peoples.* Dunedin, N.Z.: University of Otago Press, 1999.

Smith, Linda Tuhiwai Te Rina. "Kaupapa Maori Research." In *Reclaiming Indigenous Voice and Vision,* edited by Marie Battiste, 225–47. Vancouver: University of British Columbia Press, 2009.

Smith, Paul Chaat, and Robert Allen Warrior. *Like a Hurricane: The Indian Movement from Alcatraz to Wounded Knee.* New York: New Press, 1996.

Sorkin, Alan. *The Urban American Indian.* Lexington, Mass.: Lexington Books, 1978.

Stinson, Duane. "Heart of the Earth School Restructures in the Face of Financial Woes." *The Circle: Native American News and Arts,* May 2002.

Straus, Terry and Debra Valentino. "Retribalization in Urban Indian Communities," in *American Indians and the Urban Experience,* edited by Susan Lobo and Kurt Peters, 85–94. Walnut Creek, Calif.: Altamira Press, 2001.

Strong, Gabrielle. "AIFEP Changes Focus of Grantgiving." *The Circle: Native American News and Arts,* January 2004.

Szasz, Margaret Connell. *Education and the American Indian: The Road to Self-Determination since 1928.* Albuquerque: University of New Mexico Press, 1999.

Thompson, Paul. *The Voice of the Past: Oral History.* New York: Oxford University Press, 1988.

Thompson, Sally. "Survival Schools: Learning 'the Indian Way.'" In *Closing the Circle: The Indian in Minneapolis: A New Era,* edited by Betty Binkard, 18–23. Minneapolis: University of Minnesota School of Journalism and Mass Communication, 1975.

The Three Fires Culture and Education Society. "Three Fires Society: 'Our Story': The 7th Generation." Brochure, [2003?].

Trask, Haunani-Kay. *From a Native Daughter: Colonialism and Sovereignty in Hawai'i.* Honolulu: University of Hawaii Press, 1999.

Tyack, David, and Larry Cuban. *Tinkering toward Utopia: A Century of Public School Reform.* Cambridge: Harvard University Press, 1995.

Tyrell, Ian. "Beyond the View from Euro-America: Environment, Settler Societies, and the Internationalization of American History." In *Rethinking American History in a Global Age,* edited by Thomas Bender, 168–92. Berkeley: University of California Press, 2002.

Unger, Steven. "Preface." In *The Destruction of American Indian Families,* iii–iv. New York: Association on American Indian Affairs, 1977.

U.S. Commission on Civil Rights. Minnesota Advisory Committee. *Bridging the Gap: The Twin Cities Native American Community: A Report.* Washington, D.C.: U.S. Commission on Civil Rights, 1975.

———. *Bridging the Gap: A Reassessment: A Report.* Washington, D.C.: U.S. Commission on Civil Rights, 1978.

U.S. Senate Committee on Labor and Public Welfare. Special Subcommittee on Indian Education. *Indian Education: A National Tragedy—A National Challenge.* 91st Cong., 1st sess., 1969. S. Res. 80.

Van Deburg, William. *New Day in Babylon: The Black Power Movement and American Culture, 1965–1975.* Chicago: University of Chicago Press, 1992.

Vicenti-Carpio, Myla. "'Let Them Know We Still Exist': Indians in Albuquerque." Ph.D. diss., Arizona State University, 2001.

Vick, Judith. "The Press and Wounded Knee, 1973: An Analysis of the Coverage of the Occupation by Selected Newspapers and News Magazines." Master's thesis, University of Minnesota, 1972.

Vizenor, Gerald. "Avengers at Wounded Knee." In *Shadow Distance: A Gerald Vizenor Reader,* 33–43. Hanover: Wesleyan University Press, 1994.

Weible-Orlando, Joan. *Indian Country, L.A.: Maintaining Ethnic Community in a Complex Society.* Urbana: University of Illinois Press, 1991.

Westermeyer, Joseph. "Indian Powerlessness in Minnesota." *Society* 10, no. 3 (1973): 45–52.

Wilson, Angela Cavender. "American Indian History or Non-Indian Perceptions of American Indian History?" In *Natives and Academics: Researching and Writing about American Indians,* edited by Devon A. Mihesuah, 23–26. Lincoln: University of Nebraska Press, 1998.

———. "Grandmother to Granddaughter: Generations of Oral History in a Dakota Family." In *Natives and Academics: Researching and Writing about American Indians,* edited by Devon A. Mihesuah, 27–36. Lincoln: University of Nebraska Press, 1998.

———. "Power of the Spoken Word: Native Oral Traditions in American Indian History." In *Rethinking American Indian History,* edited by Donald L. Fixico, 101–16. Albuquerque: University of New Mexico Press, 1997.

Wilson, Waziyatawin Angela. *Remember This! Dakota Decolonization and the Eli Taylor Narratives.* Lincoln: University of Nebraska Press, 2005.

Wilson, Waziyatawin Angela, and Michael Yellow Bird, eds. *For Indigenous Eyes Only: A Decolonization Handbook.* Santa Fe: School of American Research, 2005.

Wittstock, Laura Waterman, and Elaine J. Salinas. "A Brief History of the American Indian Movement." http://www.aimovement.org/ggc/history.html (August 26, 2002).

Wittstock, Laura Waterman, Elaine Salinas, and Susan Aasen. "Russell Means."

In *Visions and Voices: American Indian Activism and the Civil Rights Movement*, edited by Kurt Peters and Terry Straus, 54–74. Brooklyn: Albatross Press, 2009.

Wolfe, Patrick. "Imperialism in Theory and Practice." Talk delivered at the Moore Institute in conjunction with the Sixth Galway Conference on Colonialism, National University of Ireland, Galway, June 23, 2010.

———. "Land, Labor, and Difference: Elementary Structures of Race." *American Historical Review* 106 (June 2001): 866–1006.

———. "Logics of Elimination: Colonial Policies on Indigenous Peoples in Australia and the United States." Lecture delivered at University of Nebraska, Lincoln, February 21, 1999.

———. "Settler Colonialism and the Elimination of the Native." *Journal of Genocide Research* 8, no. 4 (December 2006): 387–409.

———. *Settler Colonialism and the Transformation of Anthropology: The Politics and Poetics of an Ethnographic Event.* London: Cassell, 1999.

———. "Structure and Event: Settler Colonialism, Time, and the Question of Genocide." In *Empire, Colony, Genocide: Conquest, Occupation, and Subaltern Resistance in World History,* edited by A. Dirk Moses, chapter 4. New York: Berghahn Books, 2008.

Woods, Richard G., and Arthur M. Harkins. *A Review of Recent Research on Minneapolis Indians: 1968–1969.* Minneapolis: University of Minnesota, Center for Urban and Regional Affairs, 1969.

Index

academic performance: in public schools nationally, 75; in survival schools, 109, 175, 190, 197, 199–201; in Twin Cities public schools, 68–73, 130. *See also* discipline; evaluation

activism, AIM: criticisms of, 7–8, 151–54, 243; cultural and spiritual foundation for, 42–51, 97; as decolonization, 7, 243–45; as different from other Twin Cities Indian activism, 34–37, 50–51, 54–55, 66–67, 96–97; in global context, xiii, 239–43; motivations for, 3–6, 12–13, 42–51, 77–82, 91–97, 241–43; in national context, 5, 35–36, 66, 117–19, 136–37, 148–49, 182–86; and women, 6, 253n9. *See also* assimilation: AIM's resistance to; Banks, Dennis; Bellanger, Pat; Bellecourt, Clyde; Benton-Banai, Eddie; child welfare crisis: AIM's response to; cultural dissonance: AIM's response to; discrimina-

tion: AIM's work against; juvenile justice system: AIM's activism and; languages: AIM's revival of; prisons: AIM's activism in; settler colonialism: AIM's work against; socioeconomic disparities: AIM's work against

activism, Indian: scholarship on, 7; in Twin Cities besides AIM, 20–21, 28–31, 66–67

adult education programs, 169–71, 176, 191, 213–14

allotment, 17–19, 40, 55. *See also* colonialism; settler colonialism

Anishinaabe/Anishinaabeg: cultural revitalization of, 45–47, 50, 228–34, 237, 244, 283–84n62; definition of, xiv. *See also* Midewiwin; Ojibwes; Three Fires

assessment. *See* academic performance; evaluation

assimilation: AIM's resistance to, 7, 48–51, 54–55, 65–67, 77, 82, 97; boarding schools and, 38–41, 43–44, 55, 57, 85; federal policy of, xiii, 15–18, 22, 37, 54; survival schools' resistance to, 213, 226, 242–44. *See also* "assimilationist imperative"; child welfare crisis; settler colonialism

"assimilationist imperative," 51, 62–67; in child welfare system, 84–91; persistence of in present, 244–45; in Twin Cities public schools, 68, 73–75, 77, 80–82, 226; in Twin Cities social services, 83

Australia, 16, 87–89, 143, 243. *See also* settler colonialism

Banks, Dennis: as AIM founder, 3–5, 33, 57; as AIM organizer in Twin Cities, 31–34, 42, 82, 92–94; cultural alienation of, 42–43, 50; as national AIM activist, 2–3, 5, 8, 152–53; politicization of, in prison, 4–5. *See also* prisons

Battiste, Marie, 182, 224–27, 233, 242, 246

Bellanger, Lisa: community/cultural leadership of, 215–17, 222–23, 231; as Heart of the Earth staff/volunteer, 171, 178, 213; as Heart of the Earth student, 163, 169, 178, 199, 201–3, 205–7, 218–19; as survival school parent, 11, 209–10, 212–13

Bellanger, Pat: as AIM founder, 4; as AIM organizer in Twin Cities, 1–2, 32, 48–50, 81; childhood experiences of, 56, 58, 77–79; child welfare activism of, 91–93; educational activism of, 78–81; experience in Twin Cities, 25, 58; as survival school founder, 2, 94–96, 160; as survival school parent, 120, 201–2, 208–9; work in

survival schools, 103–4, 113–14, 116–17, 150–51, 161, 168–69, 180–81

Bellecourt, Clyde: as AIM founder, 3–5, 47–48; as AIM organizer in Twin Cities, 32–34, 37, 49–50; child welfare activism of, 91–94; cultural alienation of, 11–12, 42–48, 53–54; cultural awakening of, in prison, 4–5, 45–47; educational activism of, 81, 113; as Heart of the Earth school board chairman, 160, 164, 173, 179, 191; as national AIM activist, 2, 152–53; as survival school founder, 93–96, 102, 114, 134, 160; as survival school parent, 96, 120, 202, 209. *See also* leadership: criticism of, in survival schools; prisons

Benton-Banai, Eddie: as AIM organizer in Twin Cities, 4, 32–33, 47; childhood cultural education of, 45, 50–51; cultural/spiritual leadership of, 5, 11, 45–47, 164–68, 178, 195–96, 208, 230–34; as director of Red School House, 104, 108, 122, 124–25, 128, 164, 178–79, 186; as survival school founder, 33, 81, 95, 113; as survival school parent, 120, 209. *See also* leadership: criticism of, in survival schools; prisons

Black Power, 5, 36, 146–47, 149

boarding schools: AIM founders and, 5, 42–44, 48, 57, 77; cultural loss and, 39–44, 48, 55, 85; federal assimilation policy and, 7, 38–39, 55; survival schools as response to, 113, 130–31, 226. *See also* colonialism; languages: loss of; settler colonialism

Bug O Nay Ge Shig school (Bug School), 137, 143, 149

Central High School, 202
charter school status, 187, 192–93. *See also* funding: sources of
Child, Brenda, 6, 17–18, 40–41, 55
child welfare crisis: AIM's response to, 12, 51, 54–55, 67, 91–95; "assimilationist imperative" and, 82–89; as a national problem, 84–87; survival schools and, 82, 93–96, 212, 241; as a transnational problem, 88–89; in the Twin Cities, xii, 54, 83–84, 89–91. *See also* settler colonialism
Circle of Life school, 215
colonialism, 224–25, 237, 240, 241–42, 245; in the United States, 12–16, 18–19, 48, 51, 213, 224, 233. *See also* allotment; assimilation; "assimilationist imperative"; boarding schools; child welfare crisis; languages: loss of; "logic of elimination"; settler colonialism
community control: as decolonization, 223–26, 235–36, 244; of Indian education, 7, 117–19, 137, 182–85, 189; in survival schools, 113–18, 125, 129, 193–94, 220–23, 226, 235–36
"community-mindedness," 125, 150, 168, 196, 213, 227
criminal justice system. *See* discrimination: by Twin Cities police; juvenile justice system
cultural dissonance, 51, 61, 65; AIM's response to, 12, 51, 65–67, 97; in Twin Cities public schools, 68, 73–75

curriculum materials, 77, 79, 156, 165–68, 183, 235

Dakotas, 14–15, 18–19, 39, 143; survival schools and, 135, 140–41, 147–48, 164, 207, 214, 228; in Twin Cities, 19, 23–24, 29, 32. *See also* languages: survival schools' instruction of
Day, Charlotte, 58–60; AIM and, 92, 94, 97, 207; in conflict with Twin Cities public schools, 70–72, 90–92, 94–95; as survival school founder, 95–96, 120, 128, 209
Day, Dorene: community/cultural leadership of, 215–19, 222–23, 231; prejudice in Twin Cities and, 59–60, 121; as Red School House staff/volunteer, 186–87, 214; as Red School House student, 121, 124, 128, 156, 204–7, 209; as survival school parent, 209–13
discipline: in mission/boarding schools, 44, 57; in survival schools, 109–12, 120, 168, 175, 187
discrimination: AIM's work against, 2–3, 31–32, 34–35, 51, 152; in Twin Cities employment and housing, 3, 20, 24–25, 61, 96, 156; by Twin Cities police, 31, 87, 89, 256–57n35; in Twin Cities public schools, 3, 68–71, 82, 94; in Twin Cities social services, 3, 28, 63. *See also* prejudice
dropout rate, 68–70, 73, 75, 82, 212

employment. *See* discrimination: in Twin Cities employment and housing
evaluation: and federal funding, 180; of survival schools, 112, 197,

199–200; of survival school students, 108–9, 199–200. *See also* academic performance; discipline; instruction

extended family system: decolonization and, 225–27; as Indigenous value/practice, 20, 40, 60, 86, 87, 229; revitalized by survival schools, 113, 120, 125, 137, 175, 178, 191, 193, 196

Federation of Native American Controlled Survival Schools, 107, 185, 206

Franklin Avenue, 1, 26, 31–32, 37, 208, 218; AIM office on, 94; A.I.M. Survival School on, 94, 102

funding: conflicts over, 179–81, 185–86; Heart of the Earth closing and, 187–89, 193; lack of, 82, 102–3, 114; loss of, 153–54, 181, 184–89; Red School House closing and, 186–87, 189; sources of, 102–3, 105–6, 113, 153, 180, 183–85, 192. *See also* Indian Education Act, 1972

governance. *See* community control: in survival schools; parent–school relationships: in survival schools

Ho-Chunks, 14–15, 39, 143; survival schools and, 140, 215; in Twin Cities, 19, 23–24, 32. *See also* languages: survival schools' instruction of

housing. *See* discrimination: in Twin Cities employment and housing

Howard, Vikki: community/cultural leadership of, 214–15, 228; as Heart of the Earth teacher/administrator, 124–25, 132, 145, 150, 176, 177–78, 190

Indian Community School, Milwaukee, 118–19, 137, 145, 149, 153, 275n39

Indian Education Act, 1972 (Title IV), 105–6, 183–85. *See also* funding: sources of

"Indigenousness," 51, 54, 223–37

instruction, 107–13, 129, 172, 193. *See also* adult education programs; curriculum materials; discipline: in survival schools; languages: survival schools' instruction of; open school model; parent–school relationships: in survival schools; student–staff relationships: in survival schools

Johnson administration. *See* Office of Economic Opportunity; War on Poverty

juvenile justice system: AIM's activism and, 51, 54–55, 91–94; Indigenous assimilation and, 87–89; survival schools and, 12, 93–94, 96, 101, 189, 212, 241. *See also* child welfare crisis

Kingbird, Ona, 114, 120, 127, 130–31, 223

Lakotas, 39, 143, 152–54, 208; survival schools and, 140–42, 146–47, 164, 228; in Twin Cities, 19, 23–24, 32. *See also* languages: survival schools' instruction of

languages: AIM's revival of, 6, 48–9, 67, 82; loss of, 4, 39–44, 48, 55, 224; preservation of, 21, 29, 45,

56–57, 245; revitalization of, 1, 136–37, 185, 196, 214, 218, 225, 229–34, 240, 243–46; survival schools' instruction of, 114, 124, 127, 130–32, 151, 160–63, 167, 169–70, 177, 190, 200–204, 227–28, 241

law enforcement. *See* discrimination: by Twin Cities police; juvenile justice system

leadership: criticism of, in survival schools, 157, 179–82, 186–87, 220–22, 243; cultivation of, by survival schools, 145–51, 161–64, 198, 206–7, 213–23, 228, 230–31, 234; of Native women, 6, 118–19. *See also* activism, AIM; activism, Indian: in Twin Cities besides AIM; Banks, Dennis; Bellanger, Lisa; Bellanger, Pat; Benton-Banai, Eddie; Day, Charlotte; Day, Dorene; funding: conflicts over; Howard, Vikki; Smith, Johnny; Strong, Gabrielle; student activism

Leech Lake reservation, Minnesota, xv, 8, 215; AIM founders' childhood on, 42–43, 56–58, 77–78. *See also* Bug O Nay Ge Shig school

Legal Rights Center, 35

Little Earth housing project, 35

"logic of elimination" (Wolfe), 16–17, 38, 62–64, 84, 88, 245; survival schools' work against, 51, 198, 241–43. *See also* assimilation; "assimilationist imperative"; settler colonialism

Lomawaima, K. Tsianina, xv, 242, 245–46, 253n8

McCarty, Teresa, 182, 184, 185–86, 242, 245–46, 253n8

Mechanic Arts High School, 69, 70–72, 90–91, 92, 94–95

Midewiwin: persistence of, 45, 55–56; repression of, 41, 56; revitalization of, 11–12, 47, 50, 195–96, 210–11, 229–34

Miller, Susan, xiv, xv, 8, 143, 225, 232–33

Mt. Airy projects, 58–60, 70, 90

National Indian Youth Council (NIYC), 36, 66, 142

Nett Lake reservation, Minnesota, 58

New Zealand, 16, 87–89, 143, 235, 243. *See also* settler colonialism

Nixon administration, 36, 153, 182–84

No Child Left Behind, 187, 193

Northern Ireland, 16, 239–40, 243, 248. *See also* settler colonialism

North High School, 77, 79

O'Brien, Jim, 93, 111, 121, 123, 147, 200

Office of Economic Opportunity (OEO), 30, 75, 106, 153, 183–84. *See also* War on Poverty

Ojibwes, xiv, xv, 12, 14–18, 50, 136–37, 143, 215; AIM founders as, 3–5, 31–34, 42–43, 45, 56, 77; boarding schools and, 39–41, 55; Ojibwe culture in survival school curriculum, 104, 134–35, 139–40, 163–67; survival schools and, 11, 99, 123–24, 142, 146, 151, 177–79, 189; in Twin Cities, 18–24, 25, 29, 31, 32, 57–59, 92–93. *See also* Anishinaabe/Anishinaabeg; languages: survival schools' instruction of; Three Fires

open school model, 80, 101, 107–9, 116, 117–18, 125, 129, 190. *See also* St. Paul Open School oral history methodology, xii–xiii, 251n1, 251n3

parents: boarding schools and, 39–44, 48, 72, 85, 226; former survival school students as, 208–13; as survival school founders, 6, 95–96, 101, 103–4, 128, 208–9, 241. *See also* child welfare crisis; parent–school relationships
parent–school relationships: in survival schools, 113–18, 120, 129, 168–72, 189–93, 214, 225–27, 236; in Twin Cities public schools, 54–55, 69–76, 78–80, 89–96, 116–17, 226
pedagogy. *See* curriculum materials; evaluation: of survival school students; instruction
Pine Point Experimental Community School, 118, 136–37, 143
police. *See* discrimination: by Twin Cities police
Pourier, Joel, 187–89, 193–94
prejudice: in Twin Cities, 12, 20, 21, 35, 59–60; in Twin Cities child welfare system, 83–87, 92. *See also* discrimination
prisons: AIM's activism in, 32, 208; as incubator for Indigenous activism, 4–6, 11–12, 33, 45–47, 240. *See also* adult education programs
public schools. *See* academic performance: in Twin Cities public schools; "assimilationist imperative": in Twin Cities public schools; Central High School; cultural dissonance: in Twin Cities public schools; Day, Charlotte: in conflict with Twin Cities public schools; discrimination: in Twin Cities public schools; dropout rate; Mechanic Arts High School; North High School; parent–school relationships: in Twin Cities public schools; South High School; student–staff relationships: in Twin Cities public schools. *See also* child welfare crisis; curriculum materials; juvenile justice system

Reagan administration, 184–86
relocation policy, 22–23, 28, 62–63
Robertson, Chuck, 114, 119, 223
Rough Rock Demonstration School, 117–18, 136, 143, 148–49, 182, 185–86
Roy family, 92–94, 96, 120, 209, 265n89

settler colonialism: AIM's work against, 51, 67, 97; in postwar Twin Cities, 51, 62–64; settler colonial theory, xiii, 235, 248, 253–54n2; survival schools' resistance to, 236–37, 241–43, 245; as transnational process, 16, 87–89, 241–43, 248, 252n4; in United States, 16–18, 38, 236, 244–46. *See also* allotment; assimilation; "assimilationist imperative"; boarding schools; child welfare crisis; colonialism; "logic of elimination"
Smith, Johnny, xv, 11, 99–100, 127–28, 173–74, 189–92
social services. *See* assimilation; "assimilationist imperative"; child welfare crisis; discrimination: in Twin Cities social services; prejudice; settler colonialism
socioeconomic disparities: AIM's work against, 31–35, 37, 51, 67, 73; child welfare crisis and, 83,

85–87; other Twin Cities Indian activists' work against, 28–30, 34–35; in Twin Cities, 2–3, 12, 24–28, 96, 146

South High School, 77, 79, 199, 214

staff. *See* academic performance: in survival schools; Bellanger, Lisa: as Heart of the Earth staff/volunteer; Bellanger, Pat: work in survival schools; Day, Dorene: as Red School House staff/volunteer; discipline: in survival schools; evaluation: of survival school students; Howard, Vikki: as Heart of the Earth teacher/administrator; instruction; Kingbird, Ona; parent–school relationships; Robertson, Chuck; Smith, Johnny; Strong, Gabrielle; student–staff relationships; volunteers

Stevens Square neighborhood, 19, 28

St. Paul Open School, 80–81, 201, 223. *See also* open school model

Strong, Gabrielle, 207, 213–14, 218–22

student activism, 147–50, 175–76, 178, 205–7

student–staff relationships: in survival schools, 115, 119–25, 216, 225–26; in Twin Cities public schools, 68–75. *See also* Bellanger, Lisa; Day, Dorene; Howard, Vikki: as Heart of the Earth teacher/administrator; Kingbird, Ona; parent–school relationships; Robertson, Chuck; Smith, Johnny; Strong, Gabrielle

Summit Hill neighborhood, 26, 58

Three Fires: Three Fires Confederacy, xiv, 229; Three Fires group (Red School House), 164; Three Fires Society, 229–34. *See also* Anishinaabe/Anishinaabeg; Midewiwin; Ojibwes

Title IV. *See* Indian Education Act, 1972

Upper Midwest American Indian Center (UMAIC), 29–30, 34–35, 37, 217

volunteers: family/community members as, 104, 113–17, 120, 191, 269n27; former students as, 213, 219. *See also* Bellanger, Lisa: as Heart of the Earth staff/volunteer; Bellanger, Pat: work in survival schools; Day, Dorene: as Red School House staff/volunteer; parent–school relationships: in survival schools; student–staff relationships: in survival schools

War on Poverty, 36, 183. *See also* Office of Economic Opportunity

White, Walter (Porky), 124, 133, 164, 190, 231

White Earth reservation, Minnesota, 19, 107, 118, 134, 136, 149, 215, 244; AIM founders' childhood on, 43–44, 56

Wolfe, Patrick, 16, 38, 62, 252n4

World War II, 21–22, 24, 30, 62–63

Julie L. Davis *is associate professor of history at the College of St. Benedict and St. John's University in central Minnesota.*